LAND TOO GOOD FOR INDIANS

New Directions in Native American Studies Series
Colin Calloway and K. Tsianina Lomawaima, General Editors

LAND TOO GOOD
FOR INDIANS
Northern Indian Removal

John P. Bowes

University of Oklahoma Press : Norman

Also by John P. Bowes
Exiles and Pioneers: Eastern Indians in the Trans-Mississippi West (New York, 2007)
The Trail of Tears: Removal in the South (New York, 2007)
Black Hawk and the War of 1832: Removal in the North (New York, 2007)
The Choctaw (New York, 2010)

Library of Congress Cataloging-in-Publication Data

Names: Bowes, John P., 1973– author.
Title: Land too good for Indians : northern Indian removal / John P. Bowes.
Other titles: Northern Indian removal
Description: First edition. | Norman, OK : University of Oklahoma Press, [2016] |
Series: New directions in Native American studies ; volume 13 |
Includes bibliographical references and index.
Identifiers: LCCN 2015042399 | ISBN 978-0-8061-5212-7 (hardcover : alk. paper)
Subjects: LCSH: Indian Removal, 1813-1903. | Indian of North America—
Northwest, Old—Government relations. | Indians of North America —
Government relations—1789-1869. | Indians of North America—Land
tenure. | Forced migration — Northwest, Old. | Northwest, Old—History.
Classification: LCC E98.R4 B69 2016 | DDC 323.1197—dc23
LC record available at http://lccn.loc.gov/2015042399

Land Too Good for Indians is Volume 13 in the
New Directions in Native American Studies series.

The paper in this book meets the guidelines for permanence and durability
of the Committee on Production Guidelines for Book Longevity of the
Council on Library Resources, Inc. ∞

1 2 3 4 5 6 7 8 9 10

For Sarah, Callie, and Reese
I love you more, and that is not impossible

CONTENTS

ILLUSTRATIONS

FIGURES

MAPS

ACKNOWLEDGMENTS

I take great joy in writing acknowledgments for at least three different reasons. First, the task is an indication that I am almost at the finish line. Second, it is fun to go back through the journey of the past eight years and remember the contributions made by so many people to a project about which I am so passionate. I know that I often turn first to the acknowledgments of a new book to see who was part of the experience that made that particular effort possible. Hopefully my friends, family, and colleagues will do the same. Third, for some reason I have always appreciated the standard statement in which the author claims ownership of any flaws that exist within the book. And so instead of adding that phrase as a final caveat, let me declare right now that any errors (of which there may be some, but hopefully not many) contained within the following pages are there because of my own shortcomings and not due to any other individual's actions. I have been the beneficiary of a great deal of support in my work on this book. I hope the finished product does that support justice.

This book is the culmination of more than eight years of researching, writing, and thinking. It is difficult to claim it as my own because not a single one of those three activities did I complete in a vacuum. My research efforts were accomplished under the auspices of several different research grants. I utilized funds from the University Research Committee at Eastern Kentucky University to make trips to Ohio and to Oklahoma. A Phillips Fund for Native American Research grant from the American Philosophical Society made it possible for me to make yet another trip to Oklahoma. In Oklahoma the staff at the Oklahoma Historical Society made me feel very welcome, as did Kelli Mosteller at the Citizen Potawatomi Nation Cultural Heritage Center in Shawnee and Renee Harvey at the Gilcrease Museum in Tulsa. Nan Card at the Rutherford B. Hayes Presidential Library was especially helpful in my pursuit of all things Sandusky. At Indiana University Teena Freeman and all those affiliated with the Great Lakes and Ohio Valley Ethnohistory Collection were exceedingly generous with their time as I pored through as many of the collected materials as possible.

Additional research occurred through more informal measures, including conversations and e-mail exchanges. Theodore Karamanski shared some of his own documents, which allowed me to flesh out my analysis of Indian affairs in Michigan. Jim Rementer was generous with his time via e-mail. Some of the most important thinking that I did about my research and writing, however, occurred during the course of my participation in two different grant projects funded by the National Endowment for the Humanities and overseen by the Ohio History Connection (formerly the Ohio Historical Society). It was especially through the grant from America's Historical and Cultural Organizations, focused on the removal of Indian tribes from the Ohio country, that I had the opportunity to engage in wide-ranging discussions about the removal histories of the federally recognized tribes with ties to Ohio. My thanks especially go to George Ironstrack, Ben Barnes, Paul Barton, Chief Glenna Wallace, Richard Zane Smith, and many others for their words and their willingness to include me in the conversation. And a significant thank you goes to the staff of the Ohio Historical Connection for their hard work and generosity related to those meetings that took place in Ohio and Oklahoma.

The actual writing portion of this process also owes much to several benefactors. I am forever indebted to the National Endowment for the Humanities for the summer stipend that enabled me to begin the substantial work of putting the research into words on a computer screen. An equally important thank you to Eastern Kentucky University for the sabbatical during the autumn of 2012, which allowed me to put a huge dent in the writing, and to my department chair, Chris Taylor, who went out of her way to make sure I had the opportunity to work on this book. Indeed, I am very fortunate to be part of the History Department at Eastern Kentucky University. It is a wonderful environment in which to work. My friends and colleagues Tom Appleton, Carolyn Dupont, Nick Rosenthal, George Ironstrack, and Stephen Warren read various parts of this manuscript in the years and months leading up to its completion, and I very much appreciate their feedback. My informal conversations with both George and Steve in particular have greatly influenced the way I thought about this project and they made the end result better. I also owe a great debt to the cheerful patience of Alessandra Jacobi Tamulevich at the University of Oklahoma Press, who has supported my manuscript from the beginning and has helped bring it to life. Copyeditor Abby Graves deserves credit as well for the attention to detail and style that has made this book better.

In the years that it took me to complete this project I have also worked through a number of topics and ideas in articles and book chapters that improved greatly because of critiques and suggestions made by numerous scholars. Thanks go to the late Nora Faires and the editors of *The Michigan Historical Review* for including my work in the spring 2008 volume. Reworked pieces of that article on the impact of the Gnadenhutten Massacre appear in chapter 3. I also appreciate the editorial efforts of Bruce Vandervort and *The Journal of Military History*, where portions of chapter 4 first appeared in October 2012. The keen and knowledgeable eye of David Skaggs added significantly to my thinking about the War of 1812, and I thank him for including my chapter in *The Battle of Lake Erie and Its Aftermath: A Reassessment*, published by Kent State University Press in 2013. That chapter has been reworked and incorporated into the larger discussion of the perceived British-Indian relationship that comprises chapter 1. Yet with all of this thinking, writing, revising, and writing some more, it was not until my article on the Indian Removal Act was published in *NAIS: Journal of the Native American and Indigenous Studies Association* in spring 2014 that the central points of this book finally crystallized. The article began as a conference paper delivered at NAISA in 2011, and during the course of its journey the article benefited from the critiques and insights of several individuals. I am particularly grateful to the late Mike Green, who was generous with his time and unsparing in his feedback. I also thank Jean O'Brien, Robert Warrior, and the anonymous reviewers from *NAIS* for their constructive criticism, which made both the article and this book better. That article and its ideas can be seen in the introduction and throughout the chapters that follow.

As is always the case, mentors, colleagues, and friends have made all of this work not only possible, but also rewarding. When this book is published it will have been nearly eight years since my advisor and friend

Melissa Meyer passed away. I still hear her voice as I research and write. Colin Calloway continues to prove an invaluable source of advice and friendship and has helped me become a better scholar. I cannot thank him enough. During my visits to Bloomington several wonderful hosts made my trips more enjoyable, including Josh Paddison and his family as well as Karen Ross and Neil Pederson. In Tulsa Brian Hosmer took me to lunch and gave me a break from my research. And of course thank you to those back in Lexington, Sharon and Chris Chrisman especially, who made sure to look out for my family whenever I traveled to work on this project and poured me a glass of wine whenever I returned.

Words cannot capture what it means to me to have the support and love of my family. Jay and Taffy Bowes, Katie, Chris, Mike and Brendan Balestracci, and Suzy, Brian, and Zoey Hannen, you shine brightly in my life. Thank you for always being there for me and loving me. To Callie and Reese, thank you for reminding me every day about what should be important and that sometimes everyone needs to take a break from dinner to dance or do cartwheels. I am blessed to be your father and I am forever grateful for that opportunity. And to Sarah, I am rendered nearly speechless. Your unwavering love and support mean the world to me. Thank you, as always, for saying yes.

LAND TOO GOOD FOR INDIANS

INTRODUCTION

Certain images must not be forgotten, marginalized, or ignored in any discussion of Indian removal. Official descriptions of forced relocations, like those that immediately follow, should be read with care so that one's senses and emotions are not overwhelmed by the harshness revealed in the journals maintained by Indian agents and conductors.

In the spring of 1827 Indian agent Richard Graham wrote to Superintendent of Indian Affairs William Clark and described the condition of 227 Shawnees and Senecas encamped near Kaskaskia, Illinois. "They appear to be in a miserable condition. . . . It appears they left their villages in Ohio in Nov. and arrived at their present encampment in Feby," he penned. "They have not been able to proceed on to their place of destination owing to the extreme leanness of their horses—many of which have died for the want of means to purchase grain for them."[1] John Shelby, the assistant conductor for the removal of the Shawnee Indians from Wapakoneta and Hog Creek in Ohio during the fall of 1832, wrote in his journal on November 16, "An Indian called —— died in the wagon to day of a lingering consumption as we passed on with out a frind present except his wife to witness his last departing moments."[2] J. J. Abert reported from Arrow Ferry on the west branch of the Missouri River on November 18, 1832, "The Ottaway camp still continues healthy, but I should not be surprised if some of these Shawnees were found frozen to death to-morrow, as, on passing through their camp I found some of them rather drunk; they are a sort of over-grown children, and require continual care."[3] The

3

journal entry William Polke made on September 9, 1838, relates the omnipresent misery in the forced removal of Chief Menominee's band of nearly eight hundred Potawatomis from northern Indiana. He began the entry, "Physicians came into camp today, and reported three hundred cases of sickness. . . . A child died today," and ended it just as abruptly, writing, "A child died since dark."[4]

The history of removal is relentless in its tales of death, dispossession, and dislocation. There is horror in those accounts. There is loss and emotional trauma. There is physical violence. And the reports written by the appointed overseers of the removal of men, women, and children to lands west of the Mississippi River often contain an inherent paternalism and a measure of indifference to the pain so clearly on display. What else might explain the words of William Polke, who wrote how "the bright smiles that gild the sunny faces of our unhappy wards" gave reason to anticipate "the pleasantest and happiest of the emigrations west" only two days after describing sickness and death among the Potawatomis?[5]

[The removal of American Indians from their lands east of the Mississippi River was an act of all-encompassing violence that did not take place in an abstract world of political debates and historical narratives.] Literary scholar Scott Richard Lyons states in harsh terms, "Removal is to migration what rape is to sex." It was not antiseptic. It was not clean. In all cases it involved some manner of coercion. Removal forcefully renamed the physical and cultural landscape as it marginalized Native ways of living and being.[6] Lyons expands upon this idea, explaining, "While the original political policy was concerned with actual physical removals like the Trail of Tears, the underlying ideology of removal in its own way justified and encouraged the systematic losses of Indian life: the removal of livelihood and language, the removal of security and self-esteem, the removal of religion and respect."[7] In this light, [federal removal policy codified in the 1830 Indian Removal Act should be viewed as a continuation of, rather than a transition from, the civilization policy begun in the late eighteenth century that attacked indigenous religions, subsistence patterns, and land-holding practices.] And this wholesale dispossession continued within the histories written throughout the nineteenth century. [As a group, in fact, the self-proclaimed historians of the lower Great Lakes writing during the nineteenth century committed literary genocide by crafting origin stories of Ohio, Indiana, and Illinois that hinged on the "moment of Native dispossession and victimless settlement."[8]]

Winning the West with Words

All of this is true and all of this must be remembered. Through a general recognition and knowledge of the Cherokee Trail of Tears in particular, a surface-level understanding of the injury done to Indians through nineteenth-century forced removals continues to exist within public forums in the United States. Yet in a world desensitized to physical violence, it may have become too easy to simply acknowledge and apologize for the brutality that is seemingly confined to the past. It is far more difficult, however, for many to see and understand the complex frameworks that support the justifications behind these past injuries but which clarify the ways in which Indian removal, and its aftermath, is more than a historical episode relegated to the 1800s.

The histories of northern Indian removal illustrate those complex frameworks well, but exploring those histories requires us first to move beyond events that have been deemed representative. That means, in part, looking beyond the Black Hawk War, which far too often is presented as the northern equivalent of the Cherokee Trail of Tears. Textbooks written for college classrooms have become much better in their analysis and inclusion of Native American histories over the years, but even recent editions continue to encapsulate the northern experience in the actions of Sauk warrior Black Hawk and his followers who "refused to leave rich, well-watered farmland in western Illinois in 1832."[9] In many instances the accompanying maps do not even indicate the presence of Indians other than the Sauks north of the Ohio River.[10] Or, in addition to relying exclusively on Black Hawk to represent the northern experience, even a Pulitzer Prize–winning book might also assert that Indian removal "involved Indian tribes all over the country, but the ones with the most at stake were the Five Civilized Tribes of Cherokee, Creek, Choctaw, Chickasaw, and Seminole."[11] Perhaps the trend is not surprising when even one of the most prolific scholars of Indian removal, Grant Foreman, in 1932 wrote in the introduction to his first book on the topic that northern Indians were "weaker and more primitive" than the southern tribes, and as a result they "yielded with comparatively small resistance to the power and chicane of the white man."[12] Fourteen years later Foreman published a book focused more exclusively on northern Indian removal. Time and research may have tempered his attitude to an extent, but they did not alter his underlying assertion. He writes in the introductory chapter of *Last Trek of the Indians* that the northern removal is "a more complicated undertaking" because, unlike the southern tribes, the northern Indians failed to preserve their tribal integrity and did not share a common experience of relations with Euro-Americans.[13]

The history presented in this book addresses in more depth the "complicated undertaking" that Foreman described nearly eighty years ago. More important, it is an effort to explain that the northern removal's complexity rests not in the loss of tribal integrity or weaker condition but instead in the historical context of the Old Northwest and its Native inhabitants. History, both large and small, unfolds within a specific environment, whether it is geographical, chronological, economical, political, sociological, or more accurately, all of them intertwined. Consequently the history of Indian removal cannot be summarized or represented within a single narrative arc, especially if that arc is confined to the experience of a single tribe within a particular space in time. The removal experiences of Wyandots, Shawnees, Miamis, Delawares, Potawatomis, and others should not be tied to a removal era centered on legislation like the Indian Removal Act or bounded by the Cherokee Trail of Tears or the Black Hawk War. Therefore, even as this book addresses a more expansive chronology, it can also be said that it reveals smaller histories. In the northern states and territories in particular, removal did not occur on the grand scale seen in the southeast. Because of that smaller scale, removal was fragmented and filtered through a diverse set of political, economic, and regional interests. Dislocation in the north was enmeshed in a very different local context, and context mattered.

The ideas and arguments presented in the pages that follow have evolved throughout a gestation period that dates back to my dissertation, which became *Exiles and Pioneers*, a study that primarily addresses the postremoval experience of Wyandots, Potawatomis, Shawnees, and Delawares. As such, this current book is also the product of a long period of engagement with an ever-growing historiography. That historiography has a number of founders, but perhaps none is more influential than Grant Foreman. Foreman wrote books that defined our understanding of the larger picture of Indian removal in so many ways, and the documentary research that supports his analysis is unmatched. Decades after his books first appeared they remain a necessary reference point, and scholars will find it difficult to rise to the encyclopedic analysis he provided of Indian removal. Despite the aspects of his work that have not stood the test of time, his books should be required reading for anyone seeking to understand the detailed movements and activities encompassed by the history. Foreman is not the only scholar to have tackled the subject, however, and this book is not the first to call attention to the removal histories of the Potawatomis, Delawares, Miamis, Shawnees, Wyandots, Odawas, and Ojibwes.[14]

Despite the articles and monographs already published, bringing these histories of northern removal to the forefront still necessitates a confrontation with the framework that has long defined the most common understanding of removal in general, namely the understanding founded on the Cherokee Nation and the Trail of Tears. The scholarship examining Cherokee removal does not claim sole ownership of the narrative. As Theda Perdue and Michael Green note, "The history of the removal of the Cherokees can never substitute for the histories of the others, but it can exemplify a larger history that no one should forget." Nevertheless, [the discourse grounding the narrative, constructed primarily around the Indian Removal Act and the Cherokee experience, at times hinders a more expansive picture of the wholesale cultural and physical dispossession in the early American republic.] A focus on the 1830 legislation ties the conversation to the vocabulary used in opinion essays, congressional debates, petitions, and court cases, thus largely focusing on the history of the Cherokees and their southeastern neighbors. And the fact that the Cherokees were "masters of public relations" also provides scholars with countless documents with Cherokee voices speaking to the same issues.[15]

The Indian Removal Act was not just enabling legislation passed by Congress in May 1830. It did more than grant the president of the United States authority to arrange for the relocation of eastern Indians to lands west of the Mississippi River. The Indian Removal Act, as well as the debates and events connected to it, established a discourse that has continued to frame discussions of the historical era in which it occurred. That discourse is one layered in the language of constitutional authority, civilization versus savagery, property rights, states' rights, tribal sovereignty, and government jurisdiction. It provides the foundation for a broad conversation encompassing American imperialism during the Jacksonian Era, "a determination to expand geographically and economically, imposing an alien will upon subject peoples and commandeering their resources."[16] In addition, the process has created a powerful and tragic narrative concerned primarily with the experiences of the southeastern Indian tribes and their forced removal from the eastern half of the continent.[17]

The portrayal of the Indian Removal Act of 1830 as a watershed historical event has thus been influenced by the construction of the American national narrative as a whole. Whether it is seen as ending "the drift and indecision of previous administrations," or as forcing "the recognition that attitudes that had been vaguely and randomly expressed before had now to be consolidated into a unified, practical, and defensible national policy," the legislation has left its mark as a significant moment for federal Indian affairs.[18] Teachers and scholars have long emphasized the well-known battle among the assembled forces of Andrew Jackson, Christian missionaries, Georgia politicians, and Cherokee Indians to illustrate the bill's place within a transformative era of American history. John A. Andrew III presents Indian removal as "Jacksonian Democracy's first great crusade," which "became a key to understanding a concomitant change in American culture." Similarly, Mary Hershberger has deftly illustrated the connections between women's involvement in the antiremoval petition campaign of 1830 and the early abolitionist movement. In an impressive study of political behavior, Fred Rolater has asserted that the debates over Indian removal contributed significantly to the emergence of the second American party system. Foreshadowing Rolater's argument was Ronald Satz's foundational work on Jacksonian Indian policy, which also highlighted the broader political implications of the congressional debates over the legislation. For Andrew, Hershberger, Rolater, Satz, and others, the battle over American Indian removal influenced several vital elements of American society during a period of tremendous change.[19]

The weight given the Indian Removal Act is emblematic of the treatment granted the era as a whole. Just as the legislation became a key marker of the Jacksonian Era, removal has represented the demise of eastern Indians at the hands of Andrew Jackson and his policies. Weakening the legislation's hold on the discourse, however, grants opportunities to broaden the horizons of the historical narrative. This in turn provides for continuity instead of harsh breaks with the past and allows for the creation of a more complete national history. In more recent years narrative continuity and inclusion have been apparent in the work of American Indian history scholars who have moved beyond the traditional scope of Indian removal. However, such positive trends remain within a static historical narrative and have struggled to escape boundaries established by discipline and topic.

[American Indian history in general has developed dramatically over the past several decades, but most of the transformative work has occurred on either side of the so-called removal era, and the period of 1815 to 1848 is largely left to Jackson and Indian tribes of the Southeast.[20] It is both crucial and possible, however, to create new paths and perspectives for those studying American Indian and American history. The process begins with the assertion that, despite its relevance in the Cherokee experience in particular, the Indian Removal Act plays a smaller role in the larger history of Indian relocations in the early American republic. That statement opens up three different avenues. First, eliminating 1830 as the distinctive mark of the era creates a more extensive chronological context for Indian removal. Second, an extended chronology promotes both a more continuous narrative from the early to the late nineteenth century and a more comprehensive narrative that incorporates the American Indian communities north of the Ohio River. Third, and finally, shortening the legislation's reach opens the door to more fruitful investigations of localized power struggles that occurred during the process of dispossession and relocation both north and south of the Ohio River.

Both the events and the historiography of the nineteenth century depend on their respective partners of the previous centuries. To say that colonial American history cannot be understood without the inclusion of Native actions and perspectives therefore entails that we also acknowledge the repercussions of the colonial era that echoed well into the 1800s.[21] Indeed, the responses of American Indian communities to American expansion and removal policy cannot be separated from the world created throughout the previous decades and centuries. In both the Great Lakes region and the Southeast, Indians as individuals and communities had intricate connections to Spanish, French, and British interests during the seventeenth and eighteenth centuries. And the human legacies of these interactions, as well as the diplomatic ties, did not disappear in the aftermath of the American Revolution. Violence, as much as diplomacy, carried forward. Both literal and figurative violence played substantial roles in the migration and relocation of Indians throughout the eastern half of the continent. To a certain extent the violence of colonial conflicts had as much of an influence on nineteenth-century relocations as did the coercion of federal soldiers and state militiamen in the 1830s and 1840s.[22]

By acknowledging the influence of context and continuity in the narrative, we give voice to the unique histories of the individuals, families, and communities that lived in the Old Northwest Territory during the early nineteenth century, and we demonstrate that their choices made a difference in their experiences. The Shawnee villages of the Ohio Country in the late eighteenth century, for example, were products of a specific history, shaped not exclusively by the struggles of imperial outsiders but also by Shawnee men and women for whom movement had become "a strategy deployed to preserve what remained of their independence" in the midst of the violence of colonial North America.[23] More to the point, however, the Shawnees, like their Delaware and Wyandot neighbors in the region, existed within a stream of history related to their own movements and relationships and not a generic narrative of dispossession and European oppression. The ongoing engagement with Moravian missionaries by some Delawares and the particular relations between Wyandots and Senecas all factored into the manner in which each community thought about and responded to the changes in the world around them from the 1700s through the 1800s.[24]

As much as we want to segment our historical narratives by eras and events, the ways in which people and communities live their lives make it impossible to eliminate continuities, even if we wanted to do so. This is not meant to suggest that scholars have completely ignored such connections.[25] Yet the ongoing emphasis on the southeastern experience remains the most prominent characteristic of the historiography, and the larger national narrative remains largely unchanged.[26] A more substantial representation of the histories of Indians from the Great Lakes region has the potential to showcase continuity and context in a manner that more effectively alters our perspective on both removal and the national narrative from the late eighteenth to the mid–nineteenth centuries.

Northern removal has been neglected as a subject of scholarly analysis for the better part of the past seventy years. [The Black Hawk War, in contrast, has received an undue amount of attention, only reinforcing the belief that it was the seminal event of the Great Lakes region after 1830.] In short, the miscast and misunderstood conflict of 1832 is viewed as the only succinct way to incorporate northern Indians into the narrative framed by the Indian Removal Act. Removing 1830 as the year of transition therefore has simple but powerful consequences. It opens the narrative to the longer migratory histories of the Delawares and Shawnees, many of whom had relocated west of the Mississippi River before 1800, as well as the diverse removals of the Potawatomis and other northern communities who took advantage of local contingencies and the international border.[27]

To question chronology, however, also requires that we question authority. More to the point, to displace the timing of removal necessitates a closer examination of the power relations inherent in this history. If, as one legal scholar writes, "Despite its grand terms, the Removal Act may not have delegated any power at all," then how did the physical relocation occur? Andrew Jackson, for all that he has become the evil face of Indian removal, more often than not assigned the federal government the role of a passive actor, especially in the case of the Cherokees. In contrast to the vision of removal policy as a context within which the president abused his authority, the national debate over Indian removal actually began with a statement of federal inaction by the chief executive. Jackson advised the Cherokees and Creeks "to emigrate beyond the Mississippi or submit to the laws of those States." The federal government would not act to protect Indians, and instead would only offer the means by which Indians could escape state authority.[28] Jackson's image as the immoral mastermind is by no means entirely undeserved; yet casting him in that role has left far too many other parties blameless in the events that transpired throughout the United States and its territories. Frontier residents in the decades during and after the American Revolution shaped events well outside the boundaries prescribed by those who conceived and wrote policies in the young republic.[29] It stands to reason that the actions of American citizens in the first half of the nineteenth century helped create and sustain the long era of Indian removal as much as the soldiers acting on the orders of a distant president did. In other words, American expansion on the local, regional, and national levels has always been about Indian removal. It is not isolated to a particular moment in time, and it is not the handiwork of a lone-wolf president or Congress. Instead, removal is an ongoing historical process, from the American past to the American present, in which every generation has the opportunity to sanction or condemn the dispossession and dislocation enacted by the generation that came before.

[Rather than update prior scholarship or critique removals discussed solely within the confines of a tribal history, the chapters that follow use some, but not all, experiences of dispossession and relocation in the Old Northwest Territory to describe in more definitive terms the manner in which removal was the work of more than just a single policy or individual.] The narrative is meant to foster a realization of the manner in which Indian removal was a societal creation—the work of numerous people who were not always working toward the same goal, but who nevertheless facilitated the dispossession and relocation of thousands of men, women, and children over the course of decades. It is, in that regard, an indictment of the early American republic. Yet it is also an indictment of United States policy in the decades that followed. Removal was not simply a physical displacement, and as such, removal history should not be confined to a singular period in the American narrative. At the same time, by understanding more clearly the ways in which removal was a societal decision as much as it was a political desire of one or more powerful men, perhaps we can better understand the societal frameworks that have helped shape the treatment of American Indians throughout the nineteenth and twentieth centuries. This, then, is one way this book seeks to begin a discussion that ultimately connects the past to the present more explicitly.

[Those familiar with the scholarship of settler colonialism will see clearly the ways in which the larger historical context of removal falls very much in step with what many within that field have written.] Patrick Wolfe in particular explains quite eloquently two of the formative factors that shape the encounters between colonizers and indigenous peoples throughout the globe. Land is at the core of this relationship, for "territoriality is settler colonialism's specific, irreducible element." Just as important, however, is the fact that settler colonialism also operates on what Wolfe terms the "logic of elimination." In brief, "settler colonialism destroys to replace." Colonization that is focused on the transfer of land ownership and the creation of new societies is therefore ongoing and is not restricted to one era or place. Nor is it limited simply to land policies, for settler colonialism also encompasses missionary efforts, forced education, political assimilation, and other tools that aid in both the destruction of the old and the creation of the new. The placement of settler colonialism within a specifically American context has also influenced a number of recent studies, including Gary Anderson's work in which he provides a thorough rationale to support the use of the term "ethnic cleansing" to describe the treatment of American Indians during the course of the United States' existence. Indian removal is thus a powerful illustration of settler colonialism's theoretical framework, which in turn reaffirms that it is also, by definition, one piece of a larger process and not an isolated historical event.[30]

Yet it is just as crucial to recognize that settler colonialism as evident in American history was not and is not an all-powerful force that leaves no room for resistance or response. Kevin Bruyneel, for example, writes about "the institutional dynamics of colonial ambivalence" within the context of Cherokee negotiations with the U.S. government after the Civil War. The Cherokee leaders sought to capitalize on "the fact that the

American state was not a unitary actor with a single voice." The disconnect and differing attitudes between the various branches of the federal government allowed room for the Cherokees to maneuver in what Bruyneel has termed a "third space of sovereignty." Within the context of the Old Northwest, it is possible to see the "institutional dynamics of colonial ambivalence" writ larger, particularly once we expand our notion of "institution" beyond the bureaucracy of federal agents and agencies. Not only did the relocation of northern Indians occur in smaller numbers than with the Cherokees on the Trail of Tears, but each removal also occurred within a more fragmented framework of external and internal interests. As a result, the fractured nature of removals from the 1820s to the 1850s, as well as the experiences of those Indians who avoided removal altogether, provided more opportunities for the illumination and exploitation of colonial ambivalence.[31]

Within a complex historical process that involved numerous actors and interests, it should not be surprising that, first, there was room to maneuver, and second, not every event had a singular outcome. In exploiting the instances of colonial ambivalence, for example, Native peoples utilized a variety of strategies to achieve specific goals or just to survive. When I was a graduate student, the buzzword for those instances was "agency." More fitting, however, may be the term "adaptive resistance," for it better describes the diverse array of approaches to settler-colonial policies. Indians who accepted the presence of, or worked closely with, traders and/or missionaries to maneuver around local, state, or federal policies used the means at their disposal to do what they thought best for themselves, their family, and their community. Even those who signed treaties did not simply surrender or concede. Treaties could be instruments of gain as much as they were instruments of loss, and those treaties that were intricately connected to the removal of Indians from their lands in the nineteenth century also provided foundations for survival into the twenty-first.[32]

No book, least of all this one, can be all things to all people. The histories of removal from the Old Northwest are in many ways too diverse to discuss adequately in a single narrative. What follows is a framework within which to explain and understand that complexity. The opening two chapters provide a foundation for the more specific case studies that follow. The first chapter explores the violence of the early American republic, and the second traces the development of the rhetoric of removal. In an effort to cast the net broadly, I selected four different stories that exemplify

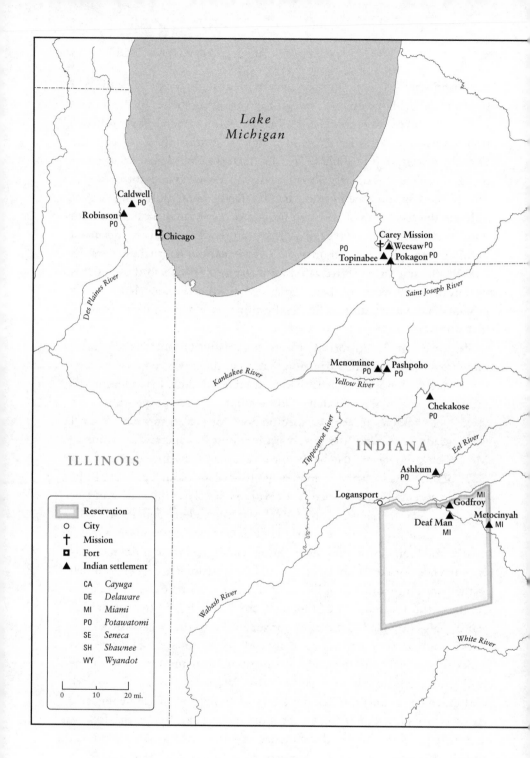

Lake
Michigan

Caldwell
▲ PO

Robinson ▲
PO

□ Chicago

Carey Mission
✝ ▲ Weesaw PO
PO ▲ ▲ Pokagon PO
Topinabee

Saint Joseph River

Des Plaines River

Kankakee River

Menominee
PO ▲ ▲ Pashpoho
Yellow River PO

▲ Chekakose
PO

Tippecanoe River

INDIANA

Eel River

ILLINOIS

Ashkum ▲
PO

Logansport ○
MI
▲ Godfroy
Deaf Man ▲ Metocinyah
MI ▲ MI

Wabash River

White River

	Reservation
○	City
✝	Mission
□	Fort
▲	Indian settlement

CA	*Cayuga*
DE	*Delaware*
MI	*Miami*
PO	*Potawatomi*
SE	*Seneca*
SH	*Shawnee*
WY	*Wyandot*

0   10   20 mi.

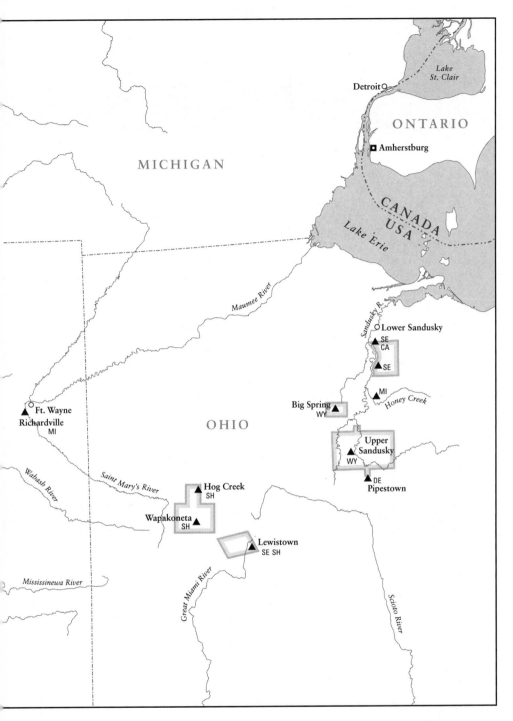

This map indicates the locations of the Wyandot, Delaware, Shawnee, Seneca, Cayuga, Miami, and Potawatomi settlements, ca. 1830, discussed throughout this book. The selective nature of this illustration means that it does not include all of the Native settlements located in Ohio, Indiana, Illinois, and Michigan Territory at that time. Drawn by Erin Greb. Copyright © 2016, University of Oklahoma Press.

Michigan Territory reservations and settlements, 1800–1855. This map brings attention
to the locations and ongoing presence of Ojibwes, Odawas, and Potawatomis on the
Lower Peninsula of Michigan into the mid-nineteenth century. Drawn by Erin Greb.
Copyright © 2016, University of Oklahoma Press.

particular elements of removal in the territories north of the Ohio River. Chapter 3 traces the different paths taken by Delaware Indians in response to Euro-American expansion and American policies in the decades prior to the Indian Removal Act. That is followed by a chapter that takes the Sandusky River region of northwestern Ohio as a focal point, an approach that considers the localized nature of removal and its impact on multiple Indian communities, including the Seneca-Cayugas and the Wyandots. Chapter 5 uses the 1833 Treaty of Chicago to explore and explain the forces that drove the diverse removals of disparate Potawatomi communities from northern Illinois and Indiana. The final case study, addressing the experiences of the Odawas and Ojibwes in Michigan Territory, analyzes the historical context and choices that enabled many Indian communities to avoid relocation west of the Mississippi River.

As in any selection process, the consequence is that other histories do not receive singular attention. Shawnees, for example, appear in smaller references throughout instead of in more developed analyses. Though I discuss the Black Hawk War, I do not examine the particular histories of the Sauks or Mesquakies. Rather than a purposeful exclusion, however, the choices I made for the case studies are meant to illustrate specific facets of a diverse and complex history. Despite the lack of comprehensiveness that even I might hope for, this book still seeks to describe broadly the manner in which all Indian communities in the Old Northwest experienced the forceful powers of settler colonialism.

The final chapter encompasses a more expansive chronology to illustrate that removal did not have a designated endpoint. Those eastern Indians relocated to lands west of the Mississippi River, from north to south, were forced by the Anglo invasion and warfare of the 1850s and 1860s to move yet again into Indian Territory. Then the allotment policies that proved so devastating to communal land ownership in Kansas Territory revisited Indian peoples on a larger scale beginning in the 1880s. Boarding schools and missionary institutions sought to remove Indian culture. Well into the twentieth century, the lands that still remained in Indian hands continued to be the target of outside interests. Within the context of the history of the United States, then, Indian removal cannot be confined to a specific chronology or geography. Instead, to paraphrase the title of the final chapter, the American era was, and is, the removal era.

1

VIOLENCE AND REMOVAL FROM LITTLE TURTLE TO BLACK HAWK

On June 11, 1782, Colonel William C. Crawford was stripped naked, had his hands bound behind his back, and was further restrained by a rope connecting his bound wrists to a post secured in the ground. The Delawares who surrounded him had captured the officer only days earlier after the Battle of Sandusky. There, Crawford's force of five hundred American soldiers had suffered a substantial defeat at the hands of the warriors of the Northwestern Indian Confederacy. Now, with Crawford at the mercy of his enemies, it became apparent that they did not intend to kill him quickly. The torture began when Delaware warriors fired powder at Crawford's naked body from point-blank range. They may have then cut off his ears. Next, in small groups they took up burning pieces of wood from the fire, advanced on the prisoner, and applied the fiery ends to his flesh. More than two hours passed as Crawford suffered repeated torture at the hands of the Delawares. Then, they scalped him, and an old woman placed ashes and embers on his back and scalped head. By all accounts he died shortly thereafter.[1]

Crawford's death scene was, and remains, iconic, as the first narrative account of the torture described above was published less than two months after the event. Dr. John Knight, a surgeon on the Crawford expedition who had also been captured, produced an account that Hugh Henry Brackenridge, through the auspices of publisher Francis Bailey, presented the American public in print. The published edition began, however, with a short letter from Bailey testifying to the purpose behind the publication.

As the American Revolution was drawing to a close, Bailey and others were upset over what they viewed as the British-inspired Indian atrocities in the Great Lakes region. And while he had heard that Sir Guy Carleton, the commander of all British forces in North America, had informed General George Washington that the Indians had been told to cease their attacks, Bailey wrote, "[The Indians] still continue their murders on our frontier." Consequently, Bailey hoped that the published narrative of Crawford's torture might "be serviceable to induce [the] government to take some effectual steps to chastise and suppress them; as from hence they will see that the nature of an Indian is fierce and cruel, and that an extirpation of them would be useful to the world, and honorable to those who can effect it."[2] This publication highlighted what many Americans viewed to be the immoral and unrestrained violence of the Indians who populated the frontiers of the American nation, which was on the verge of gaining its independence. Bailey clearly connected that violence to British instigators. The Indians were not simply savages, but savages acting at the behest of a British master.

Fifty years later, in 1832, American citizens and government officials drew similar conclusions from the actions of Sauk warrior Black Hawk and the Indians who traveled with him. Communications between American officials throughout the summer of 1832 did not hesitate to note that the Sauks who crossed into Illinois in April 1832 were members of the so-called British Band. In addition, many emphasized the fact that Black Hawk had visited British agents at Fort Malden several times in recent years. Even when the violence ended, the anxiety lingered. On August 13, eleven days after there had been bloodshed on the Bad Axe, American colonel Samuel Stambaugh turned over seven Sauk prisoners to the commanding officer at Prairie du Chien. One of the prisoners, an elderly woman, had in her possession a letter written by the former governor of Canada, Sir George Prevost, to the Sauk Indians. Stambaugh enclosed this incriminating document in a letter to his superiors but did not describe its contents. He did not need to; the implication was clear. Stambaugh even noted that he had explained to the Sauk woman "the injury these papers had done her people." From the colonel's viewpoint, two things made the letter dangerous. First, a powerful British official had written it. Second, and even more important, the letter bore the date of March 7, 1814, which meant it was composed during the War of 1812. Colonel Stambaugh's discovery and response make it evident that American perceptions of the relationship between the British and the Indians had not changed dramatically in the previous five decades.[3]

Warfare marked the people and places of the western Great Lakes region from the 1750s to the 1830s as violence under the auspices of multiple imperial struggles shaped the physical landscape. It drew, erased, and imposed political borders in territories that were more naturally delineated by rivers, portages, and lakes. The passage of time witnessed the transformation of the area known as the Pays d'en Haut into the Old Northwest Territory, and finally into the states of Ohio, Indiana, Illinois, Michigan, and Wisconsin. But perception shaped the landscape of American-Indian relations just as powerfully. Bailey's letter that introduces Knight's narrative makes clear the important image of Indians as savage agents of the British Empire. And Stambaugh, like other American officials before and after him, saw the letter held by the Sauk woman as a fulfillment of his expectations. The communication confirmed ongoing British intrigue and Indian duplicity.

In the long list of grievances comprising the Declaration of Independence, there appears the accusation that King George had "endeavoured to bring on the inhabitants of our frontiers, the merciless Indian Savages, whose known rule of warfare, is an undistinguished destruction of all ages, sexes and condition." During the war over the Ohio country in the 1780s and 1790s, the hands of British agents appeared in every Indian attack and negotiation. Americans identified British interests in the works of Tecumseh and his brother, the Shawnee Prophet, in the years leading up to the War of 1812. And in the summer of 1832 American citizens in northern Illinois saw a familiar danger in every Indian face. They asserted that the local Potawatomis and Ho-Chunks had "about as much friendship" for the Americans now "as they had during the late war with Great Britain." Therefore the Black Hawk War proved to be only the most recent in a string of conflicts encompassing more than five decades, which had been sparked by British interference and Indian treachery.[4]

More than anything else, however, Stambaugh's response to the Prevost letter illustrates the manner in which past actions, more than present realities, influenced American views of American Indians by the 1830s. Iconic images and events of a violent past had more power over American opinion than contemporary actions and truths. At the very moment that Americans declared their independence, they had classified Indians as either with the United States or against it. From 1776 to the 1830s, with few exceptions, that meant that the Indians in the Great Lakes region were either pro-American or pro-British. Indian interests and motivations outside of that colonial framework did not matter or did not exist. Wars had both immediate and long-range impacts, but most importantly, each conflict, regardless of size or participation, proved a point. Indians and whites, and more specifically Indians and frontier whites as well as Indians and British whites, needed to be separated. The Black Hawk War in 1832 sparked a widespread push for removal in the Old Northwest. Yet that conflict was not an exclusive catalyst for that push. Instead, the Black Hawk War served as only the latest confirmation of what American citizens had believed for more than five decades—American Indians were dangerous and had a suspiciously strong and enduring relationship with the British. In light of these factors, American Indians in the Old Northwest needed to be removed from the path of an expanding American nation.[5]

Crawford's death at Sandusky occurred even as the American Revolution was drawing to a close. Lieutenant General Lord Cornwallis had surrendered at Yorktown nearly a year earlier, and the first discussions leading to the Treaty of Paris had already begun. Yet the end of the Revolution did not eliminate the British presence from the Great Lakes region. Nor did it sever the connections between the British and their Native allies in the Ohio Valley. Indeed, the conclusion of the hostilities between Great Britain and the United States did not end the violence for American Indians, for the American Revolution was only part of a much longer conflict in Indian country that continued well into the 1790s and beyond.[6]

Though the end of the American Revolution did not end the warfare in the Ohio country, the terms of the 1783 Treaty of Paris definitively shaped the rhetoric surrounding that violence. At stake was the power to define the meaning of the American Revolution for the current and future residents of the Great Lakes region. Everyone from the farmers in Kentucky to the victorious general-turned-land-speculator George Washington hungered after the fertile lands north of the Ohio River. And Americans interpreted the Treaty of Paris to mean that they could now claim authority over the lands east of the Mississippi and south of the Canadian border. While disputes remained over that northern border and some other issues needed resolution, there could be no question that the British had ceded the bulk of the territory west of the Appalachians and that the United States had gained that territory through military victory.

The immediate postwar claims of the United States and its citizens were based on an unfiltered principle of conquest.[7]

Treaty commissioners of the United States made this position clear in the treaty councils held with Indians in the decade that followed. At the preliminary negotiations leading to the Treaty of Fort Stanwix in 1784, three American treaty commissioners debated this philosophy with delegates of the Six Nations of the Iroquois Confederacy who claimed to speak for themselves and the Indians of the Ohio Valley. When Seneca chief Cornplanter asserted that the Indians were a free and independent people now that Great Britain had ended their covenant and abandoned them, the American commissioners contested his interpretation. They explained in no uncertain terms that Cornplanter and his people were mistaken. "You are a subdued people," they asserted. "You have been overcome in a war which you entered into with us." To avoid any misunderstanding, the commissioners became more emphatic. "The King of Great Britain ceded to the United States *the whole*," they declared, "by the right of conquest they might claim *the whole*." Even though in 1784 the United States chose to push for only a portion of the land in question, its representatives professed the authority to take as much as they desired and needed.[8]

More than just this philosophical disagreement dogged the 1784 treaty. The very fact that there were negotiations illustrated the Americans' willingness to accept Iroquois territorial claims that had been supported by the British in the 1768 Treaty of Fort Stanwix. Yet Miami and Shawnee headmen had protested Iroquois claims since that 1768 accord and resisted the attempt by the Six Nations to exclusively negotiate boundaries. As Richard White describes it, the Six Nations and the British "spoke for peoples—the Algonquians and the backcountry settlers—whom, in fact, they could not control." If that dispute between the Iroquois and the Ohio Indians had not been clear to American officials before, it soon became quite evident. In the treaty councils of January 1786 that led to the conclusion of the Treaty of Fort Finney, Shawnee chief Kekewepellethe responded to the demands of the American treaty commissioners. "Brother, you seem to grow proud, because you have thrown down the King of England," he observed, "and as we feel sorry for our past faults, you rise in your demands on us." By the late 1780s, however, distrust had developed into outright hostility, and that fact was not lost on Secretary of War Henry Knox. In a report of May 1788 Knox addressed the growing problem with the confederacy of Indians in the territories north of the Ohio River. "[Those Indians] have expressed the highest disgust, at the principle of conquest," he wrote, "which has been specified to them, as the basis of their treaties with the United States." If the United States refused to recognize that point of contention, it should be prepared for a protracted conflict. "The doctrine of conquest is so repugnant to their feelings," Knox continued, "that rather than submit thereto, they would prefer continual war."[9]

Even as the Ohio Indians saw the conquest doctrine as repugnant, American officials in the late 1780s began to recognize it as a dream that "foundered on the weakness of the new republic." Financial, political, and military weaknesses were only a few of the problems that had manifested by the end of the Revolutionary War and the creation of the Articles of Confederation. The strength of the Indians' military resistance also sparked the Americans' change of heart. Even before the defeat of expeditions led by General Josiah Harmar and Major General Arthur St. Clair in the early 1790s, Secretary of War Knox affirmed in June 1789 that the United States had abandoned its assertion of the conquest doctrine in its dealings with the northwestern Indians. In an often-quoted phrase, Knox stated, "The Indians being the prior occupants, possess the right to the soil." In short, the Treaty of Paris in 1783 had not transferred ownership of the land from the British to the Americans. This apparent submission to Native rights to the soil did not shut the door on territorial acquisitions, however. Although Knox added that land could not "be taken from them unless by their free consent, or by the right of conquest in case of a just war," economic conditions, more than respect for property rights, held the most influence. The reality was that in the current circumstances, even if the authorities deemed the use of military force against the northwestern Indians as just, "the finances of the United States would not at present admit of the operation."[10]

Land rested at the heart of the violence in the Old Northwest during the late eighteenth century. Knox claimed that this concession of the Indians' right to the soil and the American determination to negotiate peaceful land transfers was based on a principle of justice. But military force remained viable and likely if Indians rejected American attempts to treat, a situation that made further conflict inevitable. The Northwestern Indian Confederacy, whose council fire burned bright at Brownstown, just south of Detroit, made it clear in 1786 that Americans should remain south of the Ohio River. At a December council at Brownstown, representatives from the Iroquois, Cherokee, Wyandot, Shawnee, Delaware, and five other nations crafted an address to the Continental Congress of the United States that provided the terms to ensure peace. "We beg that you will prevent your surveyors and other people from coming upon our side [of] the Ohio River," they pled, and they would do their best to prevent their warriors from raiding south of the river. If the surveyors and settlers continued to encroach, and "fresh ruptures" ensued, the confederacy would stand united, they said, in defense of "those rights and privileges, which have been transmitted to us by our ancestors."[11]

Knox's warnings, Indian petitions, treaty councils, and written agreements did not, or could not, defuse the situation. Throughout the late 1780s the Ohio Valley witnessed a rise in violence and bloodshed. Judge Harry Innes in Danville, Kentucky, assured Knox, "The Indians have always been the aggressors," and he stated that nearly 1,500 lives had been lost and as much as fifteen thousand pounds worth of property had "been carried off and destroyed by these barbarians." Yet where the records attest to the rising bloodshed caused by Indian raiding parties in the Ohio Valley, the violence was not as one sided as Innes and others made it appear. Instead it was a continuation of the war that had raged in the Ohio River Valley for more than two decades before. The Shawnee, Wyandot, and Delaware raiders of the late 1780s saw their actions as retaliation for those taken by the Virginians who greedily eyed southern Ohio. It was a cycle of violence that dismayed those federal officials who were obligated to enforce the authority of the new nation but unable to control the passions of the western frontiersmen. One of the most notorious attacks occurred in August 1788 when a force of approximately sixty men under the leadership of Patrick Brown crossed the Ohio River from Kentucky into Indiana with the sole purpose of finding and killing Indians. They killed nine friendly Piankeshaws who were members of Pacan and La Demoisel's band living near Vincennes. Brown then disobeyed direct orders from his superior officer, Jean-François Hamtramck, to desist in his efforts and led his men across the Wabash River. One year later another unauthorized expedition of Kentuckians entered the Wabash region under the leadership of Major John Hardin. Hamtramck expressed his displeasure, telling General Harmar, "It is very mortifying to see the authority of the United States so much insulted" by the actions of such expeditions.[12]

In the end, however, the U.S. government intervened on behalf of its Anglo citizens with three military campaigns in the early 1790s. The first, led by General Harmar in the fall of 1790, failed. After burning several villages and neighboring cornfields, Harmar and his men suffered an attack led by Miami war chief Little Turtle. Nearly two hundred Americans died, and Harmar retreated south to Fort Washington. The following year the governor of the Northwest Territory, Arthur St. Clair, led another expedition against the multitribal confederacy based along the Auglaize River in northwestern Ohio. If Harmar's attempt was a failure, then St. Clair's expedition was a catastrophic failure. This time approximately six hundred men lost their lives as, once again, Little Turtle and the confederate forces overwhelmed a disorganized and unprepared army of soldiers and militiamen. Only with General Anthony Wayne's campaign, which culminated at the Battle of Fallen Timbers in 1794, did the American military and the American public gain the victory they desired. After this defeat of the villages on the Auglaize, the Indian confederacy's leaders viewed peace as their best option. The Treaty of Greenville, signed in 1795, brought an end to this phase of the conflict and led to the cession of most of the present-day state of Ohio.[13]

The Battle of Fallen Timbers opened the door to American settlement in Ohio, but a closed door made a more dramatic statement. Major William Campbell, the British commander of Fort Miami, refused to shelter Native warriors fleeing the battlefield, an act that most Indian confederates viewed as a betrayal. Americans breathed a sigh of relief. Even before Harmar's expedition, Henry Knox had communicated the true intentions of the American military efforts so as to avoid any unnecessary outside involvement. The secretary of war wanted a messenger sent to the British agent at Detroit "to assure him of the entire pacific disposition of the United States towards Great Britain and its possessions." The United States could barely afford military campaigns against the Indians, and Knox was not going to risk enlarging the scope of the conflict by offending the interests of the British. Knox served until the end of 1794 and therefore must have been pleased that the American military campaigns of the 1790s had not resulted in a larger engagement with British forces.[14]

Indeed, a closer examination of the events of the 1790s reveals a complex situation in which American and British officials viewed the overall conflict as a larger dance between their respective interests. That dance is reflected most specifically in the communications and councils during the spring and summer of 1793. Harmar and St. Clair had both failed to extinguish the Indian confederacy, and Congress appropriated one million dollars for the organization of another military campaign under the leadership of General Anthony Wayne. Yet even as Wayne trained his forces at Fort Washington, Knox sent federal commissioners to meet with confederacy representatives at Sandusky in early June. The commissioners had orders to be inflexible on one principle—the time had passed when the Ohio River could remain the boundary between Indian and American lands. On this point the Americans would not relent. And even as the negotiations proceeded, General Wayne gathered his forces around Fort Washington in anticipation of the campaign that ultimately led to an American victory.

The diplomatic affairs of 1793 reveal in part that American officials were resigned to a British presence that violated the terms of the 1783 Treaty of Paris and reluctantly surrendered to British involvement in the negotiations. Knox informed commissioners Benjamin Lincoln, Beverly Randolph, and Timothy Pickering, "It is, however, probable that the British agents Messrs. Butler and McKee, will be present by the desire of the Indians. To this, you will not object, although you cannot formally admit of them, or any other British agents, as mediators or umpires." And when the commissioners reached Niagara on May 17, they received a letter from Colonel Alexander McKee informing them that the Indians would not be ready for them at Sandusky on June 1 as planned. The commissioners resorted to asking McKee for his assistance in brokering a peace and even discussed obtaining white wampum from the British agents in Detroit because they were having difficulty finding it at every other point in their journey.[15]

The commissioners' dealings with John Graves Simcoe, the lieutenant governor of Upper Canada, were just as telling. They first wrote Simcoe asking him to quell what they called "unfounded rumors," including one that Simcoe had "advised the Indians to make peace, but not to give up any of their lands." Randolph and his colleagues viewed the American negotiating points as "fair and liberal," and wanted "to embrace every means necessary to make them so appear to the Indians," including the presence of a British military officer at the council sessions. Simcoe denied giving any such advice to the Indians, but he also provided the Americans with some constructive criticism. The British had always aimed at uniting the Indian tribes, Simcoe wrote, somewhat disingenuously. That being said, he felt it within his rights to point out that "a jealousy of a contrary conduct in the agents of the United States, appear[ed] to him to have been deeply impressed upon the minds of the confederacy." The British in general, and Simcoe in particular, would not make things easy for the Americans.[16]

Rather than a single council session at Lower Sandusky, the negotiations occurred in several different sessions over the course of several months. Records of the first council at British-built Fort Erie demonstrate American discomfort with the fact that the commissioners were going to have to talk to Mohawk leader Joseph Brant and the other Indian representatives in the presence of Simcoe and several other civil and military British officials.[17] Indeed, the Americans' journal of proceedings begins with a speech made by Brant, but fails to indicate that the Americans had to wait to enter the hall until Brant had addressed the British officials. The British records show only a brief exchange in which Brant presented a belt of white wampum, declaring, "Our intention and business is peaceable," and Simcoe stated that he would be glad to hear what they had to say and returned the belt. The words appear to be of no great import, but the staging illustrates that the British stood ready to monitor the Americans.[18]

The short council at Niagara focused primarily on Indian concerns over the American military threat and whether or not the commissioners had authority to delineate boundaries between American and Indian lands.[19] Told that they did, the Indian delegates left Niagara to discuss the current circumstances in council at Sandusky. The Americans chose to move closer to the Indian negotiations, arriving at Detroit by boat on July 21 and taking a room at the home of Matthew Elliott, the assistant to Colonel McKee. Nine days later the commissioners finally heard from the Sandusky council when a Wyandot speaker named Sawaghdawunk (also called Carry One About) presented a short written message. The Treaty of Fort Stanwix had set the boundary at the Ohio River. "If you seriously design to make a firm and lasting peace," the statement read, "you will immediately remove all your people from our side of that river." So when they had asked if the commissioners had the authority to draw a boundary, the Indians had meant that they wanted the commissioners to affirm the Ohio River as the border, not draw a new one.[20]

After waiting nearly two months to hold a full council, Lincoln, Randolph, and Pickering grew irritated by the unyielding nature of the confederacy's communication. They referred to all of the previous treaties negotiated in the 1780s that had confirmed land cessions north of the Ohio River and declared, "It is impossible to make the river Ohio the boundary."[21] Sawaghdawunk countered by dismissing all of the treaties except for that of Fort Stanwix in 1768, negotiated by the British agent Sir William Johnson. The others mentioned by the Americans did not count because the few chiefs who had signed those agreements had little authority. "We are sorry we cannot come to an agreement," the Wyandot orator said. "The line has been fixed long ago." The Indian delegation returned to Sandusky, and for the next two weeks the commissioners in Detroit were buffeted by rumors. One tale held that only four of the tribes, the Delawares, Miamis, Shawnees, and Wyandots, were agitating for war, while another story indicated that the confederacy would negotiate for peace. The commissioners could do nothing but sit and wait, powerless diplomats at the mercy of the Indians and the British. Even when they expressed a desire to go uninvited to the Indian council at the rapids, the captain of the boat granted to them by Simcoe stated that he was under orders to be at their disposal with the exception of that very action.[22]

Frustrated and impatient, the commissioners finally sent word that they intended to leave. In response, two Wyandot runners arrived at Detroit carrying only a point-by-point critique of the American position. The Indians who had signed the treaties at Fort McIntosh, Fort Finney, and Fort Harmar had attended to make peace with the Americans, but "through fear were obliged to sign any paper that was laid before them." Instead of paying large sums of money to the Indians for the land, perhaps the Americans would be better served by turning their attention to those who had advanced north of the Ohio River. "We know that these set- tlers are poor," the statement read, "or they would never have ventured to live in a country which has been in continual trouble ever since they crossed the Ohio." The confederates even suggested that the United States give money intended to purchase Indian lands to the poor whites who could then buy land elsewhere. In the end, however, the confederacy's position emphasized American intransigence more than creative uses for federal funds. Because the commissioners never agreed to consider the Ohio River as the proper boundary, they would never be invited to attend a full council.[23]

The brief reply to the confederacy's message stated simply that because the Americans had at least given the Indians a chance to negotiate, they trusted that impartial judges would "not attribute the continuance of the war" to the faulty actions of the United States. In a short communication to General Wayne, written upon their departure from Detroit, Lincoln,

Pickering, and Randolph thanked the general for maintaining the peace and thus keeping them safe. A longer letter to Knox opened with a blunt statement that spoke volumes: "The Indians have refused to make peace." Both the Americans and the Indians had stood firm in their respective positions, and a refusal to budge from those terms was interpreted by the opposing side as a refusal to support a nonviolent resolution.[24]

A more transformative negotiation resulted from the Battle of Fallen Timbers, however, and the British role in the region was never far from the participants' minds. On June 12, 1795, General Anthony Wayne lit the fire at Fort Greenville in Ohio and opened a council that lasted nearly two months. The Treaty of Greenville was many things, perhaps foremost among them an accord that described a boundary line for Indian lands in Ohio entailing a cession of tens of millions of acres. Yet recent events, beyond the military victory of General Wayne's Legion, made the treaty about more than just land. Most important, the United States and Great Britain had signed what became known as Jay's Treaty in November 1794, and the U.S. Senate had ratified the agreement in June 1795. As part of that accord, the British finally began to pull out of their positions south of the Canadian border.[25] Indeed, the council at Greenville provided an important breaking point for many of the Indian participants from the British, and Anthony Wayne was more than happy to exploit any doubts in their British allies that the Indians may have shown. He read the 1783 accord out loud to reinforce the British betrayal and then added to it by pointing out how the continued British presence in the ceded lands showed their betrayal of treaties in general. He finished off with a flourish by then reading the text of Jay's Treaty, in which the British once again agreed to specific boundaries between Canada and the United States.[26]

The councils also marked a substantial turning point for some of the most notable principal men among the Northwestern Confederacy. In the process of attempting "to use the council to renegotiate their position with the Americans," many Native leaders also stated their intentions to leave the British behind. Tarhe, the Wyandot chief from Sandusky, made the most direct statement in this regard. "I view you lying in a gore of blood," he said to Wayne. "It is me, an Indian, who has caused it. Our tomahawk yet remains in your head; the English gave it to me to place it there." Tarhe then declared the Wyandots' intention to bury the tomahawk deep in the ground and develop a strong relationship with the United States. The Wyandot chief now looked at the terms of the Treaty of Fort Harmar of 1789 as fair. "You took pity on us Indians," he added. "You did not do as our fathers the British agreed you should." This was taken to an even further extent when Tarhe asserted that he spoke for the Wyandots, Delawares, and Shawnees and explained that the only problem they had with the proposed treaty was the absence of drawn boundaries between Indian lands north of the treaty line. The Wyandot chief cemented his support for the Americans on the final day of the council: "You see we all now acknowledge you to be our father," he declared. "I take you by the hand, which I offer as a pledge of our sincerity, and of our happiness in becoming your children."[27]

Tarhe's unflinching proclamation of support did not speak for all present. The Miami leader, Little Turtle, made a point of following Tarhe's declarations with a more measured assessment of American policies and discussed the numerous ways in which Wayne's statements in council demonstrated the Americans' unfamiliarity with the history of the landscape and the relations among the Indians, French, and British. The Americans had told Little Turtle and his people that the British had spread falsehoods when they said the United States just wanted the land. Little Turtle's speech implied that the proposed treaty validated those British statements. In the end, however, Little Turtle presented a calumet to signal the Miamis' intention to hold fast to the new relationship with the United States. Other speakers followed Little Turtle, reminding Wayne that this new relationship required constant maintenance. New Corn, a Potawatomi *wkama* (leader), was one of those who voiced the more prevalent feelings about British betrayals and the need for the Americans to prove themselves to be better. After agreeing to the treaty and listening to Tarhe pledge allegiance to the United States, New Corn tried to make Wayne understand the Natives' expectations. "Do not deceive us in the manner that the French, the British, and Spaniards have heretofore done," he chided.[28]

The three-year period of 1793 through 1795 therefore served as an important turning point for the triangle of British-Indian-American relations, and it appeared that the United States had isolated the Indians from their land and their allies. Yet the reach of Wayne's campaign and the Treaty of Greenville was limited to a relatively small population of Indians in the Great Lakes region. For all that the Battle of Fallen Timbers was viewed as a struggle between Wayne's Legion and the Northwestern Confederacy, the latter had long since lost its cohesiveness. Even in the long councils of 1793 the confederacy had shown signs of cracking as the Shawnees, Delawares, and Miamis pushed for the Ohio River boundary while others sought to compromise. Bands of Odawas and Ojibwes had even left northwestern Ohio and returned to their homes in the north several months before the Battle of Fallen Timbers, depleting the confederacy's fighting force by nearly half. Consequently, the resulting peace treaty signed at Greenville had a disproportional effect on the Indians of the Maumee Valley. North of the Detroit-Amherstburg corridor the relationship between the British and the Indians was largely unaffected. The United States had not pushed that far, and the fur trade under British control maintained a strong influence in the region. The British-Indian alliance in the larger Great Lakes region still survived, radiating from Niagara, Amherstburg, and Michilimackinac.[29]

From 1795 to 1805 the affected Indian communities adjusted to the terms of the Greenville treaty. Northwestern Ohio remained Indian country, but villages moved and some Indians relocated further west into central and northern Indiana along the White and Wabash Rivers. Between 1794 and 1801 most of the Delawares settled in a series of villages along the White River in central Indiana on lands allocated to them by the Miamis. Only a small band of approximately one hundred remained in a village on the Sandusky River under Captain Pipe. Those Delawares lived between the Wyandot towns at Upper and Lower Sandusky. A substantial Shawnee population resided at Wapakoneta, located on the upper Auglaize River. There, the venerated leader Black Hoof promoted a transition from militancy to adaptation and welcomed the presence of Quaker missionaries in the early nineteenth century in order to transition his people into westernized agricultural practices. Other, more traditionalist Shawnees criticized Black Hoof's maneuvers even as they struggled to gain traction in the midst of increased American settlement. Yet while the Wapakoneta Shawnees labored to meet American expectations, their relatives found the alternate path to be just as challenging. Alcoholism and violence led to death and deterioration for many Shawnees who moved their villages throughout western Ohio and eastern Indiana in the late 1700s and early 1800s in an attempt to find a suitable refuge.[30]

Within that context of struggle emerged the Shawnee Prophet. In 1805 Lalawethika (also called the Rattle), a failed warrior and hunter as well as an alcoholic, had a vision and transformed into Tenskwatawa, the Open Door. He had received a message from the Master of Life, and with that message Tenskwatawa set out to renew and revitalize the Shawnee people. The resulting revitalization movement swept through the Great Lakes region over the next five years. Even as Black Hoof and other Shawnees viewed the message bearer with skepticism, other Indians eagerly grasped this new nativist teaching that promised to return them to a better way of life. Tenskwatawa's revelations in the spring of 1805 provided the foundation for a renewal of an Indian confederacy over the decade that followed. With his brother Tecumseh expanding upon this message, the two men built an alliance that brought together Indians throughout the Great Lakes region and the trans–Mississippi West. Within the larger message of social and cultural renewal, the Shawnee Prophet also had a more pointed commentary about the Americans in particular. Whereas the Master of Life had created the British, Spanish, and French, the Americans were children of an evil spirit and should be avoided at all costs.[31]

American officials in the region did not know what to make of the Shawnee Prophet at first. William Henry Harrison, the governor of Indiana Territory, infamously failed to discredit the Prophet by demanding that he provide a miracle as proof of his power. That plan sank under the weight of a solar eclipse in June 1806. Harrison was concerned by the increasing popularity of the Shawnee spiritual leader, but he was also skeptical of the source of his power and motivation. "I really fear that this said Prophet is an engine set to work by the British for some bad purpose," Harrison wrote to the Secretary of War in the summer of 1807. British agent Alexander McKee had been spotted moving among the Indians, and traders in the region agreed, "A general combination of the Indians for a war against the United States is the object of all these messages and councils." A month later Indian agent William Wells confirmed Harrison's fears, stating his opinion, "The British are at the bottom of all of this Business and depend on it that if we have war with them that many of the Indian tribes will take an active part against us."[32]

Over the next four years the cat-and-mouse game between the Prophet and Harrison over the possible role of the British in the Indian confederacy and the looming possibility of an Indian uprising only intensified. In an exchange of letters in the summer of 1808, Tenskwatawa informed Harrison that it had never been his intention "to lift up [his] hand against the Americans," and that he and his followers were "resolved not to listen any longer to bad advice." In response Harrison confessed that he had "given credit" to the report of British involvement, but was content with the

Prophet's "solemn assurance of fidelity." "Very different however will be your lot," Harrison warned, "if you permit yourselves to be seduced by the British agents." From all appearances, Harrison never believed the Prophet separated his interests from those at Amherstburg. "I have no doubt," he reported to Secretary of War William Eustis in 1810, "that the present hostile disposition of the Prophet and his Votaries has been produced by British interference."[33]

Two things crystalized in the buildup to the Battle of Tippecanoe in 1811. First, Harrison and the Americans had been wary of the Shawnee Prophet for years and saw the potential for violence throughout that period of time. Second, and more important, Harrison saw the British as the instigators and refused to acknowledge the larger Indian interests at work. Harrison and others did not give credence to the sacred aspect voiced by the Prophet and the political aspect voiced by Tecumseh. There is no question that the British at Amherstburg maintained relations with Indians in the region and did their best to cultivate an alliance in preparation for the outbreak of war. At a private meeting held in March 1808 at Amherstburg, British agent William Claus talked to three Shawnee chiefs, Captain Johnny, Blackwood, and Buffalo, about the tensions between the British and Americans resulting from the *Chesapeake* affair (in which a British ship attacked an American ship in search of deserters) and reminded these potential allies of the problems caused by American settlement. "You must see every day," he said, "that what little is now left you is going fast," and he explained that the British were better fathers than the Americans ever would or could be. Both Tenskwatawa and Tecumseh visited the British at Malden to cultivate that relationship. In November 1810 Tecumseh spoke with Matthew Elliott and stated that while the Indians were ready and able to defend their country themselves, they expected the British would, he said, "push forwards towards us what may be necessary to supply our wants." Elliott knew he could not overtly support the Shawnee-led confederacy, but that did not mean he cut off all communications.[34]

Blinded by their British obsession, Harrison and other American officials ignored other critical catalysts of both American and Indian origin. The 1809 Treaty of Fort Wayne came under particular fire by Tecumseh and others because Harrison had coerced land cessions without the full consent of the Indian nations involved and in direct contradiction of the Treaty of Greenville. Much like Harrison's failed attempt to undermine the Shawnee Prophet's claim to sacred power, continuing to focus on the role of British intrigue in the Indians' militancy was dismissive of the spiritual foundations of the nativist movement, which had little to do with British influence. And while the Treaty of Fort Wayne marked the increased importance of pragmatic opposition under the leadership of Tecumseh, it is also true that the spiritual element of the resistance did not fade or disappear. Tenskwatawa, like other Indian prophets before him, had always connected the pragmatic and the sacred, and he had promoted pan-Indianism through notions of separate creation and cultural revitalization. For the Shawnee Prophet and his brother, the British remained a tool that could help achieve a larger goal, not the catalyst for the movement.[35]

Yet to Harrison the dangers of a British–Indian alliance became more apparent with every passing day. And even when Harrison's army defeated Tenskwatawa's physical force and his spiritual promise at the Battle of Tippecanoe in November 1811, Tecumseh's continued influence meant that the danger had not truly passed. Captain R. I. Snelling noted shortly after the battle that "all the confederated tribes had abandoned their faith in the Prophet except about forty Shawanose." And Harrison informed the Secretary of War that the Prophet was besieged on all sides by former allies who blamed him for their losses at Tippecanoe. Nevertheless, Harrison also believed that the Shawnee Prophet's downfall had not eliminated the threat, and his good friend Andrew Jackson shared that belief. In a letter of condolence on the loss of American lives at Tippecanoe, Jackson mentioned to Harrison that he would be willing to support actions to avenge those deaths. One future president wrote to the other of his hope that the federal government would act appropriately because "this hostile band, which must be excited to war, by the secret agents of Great Britain, must be destroyed." Upon the American declaration of war seven months later, Jackson and Harrison would have their chance.[36]

On June 18, 1812, President James Madison signed the official declaration of war against Great Britain. American officials first adopted a policy of promoting Indian neutrality in the War of 1812. Past experience led federal agents to argue that it was best to keep Indians out of the conflict. History informed Indians as well, and several villages of Wyandots recognized the dilemma they now faced. In the latter half of the eighteenth century most Ohio Wyandots lived in several villages along the Sandusky River, but smaller communities had also established settlements in the vicinity of Detroit. From the 1750s to the 1810s these different villages and

A Scene on the Frontiers as Practiced by the Humane British and Their Worthy Allies. In this image the British military officer accepts a handful of scalps, saying, "Bring me the Scalps and the King our master will reward you." Originally printed in 1812, this cartoon spoke clearly to Americans who saw the British behind the attacks and atrocities committed by American Indians. Courtesy of the Library of Congress, Prints and Photographic Division.

their leaders alternately worked with the French, British, and Americans. Most recently the Wyandots had suffered severe losses fighting American soldiers at the Battle of Fallen Timbers in 1794. While a number of factors influenced Wyandot diplomacy in the early nineteenth century, their location at a focal point of imperial conflict made some kind of alliance necessary.[37]

Therefore in 1812 the Wyandot residents of the Brownstown and Monguagon settlements just south of Detroit knew from past experience that neutrality would be impossible to maintain. They were trapped in the middle. This was particularly true for the family of William Walker, Sr., who at age forty-two had lived among the Wyandots for more than thirty years. Captured by Delaware hunters in Virginia in 1781, Walker's adoption by the Wyandots had been facilitated by Adam Brown, another white captive. During his time with the Wyandots, Walker had learned the language and married a Wyandot woman named Catherine Rankin. In 1790 the young couple settled just south of the main Wyandot settlement of Brownstown, near present-day Gibraltar, where Walker turned his attention to farming and raising a family. At the time war was declared, the Walkers had a sizeable farm and seven children.[38]

William Walker, Sr., had also established a reputation as a dependable interpreter. According to his son, William had Catherine to thank for this development because she was fluent in several Indian languages, and she was a valuable asset for Indian diplomacy in the region as well. William became a mediator for relations between the Americans and Wyandots, and American officials appointed him as a special Indian agent at the outbreak of war with the specific task of keeping the Wyandots near Detroit neutral. The problem Walker faced was not necessarily the intractability of the Wyandots but the simple fact that their settlements rested just across the river from the British centers of Fort Malden and Amherstburg. His troubles were compounded in July 1812 when the British attacked the Wyandot settlements under the pretext of capturing boats filled with supplies for the American army. Although Walker and other Wyandots initially repulsed the attack, they could not defeat the force that finally arrived. The British soldiers destroyed Walker's farm and took his family prisoner. By October William, Catherine, and their seven children were captives in Detroit, which was now in British hands after General William Hull's infamous surrender the month before.[39]

The experiences of the Walkers over the next several months illustrate the difficulties confronting their family in particular and the Wyandots in general. William was initially placed in a prison cell. His oldest son, John, who had been wounded while defending Brownstown, was supposed to travel by ship to Quebec with other American prisoners. Both men avoided their fates by breaking free, but neither managed to escape unscathed to American lines. John fled Detroit in early October and headed to Fort Defiance in northwestern Ohio only to be accosted by American soldiers who assumed the young Wyandot was a British spy. They then placed John in strict confinement. It took a few more months for William to manage his escape. Like his son, he headed toward the American positions at Fort Defiance. He had no identification papers on his person and therefore suffered the same fate as John. Their troubles ended only when respected citizens verified their identities and thus validated their loyalty to the United

States. For the remaining Walkers, freedom had to wait until the fall of 1813. Catherine and the other six children were released when the British evacuated Detroit, but they could not return to Brownstown. Their home had been destroyed, so they instead moved to the Wyandot settlements at Upper Sandusky in northern Ohio where they lived for the next three decades.[40]

The fate of the Walker family had shifted because of American victories on the waters of Lake Erie and on land in Upper Canada. The Battle of Lake Erie, in which Master Commandant Oliver Perry led the American fleet to defeat Captain Robert Barclay's British naval force, lasted only a couple of hours on September 10, 1813. Yet it turned the tide of American fortunes in the western Great Lakes. American domination of the lake waters meant control over the transport of goods and people. As a result, the British land forces under Major General Henry Procter surrendered their position at Detroit. They crossed the border to Amherstburg and in short order began a retreat up the Thames River through Upper Canada. General William Henry Harrison and his army were not very far behind. On October 5, at the Battle of the Thames, Harrison and his men routed the British forces and secured their hold on the region. Much has been made of these events, with Procter lambasted for his retreat and Tecumseh praised for his desire and willingness to make a stand, even though it meant his life.[41]

Yet debates over strategy tend to obscure the meaning of that campaign, and the war overall, for the Indians who were caught in the middle of a conflict they did not start or want. It would have been difficult for anyone to assume a position of neutrality in the vicinity of Detroit and Amherstburg, for circumstances had placed the Walkers and their neighbors at the epicenter of military campaigns in 1812 and 1813. But more than geography complicated matters. Their identity as Indians, or as members of Indian communities, hampered their ability to operate without external interference. The British and Americans viewed Indians as both valuable allies and dangerous enemies in the War of 1812. Particularly for Americans, however, the war and its legacy constantly reminded them of the threat posed by British support of Indian interests. In the minds of American citizens and officials, a looming British presence overshadowed Indian affairs in the western Great Lakes for the next two decades.

The Treaty of Ghent officially ended the War of 1812, but it provided little comfort to Americans living in the western Great Lakes region.

Agents in the field and territorial governors saw the British around every corner and viewed any contact between Indian tribes as the foundation of a militant confederacy that would carry on Tecumseh's work. American citizens also tended to lump Indians into a single group and seldom distinguished between tribes or bands. Into the 1830s Americans defined some Indian communities and individuals by their actions in the "late war." Most Americans expected Indians in the western Great Lakes to be faithless and easily swayed by British temptations.

The federal government sought to reestablish order in Indian affairs as soon as possible after the war ended. In the summer of 1815 treaty commissioners held councils at Portage des Sioux, Detroit, and other northern locales in order to formalize peaceful relations with those Indian nations who had allied with the British. Government agents also received specific instructions. Acting secretary of war A. J. Dallas informed the new agent for Illinois Territory, Richard Graham, that he was to execute his duties according to guidelines laid out in the Trade and Intercourse Act of 1799. Graham would particularly need to be on the alert for any individual "among the Indians attempting to mislead them, or to inspire them with distrust in the U. States." Within a year of his appointment Graham found reason to appreciate that warning. "The British traders will have to be watched very close," he wrote to his superiors in July 1816. "Those who have been trading on the waters of the Mississippi have used all their influence, which is very considerable to excite distrust among the Indians." The agent feared the economic hold of foreign traders and the ease with which they appeared to manipulate the minds of their Indian customers.[42]

Graham was not alone in his concerns. Illinois territorial governor Ninian Edwards asserted that the United States needed to eliminate all vestiges of the British. He expressed unease because the Potawatomis in northern Illinois were "invited to British Councils" and had been informed that war would be renewed. Based on the reports coming into his office, Edwards believed that the British agents at Fort Malden kept alive the possibility of a revitalized British-Indian alliance. More than anything, however, Edwards worried because he faced Indians who did not fully understand or respect American strength. The tribes in northern Illinois Territory, he wrote to the Secretary of War, "having long been, and still being, so devoted to that Nation [Great Britain], that nothing less, than an adequate display of Military power, or great liberality on the part of our

Government, can command their obedience; or conciliate their friend-ship." In short, either force or generosity was necessary to combat perva-sive British interests.[43]

Border permeability exacerbated American anxieties. The Treaty of Ghent had not ended a decades-long relationship between local Indians and their British father, and agents at Fort Malden annually distributed clothing, weapons, and ammunition to those Indians who visited their outpost. American officials like Michigan territorial governor Lewis Cass argued that it was absolutely necessary for the U.S. government to respond to this trade. More than economics underscored his opinion. The trade spawned violence against American settlers. "In nine cases out of ten," Cass asserted, "the Indians, who are guilty of these aggressions are on their return from Malden, carrying with them British presents and British counsels." The secretary of war hastened to reassure American agents in the Old Northwest, writing, "Efficient measures will be taken by the Gov-ernment, as soon as practicable, to prevent the Indians from crossing into Canada." But from Cass's position in Detroit, it was clear that government efforts would have little impact. Indians moved through the region in large numbers through the early 1820s. Although it is an admittedly inex-act measure, the numbers of Indians crossing over the Raisin and Huron Rivers in southern Michigan provide some sense of how many were head-ing north to Detroit and Fort Malden. From March 1822 to April 1823 approximately 2,000 Indians used the bridge over the River Raisin, while nearly as many used a similar span that crossed the Huron River.[44]

The Delawares, Wyandots, Shawnees, Potawatomis, Sauks, and Oda-was who crossed those bridges were not necessarily heading directly to Fort Malden. Detroit was the headquarters of the Michigan superinten-dency and therefore served as the location of annuity distributions. Nev-ertheless, the distance between the two settlements made it impossible to limit travel between them, and American officials were not the only ones concerned. The leaders of the Wyandot community at Sandusky, Ohio, wanted U.S. officials to change the annuity distribution point because of the proximity of Fort Malden to Detroit. According to Cherokee Boy and his fellow Wyandot chiefs, "Our Young Men when at Detroit frequently Visit the British Nation in Upper Canada and receive large presents from them which often Induces them to revisit the British." Further evidence of Indian visits to Amherstburg comes from the records of British agents. Captain Billy Caldwell of the British Indian Department noted that a total of 1,166 men, women, and children from eight different tribes visited Amherstburg on August 15, 1816. Caldwell's report described these visitors as "dependent Indians." The description mattered, for it differentiated those Indians who were expected from the twenty-two who visited on August 14 and were labeled "strangers." Multiple sources confirm that Indians continued to deal with the British in large numbers.[45]

Despite his concerns about continued contact between the British and local Indians, Lewis Cass, unlike other American agents, did not panic easily. He had been appointed the governor of Michigan Territory in 1813, and even as others continually warned of Indian hostilities, Cass reassured officials in Washington that "exaggerated reports" about the hostile intentions of Indians near Detroit had "prevailed." When others rushed to accuse the British of interference, Cass raised alternative justifications for Indian anger. One reason was, he claimed, the "mode in which their land has been acquired in this quarter," and the other was "the selection of persons to fill offices in the Indian Department." In other words, Indians did not need the British to tell them to be mad about the land rush and inadequately prepared agents. Yet Cass still concluded that the United States needed to improve its approach to British and Indian relations in Michigan Territory. The Wyandots at Brownstown served as the perfect example. If nothing else, the War of 1812 proved, according to Cass, that "this tract of country should be in our possession and that a white Settlement should be interposed between the British possessions on the opposite side and the Indians." Although another war was not imminent, Cass did not see the need to tempt fate or to coddle those Indians who had allied with the British in the War of 1812.[46]

Yet British infiltration and influence spanned a vast stretch of the Canadian border. The geography of the Great Lakes played a crucial role in the manner in which Indians cultivated relationships in the decades after the War of 1812. For the thirty-year period leading up to 1815, the strength of British diplomacy was not evenly spread. By the War of 1812 the strongest ties between Indians and the British rested northwest of the Detroit-Amherstburg corridor. It should not have been surprising, then, for Americans to see signs of British influence along the shores of Lake Superior and in the present-day Upper Peninsula of Michigan. On June 16, 1820, Cass held a council with the Ojibwe bands living near Sault Ste. Marie. He was in the midst of an expedition designed to introduce Indians in the far northwestern area of his jurisdiction to the reach and measures of

American policy. Henry Rowe Schoolcraft, who was officially appointed as geologist of the expedition, made telling observations of the Ojibwe delegates at the June 16 council. Schoolcraft explained their resistance to American authority by noting that the chiefs wore "costly broadcloths, feathers, epaulets, medals, and silverwares, of British fabric." And only moments after the Ojibwe delegation literally kicked aside the presents brought by the Cass expedition and left the council meeting, they "hoisted the British flag in the midst of their encampment." Schoolcraft had no doubt that the British bore responsibility for this belligerence.[47]

Hostility among the Ojibwes, Menominees, and Ho-Chunks in this region was usually attributed to the efforts of British traders affiliated with the American Fur Company and smaller trade outfits who operated out of Michilimackinac and Drummond's Island. The latter spot rests in the waterway that connects Lakes Superior and Huron, and in the decade after the War of 1812 the British maintained a garrison there to retain some measure of influence. Thousands of pounds worth of goods and provisions were distributed to thousands of Ojibwes and other Indians who traveled from up to six hundred miles away to receive those gifts every June. It appeared that Americans needed to do more to control trade relations in the northwestern Great Lakes. The first benefit of such an effort, according to Green Bay agent John Bowyer, would be the "destruction of British influence among the Indians, which is now diffused through the traders." According to Bowyer, almost all of the men involved in the Indian trade in the western expanse of Michigan Territory were "British subjects, under British influence, which . . . must operate unfavorably to the interests of the United States." Once again, Lewis Cass attempted to provide a voice of reason and argued that those men employed in the fur trade on the waters of Lake Huron and Lake Michigan were not having a negative impact. As far as he was concerned, these men were crucial to regional commerce.[48]

Despite Cass's attempts to temper the anxieties of those around him, warnings about the British filled the letters and reports of Indian agents from the latter half of the 1810s into the 1820s. The specter of a pan-Indian confederacy, another legacy of the late war, also made an appearance. American officials and citizens feared any indication that Indians were communicating with other Indians. In their minds, any element of cooperation could lead to confederacy, and confederacy inevitably signified an uprising against the United States. Cass notified federal officials in the spring of 1818 that rumors of such a possibility had begun to circulate. Reports reached his desk that a war belt of wampum from the south had made its way through the western Great Lakes. To make sure officials in Washington understood the potential problems, Cass noted that the northern Indians were "perfectly aware of the state of affairs in the South." In other words, the northern Indians knew about Andrew Jackson's military actions in Florida against the Seminoles and were worried it might fore-shadow American military action in the Great Lakes.[49]

The perceived threat of a pan-Indian uprising also endured in the very person of Tenskwatawa, the Shawnee Prophet. At the Battle of the Thames in October 1813, the Prophet had fled after the initial American charge and therefore did not learn of his brother Tecumseh's death until later. He spent the next two years trying to stay out of harm's way, and at war's end he was living near Amherstburg on the Canadian side of the border. In the late 1810s Tenskwatawa made several weak attempts to renew what had been a powerful Indian confederacy at the beginning of the decade. American officials at Detroit and British officials at Amherstburg did their best to keep track of his actions and those of his small band of followers. By the mid-1820s, however, the Shawnee Prophet had become relatively harmless in the eyes of territorial authorities like Lewis Cass. The aging visionary no longer had the religious power or authority to influence or attract Indians in the region.[50]

Tenskwatawa's power may have weakened by the late 1820s, but the memory of a British-Indian alliance never left the minds of American officials. The strength of that ongoing concern endured into the early 1830s, particularly in the case of the Black Hawk War. Despite a host of factors leading to the outbreak of violence in 1832, American citizens and officials could not free themselves from the assumption of British involvement. Consequently, any and all Indian activity in the western Great Lakes in the 1830s was placed within the framework that had existed for decades.

Tensions first began to rise in northern Illinois over the movement of Sauks and Mesquakies on both sides of the Mississippi River in the late 1820s. The Sauks had never been satisfied with an 1804 treaty that obligated them to remove from their lands east of the Mississippi when the federal government deemed it necessary. The history of that accord was rife with fraud, and the warrior Black Hawk was one of many Sauks who refused to accept its terms. Therefore, when federal officials finally decided to enforce the terms of the treaty in the late 1820s, the anger over the 1804 treaty resurfaced. Under the auspices of that agreement, American citizens began to move into the territory that was still claimed by the Sauks. When Black Hawk and the members of his British Band protested, their intransigence made American agents and military officers in the region nervous.[51]

American officials did not hesitate to point out the relationship between the potentially dangerous Indians in the 1830s and the War of 1812. The very designation of the British Band referred to the fact that Black Hawk and other Sauk warriors had allied with the British during the War of 1812. Nearly twenty years later this affiliation was used to distinguish them from the "friendly" Sauks under Keokuk who had moved west of the Mississippi River and accepted the terms of the 1804 treaty. Dangerous affiliations were not limited to the Sauks, however. Captain Richard Bell praised the decorum and peaceful intentions of the Ho-Chunks, Menominees, Ojibwes, and Potawatomis of northern Illinois and southern Wisconsin but still expressed some doubts about some of their chiefs. Black Eagle, a Ho-Chunk headman, was of particular concern. Bell informed his superior, "Black Eagle fought with Tecumsee, was a principal councilor of his, and is under British influence with his followers and receive annual stipends or presents from the British at Drummonds Island." Guilt by association, in the past and present, mattered more to Bell than apparent peaceful intentions.[52]

In the shape of the Black Hawk War, then, the traditional threats of confederacy and foreign influence returned to a region that only two decades earlier had experienced firsthand the damage done by a British-Indian alliance. Clearly, the Black Hawk War was far more complicated than presented by that narrative. Indeed, those Indians who allied with the United States during the conflict did so for reasons that had nothing to do with American or British interests. Yet that does not alter the fact that the hostilities marked a revival of longstanding American fears regarding the relationship between the British and the Indians in the western Great Lakes region. Though few could point to British responsibility for the Ho-Chunk attacks in the lead-mining region in 1826 and 1827, Americans had a recognizable target in Black Hawk and the British Band. American officials quickly revived the accusations and actions of the past. In the process they stoked the fires of rumor and panic as they painted a picture of Indian traitors working in concert with the British to once again assault the lives and interests of the United States in general and American settlers specifically.[53]

For a year before Black Hawk and his band crossed the Mississippi River in April 1832 and sparked a substantial uproar, American officials saw the British everywhere they looked. From his position as superintendent of Indian Affairs for the St. Louis superintendency, William Clark had noted in the late spring of 1831 that those known as the British Band had "been for many years in the habit of making annual visits at Malden in U. Canada." They went for the presents, but also to talk. It was because of these ongoing conversations, Clark argued, "that so little influence has been acquired over them by the U. States Agents." American officials even put in writing their determination to sever relations between the British Band and the British agents. On June 30, 1831, at a council held at Rock Island, Illinois, Major General Edmund Gaines confronted the Sauks regarding their unwillingness to surrender land that had been officially ceded in the treaty of 1804. To record their official recognition of the terms, he had the Indians sign terms of "Agreement and Capitulation." The fourth article specifically required the Indians "to abandon all communication, & cease to hold any intercourse, with any British Post, Garrison, or Town." The American government refused to tolerate any more meddling.[54]

Rumors of a growing Indian confederacy further fueled American apprehension. Agents throughout the western Great Lakes and trans-Mississippi West filed numerous reports alleging suspicious inter-Indian diplomacy. The agent for the Osages, Paul L. Chouteau, informed Superintendent of Indian Affairs William Clark in June 1831 that Sauk diplomats had crossed the Mississippi. More than a dozen Sauks had brought wampum belts to the Osages in Clermont's Town (in present-day Missouri) right after they had visited the Creeks, Cherokees, and other Indians in the region. "The arguments used by them," Chouteau told Clark, "were well calculated to rouse the savage disposition of the Osages." Undoubtedly the Sauks were laying the groundwork for a widespread Indian uprising against the United States. Such news only confirmed the suspicions of men like John Reynolds, governor of Illinois. In July 1831 he declared, "The Indians with some exceptions, from Canada to Mexico, along the northern frontier of the United States are more hostile to the whites, than at any other period since the last war." It appeared to be only a matter of time until they struck all along the American frontier.[55]

These fears of a pan-Indian uprising grew in size and scope once the British Band crossed the Mississippi River and headed northeast, up the Rock River through northern Illinois, in early April 1832. Three men informed Governor Reynolds on April 20 that they were confident "that the pottawattimes [would] join the Sacs & ha[d] little doubt that if their first effort should not prove disastrous the Winnebagoes [would] unite their forces with others." Within a month of that letter, Reynolds himself believed he had the information necessary to declare in a statewide announcement that the Potawatomis and Ho-Chunks were now allied in full with the British Band. Even as agents like Thomas Owen of the Chicago Agency counteracted such statements with a more knowledgeable assessment of the Potawatomi bands with whom he interacted, the fears of confederacy would not disappear.[56]

American officials and citizens throughout the western Great Lakes asserted that Indians in their vicinity could not be trusted. An American soldier named George McCall combined a number of these notions when he spoke about the hostility of the Sauks and Mesquakies in northern Illinois during the summer of 1831. In council with General Edmund Gaines, the Sauks professed their desire to be at peace. According to McCall, however, that was simply "Indian talk." McCall explained, "[The Sauks] are perhaps the most warlike and the fiercest as well as the most determined Indians in our country, as their conduct during the last war exemplified." Like Reynolds and others, McCall saw actions in the War of 1812 as a critical litmus test.[57]

References to the late war often included testaments to the faithfulness, or the lack thereof, of the Indians. Perhaps no one made as strong a statement as William Clark. In June 1832 he raged, "The faithless and treacherous character of those at the head of our Indian enemies appears now to be so well known as to permit an expression of the hope, that their wanton cruelties will eventually result in their own destruction." The Sauks' "entire disregard of Treaties" and their attacks on American women and children demanded a "War of *Extermination*." Even those Indian bands that had remained peaceful or supported the American effort against Black Hawk had to be watched closely. Agent Joseph Street could report from Prairie du Chien that although the Ho-Chunk bands living north of the Wisconsin River had conducted themselves well, "some individuals have been faithless to the Whites, and have given aid to the hostile Indians."[58]

The fever created by the movements of the British Band also placed the Potawatomi bands of northern Illinois in a very difficult position. Like other Indians in the region, they were guilty until proven innocent. But the guilt of May 1832 was based on the events of August 1812. In the early stages of the late war a wagon train of American men, women, and children left Fort Dearborn under an armed escort. Only a mile and a half east of the fort nearly five hundred Potawatomi warriors under the leadership of Blackbird and Mad Sturgeon assaulted the American column. More than fifty Americans died, and the Potawatomis killed some of the prisoners after herding them back to Fort Dearborn. The incident became known in the American narrative as the Fort Dearborn Massacre, and it scarred Potawatomi–American relations.[59]

Every mile the British Band advanced in the spring of 1832 brought them closer to Potawatomi villages on the Rock, Kishwaukee, and Fox Rivers. Then on the night of May 17 a runner from a nearby village arrived at Fort Dearborn to notify Indian agent Thomas Owen that a skirmish had occurred between the Sauks and a scouting party of the Illinois militia. This skirmish at Stillman's Run marked the first shots of the Black Hawk War, and word of that fight sent hundreds of American settlers fleeing to the relative safety of Fort Dearborn. It also forced the Potawatomis of northern Illinois and southern Wisconsin into a defensive posture. The same runner informed Owen that the Potawatomis had tried to "persuade them [the Sauks] from their contemplated designs" with no success. Although Owen was, as he said, "pleased to see, that the Indians of this Agency have fully evinced their determination to render no aid to the Sacs whatever," the Potawatomis knew that most citizens did not share Owen's calm demeanor. In early June, as the British Band hid in the marshes north of Lake Koshkonong in southern Wisconsin, a Potawatomi wkama named Big Foot sent a belt of white wampum and a message to Black Hawk. Big Foot wanted the British Band "to leave the Country, that the Potawatomies might return with safety to their respective Villages and plant corn before the season was too far advanced." Similar to the other Potawatomi wkamek who moved their people closer to Fort Dearborn during the conflict, Big Foot knew that even friendly Indians were in danger as long as the Sauks continued their hostilities.[60]

The Potawatomis of northern Illinois also sought to dissuade Black Hawk from his notions that the British would come to their aid. Only hours before the firefight at Stillman's Run, a Potawatomi delegation had met with the Sauks near the village of Kishkawaka, at the juncture of the Rock and Kishwaukee Rivers. At a public council the Potawatomis informed the Sauks that they could not supply them with any corn. A more important session with Black Hawk occurred in his lodge in the dead of night. While the other Sauks slept, Black Hawk asked his visitors whether they had "received any news from the lake from the British." When the Potawatomis said no, Black Hawk pressed them further. "I inquired if they had heard that a chief of our British father was coming to Mil-wâ-kee," the Sauk warrior remembered, "to bring us guns, ammunition, goods and provisions?" Once again the reply was no.[61]

This admission by Black Hawk illustrates that American officials did not invent a possible British-Sauk connection. Indeed, some actions of the British Band in the early 1830s only fueled such speculation. In the summer of 1830 Black Hawk had visited Fort Malden to ask the British about their perspective on American land policies. The British had advised him to stay at peace and trust the Americans, but American officials only knew that Black Hawk had visited Malden. In the spring of 1831 members of the British Band once again made their annual pilgrimage to Canada. American general Edmund Gaines reported that according to the Indians, the British were less neutral this time around. "Their English friends, they say, have spoken to them of an intended war with us," Gaines reported. "These speculations will serve to shew their continued, deep rooted infatuation towards England, & relentless enmity towards the United States," he concluded. The news of British hostility, however, came from the Sauks, who may have hoped they were true. At no time during the conflict of 1832 did British officials make a move to assist the Sauks.[62]

In the end, any Indian statements or actions that confirmed American expectations appeared to be built on hope more than substance. The same day that the British Band crossed the Mississippi River, Major John Bliss reported in a letter from Fort Armstrong that rumors had been circulating among the Indians in the region that the British were preparing to go to war with the Americans. The Sauk chief Keokuk even went to an American agent to learn if it was true. Upon hearing the possibility was false, Keokuk mentioned that Black Hawk and one of his closest confidants, Neapope, had spread those rumors. Then, only a few weeks after crossing the Mississippi River, the Sauks received a visit from a delegation of Americans and Ho-Chunks led by Henry Gratiot. Gratiot had orders from his superior, General Henry Atkinson, to investigate the intentions of this Sauk band that had returned with "a hostile attitude" to lands they had long ago surrendered. When Gratiot raised a white flag over his tent to signal peaceful intentions, the Sauks tore it down and raised a British flag in its place. In his journal Gratiot stated simply, "The saukees came and took it down," while in a letter to Atkinson he asserted, "Black Hawk had it taken down." Either way, this flag incident was both an act of brazen defiance and a statement that called upon one of the worst fears of the United States. It also reflected Black Hawk's hope that British support would appear in some form.[63]

As the conflict dragged on during the summer of 1832, there was as much conjecture as knowledge about the actions of Black Hawk and the British Band. American officials worried about which Indians helped the Sauks and whether or not Black Hawk would try to lead his people back across the Mississippi River or into Canada. Once the violence at the Battle of Bad Axe River had concluded and Black Hawk had been captured, American officials still tried to uncover any insidious connections and confederacies. Captain Gideon Low of the 5th Infantry continued to pursue a party of approximately ten Indian fugitives in early September. He was particularly adamant that they should be captured before they made it to Canada, their presumed destination. Prisoner interrogations revealed additional attempts to unravel the causes of the conflict. The Sauk and Mesquakie men and women held at Fort Armstrong endured a battery of questions about whether or not the Kickapoos, Potawatomis, and Ho-Chunks had helped them. The notions of a pan-Indian, anti-American sentiment and of ties to the British would not disappear.[64]

In early August 1832 the citizens of northern Illinois and southern Wisconsin Territory tried to regain their footing. After several months of tension, fear, and uncertainty, the conflict dubbed the Black Hawk War had reached its denouement. Hundreds of Sauk men and women had died on the banks of the Bad Axe River in southern Wisconsin under the withering fire of American soldiers. Scores more perished on the western banks of the river at the hands of their Menominee and Dakota enemies. The surviving members of Black Hawk's band no longer appeared to be a threat. Yet even as the fear of Indian violence diminished, the ghosts of other traditional opponents refused to disappear. The specter of the British and their unseemly influence over the Indians in the western Great Lakes region continued to haunt the thoughts of American citizens and officials.

A Sauk headman named Taimah may have summed up the problems of the Indians in the western Great Lakes region best in July 1832 when he wrote to William Clark, "You are well aware of the utter impossibility for us to refute even the most glaring falsehoods which malice or ignorance can invent." Like the Wyandots during the War of 1812, the Sauks and Mesquakies who had not joined the British Band were caught in the middle of a conflict they did not want or create. "We have from the first to last, done all in our power to prevent the rising storm," Taimah explained, "but to no purpose." The rumors of their involvement continued unabated, and the accusations of their hostility did not go away. Taimah even turned to language he knew the Americans would understand. "I am the same man now that I was in the year 1814," he reminded Clark, "when I took (as it were) my life in my hand to rescue from certain destruction the public property of the Factory." In contrast to the British Band, Taimah had helped the Americans in the late war and even saved an American trading house on the Little Moniteau River in Missouri. Just as the actions of the British Band in the War of 1812 proved their treachery in 1832, Taimah believed his past loyalty should prove his faithfulness in another time of war.[65]

Despite Taimah's eloquence, the Black Hawk War heightened fears that had been formed among Americans decades earlier and framed within the hallowed words of the Declaration of Independence. Indians could not be trusted, and just as important, behind most Indian actions were the machinations of devious British agents and traders. For American officials and citizens in the western Great Lakes region, the British-Indian alliance was an integral factor in diplomatic and economic policy from the 1770s into the 1830s. And in 1832 it was therefore a very short step from these determinations to the promotion of removal. The U.S. Congress passed the Indian Removal Act in May 1830, two years before the Black Hawk War. The first emigrant trains in both the North and the South had already crossed the Mississippi heading west before the British Band crossed the Mississippi heading east. Yet it was that eastward crossing that initiated several substantial efforts to remove Indians throughout the Old Northwest. Bloodshed had now provided a rationale to relocate Indians that went beyond land hunger, and advocating removal could now be synonymous with advocating peace. Removal would benefit both Indians and Americans by providing access to desirable lands and preventing future conflicts between Indians and American citizens. It did not hurt that it would also put more distance between the Indians and the British.

2

THE RHETORIC OF REMOVAL AND THE EVOLUTION OF FEDERAL GOVERNMENT POLICY

The Northwest Ordinance of 1787, passed by the Confederation Congress under the auspices of the Articles of Confederation, delineated the territory claimed by the United States framed primarily by the Ohio River, the Mississippi River, and the Great Lakes. The fourteenth section of that ordinance contained an explicit and implicit message for the American Indian residents of that territory. Article 3 of section 14 states directly that the "utmost good faith shall always be observed towards the Indians; their lands and property shall never be taken from them without their consent; and, in their property, rights, and liberty, they shall never be invaded or disturbed, unless in just and lawful wars authorized by Congress." The fourth and fifth articles of that same section do not mention Indians directly, but instead discuss the manner in which three to five states would be formed in the territory, and that each state would remain "part of this Confederacy of the United States of America."[1] In short, right after stating its intentions to respect American Indians and their rights, Congress declared that the fate of those lands had already been decided. Indian lands would, one way or another, end up in American hands as part of American states. Though it was never said in so many words, the very future envisioned by the ordinance did not include Indians.

The law therefore provides one logical starting point for a discussion of the rhetoric of Indian removal in the early American republic. Yet it is not the only, or even necessarily the most important, voice in the discussion. Removal rhetoric consisted of multiple ideologies and perspectives in conversation with each other over a period of more than five decades.

It invoked the devastation of past wars and the looming disappearance of wild game. It praised the wisdom of Indian communities who had already left their homes or had agreed to relocate to new homes west of the Mississippi River. Political and religious orators spoke at length about the evil influence of alcohol and the influence of bad men. All of this evolved alongside the shifting strategies of the United States first stated in ordinances like that of 1787, even as the primary goal of removing a perceived obstacle to American growth and expansion grounded both policy and rhetoric. Historian Joel Martin refers in his writing to the "gaze of development," and that gaze drove government-appointed treaty commissioners and the interests they represented at every council session with American Indians from the 1780s forward.[2]

Despite the best attempts of American officials, however, the rhetoric of removal did not have a single composer. In actions and words, both written and spoken, American Indians participated in the dialogue and shaped its delivery. Through treaty councils, written petitions, legal actions, and even self-directed migrations, Indian leaders and nations did not just receive the rhetoric but altered it as well. That influence was most evident and effective in the late 1820s when the dialogue regarding Indian removal diverged in response to the battle between the Cherokee Nation and Georgia. For nearly five decades following the cessation of hostilities between the United States and England, the rhetoric of Indian affairs had consistently addressed the commonalities of policy toward American Indians living north and south of the Ohio River. By the late 1820s, however, the discourse on the national stage emphasized the particularities of the debates engaging the southeastern tribes, specifically the arguments surrounding the Cherokees. The Cherokee Nation had adopted a constitution, and this meant that rhetoric focusing on constitutional authority and sovereign powers reigned supreme, while that highlighting civilization and justice was either tossed aside or used only when convenient. Most important, the strength of that discourse came as much from the language of resistance used by the Cherokee Nation as it did from the federal officials and others seeking to impose it. Consequently the removal rhetoric diverged, for the language of constitutional power and tribal sovereignty was largely absent from the removal debates involving northern Indians. The enforcement of and resistance to removal policies and ideologies in the northern states and territories instead maintained a much clearer continuity to the ideas grounded in the very land of the Northwest Territory, as well as the history and political frameworks of its inhabitants. Land, legacy, and a different language of resistance, then, shaped both the discussion and enforcement of removal in the Old Northwest Territory from the 1780s through the 1840s.

Although this chapter examines the development and expression of federal policy in the early American republic as it relates to American Indian removal, it does not provide an in-depth recitation of those policies because many scholars have more than capably covered that material.[3] Instead, this chapter begins with a brief overview of policy trends up to the end of the War of 1812, at which point American officials took stock of Indian affairs and assessed whether the policies of the previous four decades had accomplished their goals. The end result of those evaluations launched a more determined drive to write removal into legislation.

In July 1789, in the first year of operations under the new U.S. Constitution, Secretary of War Henry Knox outlined his perspective on the best policy for the United States to adopt toward the Indians. His message was sparked specifically by developments in the Old Northwest and Georgia. Only one month earlier Knox had reported on the ongoing hostilities with the Indians gathered into the Northwestern Confederacy. Now he showed concern about conflict between the Creeks and the state of Georgia. The message he delivered to President George Washington in both letters had a great deal to say about his perception of the realities facing the new nation in its dealings with Native peoples. The formerly weak central government of the Articles of Confederation had been strengthened by the ratification of the Constitution, but this political change had not altered the need to take a measured approach toward Indian nations residing between the Appalachian Mountains and the Mississippi River. Although war was an option, he did not believe it was the best one. Overall, Knox called for a "noble, liberal, and disinterested administration of Indians affairs." Emigration into Indian country should be "restrained and regulated," he argued, and the popular opinion that it was impracticable to civilize the Indians was "more convenient than just." During the course of this policy brief, Knox expressed the belief that, while difficult, the civilization of Indians could and should be accomplished. He spoke of missionaries and of detaching the Indians from the commercial and political interests of the British. Yet he began with an obvious starting point. "Were it possible to introduce among the Indian tribes an exclusive love of property," Knox asserted, "it would be a happy commencement of the business [of civilization]."[4]

Knox's messages to Washington contained the interwoven threads that underscored federal policy toward the Indians both north and south of the Ohio River from the 1780s forward—land, trade, and civilization coupled with the ever-present possibility of military action. Each element of the policy was predicated on one basic goal, keeping peace with the Indians in order to maintain stability as the country expanded. Negotiated treaties and structures to facilitate Indian civilization would best allow the United States to gain its footing until it was better positioned economically, politically, and militarily to deal with the Indians, or anyone else for that matter, as it saw fit.[5] "The expense of such a conciliatory system may be considered as a sufficient reason for rejecting it," Knox wrote. "But, when this shall be compared with a system of coercion, it would be found the highest economy to adopt it."[6] The policy he proposed would work as long as all involved cooperated. Yet Knox was also practical, and he supported and encouraged the use of force when deemed necessary.

From the late 1780s to the early 1820s federal officials framed U.S. policy along the lines first crafted by Knox and under the relatively broad authority granted by the Constitution to "Regulate Commerce . . . with the Indian Tribes." The Trade and Intercourse Act, first passed in 1790, and revised repeatedly into the 1830s, was one illustration of this policy's evolution in its efforts to regulate the economic, social, and political relations in Indian country by reinforcing the supreme authority of the federal government in Indian affairs. And it aimed to regulate both sides of that intercourse, meaning that the federal government not only wanted to oversee Indian activity but also hoped to control the actions of frontier whites who had already illustrated a tendency to ignore treaty agreements. In its first iteration this legislation focused on commerce, land sales, and criminal activity, but over the ensuing decades its scope expanded. As Francis Paul Prucha so ably puts it, "Originally designed to implement the treaties and enforce them against obstreperous whites," the Trade and Intercourse Acts "gradually came to embody the basic features of federal Indian policy." The legislation became concerned with more than just sweeping regulations, and in 1793 even specifically addressed the purchase of horses from Indians. Each new version, however, emphasized peaceful interactions and federal oversight that aimed to reduce the potential for conflict from the Great Lakes to the Gulf of Mexico.[7]

One of the ways in which the Trade and Intercourse legislation evolved over the first decade of its existence was the level of detail regarding land sales, non-Indian settlements, and boundary integrity. The military conflicts in the Old Northwest in the early 1790s provided one catalyst for those revisions, but even the 1795 Treaty of Greenville, which signaled the end of that episode, only proved a temporary respite from the relentless pursuit of Indian lands via "justified" warfare and government treaty. From 1795 to the opening salvos of the War of 1812, land remained the primary concern. The policies of the federal government during the two presidential terms of Thomas Jefferson best demonstrate that trend. The 1790s may have seen the initiation of a civilization policy pushed by Knox and Washington, but in early 1803 Jefferson made the most eloquent and infamous statement regarding the connection between civilizing efforts and desire for Indian lands. Writing to governor of Indiana Territory William Henry Harrison, Jefferson stated, "When they [the Indians] withdraw themselves to the culture of a small piece of land, they will perceive how useless to them are their extensive forests, and will be willing to pare them off from time to time in exchange for necessaries for their farms and families." That statement was one of many made by Jefferson in a letter that he told Harrison was "private and friendly," and not to be considered a statement of official policy.[8] Though it may not have been an official directive, Harrison's actions from 1803 forward, including his treatment of the Indian confederacy built by Tenskwatawa and Tecumseh, demonstrate that he took the principles of Jefferson's plan to heart. Indeed, much of the Indian unrest and anger fueling support for the confederacy, which led to the Battle of Tippecanoe in November 1811 and helped spark the War of 1812, came from the numerous land cession treaties arranged by Harrison.[9]

Once the War of 1812 came to its conclusion, the federal government reevaluated the effectiveness and credibility of many policies that had become standard since the late 1780s. In the words of Reginald Horsman, the "years of conflict from 1809 to 1815 served to confirm the frontiersmen and their representatives in their hatred of the Indians and in their belief that the policies developed by Knox and Jefferson were wrong because they envisioned a future in which transformed Indians would retain land desired by frontier settlers."[10] Obvious failed policies, as well as the specific consequences of the War of 1812, forced the federal government to address its handling of Indian affairs. The end of that conflict had led to a substantial demographic expansion into the lands between the Appalachian Mountains and the Mississippi River, and the years 1816 to 1821 saw the admission of Indiana, Alabama, Illinois, Mississippi, and Missouri into the Union. This demographic and political expansion placed increasing pressure on federal, territorial, and state governments to negotiate the relationships with American Indians, both north and south, and thus forced the federal government to assess the past, present, and future of Indian affairs.

The causes of the War of 1812 rested in part on American commerce, and its conclusion had an impact on one particular longstanding trade policy. The factory system had come into being during the Washington administration as the United States strategized the best way both to separate the Indians from Spanish, French, and British traders who might help undermine the new American state and to provide a foundation for good relations with the United States. During the congressional discussion of the issue on March 2, 1795, Representative William Montgomery of Pennsylvania asserted, "It is as clear as a sunbeam that the establishment of a trade must be the foundation of amity." The first act authorizing President Washington to purchase goods for this purpose passed through Congress the very next day. A full year later the legislators approved a more developed bill that called for specific posts "on the western and southern frontiers, or in the Indian country," in which government employees would conduct trade on the public account, and not for personal profit.[11] Thus was born an infrastructure that over time included twenty-seven different trading posts, not all of which operated at the same time, stretching from southern Georgia to the upper Mississippi River. By the end of the War of 1812, however, "the factory system was doomed," in part because "the war had ended the Indian threat to national security," and thus weakened many concerns about the influence of foreign traders.[12] The system did not die quickly. Thomas McKenney became head of the Office of Indian Trade in 1816, at the beginning of the factory system's decline. Five years later McKenney reported, "Our commercial relations as they now exist have their blessings overbalanced by their curses." The biggest problem, from his perspective, was that the government system did not do enough to regulate private traders, and therefore the Indians were "the perpetual victims of their speculations and frauds."[13]

Even as McKenney pushed for greater regulation, however, members of Congress urged the absolute eradication of the government factory system, and the Committee on Indian Affairs submitted a bill to the Senate on February 25, 1822 to accomplish that goal. Senator Thomas Benton, one of the primary leaders of this charge, argued that the system had been abused, most particularly through the self-aggrandizing practices of McKenney. McKenney, Benton argued in a long address on March 25, had used the system for private gain and had not purchased goods that were actually of use to Indians. In the end, the Missouri senator concluded, the system had failed. It had failed to remove British traders, it had failed to keep the Indians at peace, and it had failed to "create respect and attachment for the American government" in the hearts of Indians. Although there was significant back and forth on the bill, it finally passed on May 6, and the official deadline for the closing of the factories was set for June 3, 1822. No longer would the government advocate government-subsidized trade as a means of cultivating good relationships with Indians. More to the point, it appeared that the discussion of the policy had become more about money than anything else. Indeed, the final accounting of this ill-fated federal policy literally rested in the hands of accountants. The report detailing the liquidation of trade goods in late 1824 and early 1825 focused on the financial side and provided not even a little theorizing about the influence of the factories on Indian affairs.[14]

In the midst of this trade policy's death throes, another longstanding approach received a new official blessing. On January 15, 1819, Representative Henry Southard introduced a bill for consideration from the Committee on Indian Affairs that authorized President James Monroe "to select such tribes of Indians as he may think best prepared for the change, and to adopt such means as he may judge expedient in order to civilize the same." The act, officially known as "An Act making provision for the civilization of the Indian tribes adjoining the frontier settlements," passed the House and the Senate by March 3, 1819.[15] The bill's language fit well within the rhetoric of the day. In short, the United States government would support actions to civilize the Indians, to work "against the further decline and final extinction of the Indian tribes adjoining the frontier settlements of the United States." This included instruction in proper agricultural practices as well as reading, writing, and arithmetic lessons targeting Indian children. Ten thousand dollars a year aimed to support the efforts of "capable persons of good moral character."[16]

The Civilization Fund Act, as it became known, was a fascinating piece of legislation for two particular reasons. First, it was not a new policy, as missionaries had long worked among Indian tribes. Second, and even more important, in many ways the ideology supporting this legislation expired before the ink was dry on its first printing. The appropriations made under the act provided the means for establishing missionary establishments in the North and South, but it was merely a confirmation of a centuries-old notion about the necessity of overhauling the Indians' way of life. Most important, it did not change the larger belief that Indians were obstacles to progress and needed to surrender unimproved lands.

Talk of removal was nothing new, either, but the discussions took on a new earnestness after the War of 1812. It began with a report from the Committee on Public Lands to the Senate on January 9, 1817. Asked to comment on the "expediency of authorizing, by law, an exchange of territory with any of the Indian tribes," the committee recommended that "an appropriation be made, by law, to enable the President of the United States to negotiate treaties with the Indian tribes, which treaties shall have for their object an exchange of territory owned by any tribe residing east of the Mississippi for other land west of that river." In reaching this decision, the committee relied on what it described as the "evils and inconvenience resulting from the irregular form of the frontier." The patterns of settlement and expansion that had predominated in the decades before the American Revolution were altered by the Treaty of Paris in 1783 and the Louisiana Purchase, which had not only added significantly to American territory but had also brought a number of non-Indian towns, like Vincennes and St. Louis, under American authority. The jagged nature of non-Indian settlements west of the Appalachians led to increased interactions, and according to the committee members, this was having a detrimental effect. "It is an intercourse by which the civilized man cannot be improved," the report stated, "and by which there is ground to believe the savage is being depraved." American independence had led to dramatic expansion and incorporation, which required the federal government to take more direct action to save both the Indian and non-Indian residents through the removal of the Indians. The committee decided it should be accomplished by treaties and negotiated consent, yet regardless of the specific approach, it should be accomplished.[17]

More and more Americans believed and asserted that Indians were on the verge of extinction. By the mid-1820s, however, government officials no longer tried to blame cultural differences for the problem. President Monroe and Secretary of War John C. Calhoun viewed the relocation of eastern Indians to lands west of the Mississippi River as the next favorable policy. It was not that civilization had not worked. Nor was it that the efforts to civilize the Indians should stop. Calhoun even reported, "Almost all of the tribes proposed to be affected by the arrangement, are more or less advanced in the arts of civilized life." Instead, another issue predominated. "One of the greatest evils to which they are subject," Calhoun reported, "is that incessant pressure of our population, which forces them from seat to seat." As a result of this pressure, the Indians did not have the ability, if they stayed where they were, to successfully master the civilized arts that Americans were apparently so desperate they learn.[18]

Therefore, as President Monroe reported to the Senate near the end of his presidential tenure, removal "would not only shield them from impending ruin, but promote their welfare and happiness." Yet in Monroe's explanation, as well as in the supporting documents from Calhoun and McKenney, one important characteristic was missing from the removal debates that encompassed Congress and the nation in 1829 and 1830 but would soon become very clear. Government officials back in early 1825 had not discussed issues of sovereignty or government authority. Calhoun had proposed that federal authorities possibly unite the removed tribes under an "enlightened system of government and laws" that would not necessarily compromise each tribe's independence, but he did not view removal as an issue intertwined with sovereignty.[19] By the time Andrew Jackson took the oath of office as seventh president of the United States, however, the rhetoric had taken a dramatic turn.

Theda Perdue and Michael Green write that what gave the debate of the late 1820s and early 1830s its drama was that "it was less about Indian removal than it was about Cherokee removal."[20] This is very true, especially in terms of the rise of sovereignty as a political and rhetorical subject of overwhelming importance. Both the subject and terms of that debate had four interconnected origins. The Cherokee Nation's constitution and its assertion of sovereignty struck the first note. Second, the subsequent development of and deliberation over removal policy within the federal government reflected a distinct response to the Cherokee statement of sovereignty. The public sphere provided the third part of the conversation, with Christian missionaries in particular serving as a dominant voice. Legal ideologies and judicial rulings supplied the fourth and final element.

Together, the intertwined dialogue of these four spheres created a common language by the 1830s, which bounded the debate over Cherokee removal in particular and Indian removal in general.

The very first issue of the *Cherokee Phoenix*, published on February 21, 1828, connected the rhetorical strands prevalent both before and after the adoption of the Cherokee constitution. On page 3, under the title "Indian Emigration," the paper assessed the current dialogue about possible Cherokee removal. More specifically, the paper rejected what it viewed to be the "new turn" in the federal government's policies regarding civilizing Indians, in which the Indians were told, "Their case is hopeless, whilst they retain their present relation to the States." *Cherokee Phoenix* editor Elias Boudinot did not see the logic in that framework. "We have always thought that we were related to the General Government, and not to the states," the paper asserts. No clearer statement of that fact had been made than that of July 24, 1827, when the Cherokee Nation officially enacted its constitution. Opposition to this political maneuver did not make sense to the Cherokees. "It is well known that we always have had the right of passing laws for ourselves," the *Cherokee Phoenix* states, "and regulating our affairs, or at least this right has never been as we know, denied us. Why is this cry made now at this late hour?" The constitution clearly asserts the sovereignty of the Cherokee Nation, a sovereignty that the Cherokees correctly understood to be longstanding and reflective of a special relationship with the federal government, outside of relations with Georgia.[21]

Georgia responded quickly to the Cherokee constitution, and its state legislature passed a series of laws in December 1828 extending jurisdiction over the Cherokee lands and people within the state's boundaries. Georgians, as Wilson Lumpkin would later explain, took particular issue with the fact that through their constitution the Cherokees "claimed the right to govern themselves independently of all other governments whatsoever."[22] Yet Georgia's action was only the first decision that initiated the movement toward the Indian Removal Act. President Andrew Jackson made the second by refusing to protect the Cherokees from that extension of state law and calling for the passage of federal legislation to authorize the relocation of Indians west of the Mississippi River. These actions placed the Cherokees in the middle of a heated debate in 1829–1830 over the principles of state jurisdiction, federal power, treaty rights, and tribal sovereignty. The spotlight has been on the Cherokee experience ever since.

In April 1829, just about a month into the new administration's first term, Secretary of War John Eaton informed the Cherokee Indians that they did not have a firm legal standing against Georgia in their fight over jurisdiction. Writing on behalf of the president, Eaton advised the Cherokee leadership that by adopting a constitution and proclaiming themselves to be an independent nation they had made a mistake. "The arms of this country can never be employed," Eaton explained, "to stay any state of this union from the exercise of those legitimate powers which attach, and belong to their sovereign character." The Indians were merely occupants; the states were sovereign, and the federal government would not interfere. Only eight months later Jackson delivered the same message in remarks prepared for Congress. The congressmen read that the president had already advised the Cherokees in Georgia and the Creeks in Alabama "to emigrate beyond the Mississippi or submit to the laws of those States." In unambiguous terms the president set the tone for Indian Affairs during his eight-year tenure.[23]

The new administration's position sparked a flurry of opposition outside the nation's capital. Most notable were the efforts made by Christian missionaries, especially those affiliated with the American Board of Commissioners of Foreign Missions (ABCFM). Jeremiah Evarts, the organization's secretary from 1821 to 1831, led the ABCFM in mobilizing the northern public to an impressive extent. Petitions against the passage of removal legislation began flooding Congress well before the bill was even presented to the Senate. Most memorials were similar to the one signed by students and faculty of Amherst College in Massachusetts, who prayed "that the faith of the nation, which has been so solemnly pledged for the protection of the Indians, may be rigidly sustained, and all their rights guarded with the fidelity which becomes the spirit of a just and magnanimous people." For the most part these documents petitioned for the protection of the Cherokees' natural and treaty rights. The overwhelming majority sought to derail all efforts to propose and pass removal legislation. But Evarts did not rely only on petitions. His "William Penn" essays, published in the *National Intelligencer* from August to December 1829, articulated in detail the rights of the Cherokees to their land and the obligations of the federal government created by all ratified treaties.[24]

Proremoval politicians also found support among Christian ministers. Reverend Isaac McCoy was a Baptist missionary whose activities in northern Indiana led him to support removal. In spite of his personal experience with Potawatomis and Odawas, however, McCoy emphasized the circumstances of the Cherokees. He had praise for the advances they had made and knew they would make the right choice. "Men capable of forming themselves into an independent government," McCoy stressed, "can easily enough perceive the incongruity of the supposition, that an independent state can exist within the acknowledged boundaries of another independent state!" The Baptist missionary believed that the only feasible plan for the Indians entailed relocating them to the western territories.[25]

Prominent Jacksonian appointees, including Michigan territorial governor Lewis Cass, also entered the fray. In an article published in the *North American Review* in January 1830, Cass reiterated some of McCoy's key points. He summarized the diminishing Native populations and the negative impacts of disease and alcohol. The failure of civilization efforts should not be blamed on the missionaries, Cass noted, but they were failures nevertheless. Then Cass made the requisite shift in his discussion. After assessing the character and condition of Indians in general, Cass transitioned into an analysis of jurisdiction, state power, and federal authority. Like-minded congressmen would borrow from him just as their opponents would borrow from Evarts. "What Indian has ever been injured by the laws of any state?" Cass inquired. "If these Indians are too ignorant and barbarous to submit to the state laws, or duly estimate their value, they are too ignorant and barbarous to establish and maintain a government which shall protect its own citizens, and preserve the necessary relations and intercourse with its neighbors." Like McCoy, Cass asserted publicly that removal was the best and only recourse for the preservation of eastern Indians.[26]

The Committee on Indian Affairs in the House of Representatives then took the torch and produced a report on Indian removal on February 24, 1830. In that report the committee stated that they would not have felt it necessary to even undertake such an analysis were it not for the strong opposition to Jackson's statements encouraging Indian removal. Because of that strong opposition, however, they took all of the arguments and facts at hand under consideration. The report was wide ranging, but it addressed the very foundations of each state in the Union that were "laid by Christian and civilized nations, who were instructed or misled, as to the nature of their duties by the precepts and examples contained" in the Bible. The committee also declared that it based its analysis in historical precedent. "It is not, therefore, so important to attempt a definition of the nature and obligation of any abstract principles, about which there will always be conflicting opinions," the report read, "as to state, with as much precision and certainty as possible, the interpretation of those principles, which are to be found in the maxims and practices of those civilized societies which settled this part of America, and those which have since sprung up, in relation to Indian rights." And according to the committee, one of the core legacies of the colonial era, "the fundamental principle, that the Indians had no rights, by virtue of their ancient possession, either of soil or sovereignty, ha[d] never been abandoned, either expressly or by implication." The committee had arrived at the underlying determination that would frame and shape its overall conclusion. Instead of judging such a principle right or wrong, the congressmen determined that because the practice had always been to say that the Indians had no rights, there was no need or reason to argue in 1830 that their right to the land or sovereignty was valid or deserved recognition.[27]

The Committee on Indian Affairs sought to deflate the balloon of any humanitarian arguments by rooting their conclusions in the disregard for Indian land rights and sovereignty from the first English settlements at Jamestown and Massachusetts Bay. Because Jackson had made reference to humanitarian concerns, and the petition drive led by Evarts raised similar issues, the committee members felt it necessary to touch on the topic. Yet not until page 20 of the 32-page report did the committee address Indians facing poverty and suffering if they remained on their current lands. And on page 25 appears the tried-and-true phrase, "If they remain where they are, the experience of two centuries has shown, that they eventually must perish." Instead, then, Congress wanted the debate to center on the principles of property and government. For the committee, at least, the endgame was inevitable. "From the time of the first permanent lodgement of the white man upon these shores," the report noted, "the destiny of the red man was placed, perhaps, beyond the reach of human agency." Treaties, rather than a recognition or indication of an Indian nation's sovereign status, were "but a mode of government, and a substitute for ordinary legislation." And when it came to any discussion of jurisdiction relevant to state and federal authority, the "superior right of the State to the control of every inhabitant within its territorial limits, whether citizen or alien, must prevail over every inferior or inconsistent claim." Based on the history of Indian relations in North America presented in the report, Indians had an inferior claim.[28]

As a result of this ongoing dialogue, when the formal debates over the Indian Removal Act finally began in April 1830, congressmen on both sides had numerous speeches, letters, essays, and other publications from which they could draw. Despite the well-orchestrated petition campaign, however, few congressmen attended to the concerns of the citizens who argued for a moral and Christian perspective. Representative Edward Everett of Massachusetts most famously devoted time in his speech to the brutal impact of the bill under discussion. "A community of civilized people, of all ages, sexes, and conditions of bodily health, are to be dragged hundreds of miles, over mountains, rivers, and deserts, where there are no roads, no bridges, no habitations," he reminded his audience, "and this is to be done for eight dollars a head; and done by contract." The congressman elaborated further and forced his audience to picture the fate of the infirm and elderly who would be forced west at the mercy of private conductors operating at their economical best. "Removal is a soft word," he chastised, "and words are delusive."[29] His language of civilization and the humanitarian disaster that removal would create did not hold sway, however. Instead, most speeches made in the houses of Congress that spring primarily focused on questions of sovereignty and power in multiple contexts. Speaker after speaker lectured on the autonomy of Indian tribes and their claims to the land. Others placed state sovereignty at odds with federal authority in Indian affairs as outlined first by the Articles of Confederation and then by the Constitution. Historical events and the precedents set by British rule and colonial land policies also came under consideration. All of these issues emphasized the colonial and recent history of the European and American authority as well as the specific actions of Cherokees, Georgia state officials, President Jackson, and Congress.[30]

The debate, therefore, occurred on two distinct levels. First, the politicians focused on the definitions and limits of federal power, constitutional authority, and tribal sovereignty. Second and most important, they framed their discussion almost exclusively within the context of the southeastern United States. Senator Theodore Frelinghuysen of New Jersey asserted the sovereignty of the Cherokee Nation over their lands and offered an amendment to the bill that would protect tribal sovereignty should the Cherokees choose to reject a treaty or refuse an agreement arranging for their removal. Frelinghuysen was determined to ensure federal protection of Cherokee sovereignty that had been recognized and upheld by several treaties.[31] Proremoval senators emphasized the constitutional foundations of, and limitations on, federal authority in the early republic as it related to treaties with the Cherokees. "A treaty cannot be said to be made under the authority of the United States, when its provisions are contrary to the constitution," Robert Adams of Mississippi declared. According to Adams, once the Indian tribes declined in power and numbers, they became subject to the authority of the states and vacated any special relationship with the federal government. Consequently, any treaty, like that made at Hopewell in northwestern South Carolina with the Cherokees in 1785, undermined the proper measures of authority, and the alleged diminished capacity of the Cherokees in 1830 weakened, if it did not completely eliminate, the power of treaties they had signed decades earlier. "So far as they affect the legislative sovereignty of the States," Adams concluded, the treaties "are not consistent with the constitution; and as respects the States, they are not binding on them." In an argument that ignored the economic, political, and cultural changes that had appeared to strengthen the Cherokee Nation in the early nineteenth century, Adams alleged that time and circumstances had eroded the relationship initially built by the early treaties.[32]

The entirety of the debate never drifted far from those core issues, and the legislation finally came to a vote. Twenty days after it first took up the discussion on April 6, the Senate ended its debate with a favorable decision of 28–19. The bulk of the deliberations within the House of Representatives took place during the last two weeks of May, ending with that legislative body's favorable vote of 103–97 on May 26. Yet neither the national discussion of the policy nor the argument over sovereignty ended as a result of the congressional action.[33]

The legal realm in general, and the Supreme Court in particular, appeared to provide the final statement about tribal sovereignty within the American context. During the course of the debates, Representative Thomas Foster of Georgia quoted extensively from the Supreme Court decision in *Johnson v. McIntosh* to assert the dominion and jurisdiction of the federal government over Indian lands.[34] That pivotal 1823 ruling was one of several decisions made in federal and state courts in the 1820s and 1830s that sought to establish "the place of the Native American and the Indian tribe in the American constitutional system."[35] The two other prominent Supreme Court cases connected to removal came in the two years after the Indian Removal Act was passed. In *Cherokee Nation v. Georgia* the Supreme Court ruled that the Cherokees did not have legal standing due to their status as a "domestic, dependent nation." And though the *Worcester v. Georgia* decision in 1832 asserted that "Indian nations had always been considered as distinct, independent political communities" and that Georgia did not have jurisdiction on Cherokee lands, the nonenforcement of the *Worcester* ruling strengthened the influence of *McIntosh*.[36] Southern courts in particular "filled the legal vacuum created by the general disavowal of *Worcester* and provided legal legitimacy to the state legislative assault on Indian rights." Southern judges proved more than capable of promoting the interests of southern white citizens at the expense of tribal sovereignty.[37]

From 1827 to 1832—from the proclamation of the Cherokee constitution to the announced decision in *Worcester v. Georgia*—the national rhetoric regarding removal shifted because of decisions made within a specific context. Senators, representatives, missionaries, and citizens argued over executive power, tribal sovereignty, treaty authority, and states' rights as they related to Georgia and the Cherokees. And the Cherokees under elected principal chief John Ross clearly participated in this dialogue. The constitution adopted in 1827 was the culmination of political transformations occurring over the course of decades, and it reflected the significant effort to protect the Cherokee Nation and its lands. Yet while the Cherokee Nation had always been sovereign, the new constitution expressed that sovereignty in terms and structures more familiar to Americans, in a manner entwined with Western political and legal thought. As Mark Rifkin writes, "Cherokee expressions of collective identity, of their 'national character,' were caught within the vicissitudes of U.S. law and policy." By turning to the American court system to battle Georgia's jurisdictional assaults, then, Cherokee resistance facilitated the debate's shift to a dialogue built around sovereignty, states' rights, and constitutional authority.[38]

Because context mattered, then, the regional context and enduring colonial frameworks in the Old Northwest Territory had a distinctive influence on the removal rhetoric as well. American citizens did not enter a virgin wilderness devoid of any prior history, nor did they encounter a population of Native peoples unaccustomed to Euro-American desires and demands. Instead, American citizens and officials had to deal with the diplomatic and political savvy of the men and women who were products of a world that has been captured so well by Richard White's *The Middle Ground*. Yet as White has also emphasized in the years since its first publication, his book analyzes "a quite particular historical space that was the outcome of" the process of creating the specific middle ground his book describes.[39] In other words, the responses of Miami, Ojibwe, Wyandot, and other Indian communities to American expansion and removal policy cannot be separated from the intricate world created over the previous decades and centuries. Therefore, when the national debate over removal shifted to sovereignty and constitutional authority, the discussions north of the Ohio River did not shift with it, in part because of the legacies of colonial frameworks. And just as the Cherokees altered the terms of the debate in their particular context, the different Indian communities in the Old Northwest shaped the debates around removal in theirs. The language of sovereignty existed north of the Ohio River. Indeed, Indiana governor Noah Noble stated in his annual message of 1832 that the diminished numbers of Miamis, as well as "their present condition, circumstances and habits," prohibited the idea that they were "capable of exercising any attribute of sovereignty."[40]

Yet while the Miamis asserted sovereignty as a means of resistance, it was not because they believed it had been diminished. Nor did the Miamis necessarily define or conceive of sovereignty in the same manner in which the Cherokees and Governor Noble utilized the term. Vine Deloria, Jr., has argued that whereas "sovereignty originated as a means of locating the seat of political power in European nations, it has assumed the aspect of continuing cultural and communal integrity when transferred to the North American setting." In the legal and political arenas sovereignty is part of a contested discussion. But sovereignty is not solely expressed legally or politically. While it is true, then, that the Miami response to American removal efforts reflected their particular views of the past, present, and future, that historical context did not exclusively shape their actions. Miami adaptive resistance in the early nineteenth century articulated a sovereignty that was not adversarial but that revolved "about the manner in which traditions are developed, sustained, and transformed to confront new conditions."[41] This broader conceptualization of sovereignty underscores the events that spanned three decades and encompassed the influential leadership of Chief Jean Baptiste Richardville, the deliberation over Indian participation in regional economic development, and the ability of individual Miamis to maintain possession of even small sections of land.

In the fall of 1826 Lewis Cass, James Ray, and John Tipton held a council with Potawatomis and Miamis on the Wabash River in northern

Indiana near the mouth of the Mississinewa River with the intent of obtaining land cessions and encouraging removal. The journal of those negotiations provides a valuable introduction to the rhetoric of the next two decades. When the council began on October 5, Cass, who at the time held the position of governor of Michigan Territory, made the first address. He read from a prepared speech that might as well have been the template for all similar councils. There is a certain rhythm to the presentation of a written speech, and one can imagine listening to the familiar rhetoric coming from Cass's mouth and the cadence that took over as he spoke. He referenced decreasing wild game as well as decreasing Indian populations, and he compared them to the increasing non-Indian population that was eager to make better use of northern Indiana. "You must all see, that you cannot live in the neighborhood of the white people," Cass read aloud. Theft, destruction, and conflict were inevitable. "Besides," Cass remarked, "when you divide our settlements, we cannot have roads and taverns and ferries, nor can we communicate together, as you know it is necessary we should do." But it was whiskey that proved to be the most dangerous issue facing these Indians. "There is but one safety for you," Cass declared, "and that is to fly from this mad water."[42]

The last third of his speech reinforced the crucial aspects of the American government's stance on removal, which, while still not an officially adopted policy, was clearly on the minds of its commissioners. Cass encouraged them to move west to good lands and let the president protect them. The land, he said, "will be yours, as long as the sun shines, and the rain falls." And as they considered their response, he reminded them, "You must go before long.—You cannot remain here.—You must remove or perish." Besides, the isolation would only get worse. "The Delawares have gone, the Shawnese are going.—Be wise." The time had come for the old men to dictate the terms, he declared, and the young men "must do, as in former times, when the old men had power, and the young men were wise." As indicated by Cass's comments, the assembled commissioners believed they had wisdom to impart—the Potawatomis and Miamis needed to understand that only removal would solve the problems they faced.[43]

Following a break of nearly six days, the Potawatomi and Miami delegates delivered their response. Both refused to sell, but Meehcikilita (also called Le Gros), the speaker for the assembled Miamis, delivered a detailed explanation for the decision. "You handed it [the pipe of peace] to us to smoke, as an emblem of peace and charity," Meehcikilita declared, "but we find it was intended for our destruction and misery." Any decline was not an indication of self-destruction, as Cass implied. Whites made the liquor that was so harmful, and whites drove away the animals. As for the land, not only had their Miami forefathers told them to hold on to the land given by the Great Spirit, but their Great Father also, he said, "told us to think a great deal of our land, and not to dispose of it . . . that we should live by each other, like brothers, and sell and exchange our property as we choose." Now, Meehcikilita stated, "We want to live like neighbours, and barter and trade with each other, if we can agree, if not, to part peaceably and each keep his own." The Miami orator had begun his remarks with the statement, "I shall repeat to you some of your own words," and he then refuted Cass's arguments by reviewing the very government policy that had been pushed for decades.[44]

Confronted by Indians calling them hypocrites, both Ray and Cass moved beyond inevitability and turned to two trusted approaches—military might and money. "We could take possession of your country by force and hold it," Ray stated, "if we did not respect your rights." Cass then stepped in to remind the Potawatomis and Miamis of the late war and the negotiations at Greenville in 1814. "We fought with you, and we conquered you," he reminded them. He similarly invoked the benevolence of the United States. "We could have taken all your land. But we let you alone—we did not take a foot of it. We have never taken one acre of land, and we never will take any, without your consent, and without giving you full consideration for it." Cass then further reinforced American benevolence by remarking on the appearance of the Indians at the council, who he said were almost unrecognizable in "so many hats, so much silver work, so many blankets, and ornaments, and red leggins." What might explain it? Could the price of muskrat pelts have risen to a dollar, perhaps? No, it was in fact government annuities coming out of the 1818 treaty at St. Mary's that had allowed the Indians such finery. And now it was time for another good bargain, one that would, he said, "make you richer than if you had every musk-rat caught between the Wabash and Lake Michigan."[45]

Within the next two weeks both the Potawatomis and the Miamis agreed to terms. The Potawatomi treaty made sizeable land cessions even as it set aside land grants for numerous individuals, including fifty-eight "Indians by birth" who had studied at the Carey Mission School run by the Baptists on the St. Joseph River. And though they did not get all that they wanted, the Potawatomis requested a permanent annuity, for they knew from past experience that as soon as an annuity expired, the Americans would ask them for more land. The Miamis still firmly refused to sell as of October 16, but when the council returned on October 23, a treaty had been negotiated through discussions not kept in the official record. The treaty created ten different reservations ranging in size from one section of land to thirty-six sections. Both the Potawatomis and Miamis agreed to cessions, but neither agreed with the commissioners' stated position that removal was both beneficial and inevitable.[46]

Those reserves created by the 1826 treaty with the Miamis became a point of contention over the next two decades as state and federal officials sought to obtain all of the Miami lands. That lengthy process revealed a focal point of the removal rhetoric in the region—Indian land use versus economic development. Seven years after the 1826 agreement, Commissioner George Porter reported, "Lands contained in the Miami Reservations are very valuable, and as the line of the Canal which the State of Indiana is constructing passes through a large body of them, it is very desirable as well for this as other obvious reasons that a cession of them should be obtained if practicable." Porter knew that the federal government as well as the government and citizens of Indiana hungered for the Miami lands. He also knew that the influential chief Jean Baptiste Richardville was too smart to accept anything but the best price for them. Despite his lack of confidence about the possible results, however, Porter decided to try to negotiate a cession.[47] In a council held in mid-October 1833, Porter came to the Miamis fresh from a successful treaty negotiation in Chicago in which he helped arrange for the removal of several thousand Potawatomis, Odawas, and Ojibwes. In Indiana, however, he came up against a Miami community who had little interest in land cessions, especially if it meant relocating west of the Mississippi. Acknowledging that other tribes had already agreed to move west, the Miami speaker, Chapine, asserted, "Your red children here the Miamis have no idea to follow their example." And after several days of talks, their attitude had not changed. They would not give up what Chapine described as a "fat country."[48]

As the struggle over these Miami lands continued, however, a more important element of the discussion crystalized. It was not just a physical or geographic issue in which Indiana wanted to build the Wabash and Erie

Canal and the Miami land title obstructed that progress. The underlying principle was also ideological. Indiana wanted the Indians removed from the lands even as the Miamis believed they could stay and participate in, or at the very least profit from, the development of the region. That part of the dispute became clearer with the next round of talks. On January 6, 1834, the Indiana state legislature composed a memorial urging the federal government to extinguish the Miami land title. Chief Richardville and the Miamis had a much different perspective. According to Richardville, through the treaty of 1826 the Miamis "intended to grant to the state of Indiana permission to make a road and Canal through their reserves to use as much land as would be actually necessary for the occupancy of either or both and no more." The Miamis appealed directly to Secretary of War Lewis Cass to "interfere with the State authorities," not only because he was a prominent federal official, but also because he had been one of the treaty commissioners for the 1826 accord and should best understand the meaning of that treaty.[49]

Rather than intervene on behalf of the Miamis, Lewis Cass supported Indiana's push, and in July 1834 authorized William Marshall to commence negotiations with the Miamis and Potawatomis. Marshall was to explain that the federal government wanted to purchase their lands and remove them west of the Mississippi River. The commissioner's early attempts to convince the Miamis failed, especially when he offered a price of fifty cents per acre for lands that the Indians knew could sell for at least ten times that amount. Richardville informed Marshall that the Miamis would sell a portion of their lands if the government offered at least one dollar per acre. Not waiting for final approval from his superiors, the commissioner made the deal, purchasing approximately 200,000 acres, at a price "a fraction less than one dollar per acre." Marshall had not been able to arrange for the Miamis to remove, but he was sure that circumstances would soon eliminate any resistance. "The influx of the white men crowding around them on all sides destroying the game," he reported, "will speedily render the chase so unproductive as to compel the Indians, either to turn their attention to agriculture for a subsistence, or sell their remaining lands and remove to a country where game is more plenty."[50]

Federal officials usually viewed any and all land cessions positively. But this treaty, by arranging for numerous land grants for individual Miamis, facilitated the ongoing Miami efforts to resist emigration, and in the spring of 1836 the federal government sent Henry Ellsworth to alter the terms. The most important objection to the treaty was, Ellsworth told the Miamis, "that in a great many instances reserves are not beneficial to the Indians because in this way they are often cheated." Ellsworth's appeal did not mention the real motivation. That was left to Indiana politicians like Senator John Tipton, who noted that the Miamis had reserved "some of the best and most valuable tracts, situated on and near the line of our Canal," which was one of the reasons why the federal government wanted to prohibit such provisions in the future. Ellsworth's trip was thus an attempt to correct Marshall's mistakes by revising the treaty and quieting Indiana protests in the process. The Miamis refused to budge, and their speaker, Miinciniikia, declared, "My Father, since you are not satisfied with the treaty made and concluded by us we should be pleased to have it returned. It would gratify us—as it appears you do not care much about our land." When Ellsworth continued to press, Richardville stepped in to end the conversation. Asked by Ellsworth if there was anything more that could be done, Richardville replied, "There is nothing more."[51]

By the time the Senate finally ratified the treaty, however, another treaty was in the works. The new accord, signed in early November 1838 and ratified the following February, carried over the same issues even as federal officials proclaimed it brought the Miamis one step closer to removal. In his official report at the treaty's conclusion, Commissioner Abel C. Pepper spoke at great length about the fertility of the lands acquired and the manner in which the cessions further isolated the Miamis, cutting them off completely from the Wabash River and almost completely from the Mississinewa River. Yet he had to confess his inability to keep out provisions creating a reservation for Metosina's band as well as land patents for several other Miamis. "In fact," Pepper reported, "my opposition to this provision and the determination with which the chiefs clung to it, has been the principal cause of the prolongation of the time occupied in consummating the treaty." Even more important, "To have insisted upon a modification which would obviate the objections of government, would have proved fatal to further negotiation." Pepper did not actually have a problem with the practice, stating that it did not necessarily prevent the transfer of land because the grantees often sold their section before the treaty was even ratified. And because the reservations had become an expected part of the negotiations, he believed it was better to obtain the consent of chiefs through granting the provisions than to not get a treaty at all.[52]

The forces at work and the content of the debates over the next decade continued to illustrate the Miamis' strategy of adaptive resistance and the assertion of a sovereignty grounded in communal integrity even as the American rhetoric had not changed. The pressure on the diminishing Miami land base grew exponentially in the aftermath of a demographic explosion that saw the non-Indian population of northern Indiana increase nearly twenty times over in the ten years from 1830 to 1840. Federal officials continued to report that removal was the best solution to their numerous problems. "The habits of these Indians, and their situation, surrounded as they are by white settlements," Samuel Milroy reported in 1840, "are certainly the best illustration of the injurious effects of the contiguity of Indians to whites." Yet despite declining numbers, ongoing problems with the alcohol trade, and an 1840 treaty that stipulated their removal within five years, the Miamis remained in Indiana. Dissatisfied with federal government inaction and Miami intransigence, the members of Indiana's congressional delegation hounded Secretary of War William Wilkins, who then instructed Commissioner of Indian Affairs T. Hartley Crawford in May to hire a removal conductor and take immediate action to try and remove the Miamis later that fall. But the desires of federal and state officials could not change two particular factors. First were the efforts of Jean Baptiste Richardville to secure land and a home for his family, which continued after his death in 1841. Second, the debate over removal had become entangled in the financial relationships between the traders of northern Indiana and the Miamis. The merchants, who had filled up their account books with transactions, both valid and inflated, did their best to hinder removal for as long as it was a lucrative position to take. Just as important, individual Miamis continued to do business with these traders despite these issues because of longstanding relationships and the possibility that those connections might enable further resistance.[53]

Miami persistence in Indiana depended on several factors, not the least of which was the ability to maintain a land base, no matter how small. The sixth article of the 1838 treaty exempted Jean Baptiste Richardville and his family from removal. Richardville was almost eighty at the time, but age alone did not account for this treatment. The son of a Miami woman and a French trader, Richardville had tremendous stature as an influential merchant and Miami leader. John Tipton referred to him as "one of the most shrewd men in North America." In his later years, however, Richardville appeared to come to a determination about removal. To the extent that it was possible, he was going to secure a place for his family in Indiana. But for the Miamis as a tribe, he informed Indian agent Samuel Milroy in the summer of 1840, he considered "the sale of their lands and removal to the West, as the only mean that [would] preserve them as a separate Tribe." As such, Richardville was a driving force behind the 1840 accord, which was ratified only six months before his death. Richardville's son-in-law and his successor, Francis Lafontaine, built on that legacy by facilitating removal even as he took advantage of the favorable terms negotiated by Richardville. Agent Allen Hamilton reported in the summer of 1844, "Lafontaine seemed favorably disposed towards that object [removal], agreeing with me as to the necessity of an early emigration on account of the Indians themselves." One year later, however, Lafontaine composed a letter requesting of the president of the United States, "Permit that my relations should be allowed to stay with me and not to go to the country set apart for our tribe West of the Mississippi." Those protected by the treaty could stay. The remainder of the Miamis would be subject to removal.[54]

The 1840 treaty did not just protect Richardville and his family. Both Francis Godfroy and Meshingomesia received land grants that allowed them and their families to remain in Indiana. In 1845, upon the petition of a hired attorney, Congress passed a joint resolution that exempted an elderly woman named Maconnoqua and her family, twenty-one people in all, because of the woman's age and her daughters' ownership of a treaty land grant. Born Frances Slocum in Pennsylvania, Maconnoqua had grown up among the Miamis after her capture at the age of five. She married a Miami named Deaf Man and lived the rest of her life as a Miami woman. Upon the public revelation of her personal story in the late 1830s, her biological brothers and sisters sought first to "save" her from captivity (which she refused) and then lobbied Congress to allow her to remain in Indiana. Overall, approximately 150 individuals avoided removal under the auspices of specific treaty resolutions and other government legislation.[55]

The explanations for those exemptions at times relied on the notions of "hiding in plain sight." Godfroy, for instance, lived in a frame house and cultivated the soil in a manner similar to his white neighbors. Maconnoqua similarly resided in a double log cabin in her late husband's village, which included a number of other small log cabins and a corncrib. Yet the presentation of whiteness does not adequately explain the circumstances that allowed for the Miamis to avoid removal, especially because those

This painting by George Winter, titled *Francis Godfroy, War-Chief*, was one of several he painted of Miamis who were present at the negotiations of the Treaty of Mississinewa in 1826. Courtesy of the Tippecanoe County Historical Association, Lafayette, Ind.

Miamis who remained made no effort to hide. Instead, the successful resistance was a more effective illustration of adaptation and a conscious desire to live as neighbors. The Miamis were one of many tribes in the Great Lakes region who had shown an ability and a willingness to adopt material goods and incorporate European ideas into their traditional practices. In the early to mid-nineteenth century, as illustrated both in the 1826 council statements of Lewis Cass and in the 1830s paintings of American artist George Winter, these material adaptations could be viewed in the clothing worn by Miami men and women and the houses in which they lived. The assertion by Richardville that the Miamis could live well as neighbors was also a position affirmed in the very manner in which Maconnoqua resisted her biological family's efforts to save her from supposed captivity. She had no desire to leave her children and relatives for a white family she did not know. In the process she asserted her identity as an Indian woman, confident in her ability to remain in Indiana and live as she had been living.[56]

Some of those living near the Miamis were merchants, however, and their shifting relationship over time became more clearly defined by financial interests. By the 1820s, as the decline of the wild game population weakened fur trade profits in northern Indiana, merchants found new avenues for wealth in the annuity payments distributed under the treaties signed by the Miamis, Potawatomis, and other Indian tribes. Consequently, those merchants viewed removal solely through this financial lens. In one of the most egregious examples of such interests, a report was filed in 1842 by federal commissioners who investigated trader claims under the 1840 Miami treaty. It declared that the Indians owed approximately $450,000 in total for debts incurred before and after the treaty. According to the account books, half of that sum allegedly resulted from transactions after 1840. Traders such as brothers William and George Ewing wanted to make as much money as possible before the Indians left the state, and if an ongoing Indian presence meant potential revenue, then traders saw no need to support removal. Thomas Dowling, who had hoped to manipulate the system by obtaining the removal contract and then selling it to the highest bidder, tried to make federal officials recognize the power wielded by these men who were "disposed to keep the Indians from removal." Not only did those traders seek profit from ongoing annuity payments, but many also had individual claims and "fear[ed] that their removal from the State [would] embarrass their security." Indeed, as far as Dowling was concerned, the only way to remove the obstacle to his speculative venture and the physical removal of the Miamis would be to cut off annuity payments east of the Mississippi River, "for if the Indians [had] no means, the Traders [would] let them go." It was not even that clear cut, however, and late in 1846 Indian agent Joseph Sinclair continued to report that the traders around Peru, Indiana, told the Indians that if they refused to remove until their debts were settled that President Polk "would reconsider the whole matter." The traders hoped to squeeze every last drop they could get out of the Miamis, and the Miamis hoped that their lies might somehow be true.[57]

The Miami removal created in this context was a complicated and tragic mess. Only when the Indian Office declared that the tribe would not receive their annuities until they crossed the Mississippi did momentum begin to build. Yet as of early June of 1846 the Miamis continued to stall Sinclair, telling him that they needed more time to dispose of their property before they headed west. The Miamis also noted in council that they wanted to delay the journey so that they did not arrive at their new homes "in the hottest and most unhealthy season of the year." Two months later, even as Sinclair threatened the Miamis with removal by force, Lafontaine protested their treatment at the government's hands, expressed the desire to obtain more removal exemptions for his friends, and stated simply that the Miamis "could not remove now." Yet the local population and the officials in charge of the move refused to wait any longer. Joseph Sinclair noted on October 1 that arrangements had been made for the use of mounted dragoons if necessary, and according to the official muster roll, soldiers drove 315 Miami men, women, and children aboard three canal boats in Peru, Indiana, to begin the journey on October 6. They transferred to a steamboat in Cincinnati six days later, passed through St. Louis by October 23, and ended the boating part of their journey on November 5. After a journey of 27 days, during which approximately 16 Miamis died of sickness, 323 emigrants disembarked at present-day Kansas City. On November 9 they arrived at their western reservation after traveling fifty miles inland. Although the conductors had gathered as many of the Miamis as possible, this emigrant party did not include all of those individuals covered by the treaties, and Alexis Coquillard had to return to Indiana in 1847 to force the remainder of those who had not obtained an exemption to move west.[58]

From the first efforts to the final use of force, the narrative of Miami removal encompassed familiar elements of a larger framework. Government officials discussed the inability of Indians to survive in the face of American expansion and the vices it brought. Local citizens spoke of the Miamis as an impediment to progress, and state politicians spoke about enforcing treaties. For their part, the Miamis most often asserted their ability to coexist with their neighbors and found ways to prove that fact by holding onto as much land as possible and maintaining relationships with local traders. Jean Baptiste Richardville in particular led the Miami efforts to shape the terms of the struggle.

Sovereignty and constitutional authority did not shape the discussions in northern Indiana in the way that they did the larger national narrative. This is not because the Miami leaders did not understand tribal sovereignty within that particular framework, as Richardville made very evident during a council held in September 1832 at the Forks of the Wabash. "You say your laws will be extended over them [the Miamis] if they remain," Richardville declared following a speech by Commissioner John W. Davis. "This cannot be done—There is no power to do this—We are governed by our own laws and subject to none other." The Miami leader spoke for the Miamis, not just for himself, and they understood this conception of tribal sovereignty.[59] Yet rather than resist federal and state policies by asserting that sovereignty in an American court of law, the Miamis emphasized their desire to retain communal integrity and live beside their non-Indian neighbors through different means. Within the regional and tribal history of the Miamis are stories of adaptation and coexistence, and these are the trends that influenced their response to removal policy. Context mattered. It mattered for the Miamis, and it mattered for all of the peoples whose stories appear in the chapters that follow.

3

THE DELAWARE DIASPORA IN AND OUT
OF THE EARLY AMERICAN REPUBLIC

The history of Delaware Indian removal is best framed by statements made about the Delawares' past by Delaware men and women of the present. James Brown and Rita Kohn's *Long Journey Home*, a collection of oral histories from the post–Civil War era to the present, offers just this type of statement. In one account Curtis Zhuniga, former chief of the Delaware Tribe based in Bartlesville, Oklahoma, traveled along the various routes taken by his ancestors in Indiana, Ohio, New York, and Pennsylvania. Contemplating his ancestors' migrations, he said, "I think that the Delaware leaders were looking for, first of all, water, a place to set up a village near water; second, cover, mainly for physical protection; and third, I think that they were always looking for a place to grow crops. With those things in mind, the rest of it was really more instinctive." Chief Zhuniga's description is one that strikes at the core of the removals, which is often missed in the attempts to write sweeping histories of past events. First and foremost, Delaware men, women, and children in the eighteenth and nineteenth centuries were looking for a good place to live. They needed food, water, and protection. Building on that foundation, the stories told by tribal member Annette Ketchum speak to other integral elements of those historical movements. In her interview she refers to Mekinges, the daughter of Chief William Anderson and the wife of Anglo trader William Conner, who left her husband and traveled with their children on the road to Missouri when the Delawares were forced west in the early 1820s. "Being a part," Ketchum asserted, "staying with, going with the tribe is most important." The decisions made by individual Delawares like

Mekinges played a critical role in maintaining a Delaware community during a prolonged period of constant relocation and hardship.[1]

It makes sense to start an examination of Indian removal with the Delawares, largely because of their movements in the centuries prior to the passage of the Indian Removal Act. These people, who called themselves Lenapes and were labeled by Europeans as Delawares, were no strangers to the impact of colonization and the dispossession that came with it. By the time Congress finally passed the legislation in May 1830 that would become the symbol of removal policy, most Delawares had long since made their homes in locales outside of the eastern half of the continent, and in several cases beyond the borders of the United States. The Delaware experience therefore transcends the traditional chronological and geographic conceptions of removal. More important, however, is the story told by that Delaware experience, especially in the context of the Revolutionary War and the early American republic. The vast dispersal of Delawares during the late eighteenth century had a dramatic impact and left an enduring legacy. Yet what comes across most clearly over time is the manner in which the Delawares remained Delawares and remained connected to each other and other tribes. By the mid-nineteenth century, because of the violent forces of American expansion, one could find Delawares throughout the North American continent. Despite the dramatic change and enormous pressure on their lives and lands, they remained Lenape. The long road of violent dispossession had scattered the Delaware polity but had not removed the identity of the Lenape people as individuals and as a larger community. Rather than serving as an isolated example of removal within the early American republic, then, the Delaware relocations during this era are better viewed as part of an ongoing response to more enduring trends of both community formation and Euro-American expansion.

Two critical aspects of the Delaware removal experience were their internal and external relationships. It was not until a period of coalescence in the Ohio country during the mid-eighteenth century that the Delawares developed a more noticeable political structure that provided some manner of tribal cohesion among different settlements. What had once been a looser collection of villagers who spoke the same or similar dialects became a larger group of Delawares who lived under the leadership of men serving at the head of the Wolf, Turkey, and Turtle clans. This transformation of internal relationships occurred gradually, and during that time the Lenapes constantly had to move. Just as migrations were not new to the Delawares in the late eighteenth century, neither was diplomacy with the people on whose land they lived. This had been the case since the mid-seventeenth century, when the Unami- and Munsee-speaking villagers—who might be termed the proto-Delawares—were forced from present-day New Jersey, New York, and eastern Pennsylvania because of the onset of English colonization following the earlier forays of the Swedes and Dutch. In the late 1600s the Delawares, along with other tribes such as the Shawnees, lived within the sphere of influence of the Iroquois Confederacy. By the outbreak of the French and Indian War in 1754, the Delawares had begun to establish villages on lands claimed by the Wyandots. The onset of the American Revolution therefore found Delaware villages in two general clusters. The first was along the Tuscarawas and Muskingum Rivers in eastern Ohio, and the second was in the vicinity of Upper Sandusky.[2]

Even as the Delawares gathered together, familiar forces and pressures threatened disruption. Violent and land-hungry expansionists had long been part of the Delaware experience. And Christian missionaries once again delivered their message in an effort to change Delaware lives. But in the late eighteenth century these forces provoked an unprecedented scattering of the Delaware people. The violence of the 1770s and 1780s, most importantly that paralleling the American Revolution, did not simply bring one more series of Delaware relocations. It led some Delawares to cross the Mississippi River into Spanish territory and others to journey into Canada. And when the Delaware clan leaders sought to regroup on the White River in Indiana Territory during the early nineteenth century, they were dealing with dispersals that would forever alter their communal relations. Yet what had been true in the past held true over the course of the decades that followed. The connections remained. Ultimately, three factors defined the Delaware relocations from the 1780s to the 1830s— violence, internal relationships, and external diplomacy. Therefore, while the Delaware diaspora that began in the late eighteenth century was both sparked by and maintained by substantial violence and dispossession, the substance of Delaware relationships and diplomacy meant that this trauma did not end the Delawares as a people.

On March 24, 1801, five canoes entered the Muskingum River at Goshen in the Ohio country, carrying fifteen Delawares and six non-Indian Moravians. Their destination was the new home selected for them near the recently established Delaware settlements on the White River in the Wabash River drainage. It was a journey of more than four hundred miles by canoe, which took more than two months to complete. Entries from the journal kept by Brother John Peter Kluge reference the landscape they passed and the people with whom he traveled. On the third day of the journey the party paddled by "the former Indian town, Newcomera," which had once been the home of a Delaware band under the leadership of the late Netawatwees. Later that day they passed "White Eyes Town," and as the canoes continued their route, one of the Delaware converts pointed out the location of his former home. Early the next morning the party reached the site of Goschachgunk, more familiarly known as Coshocton, a prominent Delaware town that had been destroyed during the course of the military expedition led by American colonel Daniel Brodhead in the spring of 1781. The waterborne caravan next passed the now-overgrown town of Gnadenhutten, the site of an infamous massacre in March 1782. It was a small group of missionaries and their Delaware converts that made this journey to present-day Indiana, and on their way out of Ohio they paddled through a landscape that had been shattered by violence and renamed by its new inhabitants. One can imagine similar experiences being part of the journeys that had brought the Delawares to the Ohio country in the first place.[3]

The movement of canoes, especially when given the advantage of going with the current, evokes the image of a placid migration. Yet in passing by the former settlements of Goschachgunk and Gnadenhutten, the passengers in those canoes could not ignore the violence that marked the landscape. The Moravian emigrants were not moving to the White River because they had just suffered an attack, but that did not mean that violence was not a factor in their decision to leave the Muskingum. The journey of this small Moravian community at the beginning of the nineteenth century also testified to the scattered nature of Delaware movements and the problems faced by those Delawares hoping to unify their community.

In the introduction to his piece on the Delawares in the *Handbook of North American Indians*, Ives Goddard writes that Delaware history "involves the repeated divisions and consolidations of many villages and of local, political, and linguistic groups that overlapped in complicated and incompletely known ways." Indeed, it does not take much reading in the historiography of the Delawares to recognize the difficulty of encapsulating the movements and locations of Delaware peoples from the seventeenth century forward. Nevertheless, the shattering events of the 1770s and 1780s mark a critical turning point. The Delawares had just experienced a period of tribal coalescence during the mid-eighteenth century in western Pennsylvania and the Ohio country, and they had largely broken free from the Iroquois Confederacy, which had shaped their diplomacy and politics for nearly a century. Then, the American Revolution complicated an already difficult situation, as the British to the west and the Americans to the east vied for their support. In the midst of that diplomatic tug-of-war and increasing violence, Gnaddenhutten was more than just an isolated tragedy. It was a powerful blow that exacerbated a period of traumatic violence.[4]

The story of Gnadenhutten is a familiar tale that is no less shocking with each retelling. As winter turned to spring in March 1782, both American and British officials grew increasingly aware that the end of the Revolution was nigh. For Indians in the Ohio Valley, a place that had been a war zone for the better part of four decades, the notion of violence coming to an end was less likely. The geography of the American Revolution undermined attempts at neutrality, and increased raiding on both sides of the Ohio River by war's end only made the situation worse. Constant rumors and misunderstandings further complicated life for Indians living at the various Moravian communities, including Gnadenhutten. "Two powerful and mighty spirits or gods are standing and opening wide their jaws toward each other to swallow," Wyandot headman Half King told the Moravians at Gnadenhutten in the summer of 1781. "And between the two angry spirits, who thus open their jaws, are you placed; you are in danger, from one or from the other, or even from both." Half King and the Wyandots at Upper Sandusky knew the situation well, for they had participated in battles on behalf of their British allies. More important, however, was the advice given by those British-allied Delawares who did not live with the Moravians. Shortly after Colonel Brodhead had ravaged the Delaware towns along the Muskingum, the head war chief, Buckonga-helas, explained to the Moravian converts that he had chosen to side with the father instead of the son in this "family quarrel." He then urged the Indians to join him and other Delawares then living in the Ohio interior where, he said, "Your women and children, together with yourselves, will live in peace and safety; where no long knife shall ever molest you." Despite the impassioned speech, the Moravians declined the offer.[5]

In September 1781 a force of Delawares and Wyandots, acting upon the orders of the British commandant at Detroit, rounded up Moravian missionaries, such as David Zeisberger and John Heckewelder, as well as their Native converts. While Zeisberger and Heckewelder were taken to Detroit, the rest of the Moravians were placed in a settlement on the Sandusky River, which they called Captives Town. The strategy made sense because the British did not want the Moravians to alert Americans at Pittsburgh and elsewhere about British-Indian war parties. Native war parties continued to conduct raids across the Ohio River, passing through or by the Moravian towns while going and returning. The strategy also created tremendous hardship for the Moravian Indians who had been moved to Captives Town. Within months the Indians suffered from starvation, and by early January some had begun to make the five-to-six-day journey back to their former homes on the Muskingum to gather what might be left of their corn. With every week that passed, more and more Indians left their Sandusky captivity to harvest what remained of their crops.[6]

It is because of that hunger and desperation, therefore, that the village of Gnadenhutten had a population of approximately ninety men, women, and children in early March 1782. They had returned to the Muskingum despite the fact that they knew it could be dangerous, and they remained despite having been warned to leave. Only days before the massacre, in fact, four warriors from the Sandusky towns had informed the men and women gathering their corn at Gnadenhutten of potential danger. These four men had taken a white woman and child captive on the southern side of the Ohio River, and then, according to John Heckewelder's account, "killed and impaled [the prisoners] on [the northern] side of the Ohio river." These four men had believed they would be followed, so the dead bodies impaled on stakes were meant as a message for their pursuers to see. They had been right. A rapidly organized force of American militiamen under the command of Lieutenant Colonel David Williamson had marched into the Ohio country seeking to punish those responsible for the recent raid. The Indians at Gnadenhutten were deemed guilty by association, and the Americans systematically killed ninety-six men, women, and children. Two young men managed to survive, and it was from these two that the details of the massacre came to light. The details did not reach the Sandusky settlements for more than a week, and only then did Zeisberger, Heckewelder, and their colleagues learn about the horrific slaughter on the Muskingum.[7]

In the aftermath of the Gnadenhutten massacre, Native Moravian converts throughout the Ohio country faced two questions. The first was whether or not they should continue to stay with the Moravians. The second was where they might avoid the dangers that confronted them. Neither question had an easy answer. David Zeisberger may have stated it most eloquently in early April, less than a month after the massacre, when three converts informed Zeisberger that Half King had told them to find a place to live away from the Moravian towns and that they were considering a move eastward to the Maumee River. "In this matter we could not advise them," Zeisberger wrote, "since we did not ourselves know where there was a quiet place for them to find, for the world is on all sides too narrow for us." It was unclear who might provide better protection and what location might provide better refuge.[8]

Yet the underlying concerns evident in these questions did not pertain exclusively to the Moravian converts. The conflicts that traversed the Ohio country in the 1780s raised the same fundamental questions for all Indians. European colonization had long since pushed Delawares' ancestors out of New Jersey, and from the late 1600s to the mid-1700s imperial warfare and colonial land hunger had driven them from Pennsylvania. Now, it seemed, devastating violence would do the same in Ohio. This time the Delawares would travel far greater distances in search of security and safety. Three distinct yet interconnected Delaware trails—north to Canada, west to Indiana, Missouri, and Kansas, and southwest to Spanish Louisiana and Texas—reveal the lengths to which Delaware men, women, and children traveled in their attempts to escape the violent reach of expansionist fervor in the early American republic. The same three trails illustrate the negotiations necessary to the border crossings that the different Delaware communities made over the course of this dispersal. Ultimately, the Delaware relocations in the five decades following the declaration of American independence had a common origin in the destroyed towns along the Muskingum River valley and the blood-stained village of Gnadenhutten. Just as important, the three trails, and the complex manner in which they separated and intersected over the decades, illustrate a removal history in which diplomacy was essential to avoiding the reach of the United States and establishing a safe home.

The first trail took those Delawares who chose to remain connected with the Moravians to Canada. For much of the 1780s the Moravian refugees from towns on the Tuscarawas and Muskingum Rivers struggled to find a home. In mid-April of 1782 some converts had moved to live among the Shawnees, and others had moved to the towns on the Maumee River. The Moravian missionaries had not given up hope that they could reestablish their Christian communities, but they struggled to identify a proper location. In late July 1782 Zeisberger and others selected a site on the Clinton River about twenty-three miles northwest of Detroit, a far distance from the Sandusky villages that they had found so hostile to their interests. This mission, soon labeled New Gnadenhutten, was their home for nearly four years, and during that time the community grew slowly. Only fifty-three individuals lived at New Gnadenhutten when 1782 came to a close, and at least one reason for the slow growth came from dissension within the Sandusky villages. Zeisberger estimated that feelings about the Moravians were evenly split. On one hand, Delaware leaders told their people to prevent their friends and relatives from rejoining the Moravians, asserting, "They were no longer safer with the English than with the Americans." On the other hand, a Delaware headman named Lennachgo criticized such sentiments and chastised Delaware and Wyandot warriors for their complicity in the violent events of 1782. "Who brought to destruction the believing Indians on the Muskingum?" he demanded. "Have the white people done it, whom we call Virginians? Answer, No. They have not done it, but you are they who have killed them." Such internal dissension over where and with whom the Delawares should live only worsened in the context of the external struggles.[9]

The four-year stay on the Clinton River was marked by growth, adaptation, and anxiety. The residents had to grow a different type of corn, one that ripened earlier than that which they had used in their fields on the Muskingum. They had to adjust to new neighbors, the Ojibwes, in whose territory they now resided, and despite their hopes, missionaries and converts alike began to realize that they would not soon return to Ohio. The mission relied on Detroit for news, and conversations in that town centered on the possibility of an Indian war throughout the Ohio Valley. Although these circumstances kept them away, it was also difficult to remain on the Clinton River. New Gnadenhutten rested within Ojibwe territory, and at the end of 1785 the local Ojibwe leader who had welcomed their presence passed away. His son now had authority, and he "had it in mind to say to [the Moravians] towards spring to go over the lake again away from his land." Word also reached the Moravians that other Indians living to the north and west had "already killed many white people" and might prove dangerous to both the missionaries and the Native converts in the near future. In light of these political changes, the Moravians closed New Gnadenhutten in the spring of 1786.[10]

From April 1786 until May 1787, Zeisberger and his followers slowly journeyed back into the Ohio Country. There they found themselves once more at the center of a struggle. Lieutenant Colonel Josiah Harmar advised the Moravians that they could return to their old site on the Muskingum River under the protection of the United States. Three different Delaware headmen—Pipe, Welandawecken, and Pomoacanthe—told the Moravians, "For the present ye can nowhere live so quietly and securely as near us on the Sandusky River." The Delaware leadership hoped to bring their people back together. But a Moravian convert named Weschnasch (also called Frederick) informed Zeisberger that the headmen had deceived the missionaries. The Wyandot, Delaware, and Munsee villages would be much closer than expected, which meant the Moravians could expect to be plagued by alcohol and harassed by outsiders. Instead of Sandusky, then, the Moravians stopped on the banks of the Huron River and prepared to plant their crops. This location, soon dubbed New Salem, became their home for the next four years. Its population fluctuated, totaling 200 at the end of 1790 but dropping to 158 one year later. The violence that once again enveloped the Ohio Valley had sent new waves through the region.[11]

Delaware warriors participated in the military victories against Harmar and St. Clair in 1790 and 1791, and Delawares lived in the villages along the Auglaize River at the heart of the Northwestern Confederacy. The Moravians, however, sought to stay clear of the conflict. Three converts, named Samuel, Stephen, and Joshua, delivered a message of their peaceful intentions in January 1791 to Delaware, Wyandot, and Odawa headmen, using a threefold string of wampum to ground their message. The recent campaign against Harmar's army represented another storm that had come to the region, and the Moravians wanted advice. They asked "how in the future" they could "best and most fittingly remain in quiet." It would not be easy. Only five months later the Moravians received word from the confederate villages along the Miami River that they should "help fight for their land against the Americans." It seemed that as long as they stayed in the area they would not be able to find peace. Ohio was too dangerous, both for the physical and spiritual wellbeing of their community.[12] Several months after the momentous victory over St. Clair's forces, and what might be viewed as the peak of the confederacy's confidence, Zeisberger and the other Moravian missionaries sat down with their Native assistants and proposed a move into British territory. The assistants supported leaving their home in Ohio for the possibility of peace in Canada. "They thought also that if we dwelt on Indian land we should have little quiet," Zeisberger remarked, "for they [the Delawares, Wyandots, and others] would always have much to say to us, and would wish to force us into the war, which, on English ground and soil, we should not so much have to fear, for they would have nothing to say to us." The Moravians arranged the logistics of the move with British agent Alexander McKee in March, and by the beginning of May 1792 they began to build their new settlement north of the Thames River in what was known as Upper Canada.[13]

The Moravian Delawares left Ohio at a time when their relatives on the Sandusky and Maumee Rivers were confident in their abilities to beat back the forces of American expansion. Three years later the campaign by Anthony Wayne's American Legion and the British betrayal had brought them to the treaty ground at Greenville, Ohio. Delaware representatives did not speak much at the council that solidified the cession of millions of acres in Ohio, but toward the end of the talks war chief Buckongahelas declared, "I will, for the future, be as true and steady a friend to the United States as I have heretofore been an active enemy." Buckongahelas was one of fourteen Delawares who made their marks on the Greenville accord. As of 1795, then, the Delawares in the Ohio country had declared their enmity toward the United States to be a thing of the past. They now looked to the future.[14]

That future for the Delawares involved the growing American encroachments both within the context of the Greenville land cessions and without. For many Delawares that meant another relocation. This time the destination was the White River in northern Indiana, and they were not strangers to the waterways of the region. Delaware settlements could be found at several locations in present-day Indiana prior to the Treaty of Greenville. Two villages, of about forty-five houses total, were located on the St. Mary's River, only three miles from its confluence with the Wabash, and these had been established in 1787. A third settlement known as Delaware Town encompassed approximately thirty-six homes located on the east bank of the St. Joseph River, north of Fort Wayne, and had been established in 1785. Six years before that, in 1779, the military expedition of George Rogers Clark had attacked and destroyed a Delaware town at the forks of the White River southeast of Fort Vincennes. Because of this prior history, it made sense for the Delawares to seek refuge on those waterways in the aftermath of the Greenville treaty. By the spring of 1796 approximately twenty Delaware families had returned to the White River near Vincennes and made their homes on the site that had once been attacked by Clark. The bulk of the Delawares, however, made their homes further north. By 1800 there were at least nine different Delaware towns located in central Indiana.[15]

The terms under which the Delawares gradually shifted their homes remained in contention for several decades, largely because they "had no land of their own and resided in Indiana Territory by the sanction of a host tribe and the blessings of the United States government." Indeed, the Delaware relocation into Indiana did not simply happen. It was based on at least two different agreements between them and the Piankeshaws and Miamis, respectively. As early as the 1770s the Piankeshaws had permitted the Delawares to establish settlements on the southernmost portions of the White River and between the White River and the Wabash. The Miamis had also agreed to open their lands to the settlements of the Delawares after the Treaty of Greenville. However, during the first decade of the nineteenth century it became obvious that the parties disagreed over whether or not the Delawares were occupants or owners of the lands in question. It remained a crucial distinction, especially during a period of time when William Henry Harrison, the governor of Indiana Territory, was doing his best to advance the Jeffersonian agenda of obtaining Indian lands.[16]

The story behind these negotiations begins with the historical connections among the Piankeshaws, Miamis, and Delawares. Although referred to by American officials as a separate tribe in the 1795 Treaty of Greenville, the Piankeshaws were closely related to the Miamis. According to what Miami informants told C. C. Trowbridge in the early 1820s, the Piankeshaws originated in a settlement established by a man who had come from a Wea village consisting of those who had left the Miami towns on the Wabash when the surrounding environment could no longer support the growing population. Consequently, the Miamis, Weas, Piankeshaws, and Kaskaskias were all tribes of Wuyautonoa, or the Miami Confederacy. Those same Miami informants echoed the familiar refrain that the Delawares were viewed as grandfathers within the context of inter-Indian diplomacy. This meant, among other things, that the Delawares were given seats of honor at treaty councils as a sign of respect by other tribes. But more than just respect shaped this relationship. William Keating described it in more depth following a visit to Fort Wayne in 1823:

> All the Indians of this part of the country recognise their alliance with the Delaware Indians, whom they seem to consider as their forefathers, applying to them in councils the appellation of "Grand Fathers," and recognising their right of interfering and of deciding in last resort in all their national concerns. This right extends, however, only so far as to make their approbation necessary to the adoption of any important measure. Should it be withheld, the matter is again referred to the nations for consideration, in their separate councils, and should they persevere in the measure, it would bring on a separation of the alliance, and the nation refusing to submit to the decision of their grandfathers would be considered as strangers.

Based on this status, and the respect and authority it entailed, it is therefore not surprising that both the Piankeshaws and Miamis would have generously permitted their grandfathers to establish homes in their respective territories at different points during the eighteenth century.[17]

The Delawares complicated the situation, however, when they signed treaties that ceded the very lands on which they had recently been permitted to live. For example, the sixth article of a treaty signed by the Delawares in August 1804 states specifically, "The Piankishaw tribe have hitherto obstinately persisted in refusing to recognize the title of the Delawares to the tract of country ceded by this treaty." That same treaty, in which the Delawares ceded territory between the Ohio and Wabash Rivers, notes that the Miamis "explicitly acknowledged the title of the Delawares at the general council held at Fort Wayne in the month of June, 1803." Consequently, it reads, "The said United States will in future consider the Delawares as the rightful owners of all the country which is bounded by the white river on the north, the Ohio on the south, the general boundary line running from the mouth of the Kentucky river on the east, and the tract ceded by this treaty, and that ceded by the treaty of Fort Wayne, on the west and south west." Clearly not all of the relevant parties were on the same page. Yet, from the perspective of the United States, the Delawares had valid claims to land in the territory.[18]

Yet the federal government's attribution of authority had more to do with Harrison's willingness to pressure Delaware leaders into ceding land than it did with the legitimacy of their claims. The circumstances fit well with other treaties conducted during Harrison's tenure. In the spring of 1805 the Delawares sent a message to the Miamis through the medium of traders John Conner and William Wells. The Delawares knew that the Miamis were angry about the cession of the 1804 treaty and asserted that they did not know that had been the intention of the meeting at Vincennes. According to their message, Harrison told the Delaware delegates that they were putting their marks on "an instrument of writing to keep peace and friendship among" the Indians in the region. More to the point, they directly stated their understanding, saying, "We have not in our power to sell land." When William Patterson, the Delaware delegate who carried the message, delivered the letter, he explained to the Miamis, "Friend and Brother! My chiefs declare to you that they are not willing to sell the lands on the Ohio from the mouth of the Wabash to Clarks Grant at the Falls and that they consider it out of their power to do any such thing without the consent of the other nations in this country." Harrison showed no qualms about overriding such concerns. To quiet Piankeshaw dissent, he simply pressured them into a separate treaty that ceded the same land that had already been surrendered by the Delawares.[19]

The treaty of 1804 continued to send ripples throughout the region. When Secretary of War Henry Dearborn received word of the Delaware complaints, he told Harrison that the governor needed to get all of the Indians in the same place so that he could make the Delaware leaders recant their position. The administration would not believe the "false or improper representation of [Harrison's] conduct," and instead would refuse to negotiate with any Indian headmen "who so far degrade[d] themselves, as to deny their own doings." The result of this was an accord signed in 1805 that became known as the Treaty of Grouseland. Harrison believed that the council "had a most beneficial effect" and concluded that "every improper prejudice ha[d] been removed" from the minds of the Indians involved. The Miamis, Weas, and Piankeshaws affirmed their confederacy while also acknowledging the right of the Delawares to cede the lands that they had in 1804. But Harrison's efforts to smooth over the dissension caused by the repeated land cessions did not work. When the council was over, the Delawares reported that the Potawatomis and Miamis "told the Governor that the Delawares no longer possessed any land of their own, consequently had no right to live on the White River; that they had merely allowed the Delawares to live on it but had never given it to them;

that they wanted to have this land back again because the Delawares, without their consent, had begun to sell the land." In a short period of time the Delawares had seemingly worn out their welcome, and the Miamis did not hesitate to let their grandfathers know that they had done wrong.[20]

Internal affairs in the White River villages showed similar signs of unrest, as some Delawares began to question the decisions made by their leaders. At the time the Delawares moved to Indiana, Buckongahelas held an undisputed position as the war captain, but the principal chief of the White River towns was Tetepachsit, the speaker for the Turtle clan. A younger chief named William Anderson (also called Kikthawenund), who had become a chief among the Unami Delawares before the Treaty of Greenville, ascended to the position of first chief among the White River towns at some point during the first decade of the nineteenth century. Therefore concerns about land issues and possible relocation were in part connected to generational disputes entangled with transitions in leadership within the Delaware communities. "The Delawares are indeed extremely restless and uneasy," Harrison reported in early August 1805. "They are much dissatisfied with the Miamies and all the young men are very desirous to join their countrymen on the west side of the Mississippi." The older Delawares, however, showed no desire to leave Indiana, and Harrison was not the only one to notice the problem this caused. According to the Moravian missionaries on the White River, following the Miamis' pronouncement the Delawares wanted "to move to the Mississippi, if the afore-mentioned Indian nations [would] not give them anew the land on the White River where they live[d]." Amazingly enough, Harrison did not directly encourage the Delawares to leave, but instead requested advice on the matter from the Jefferson administration.[21]

Any potential movement west of the Mississippi River involved more than a simple relocation because the western landscape was not an empty wilderness waiting to be tamed. Delawares who had first moved to Spanish Louisiana in the 1780s now faced a growing American presence and intertribal conflict. The presence and concerns of these western Delawares were also connected to the violence of the late eighteenth-century Ohio country. In early March 1782, only three days before the massacre at Gnadenhutten, Delawares had comprised part of a delegation of forty-four eastern Indians who met with Spanish authorities to discuss the possibility of obtaining land in Spanish Louisiana. According to Spanish lieutenant governor Don Francesco Cruzat, the Delaware, Shawnee, Chickasaw, and

Cherokee visitors had represented the interests of more than just their four communities, and they had wanted "a firm and sincere peace with the Spaniards." Cruzat had viewed their visit as important to Spanish interests and given them gifts. By the end of the decade at least one small community of Delawares was living and hunting "twelve leagues below the mouth of the Ohio" on the western banks of the Mississippi River. The initial venture of this small group became a much larger emigration in the mid-1790s after Governor-General Don Francisco Luis Hector, the Baron de Carondelet, provided a land grant to the Delawares and Shawnees in the vicinity of Cape Girardeau in January 1793. In the years that followed, a growing trickle of Delawares made their way from the villages in Indiana to the newly established settlements in Spanish territory. Franco-American trader Louis Lorimier noted that parties of anywhere from five to seventeen families were traveling during the spring and summer of 1794. It is unclear how much Lorimier may have communicated with these Delaware emigrants because he did not record any stated reasons for their relocation. However, at least one Delaware man back east had explained the departure to his former British allies quite clearly. The man asserted that in the aftermath of Fallen Timbers the British had betrayed them for years. "Therefore," he said, "we will go away and leave the fighting to you."[22]

Yet Spanish Louisiana could not provide a refuge from violence for two reasons. First, the Spanish wanted to use the emigrant Indians for their own purposes, specifically to protect Spanish settlements from the Osages. Second, even without Spanish desires, the presence of the eastern Indians created a competition over resources with the Osages. The Delawares were only one of several eastern tribes that sought territory west of the Mississippi River. As a result they sought to work together against the hostility of the Osages. Early attempts by the Spanish to use emigrant Indian auxiliaries against the Osages had increased tensions with the Delawares, and the rising tensions highlighted the communication networks that were in place across the Mississippi River. An unidentified Indian from the western territories arrived at the White River settlements in November 1803, bringing wampum and a message of war to the Delawares and others. The Osages had shown little respect for the eastern emigrants, and the Cherokees, Shawnees, and others believed the time had come to act. Their appeal to the Delawares in Indiana played on the very issue of land. The messenger specifically stated that if their grandfathers would join in the fight, "they would then kill all the Hoschaschi [Osages] and give their land to their grandfather, since he had no land of his own." Inspired by the cause, the Delawares accepted and began preparations for war. Moravian missionaries predicted that there would be "a great deal of bloodshed after New Year among the Indian nations."[23]

The all-out war predicted by the Moravians did not come to fruition in the early months of 1804, but the efforts to engage the Indiana Delawares in the fight against the Osages did not disappear. By the fall of 1805, in fact, the appeal for warriors was once again tied to an invitation to relocate. A Delaware man from the western settlements arrived on the White River in October 1805 with two purposes. First, he carried two Osage scalps and invited the Delaware warriors to "taste the soup which they would make" of the Osages. This appeared to have the desired effect, and the young warriors expressed a desire to go to war. The second purpose involved relocation and connected that migration to territory. The Delaware messenger urged his relatives "to move to the Mississippi where they would have their own land." Rumors began to spread that the Delawares in Indiana were seriously considering leaving the region and moving west in the spring of 1806.[24]

The messages sent by Delawares west of the Mississippi arrived as the Miamis and Potawatomis informed the Delawares in Indiana that they no longer had any land. This turmoil also coincided with news of Tenskwatawa's teachings among the Shawnees in Ohio. In late November 1805 the Delawares at Woapicamikunk welcomed the Prophet and many of his Shawnee followers. It was at this time, then, that the Delawares on the White River would have first heard the message that would become the cornerstone of the confederacy that Tenskwatawa and his brother Tecumseh were fashioning. What remained unclear was the extent to which the Shawnee Prophet's teachings fit into the desires and plans of the Delawares. "Schawanos are gathering together and upon the advice of their teacher plan to build a large town, not far from Greenville, that is to remain a hundred years," the Moravian missionaries reported. "To this project they have also invited the Delawares. These, however, are divided in their opinions: some want to go with the Schawaonos; others desire to move to the Mississippi."[25]

The differing opinions about relocation quickly became subsumed, however, in the investigation and trial of witches on White River in the spring of 1806. Only four years earlier, the communities had sought an answer when disease swept through several Delaware towns. While some blamed the Christian Indians in their midst, the chiefs blamed two different old women, a Nanticoke and a Mingo who were "reported to have said they wished to harm the Delaware nation." Then it was reported in the summer of 1805 that, even as a bilious fever took the lives of Delawares and other Indians in the vicinity, the Shawnees had taken action to combat what they viewed as sorcery. According to the Moravians, the Shawnees had "already killed two Wyandottes who were alleged to be guilty of mixing poison." The Delaware towns along the White River had heard the teachings of prophets within their own communities, including most notably a Munsee woman who had once been baptized by the Moravians and given the name Beata. Her vision in early 1805 led her to preach that the Delawares had to "live again as in the olden times, and love one another sincerely." Word of Beata's teachings even reached the Wyandots, who hoped she could visit them in order to root out the witches in their midst. The Delaware chiefs, however, stated that because they had a particular need of Beata's knowledge, especially in regard to upcoming religious ceremonies, they could not allow her to leave.[26]

The trials and executions among the Delawares in early 1806 were not simply manufactured as part of, or in reaction to, the Shawnee Prophet's teachings. Nor did they represent a new cultural development. They were, however, part of a larger shake-up within the Delaware towns of the White River that led to several key events. In the spring of 1806 the Delawares participated in witch hunts that led to the execution of at least four members of their community. The executions took place in mid-March, following a gathering of all Delawares at Woapicamikunk where the accused were brought before the Shawnee Prophet for judgment. All four were deemed in some manner responsible for the problems experienced by the Delawares, including outbreaks of fatal disease and loss of land. The latter issue in particular explained the accusations made against Principal Chief Tetepachsit, who was found guilty, carried to the Moravian mission on the White River, hit in the head by a tomahawk, and burned to death in a fire that grew so intense it spread to the woods south of the village. Tetepachsit's nephew Billy Patterson was also found guilty of sorcery and executed. Among other crimes, both Tetepachsit and Patterson were connected to land cessions in the 1804 treaty. Having failed to protect the land, Tetepachsit, as the first Delaware signatory on that accord, had been a glaring target.[27]

Yet out of these executions seemed to emerge a stronger Delaware community. According to Anthony Shane, who was interviewed by Lyman Draper in 1821, the executions stopped suddenly when George Girty saved his sister (Tetepachsit's wife) from death and declared, "The Prophet was a devil come among them and we are killing each other." The Moravians heard a different tale. According to their sources, the executions stopped when the friends of accused chief Hockingpomsga "took their weapons, sprang in the midst of the people and threatened to kill anyone who should take part in this murder." Either way, the executions stopped, and the Delawares worked to repair the damage. Although younger Delawares vowed to keep pursuing possible witches, they held a council in August 1806 with the older chiefs in which they presented the elders with strands of wampum "to cheer them up." The older chiefs then began to reject the forces that they believed disrupted their people, starting with the Moravians. Their initial invitation to the Moravians to establish a mission on the White River had been motivated by a desire to bring as many Delawares and Munsees together as possible, but by 1806 the Moravians had proven to be too much of a divisive presence. Even the late Buckongahelas and Tetepachsit, two of the chiefs who had invited the missionaries to the White River, had sought to limit the influence of the Christians on their people. The invitation had always been more to bring the Delawares together than to welcome the missionaries. Hockingpomsga and William Anderson now made sure that the Moravians left and that in their departure they did not take with them more than they deserved. On September 16, 1806, the Moravian mission on the White River officially closed its doors. The Delaware leaders were intent on both removing the missionaries and reasserting their traditional religious practices as taught by Beata. The expulsion of the missionaries and the renewal of traditional practices indicated a renewal of the Delaware community as a whole.[28]

The Delawares would need that strength in the years ahead, for questions remained about the possibility of a relocation to the western territories as well as claims to the land on which they lived along the White River. Although Governor Harrison showed some concern regarding the extent of Delaware involvement with the Shawnee Prophet during the summer of 1807, he was relatively confident in the friendliness and authority of Chief William Anderson. Harrison was also heartened by the continued belief that the Delawares were planning on leaving Indiana Territory for the White River in Missouri Territory. "I can see no injury that will result to the United States from this removal," he informed the Secretary of War. "On the contrary it will leave vacant a fine tract of country immediately contiguous to the settled parts of the State of Ohio and the upper county of this territory." Harrison just wanted to know whether or not the administration supported this move.[29]

The relocation posited by Harrison did not happen. In the summer of 1808 the western Delawares informed their relatives on the White River that the Great Osages had cast off any stated allegiance to the United States. Missouri Territory's governor, Meriwether Lewis, in council with the Delawares, Shawnees, Kickapoos, and others, had then declared that this renegade band of Osages was "no longer under the protection of the government of the U'States," and that the eastern emigrant Indians "were at liberty to wage war against them if they thought proper, under this restriction only, that they should attack in a body sufficiently large to cut them off completely or drive them from their country." Now that the Americans had given the green light for an all-out attack, the eastern Indians appeared happy to comply. In the fall of 1808 the Delawares in Indiana attempted to organize the Miamis, Potawatomis, Shawnees, and Wyandots to go to war west of the Mississippi River. Yet Lewis's summertime encouragement turned to President Jefferson's discouragement at year's end. The United States used the threat of war to persuade both the Great and Little Osage bands to negotiate, and the resulting November 1808 treaty placed the Osages under the protection of the federal government. Jefferson could then override Lewis's message by stating that the Indiana Delawares did not have any right to attack the Osages on the other side of the Mississippi. Now, if the Delawares made what Jefferson considered an unjust war on the Osages, their Great Father would, he warned, "send upon your nation famine, sickness, or the tomahawk of a stronger nation, who will cut you off from the land." Under these altered circumstances, the Delawares and others chose not to make war on the Osages.[30]

While the Osage treaty doused one potential conflict, an 1809 accord involving the Indiana Delawares paved part of the road toward the Battle of Tippecanoe. It began with an agreement settling land-claim questions. Little Turtle confirmed in 1808 that the Miamis had agreed to grant to the Delawares, Mohicans, Munsees, and their descendants a portion of the land on the White River in Indiana Territory. After the troubles of the previous years, the Miamis made this commitment on the condition "that neither they the said Dellawares Mohiccaners, and Muncies, nor their descendants [should] ever alienate the Lands to any other persons or purposes whatsoever, without the concent of the said Miamies and the said Chiefs." That particular condition mattered much sooner than any of the Indians might have anticipated. In September 1809 delegations of Delawares, Miamis, and Potawatomis gathered at Fort Wayne to discuss proposed land cessions with Harrison. The resulting treaty has been described as "the climax of Harrison's seven years of negotiations with the Indians of the Wabash and Maumee valleys." Through this agreement the federal government obtained land cessions that it did not need and, in the process, provided further fuel to the movement led by the Shawnee brothers. The first two articles of that treaty make two statements about the Delawares' right to the lands. In the first article the Delawares, along with the Potawatomis, are designated as allies of the Miami and Eel River Indians and therefore party to the cessions of land described therein. More importantly, the second article declares, "The Miamies explicitly acknowledge the equal right of the Delawares with themselves to the country watered by the White river," and "neither party shall have the right of disposing of the same without the consent of the other." The five Delaware men who put their marks on this treaty affirmed an important relationship between the Delawares and the Miamis. Yet an additional supplement to the treaty complicates the picture somewhat. The main text of that supplement begins by saying that "as the greater part of the lands ceded to the United States, by the treaty . . . was the exclusive property of the Miami nation and guaranteed to them by the treaty of Grouseland," the federal government would provide the Miamis with some additional compensation.[31]

The Delawares present at the negotiations of the Treaty of Fort Wayne said little during the course of the council. As Harrison pushed the Miamis to agree to terms that they despised, the Delawares remained silent. In fact, the longest recorded Delaware statement came from an unnamed chief who said that his people "had always listened to the voice of their Father and were now willing to agree to his proposals." The Delawares under Anderson appeared to be building up their credibility as a neutral party in the ongoing tensions, if not as a strong American ally. From Harrison's perspective, the Delaware acquiescence had a lot to do with the fact that the treaty not only provided them with an additional annuity but also confirmed their equal right with the Miamis to the White River lands. And in the governor's eyes, now that the Delawares had an equal right to the territory, they could sell it. The 1809 treaty would "facilitate the acquirement of this valuable country by the United States, as the Delawares [had] for a long time a desire to remove to the west of the Mississippi."[32]

Even as the Treaty of Fort Wayne strengthened the movement driven by Tenskwatawa and Tecumseh, it also separated the Indiana Delawares from them. The very first time Tecumseh met Harrison in person, in August 1810, he addressed the 1809 land cessions at length. Those land cessions had been made by only a few men who had been pressured to do so, Tecumseh asserted. "But in [the] future," he said, "we are prepared to punish those chiefs who may come forward to propose to sell their land." He also warned Harrison about any similar negotiations in the future. "If you continue to purchase of them it will produce war among the different tribes," Tecumseh declared, "and at last I do not know what will be the consequence to the white people." Over the next year the machinations of the two Shawnee brothers brought together a large force of Indians at Prophetstown, and in November 1811 an American force under Harrison engaged and defeated those Indians at the Battle of Tippecanoe. The Delawares did not join the Prophet. Instead, some Delawares may have even served as diplomats, spies, scouts, and messengers for the American forces. Harrison believed that the Delawares, "having suffer'd more than any other in the former wars, were better able to appreciate the evils that a recommencement of hostilities [would] bring upon them."[33]

Yet the actions taken by Delawares in Tippecanoe's aftermath demonstrate that their efforts to avoid war should also be seen within their traditional roles as grandfathers and mediators. The best illustration of this role came in May 1812, when representatives from twelve different tribes met in council at the confluence of the Mississinewa and Wabash Rivers near Peru, Indiana. It was a council at which Tecumseh engaged in a heated debate with the Potawatomis over the actions of and accusations against the Shawnee Prophet. The Delaware delegates, viewed as the respected grandfathers by all present, tried to soften the rhetoric and repeated the call for peace that had opened the council. Rather than blame specific actors, the Delawares proposed that "both the red and white people had felt the bad effect of his [the Shawnee Prophet's] counsels." The Delawares did not want to go to war and hoped that their neighbors would share this sentiment.[34]

Delaware diplomatic efforts also reflected the dangers presented by their geography once the United States declared war against England. That became particularly evident in the fall of 1812 when now–General

William Henry Harrison directed Colonel John C. Campbell to attack the Miami villages on the Mississinewa River. Although his route would take him near the White River, Campbell was ordered to stay away from the Delawares who had "been directed to leave their Towns and retire to the Shawanee establishment on the Auglaize River." By the beginning of 1813, the Delawares abandoned their homes on the White River and crossed the border into Ohio. Following more than a year of extensive lobbying by American officials in the region who wanted to strengthen their connections with Native communities at a time of war, approximately nine hundred Delawares established temporary homes near Piqua, Ohio, to avoid military conflict and prove their loyalty to the United States. Yet despite everything, Harrison was not fully convinced. "Their chiefs are men of principle," he opined, "but the greater part of their warriors are attached to the enemy and would join them whenever an opportunity offered." In order to address those concerns and protect their interests, then, the Delawares found it necessary to become actively involved in the fighting. In August 1813, a force of nearly two hundred Shawnee and Delaware warriors left Piqua to join Harrison's army as he prepared to move on Detroit.[35]

Harrison's campaign in the fall of 1813 did many things, including drive British forces out of Detroit and Upper Canada. It also brought war to those who had hoped to avoid it, such as the Moravians who two decades earlier had made their homes at Fairfield on the Thames River. By the dawn of the nineteenth century the Fairfield community of Moravian missionaries and their converts had found the stability and security that had eluded them in the Ohio country. Although rumors of war still reached them from time to time, the Moravians had escaped the day-to-day violence that had been a problem in the 1780s and 1790s. Tensions between the United States and Britain remained worrisome, but these difficulties were not significant factors in the Moravians' daily lives. That situation gradually changed, however, until the war could not be avoided.

The Moravians maintained a mostly benign relationship with the British officials at Fort Malden. Disagreements centered on whether or not the Moravian converts deserved gifts and to what extent British settlements and expansion would affect the residents of Fairfield. In the fall of 1802, at the time local Indians assembled at Malden to receive gifts from the British, Alexander McKee attempted to define the relationship in the British terms. He asked the missionaries to tell the Indians to no longer request clothing from the British. "They are looked upon as civilized Indians," McKee wrote, "and do not count among those who get presents from the king." As far as British officials were concerned, the Moravian Indians had been given land, and that should be sufficient for them to survive. Meanwhile the Indians at Fairfield wanted to receive gifts from the British but were reluctant to accept other aspects of their location and relationship. They made their feelings particularly clear about the road that lay on the south side of the Thames River and connected Detroit to Lake Erie. Brother Gottfried Sebastian Oppelt wrote that the Indians had two primary objections: "First, because the road is only used by whites and the Indians have a certain dislike for them. Second, they are afraid that, in time, they will be subject to the white men's laws for which they show great disdain." Experience informed them well, and they did not want to relive the problems of the past.[36]

The British officials at Malden did not want to be economically responsible for the Indians but also did not want to lose them as a source of trade goods and as possible wartime allies. This concern first arose in June 1805, when it became clear that some Indians who had been kicked out of Moraviantown for breaking regulations had complained to McKee. According to the missionaries, McKee then "took them [the Indians] into his care because the government does not like to see Indians go over to the American side." But the real British interest did not begin until the *Chesapeake* affair in 1807 raised the temperature of British-American relations. This attempt by a British naval ship, the HMS *Leopard*, to seize alleged deserters from the USS *Chesapeake*, an American vessel, drew a harsh response from President Thomas Jefferson and the American public. In the event of another war, British officials wanted to make sure the Indians took the proper side. Neutrality was not a consideration. British officials hoped to agitate the Indians in the region by reminding them of the past sins of the Americans. This policy entailed diplomacy with Indians still living in the United States, and as British superintendent Matthew Elliott gained more influence, it also involved more direct communication with the Shawnee Prophet and his brother. Tecumseh even visited Amherstburg to talk to Elliott in June 1808.[37]

Although the Moravians at Fairfield lived under British rule and were located only a short distance from Amherstburg and Fort Malden, their responses to events did not always mirror those of the British. Indeed, Elliott and British officials did not focus their diplomatic efforts on the

Moravians who preached neutrality but on the Shawnees and others whom they hoped they could convince to go to war. The Moravians therefore experienced these signs of approaching war through a different lens. In May 1806 they heard from a French trader about the witch hunts and executions on the White River. This news was particularly disturbing because among those burned for sorcery was a former Fairfield resident named Joshua. Yet the Moravian diarists at Fairfield did not mention the Shawnee Prophet, perhaps because they had their own prophets in the region. Onim, an alleged troublemaker of long standing, began preaching at the Munsee town in Upper Canada in 1807. The measures he provided for his followers included a list of eighty different acts he considered to be sins. The Moravian missionaries saw it as a time for their converts to properly defend the faith and were proud to report that one man named Joseph had told the Munsees, "Everything that your teachers say are lies and come from the devil."[38]

Even in the midst of the growing unrest, however, the Moravians maintained their distance from the Prophet's movement and the concerns of their southern relatives. Yet when war broke out in 1812, it shattered the increasingly uneasy peace of the early 1800s. Two decades after they had settled on the Thames, the Moravians once again found themselves in the middle of a war zone, and although neither the British nor the Americans viewed them as vital to the conflict, neither side fully trusted the Moravians' declared neutrality, either. The British in particular wanted a commitment of support from the young men of Fairfield. As the war drew closer and closer to their doorstep, the Moravians realized that Upper Canada could no longer provide refuge.

The war first arrived in the form of rumors, progressed to recruitment of their Indian converts, and then became an all-out disaster. It was not until July 1, 1812, that the Moravians at Fairfield received reliable news that the United States and England had been at war for about a month. They were not the only ones unaware of the war's beginning, though, for the British at Malden did not call the local militia to report to the fort until July, either. Within only a week or two, the rumors of imminent American attacks had the Native residents of Fairfield on edge. On July 16 the Native converts gave all of their belongings to the missionaries for safekeeping and fled into the woods. However, as their fears rose, they retrieved their belongings from the Moravians and hid them in the woods instead. The Indians would not risk another Gnadenhutten. By the end of July 1812 a constant stream of Senecas, Munsees, and Ojibwes passed through Fairfield on their way to Malden, and in mid-October, an untold number of Moravian Indian men left the community to join the war on the British side. In early January 1813 Captain William Caldwell of the British Indian Service was traveling through the Indian towns along the Thames River collecting the men for military service.[39]

Anxiety increased as British forces gave ground in the Great Lakes in 1813. Matthew Elliott, now a lieutenant colonel in the British Army, "sent wampum made with red vermilion indicating that all menfolk from [Fairfield] and above [Muncey Town] should come to Malden," in early April. Five months later Christian Friedrich Denke's entries in the mission diary became shorter as war reports worsened, and on September 29 he revealed his misgivings. "Because of the demolition of Fort Malden and the evacuation of English troops from both Malden and Detroit, as well as the landing of the American fleet, we started to worry about our fate." Fleeing British soldiers turned Fairfield into a field hospital, and with that, the supposed neutrality of the mission disintegrated. "All Indian brethren left Fairfield and took their cattle with them" on October 4. Over the next several days, chaos reigned. The Americans under William Henry Harrison defeated General Henry Procter's British forces in a battle about two miles below Fairfield, which destroyed the settlement. As the Native residents fled into the woods, Brother John Schnall and his fellow Moravian missionaries welcomed the victors. Yet the initial kindness of the American soldiers quickly deteriorated into accusation as they charged the Moravians with hiding British soldiers and goods. On the second day of occupation soldiers ransacked homes and pillaged the food stores. On the third day the missionaries were unceremoniously "booted out" of their town. The fourth day saw Fairfield consumed by flames.[40]

In a situation eerily similar to that of 1782, members of the Fairfield community dispersed throughout the region in the wake of this disaster. With good reason, Brother Schnall, his wife and daughter, and Brother Michael Jung feared for their lives and those of their community members. Schnall's small party took twelve days to travel to Pittsburgh before heading to Bethlehem, Pennsylvania. Meanwhile, just days before Fairfield's destruction, Denke and the greater portion of the congregation had traveled east and headed toward Niagara. Although they managed to stay ahead of the Americans, they could not escape the bedlam brought by war and the retreat of the defeated British forces. "The dispersal has torn families apart," Denke reported. "Some children are without parents, married people are separated and old widows deserted." Yet the Moravians and their community served as a beacon for refugees of the war in Upper Canada. At the end of 1813, as Denke gathered the lost souls in Dundas, he counted 160 men, women, and children, 34 more than had lived at Fairfield at the end of 1812. At the war's conclusion Denke and his congregation returned to the Thames River. In 1815 they rebuilt their settlement south of the river and called it New Fairfield.[41]

The Delawares living in Indiana Territory and Ohio also sought to regroup at war's end, a task that included coming to terms with the United States. Delaware leaders made their marks on two different agreements, in July 1814 and September 1815, respectively. In the case of the former, in a council held at Greenville, Ohio, Harrison and Michigan territorial governor Lewis Cass sought to affirm and reward the friendship of their Indian allies and to enlist their aid in the fighting to come. Before the sessions even began, Harrison presented each delegation from the Delawares, Shawnees, and Wyandots with a large silver pipe, "elegantly ornamented, and engraved with devices emblematic of the protection and friendship of the United States." The war was not done, and the Americans wanted to make sure that their Indian allies recognized the need to combat both the British and their Indian allies. The subsequent treaty, negotiated in September 1815, occurred after the war had officially ended, and it included those Indian bands who had "associated with Great Britain in the late war between the United States and that power, and [had] manifested a disposition to be restored to the relations of peace and amity with the said States." Despite the intent of focusing on those who had joined with the British, the commissioners, William Henry Harrison and John Graham, thought it best to invite their Indian allies not only because they expected to be included, but also because "many individuals belonging to the friendly tribes had taken up arms against the United States, and could only in this way be fully restored to their former situation."[42]

By 1815 many of the Indiana Delawares had left Piqua and returned to the White River, where the first order of business was rebuilding the villages destroyed by American military expeditions. William Anderson had become the definitive first chief of the Indiana towns at this point, his leadership abilities proven by the survival of the Delaware community through the war. Yet within just a few years Anderson made decisions that put him in the Americans' good graces and at great risk among his own people. Indiana became a state in 1816, and the interests of its citizens rested in opening up more territory and removing Indians from their midst. It is not surprising, then, that three treaty commissioners came calling at the Delaware villages on the White River during the fall of 1818. The first article of the resulting treaty was succinct: "The Delaware nation of Indians cede to the United States all their claim to land in the state of Indiana." The simplicity of that statement belied the complicated nature of the negotiations, however, especially because Delaware land claims were still intertwined with those of the Miamis. In addition, Indian agent John Johnston later confessed that he and the three treaty commissioners gained the Delawares' agreement by bribing two of the principal chiefs. Anderson received an annuity of $360 and Lapanihilie (also called Big Bear) received $140. "On this part of the negotiation the personal safety of the Chiefs required the utmost secrecy," Johnston admitted. "I presume there is no record of the stipulation in the journals of the commissioners." However, the journal of the commissioners is not a part of the official record at all, and in subsequent months Anderson never let on what had taken place. Indeed, when the Reverend Isaac McCoy stayed at Anderson's house in December 1818, the Delaware chief discussed the late treaty, saying, "The white people now claim our country, and desire that we should leave it— and now we know not what to do! I think that the men who made the bargain with us have done wrong, and that they had not been authorized to purchase our country; and I hope the transaction will not be approved by Congress." At the end of 1818, then, with the compliance of two of their leading chiefs, the Delawares committed to leaving Indiana within three years.[43]

The 1818 treaty arranged for the removal of the Delawares but did not state their specific destination other than west of the Mississippi River. Two years after the treaty was signed federal officials were sending letters back and forth across the Mississippi, trying to figure out what would and would not work. Despite the fact that, as one scholar has written, "Arkansas was the government's destination of choice for removed tribes" following the 1808 treaty with the Osages, some clear questions remained. Based on an earlier suggestion by his neighbor to the north, William Clark, governor of Arkansas Territory James Miller mentioned the land north of the White River and east of the Osage boundary as a possibility. "As I have no map or chart of this country I cannot designate the place specifically," Miller admitted. "Neither have you informed me, nor have I acquired by any means, a knowledge of the quantity of land, which is to be given to the Delawares." If nothing else, what was obvious was that the placement of the Delawares would require some thought because of two omnipresent issues. Americans were flooding into Missouri Territory, and the land first obtained by the Delawares and Shawnees under Spanish authority was becoming less and less hospitable. This is why federal officials sought locales far removed from the banks of the Mississippi River. Yet any interior location would also have to take into account the boundaries of Osage land claims and hunting territories. The prolonged and recent history of violence between the Osages and eastern emigrants made this particularly crucial to keep in mind, because those Delawares moving from Indiana would not be coming into the region with a clean slate. They would be joining the Delawares who had moved west earlier.[44]

The reunion of these two communities did not occur along the western banks of the Mississippi River where the western Delawares had first made their home in Spanish Louisiana. A lot had changed for those Delawares in the years since they first migrated west in the late eighteenth century. War with the Osages was only one element. By the early 1820s, the Delawares, Shawnees, and others living in the new state of Missouri now had to deal with a tidal wave of American emigrants. Even before the War of 1812, the movement of non-Indians to Missouri Territory and their settlement near Indian towns, including those of the Cherokees and Delawares on the St. Francis River, had led territorial governor Meriwether Lewis to issue a proclamation "requiring the said intruders on the public lands of the United States, at the towns and places aforesaid, or within five miles or either of the same, to depart therefrom, at their peril." Two years later, however, the new territorial governor, William Clark, confirmed that the Shawnees and Delawares living on their 1793 land grant in the Cape Girardeau region were upset at the numbers of American settlers encroaching on their land without consequence. According to Clark, they were anxious and hoped "that the government would confirm them in the possession of that Land, or assign them another place out side of the Settlements." Yet it was in the aftermath of the War of 1812 that the push to claim Indian lands by Missourians really began. The Missouri Territorial Assembly argued in early 1816 that unclear Indian land claims made life extremely difficult for new non-Indian residents. The assemblymen thereby requested Congress to take action to place the Indians "in the unsettled parts of the Territory," a move that would not be difficult, especially because many Indians had already moved, evacuating several of their old villages. The assembly reiterated the call through new resolutions that passed one year later.[45]

In the late 1810s the Delawares in Missouri Territory occupied a number of towns. According to government treaty commissioners, the Delawares abandoned their claims to the Cape Girardeau lands in 1815. Christian missionaries told a different story, reporting that in 1818 approximately two to three hundred Delawares still lived in the Cape Girardeau region, and they expressed interest in obtaining a teacher for their children. More to the point is that in the 1810s, because of the pressure brought by the encroachment of American citizens, the Delawares living west of the Mississippi River began to search for new homes. As of the summer of 1817 approximately six hundred Delawares were living in villages on the St. Francis and White Rivers. Not all of the Delawares on those waterways were recent migrants from Cape Girardeau. Indeed, a band of Delawares had been granted permission by the Spanish governor of Orleans in 1796 to establish settlements on the White River after the Quapaws had rejected a joint Delaware-Cherokee request to live above the Quapaws on the Arkansas River. By 1818 the sentiments of some of the western tribes had changed, however, as a delegation of Arkansas Indians expressed an interest in having the Delawares and Shawnees from Cape Girardeau settle among them.[46]

Based on these developments, it would initially appear that the southwestern corner of Missouri and the northwestern corner of Arkansas Territory had become the next safe haven for the Delawares and other eastern Indians. Yet while the Osages had ceded much of this territory in their 1808 treaty, they had retained hunting rights. Another potential problem arose from Osage beliefs that they had ceded the territory to make room for non-Indian neighbors, and not the Cherokees or Delawares. As a result, Stephen Long reported, "They are not a little disappointed and chagrined, at the arrangement recently made with the Cherokees, their inveterate enemies, by which the latter are permitted to settle upon the Lands formerly owned by them and are by this means placed in a condition to annoy them exceedingly, which has been done of late, on repeated occasions." The Osages referred specifically to an 1817 accord that arranged for the emigration of several thousand eastern Cherokees to join their relatives already living west of the Mississippi. The treaty made reference to granting the western Cherokees lands on the Arkansas and

White Rivers to match those ceded in the East. This treaty and the subsequent emigration increased the number of Cherokees on the Arkansas, already estimated at 6,000 in the summer of 1817. It was one of several factors that led to renewed hostilities between the Osages and the Cherokees. And the Cherokees, as they had done before, called on the Delawares and Shawnees for assistance. The resulting conflict lasted from the late 1810s into the mid-1820s.[47]

By 1822, then, approximately one thousand men, women, and children who had left Indiana under the terms of the 1818 treaty joined the settlements of the Missouri Delawares who had been pushed into the southwestern corner of the state. This meant that nearly 2,500 Delawares, in multiple villages, now lived west of the Mississippi River. As had happened with great frequency in prior decades and centuries, they lived in a violent place. Within months of their arrival, Anderson and the Indiana Delawares met the Osages in council to delineate hunting territories in the Ozarks, but the attempt to avoid conflict failed. The resulting violence claimed many Osage and Delaware lives, including that of Anderson's son. War with the Osages was only one of the reasons why this reunited Delaware community did not stay in Missouri past 1829, however, for a combination of events made life in the Ozarks difficult. As early as February 1824 Anderson and other leading Delawares informed Superintendent of Indian Affairs William Clark, "A number of our people died just for the want of something to live on." Flooding the previous summer had destroyed their cornfields, and the hunting in the vicinity was poor. Overall, the Delawares noted, "We have got in a Country where we do not find as was stated to us when we was asked to swap lands with you." To make matters worse, the tendrils of American expansion began reaching into southwestern Missouri through the movements of traders and farmers. The Delaware settlements in southwestern Missouri did not last a decade.[48]

It is possible to follow the trail of the Delawares out of Missouri by tracking the movements of Anderson and his people, who left the state in 1829 under the auspices of the Treaty of Council Camp, which granted them a reserve just west of the Missouri border and north of the Kansas River. Yet years before Anderson and other Delaware headmen negotiated another exchange of land, other Delawares had already made another choice. Instead of working with the United States government, these Delawares relocated south and west into territory claimed by newly independent Mexico. Their journey into Mexico displayed a number of continuities in Delaware history. The willingness of the Delawares to promote their interests by utilizing international boundaries was not new, nor was the relationship with both Shawnees and Cherokees who had also chosen to immigrate to Mexico. Most important to this discussion, the migration to Mexico revealed once more that the Delawares' constant search for refuge was haunted by the nonstop expansion of the United States and its citizens.[49]

In October 1824 an unnamed Shawnee headman used a Mexican intermediary to petition the alcalde of San Antonio. In that petition the Shawnee leader made clear his people's desire "to place themselves under the protection of the Mexican Government." This was a request for land, but not just for Shawnees. "They pray the Government that the conditions of the grant may include all their allies and friends who may follow them," the petition explained. The governor of Coahuila and Texas, Rafael Gonzalez, approved the request in December 1824, and by the end of 1825 two different Shawnee bands had established villages in eastern Texas, and a band of Delawares lived on a creek in present-day Red River County. A report of July 1827 indicates that within two years approximately 250 Delaware families had settled in the region.[50]

The international border did not provide the desired distance from American land hunger and expansionist tendencies. This fact became particularly evident in 1828 as the Delawares and Shawnees in the Red River region were caught up in disputes with American citizens and border crossings by the American military. The citizens of Miller County, Arkansas, located in the southwestern corner of the territory, were displeased with the growing presence of Indians in their vicinity. George Gray, the Indian agent at the Red River Agency, described the situation in clear terms: "It appears to be the whirlpool that is sucking within its bosom, the restless and dissatisfied, of all nations and languages; parties of broken up tribes are continually pouring in, and it is become a receptacle for detached parties from all parts. Delawares, Kickapoos Shawanese Choctaws and others are day after day settling around us." The citizens of Miller County, meanwhile, complained to their governor that the Indians were settling amongst them without any pretense: "All done under the Authority of his Excellency Don Jose Antonio Saucedo of the Department of Texas who has given them a permission in writing, dated the 20th March 1827 at Nacogdoches to settle at this place (pecan point) until the line between the two Governments shall be run, then they are to be confirmed in their title." The Shawnees in particular defended their claim to the land under Mexican authority and told the white settlers that if they did not like it they did not have to stay. These tensions led to a questionable military action undertaken by Colonel Wharton Rector, Jr. Requested by the governor to investigate the problems at Pecan Point, Rector found that the Indians had threatened to drive the whites from the south side of the Red River, "Saying That the Country belonged to them." Rector proceeded to gather the Indian leaders of the villages to order them from the country. The Delawares "agreed to do so immediately," but the Shawnees refused. Captain Russel B. Hyde, the commander at Cantonment Towson, did not support Rector's desire for direct action, and explained that the "Indians against whom Mr. Rector had declared War were none of them within the limits of the United States. They were on the South Side of Red River in the Province of Texas at least 50 miles above where the Spanish line will strike Red River." The Adams–Onis Treaty of 1819 had supposedly finalized this boundary line, but the confusion and tension surrounding the Delaware presence indicated that the border remained a contested space a decade later.[51]

It was not simply a matter of American officials reaching across the border into Mexican territory, for the Delawares also faced pressure from American citizens seeking land grants from the Mexican authorities. Indeed, the 1827 report indicating the number and location of Indians in the northeastern corner of Texas came from three American men living in Texas—David Burnet, Benjamin Milam, and Stephen F. Austin. Burnet had first entered Texas during the Mexican Revolution, and by 1827, three years after the Mexican government adopted its constitution, was a powerful landowner. Milam was similarly positioned. He had led trade expeditions to the Comanches in the 1810s and then joined the revolutionaries in the latter stages of their uprising against Spain. Austin's name is perhaps best remembered among the three, for it was his father, Moses, who initiated negotiations in 1820 to arrange for some of the first land grants for American immigrants in Texas. The report written by these three men in 1827 not only provided a brief census of the Indian population of Texas, it raised a warning flag. The three Americans had "a deep and lively concern in all that relate[d] to the welfare of their adopted country," and because of this "regard for the future advancement and tranquility of Texas," felt it necessary to oppose any Mexican policy that would allow Indians to continue to settle in the region. Those Indians in the process of being removed from the eastern United States should remain in American territory under the jurisdiction of the United States government. And the Indians, like the Delawares who were already in Texas, should be encouraged to leave, so as "to save the peaceful Citizens of Coahuila and Texas . . . from the *tomahawk and scalping knife* of a ruthless, infuriated and savage foe."[52]

Burnet, Milam, and Austin painted a misleading picture of the Indian presence in order to promote their desire for land. Mexican authorities had welcomed the eastern Indians in the hope that they could provide a buffer against the Comanche bands that had raided the Texan settlements for decades. The Delawares who had settled south of St. Louis in the 1780s were asked by Spanish authorities to protect St. Louis and its environs from attacks by the powerful Osages. Forty years later their descendants in Texas received a request to do the same against a different western Indian nation. In contrast to the sentiments expressed by Burnet and his colleagues, even some American immigrants to Texas hoped to benefit from the presence of the eastern Indians. A small number of men, intending to lead a revolt against the Mexican authorities in the town of Nacogdoches in 1827, actively sought the favor of Cherokee, Shawnee, and Delaware warriors in the area. If nothing else, the Delawares who moved to Mexico hoping for a safe haven would get no respite from the battles over power and land. Instead they faced yet another struggle to avoid relocation, and the situation worsened once Texas declared and won its independence from Mexico in 1836.[53]

Further to the north in American-claimed territory, nearly all of the Delawares who left southwestern Missouri for the Kansas River under the leadership of William Anderson had arrived by the fall of 1831. "I hope if the Government fulfill all their promises," Anderson reported to Secretary of War Lewis Cass, "that before many years the balance of my nation who are now scattered some on Red River and some in the Spanish Country will come here on this Land." While the game appeared scarce in the region and the men had to travel long distances to hunt, he claimed, "The land is good and also the wood and water," so it appeared that the Delawares would be able to provide for their families once they had situated themselves better. In addition, Anderson had taken the opportunity to tell the government surveyors who measured off the Delaware lands, "I wished Congress to put a strong word in our hand so that we could live here forever in peace and never to be removed." For the better part of three decades Chief Anderson had attempted to reunite the Delaware communities that were now spread across three countries. A permanent home on the Kansas River presented one more opportunity.[54]

William Anderson died not long after that letter made its way to Cass, however, which meant he did not live to see his hopes go unfulfilled. The reserve in Kansas did not become a gathering point for all Delawares who had established new homes beyond the American northern and southern borders. Instead, Delaware families and individuals turned to places they felt offered them the best site to provide security and sustenance for their families. Charles Henry Killbuck, a Moravian convert, was one example of this. In 1801 he left Fairfield on the Thames and took up residence in one of the Delaware villages on the White River in Indiana at a time when Moravian missionaries moved there as well. In the wake of the 1818 treaty Killbuck did not want to move west of the Mississippi River with his relatives, and in 1823 he was one of a party of Delawares and Munsees who signed an agreement with the United States government through then–Michigan territorial governor and superintendent of Indian Affairs Lewis Cass. For the time being, they were going to move to Canada and live with their relatives at New Fairfield, the town rebuilt after the destruction of the War of 1812. However, the terms of the 1823 agreement also provided financial support for relocation to the western territories if, at some later date, Killbuck and others changed their minds.[55]

As of May 1830, the month when both the Senate and the House voted in favor of legislation that became known as the Indian Removal Act, Delawares lived along the Red River in northern Mexico, along the Thames River in Upper Canada, and on the Kansas River just west of the Missouri border. These were not the only places inhabited by Delawares, nor would they necessarily be the settlements these Indians would occupy thirty years later. In the 1850s in Texas and in the 1860s in Kansas the disparate Delaware communities endured another series of forced relocations under the auspices of federal policy. Those later removals were yet another reminder that, if 1830 marked a particular turning point in the longer Delaware experience with dispossession and relocation, it was not a direct result of the Indian Removal Act. Delaware removal was defined as much by what happened before 1830 as it was by what came after 1830, and during that time the Delaware history was as much about the relationships within and without the community as it was about the development of particular federal policies.[56]

4

SANDUSKY RIVER REMOVALS

In the fall of 1817 American treaty commissioners held a council near what would soon be Sandusky, Ohio, with delegations from several Indian tribes. At first glance, the council provides insight into the expansion of American settlement into the Old Northwest after the War of 1812. Ohio entered the Union in 1803, but the northwestern portion of the state had been Indian country for much of the fourteen years that followed. By 1817, however, the developing interests of the young American nation required the cession of Indian lands. Events during the War of 1812 had illustrated the dangers of poor communication and underdeveloped infrastructure in the region, and politicians and military officers alike clamored for the construction of roads, forts, and settlements to protect against future threats, especially from the British in Upper Canada. The cessions gained in the 1817 treaty were substantial, and they set the stage for the dramatic growth of American settlements along the southern shores of Lake Erie and the removal of Indians over the next two decades. Yet the treaty was more than just an expression of national interest and federal power. The details and circumstances of that accord illustrate the extent to which national desires masked the intertwined local interests that drove these developments.

By the time the United States declared war against England in June 1812, the residents of the Sandusky region had long lived with warfare sparked by the larger forces of settler colonialism. This time, however, things were different, not because of fluctuating levels of violence and bloodshed, but because of the ripple effects created by the war and the treaty that brought it to a close. In the early stages of diplomatic negotiations the British had insisted on the establishment of a territory located between the United States and Canada to be held exclusively by their Indian allies. Instead of remaining steadfast to this proposal, however, the British sacrificed a promise made to those allies and agreed to an article stating that the Indians should "enjoy all the rights and privileges they enjoyed before the war." That vague and empty statement would not protect the rights and interests of Native peoples, and the Treaty of Ghent could not reverse what the war had transformed. In the years that followed, the Wyandot, Seneca, and Delaware residents of the Sandusky River region found themselves under increasing pressure on a rapidly diminishing share of the lands set aside in previous treaties.[1]

In 1815 Ohio was little more than a decade old, which meant that Ohioans were still seeking to establish their state in much the same way that Americans as a whole sought to strengthen their nation. The pressure placed on Indian lands thus occurred at a critical confluence of state and nation building in the early American republic. Indeed, federal policy regarding land sales had such a dramatic effect in Ohio that the settlement of the landscape "happened with unprecedented speed and thoroughness," leaving scant acreage available for sale by 1830. From the passage of the Land Ordinance of 1785 to the 1820s, federal land policy was in large part dependent on the idea of increasing federal revenue through organized land sales and surveys. This promotion of settlement in the Old Northwest contributed greatly to the development of Ohio, even though land speculators and squatters often undermined the proposed equitable and affordable distribution of land. As of 1821, eight different land offices operated in the state. All told, in the first two decades of the nineteenth century those offices accounted for the sale of more than seven million acres, or the equivalent of roughly two-thirds of available federal lands.[2]

These, then, were two prominent forces pulling non–Indians into Ohio and driving Indians out during the first four decades of the nineteenth century. Rather than address all of Ohio, however, this chapter focuses on the Sandusky River region in the northwestern part of the state in order to showcase the power structures and circumstances that framed the experiences of Delawares, Senecas, and Wyandots from the 1810s to the 1840s. The similar obstacles those three different communities faced illustrate that they confronted pressures from local, state, and federal trends. In part, this focus demonstrates the manner in which the distinctive political, legal, geographic, and social contexts of the Sandusky region shaped these unique removal narratives. The timing and circumstances surrounding the respective removals of these three Native communities in turn reveal the relative capability and desire of the Delawares, Senecas, and Wyandots to maintain a presence along the Sandusky River and to combat the persistent encroachment of non-Indians. At the center of it all were the competing visions of the future of Ohio. "In a few years," the *Cincinnati Gazette* reported in the fall of 1818, "these almost interminable forests will be converted into flourishing towns and villages and cultivated farms; the silent footsteps of the savage will give way to the resounding of the axe, the din of industry, and the bustle of commercial enterprise." The world that white Ohioans sought to create in the early nineteenth century could only come to pass once the Indians yielded to its inevitability.[3]

From its origins at Walton Lake, in present-day Richland County, the Sandusky River winds its way along nearly 150 miles of northern Ohio before making its entrance into Sandusky Bay in western Lake Erie. On the way, it cuts through the counties of Wyandot, Seneca, and Sandusky and runs along numerous towns, including Tiffin, Upper Sandusky, and Fremont. The region has a long history of both Indian occupancy and European trade relations, especially because it became a site of strategic importance between the French and English colonial enterprises during the seventeenth and eighteenth centuries. Sandusky Bay first appeared on a 1683 European map that was a product of an expedition in which René-Robert Cavelier, Sieur de La Salle, traversed the waters of Lake Erie in 1679. Both French and English traders were active in the region throughout the early eighteenth century, and a map from 1733 provides the first named register of Sandusky. More detailed examinations by Europeans appeared in the late 1730s as the region became home to Wyandots who sought to escape the violence of the latter stages of the Mesquakie Wars around French Detroit. The Wyandot settlements focused around the leadership of a man named Nicholas (also called Orotony). He courted the English, and for much of the 1740s he worked to build an Indian confederacy to defy the French. When his efforts to bring the English into the region to counteract the French failed to secure his position, in 1748 he burned all the buildings at the mouth of the Sandusky and headed to the White River in present-day Indiana.[4]

The Wyandots did not leave with Nicholas, however, and instead maintained villages along the Sandusky River for nearly a century after his departure. A map from 1755 marks two different Wyandot villages, one near the mouth of the Sandusky and the other in the vicinity of present-day Fremont, or Lower Sandusky. The 1755 map also reveals some of the connections in the region, as the mouth of the Sandusky to the Detroit River is labeled with the information, "The Indians cross here using canoes to jump from I[sland] to I[sland]." Such travel was important, for the Wyandot population was not confined to northern Ohio. In 1790 the English government of Upper Canada established a reservation of 24,000 acres between Sandwich and Amherstburg, and another portion of the Wyandot population resided in the villages of Brownstown and Monguagon, south of Detroit.[5]

The centrality of the Sandusky villages placed them at critical travel routes during times of both peace and war, and many references to those Wyandot settlements in the mid-to-late eighteenth century come from captivity narratives. Colonel James Smith, a Delaware prisoner, passed through Lower Sandusky during the mid-1750s and later remembered the rich soil of the flood plains near the Wyandot town of Sunyendean, located just south of the mouth of the Sandusky River. Less than a decade later an Englishman named John Montresor stated that the Wyandots on Upper Sandusky lived in a bountiful place that was "covered with Game," and described the land as "extremely rich, interspersed near the borders of the Rivers and lake with large tracts of meadow." Their location along the Sandusky River allowed the Wyandots to have a plentiful existence and also allowed them access to the Ohio River and the Great Lakes. Upper Sandusky—whose name refers to its location on the upper portions of the river, farther into the interior than Lower Sandusky—also served as the focal point of the Northwestern Indian Confederacy during and after the American Revolution. Lower Sandusky became the seat of the Wyandots' principal war chief, whereas Upper Sandusky was the seat of the principal civil chief. Into the 1790s this meant that Tarhe (also called the Crane) resided at Lower Sandusky and Half King at Upper Sandusky.[6]

The Seneca and Delaware villages on the Sandusky River were of later origin. The exact timing of the Senecas' arrival is difficult to pinpoint, as is the exact composition of the community that federal officials labeled the Senecas of Sandusky. Indian agent John Johnston stated, "About the time of the revolutionary war 500 Senecas by the permission of the Wyandotts became located on Sandusky River within the limits of what is now Seneca County Ohio." Other references simply state that the Wyandots granted land to the Senecas "many years before the treaty of Brownstown was made" in 1808. The population was augmented during the decade after the Brownstown accord in part by the emigration of Cayugas from the Buffalo Creek Reservation in New York. By 1819 the village known as Seneca Town was home to 248 men, women, and children and was one of two primary settlements on the reservation created for the Senecas of Sandusky in the 1817 Treaty of the Maumee Rapids. That same accord set aside approximately one thousand acres south of the reservation along Honey Creek, and there 57 Mohawks made their home.[7] These Mohawks, most of whom had only recently arrived in the region from the Grand River Reservation in Canada via Monguagon, had received permission from Michigan territorial governor Lewis Cass to establish a new home in Ohio. The Mohawks testified that they had found themselves in "a bad situation" at Grand River and wanted to move to Sandusky where, they said, "some of our own kind of people is living and become one body." By 1829 Seneca Town had a population of 322, all of whom, according to John Johnston, went "under the name of Senecas," though that number included Senecas, Mohawks, Cayugas, Oneidas, and at least one family of Onondagas.[8]

The Delawares had established their home just south of the Wyandots at Upper Sandusky on a tract of land that measured about three square miles. Their settlement had its origins in a 1778 migration undertaken by a party of Delawares and Munsees under the leadership of Hopocan, who was also known as Captain Pipe. This band had allied their interests with the British and decided to settle near the similarly minded Wyandots in the Ohio country during the early stages of the Revolutionary War. From that point forward the Delaware settlement was generally referred to as Captain Pipe's Town, or just Pipestown. The town's status evolved through the petition of Montgomery Montour, a Delaware resident who, along with approximately one hundred other Delaware men, women, and children, took issue with two different treaties ratified in April 1806, which were signed by Delaware chiefs and ceded land that included Montour's home on White Woman's Creek south of Upper Sandusky. Unhappy with the fact that the Delaware signatories had agreed to such cessions without acknowledging the presence of two Delaware towns on those ceded lands, Montour asked Congress to secure to the Sandusky Delawares their homes along White Woman's Creek. His petition assured Congress that "his people love[d] the white people, and wish[ed] to be settled near them, and even round about them they earnestly wish[ed] to learn agriculture and other improvements of life and manners, from the white people: in short, as soon as convenient, to become willingly one people with them." Despite the fact that he believed the claim was based solely on Montour's assertion, and not necessarily on a legitimate title, Secretary of War Henry Dearborn felt it best to support the petition. On March 3, 1807, Congress passed a law designating thirteen sections of land for the Delawares and their descendants at White Woman's Creek. Ten years later, in the treaty of 1817, the Delawares surrendered those thirteen sections in exchange for three square miles, to be equally divided among seventeen different Delawares, including Captain Pipe (also called Tahunqeecoppi), the namesake of the Delaware chief who led that 1778 migration to the Sandusky River.[9]

The Sandusky River region in which the Wyandots, Senecas, and Delawares made their home was the specific target of only one concerted British assault during the War of 1812. Nevertheless, neither the Indian nor the non-Indian residents of the region escaped the conflict unscathed. Within a few months of the war's outbreak in June 1812, the Wyandots, Senecas, and Delawares all feared that their respective towns might be vulnerable. They were not alone in their fear, for even the small American military garrison stationed at Lower Sandusky had evacuated by late August. Tarhe, the Wyandot principal chief at Upper Sandusky, turned to American officials with the expectation that they would help protect friendly Indian communities. Even as the Americans prepared to abandon their simple fortifications at Lower Sandusky, he declared, "I hope you now will listen to me that you will medently send on to me men to build a garrison large enough to hold the Windots Senecca and [illegible] at my town upper Sandusky." The Wyandot chief, who had long advocated a strong alliance with the United States, now hoped that American officials recognized the necessity of providing asylum for the Seneca and Wyandot refugees moving south to the relative safety of the interior.[10]

The federal government needed to move quickly, because after General William Hull surrendered Detroit that September, the situation worsened. Rumors raced throughout the region that British forces might move into northwestern Ohio any day and, according to the Moravian missionary Abraham Luckenbach, the "Wyandottes in the Lower Sandusky fled to the Upper Sandusky, as did also the Senecas. They drove their cattle before them and everybody had to look out for himself." By January 1813 General William Henry Harrison had received letters from former residents of Lower Sandusky such as Elizabeth Whitaker, a widow who pleaded for assistance since the British forces had burned down her home. "To ad[d] to my difficulty and sorrow," Whitaker explained, "your arme has taken my corn and hogs that the ennimy had left." For the next seven months, however, Harrison's time and efforts were dedicated to repulsing British assaults on Fort Meigs, while an American command of approximately 160 soldiers occupied Fort Stephenson, located on the western bank of the Sandusky River. The British forces, after failing to take Fort Meigs, made one effort in August 1813 to take Fort Stephenson and failed. Devastating naval losses on Lake Erie one month later ended any further British efforts in northwestern Ohio.[11]

The ebb and flow of these military campaigns led to a similar ebb and flow in the movements of northwestern Ohio inhabitants. Four months after the British failed to take Fort Stephenson, Ohio governor Return J. Meigs received a petition from fourteen men who had established homes at Lower Sandusky within the boundaries of the Wyandot reservation. These men and their families had been "severe sufferers since the commencement of the present war, and even prior to the declaration thereof." They had moved to Lower Sandusky to be under the protection of the American military forces, and now hoped to remain. "We do not, neither can we, attempt to claim any legal right to the ground or spot of earth on which we have each and individually settled," they humbly stated. "But the improvements which we have made, and the buildings which we have erected, we trust will not be taken from us without the interference of legal authority." As of mid-1814 approximately eighty families had built cabins at Lower Sandusky, all with the consent of the military commanders at Fort Stephenson. According to Thomas Hawkins, a former lieutenant in the U.S. Army, these preemption rights to the Wyandot lands were "by each succeeding officer sanctioned and each Refugee found protection until the Reservation became thickly populated." Hawkins had even erected a sawmill and made plans with one of Fort Stephenson's officers to survey a town they intended to name Croghansville in honor of George Croghan, the officer who had led the defense of Fort Stephenson. Everyone involved believed that they would receive official confirmation of their preemption claims once the war was over. Hawkins and his fellow squatters saw a prosperous future in Lower Sandusky and only hoped that the federal government would recognize that truth and allow them to purchase the lands they had worked so hard to improve.[12]

Not surprisingly, these settlements threatened to destabilize relations with the Wyandots and their neighbors. From late August into September 1815, William Henry Harrison and John Graham met in council at Fort Wayne in Detroit with representatives of the Wyandots, Shawnees, Delawares, Senecas, Potawatomis, Ojibwes, Miamis, and Odawas to finalize the peace that had been brought about by the Treaty of Ghent. In that council Tarhe spoke for those Indians who had allied with the Americans and chastised those who had sided with the British. Yet the Wyandots also had a number of justifiable complaints they did not air during the meeting. The first addressed the road that had been surveyed to run from the rapids of the Maumee to the western edge of the Connecticut Reserve. At the point it would cross the Sandusky River, the Wyandots argued, "It will injuriously interfere with the settlements of the Senecas." The Indians had understood that the road was supposed to take a different path, and they wanted it corrected. In addition, Tarhe and the Wyandots protested the continued presence of trespassers on their lands who had "considerable farms" and who "employed themselves in hunting and destroying the animals which were so necessary" to the Wyandots. Harrison and Graham stated that the Indian complaints should be addressed. "Good policy, as well as justice, requires this," they wrote, "as a contrary conduct would have the effect of procrastinating a further extinction of title to lands, which is now so ardently desired by the citizens of Ohio."[13]

It initially appeared that the commissioners' recommendations had been heard, for on December 12, 1815, President James Madison issued a proclamation "commanding and strictly enjoining all persons who have unlawfully taken possession of or made any settlement on the public lands as aforesaid forthwith to remove therefrom," and asserted that any who did not remove would be punished as the law directed. American citizens in Ohio responded to this proclamation by reasserting the importance of the region's development to the state and the nation. Thomas Hawkins lobbied William Crayton, a congressional representative from Ohio, to aid the squatters. This assistance would be important to more than just the refugee families, of course. As Hawkins was quick to point out, the development of Lower Sandusky would be crucial in the years to come. "It is the opinion of every reflecting mind," he asserted, "that the time is not far distant when this will be the deposit for all the goods that enter the Western world." Hawkins's prediction was based on more than just the commerce already in existence. He referenced with confidence the plans for the Erie Canal and the "spirit of New York in opening a Communication to the lake," making sure Crayton understood the national implications of this request.[14]

This increasing pressure coincided with the death of Tarhe in November 1816, a loss from which federal officials hoped to benefit. The Wyandots "held several councils" in the aftermath of Tarhe's death, commissioner Duncan MacArthur informed acting secretary of war George Graham, "and a large Majority of them" were in favor of "leaving the Sandusky and for going to White River, or still farther on westwardly, to where the game is more plenty." The moment appeared ripe for obtaining land cessions from all the Indians living along the Sandusky River who had taken their prompts from venerable Wyandot Chief. According to Graham, the time had come for the Wyandots to make a choice about how they were going to live the rest of their lives in relation to the United States. On March 23 he sent a letter to Lewis Cass that laid out some instructions for approaching the Indians in Ohio about land cessions. "The negotiations should be founded," he stated, "on the basis that each head of a family who wishes to remain within the limits ceded should have a life estate in a reservation of a certain number of acres, which should descend to his children in fee . . . and that those who do not wish to remain on those terms should have a body of land allotted to them on the west of the Mississippi." Those proposed terms represented the government's ideal scenario, so if the Wyandots and others were not willing to go that far, the letter indicated, Cass should focus on a partial land cession. Obtaining this territory in northwest Ohio would connect the population of Ohio to that of Michigan Territory and therefore further unite American citizens in the Old Northwest.[15]

Yet the government's opportunism foundered when the Wyandots took issue with what they perceived to be departures from diplomatic protocol. The Wyandots' interpreter, William Walker, Sr., wrote to Lewis Cass in late May 1817, informing him that they were not pleased with the most recent attempts to discuss a possible treaty. The Wyandots had received a message of a threatening nature regarding those potential negotiations. Walker reported, "They very well know that whenever the Government wanted to inform them of any business of importance that it was a practice to send a written speech accompanied (with a token) of the importance of the object." They would not respond to any messages that did not follow customary diplomatic measures. A confused Cass only learned weeks later that a man named Paul Butler had attempted to stir things up by sending a letter under Cass's name stating that the United States was "determined to purchase the Country at any price." Faced with a delicate situation, Indian agent John Johnston informed Cass that he was going to try and lay a better foundation for negotiations by sending Shawnee headman Black Hoof to Sandusky. Black Hoof, who had convinced his band at Wapakoneta to accept Quaker missionaries and learn to farm in the American way, became the agent of American interests.[16]

American officials utilized multiple approaches to overcome the Wyandots' resistance to land cessions. In addition to sending Black Hoof, Johnston urged that the treaty negotiators focus on the Wyandot chiefs because gifts and land grants might serve the purpose well. The chiefs, however, were not the only problem. "I learn Mrs. [William] Walker is an enemy to the Treaty," Johnston reported to Cass. "In short every engine, short of coercion, must be put in motion or the object will fall thro', and much delicate management will be necessary least it should be hereafter alledged that the Indians were forced." Johnston believed that, similar to the careful handling of the chiefs, land grants might appease the opposition of the powerful Walker interests. Johnston also found another ally in the person of Elizabeth Whitaker, the same widow who had petitioned General Harrison in January 1813. She had been born Elizabeth Fulks and was captured by a Wyandot war party in 1782 near Cross Roads, Pennsylvania. After being adopted by the Wyandots, she married another captive named James Whitaker at a Catholic ceremony in Detroit in 1786. The two settled in a log cabin at Lower Sandusky and raised eight children among the Wyandots. As a result she had become a respected member of the Wyandot community. In a letter to Cass on June 14 Whitaker reported, "[I] returned from Upper Sandusky the 11th of this Month after having been there seven days doing all in my power to promote your designs and I have the satisfaction of informing you that prospects appear flattering." She would later attend the council held by the chiefs and report on all that she saw and heard.[17]

From June 20 to June 28 Elizabeth Whitaker visited Upper Sandusky and talked to three of the Wyandot headmen. During the course of her consultations with those men she found them amenable to negotiations. Yet while the specifics of their discussions are not known, Whitaker relied strongly on her relationship with the chiefs and their trust in her. The Wyandots wanted to know whether it was "their Father the President" who wanted "the Land for the use of his children" or whether individuals desired "to speculate on it" as they had been told. This information was very important to them. Whitaker took it upon herself to pledge, "It was not the intention of Government to obtain their Lands for speculation nor would individuals be permitted to obtain it for that purpose." Whitaker had a strong relationship with the Wyandots, but it is unclear if her statements illustrated a naïveté about possible speculation or her willingness to manipulate the situation for personal benefit. The widow had lost her home, her fields, and most of her property in the British campaign against Lower Sandusky in the late war, and she justifiably saw financial security and salvation in a treaty. Her prediction of fruitful treaty negotiations ultimately proved correct, as Black Hoof also reported to Johnston that the Wyandots and William Walker appeared willing to talk.[18]

At the end of September 1817 commissioners Lewis Cass and Duncan McArthur sent the treaty they had negotiated to the War Department. The accord encompassed twenty-one distinct articles and an even greater number of interests. The Wyandots ceded territory between the southern shores of Lake Erie and the northern boundaries of Upper Sandusky, and the Senecas of Sandusky secured a tract of 30,000 acres adjoining the Sandusky River. Cass and McArthur heralded the land purchase, seeing it "as the great connecting link which b[ound] together [the] northwestern frontier." Though pleased with the result, the commissioners were also concerned that some might view the treaty as providing too-liberal terms to the Wyandots. That tribe was set to receive an annuity of $4,000 in perpetuity for their cession. Everyone should be aware, the commissioners explained, that the Wyandots, Senecas, and Shawnees had shown themselves to be shrewd negotiators. "By frequent communication with our citizens," they stated, "they perfectly well know upon what terms the United States sell their land; and they also know the extravagant rate at which the reservations at Sandusky and this place are sold. This knowledge led them to expect a compensation for the land far exceeding any thing which is secured to them by treaty."[19]

Cass and McArthur were less aware of Indians who criticized the treaty's terms. In November a delegation of Wyandots, Senecas, and Delawares made an unannounced journey to Washington. Agent John Johnston did not learn of their departure until well after the fact and explained to Cass that the trip "was undertaken with so much secrecy and dispatch" that he had no "power to counteract it." Johnston did not know their motivations but expected they wanted "to procure some modification of the part of the treaty relating to their reserves and to get Young Walker made Agent at Upper Sandusky." Although no records exist of the exact conversations held with that delegation of Indians, the treaty signed at St. Mary's in Ohio, almost exactly a year after the 1817 accord, provides a good clue. The 1817 treaty had granted land in fee simple, thus attempting to institute personal property ownership among the Ohio Indian communities. The 1818 treaty altered that in its very first article. Signatories to the latter treaty, including Cass and McArthur as well as Wyandot, Odawa, Shawnee, and Seneca representatives, agreed, "The several tracts of land, described in the treaty to which this is supplementary . . . for the use of the individuals of the said tribes, and also the tract described in the twentieth article of the said treaty, shall not be thus granted, but shall be excepted from the cession made by the said tribes to the United States, reserved for the use of the said Indians, and held by them in the same manner as Indian reservations have been heretofore held." The 1818 supplemental treaty voided the notion of individual ownership and returned the reserve lands to the communal ownership of the Native communities. Other adjustments, including the creation of reservations for the Wyandots at Solomonstown and on Blanchard's Fork, mattered, but the reversal of private ownership was particularly important. Cass and McArthur also indicated, in their best bureaucratic language, that the Indians had a fixed position on removal. The two commissioners raised the idea and reported it was "received by them with such strong symptoms of disapprobation, that we did not think it proper to urge them too far upon the subject." Both men believed this attitude would change. "As our settlements gradually surround them," Cass and McArthur wrote, "their minds will be better prepared to receive this proposition."[20]

The 1817 Treaty of the Maumee Rapids thus served as end point and catalyst. It confirmed lands to those non-Indians who had rushed to Sandusky during the late war, and it opened a new world to those who saw economic opportunities in northwestern Ohio. As a result, the 1820s proved to be a critical decade for the Indians living along the Sandusky River. The town of Sandusky was first plotted on October 27, 1817, but was not officially incorporated as Lower Sandusky until 1830. Sandusky County was officially organized on April 1, 1820, and neighboring Seneca County was officially organized on January 22, 1824. According to the 1820 census, Sandusky County contained 852 non-Indian citizens. Ten years later the county population numbered 2,851, while adjacent Seneca County had a population of 5,159. As this population grew in those and the surrounding counties, the state and national governments focused on developing a transportation corridor along the southern shores of Lake Erie, even as the impending completion of the Erie Canal increased the desire of American citizens to populate and develop the region. And though the 1817 treaty secured land to the Wyandots, Senecas, and Delawares, they could not ignore the world pressing in around them and how such developments threatened the future of their communities. Tall Man, the principal chief at Seneca Town, along with fourteen other leading men said as much in a letter addressed to President James Monroe in early 1824. "Our hearts are often made sick," they stated. "Whitemen passing through our Land often say this land is too good for Indians—We fear that we will soon be driven from this country unless you help us."[21]

By the end of the decade those fears were realized, and both the Senecas and the Delawares had decided to leave Ohio. Ongoing property loss suffered at the hands of non-Indians was one of the more obvious factors driving their respective decisions. As early as 1819 John Johnston expressed the need for another agent to protect the Senecas. White men in the region had been killing the Indians' hogs and cattle, and, Johnston asserted, the "character of the Government of the U.S. requires that they should not be left thus exposed to the inroads of the wicked and abandoned portion of our species." A year later the problems continued and Johnston reported the death of a Seneca man's oxen "under very aggravating circumstances" near Lower Sandusky. As far as the agent was concerned, there was "nothing so embarrassing to the Agent for Indian affairs in Ohio, as the conflicting claims of the whites and Indians for depredations." And while members of both communities suffered losses, the assaults on Indian property had become more frequent by the mid-1820s, owing, the agent said, "to the near approach of our settlements to their towns." Friction between whites and Senecas often revolved around hunting territories. James Montgomery, the assistant agent for the Senecas, compiled a list of property that had been taken and/or destroyed from that community from 1824 to 1827, and it included numerous horses either stolen or killed. "The general opinion of the white people," Montgomery reported, "is that they were shot by some white hunter." The agent had one white man tell him "that a neighbor of his said he would kill the Indian Horses if the[y] continued to hunt near him." That list of twenty claims, totaling more than $500, was only a fragment of the losses declared by the Senecas. As the white population grew, agent John McElvain explained, it simply required "more vigilance, prudence & management on the part of the agent to protect the Indians & their property."[22]

For the Delawares living on their small reserve south of the Wyandots at Upper Sandusky, encroachment and property loss were only two pieces of a much more complicated puzzle. Knowing that the Delawares in Indiana had moved west of the Mississippi River in 1822, the chiefs and headmen at Sandusky expressed in September 1828, "We are now desirous of following and uniting ourselves with them that we might again become one people." John Johnston estimated that nearly 130 Delawares and Munsees would be a part of the removal, and by the following spring he reported, "A messenger from their nation on the Arkansas is waiting to conduct" the Ohio Delawares to the west. Yet the Sandusky community needed to coordinate plans with relatives living further north. In fact, when John McElvain traveled to the Sandusky reserve with the intent of arranging a treaty in June 1829, he found "that almost the whole nation had taken a visit to Canada." By mid-July most, but not all, of the Delawares had returned from Canada and were "anxious to sell their lands." On August 3, 1829, seven Delaware Indians led by Captain Pipe made marks on a treaty that ceded their Upper Sandusky lands. Captain Pipe and the Delaware men, women, and children decided to leave Ohio behind to join Captain William Anderson and other Delawares, who themselves were on the verge of signing a treaty that would relocate them once more to the Kansas River west of the Missouri border.[23]

One year after agreeing to leave Ohio, however, the Sandusky Delawares had not moved. The Delawares could not "bear the idea of leaving a single one behind," and were still working to get their northern relatives to join them. McElvain tried to facilitate the process in the spring of 1830 by sending the Piqua Agency's interpreter, William Walker, Jr., to Canada to bring back any Delawares from the Thames River villages who wanted to relocate west with the Ohio party. As of August, McElvain was convinced that if he did not personally conduct them, they would "halt at the first good hunting ground they f[ound], spend the winter there, and return on [Ohio's] hands in the spring." Although the Delawares had left their settlements on the Sandusky at this point, they had now established an encampment at Wapakoneta among the Shawnees. The ongoing delay convinced McElvain that it was "useless to think to remove them all at the

same time, without holding out to them some appearance of compulsion."
Yet the agent also recognized that any use of force might damage future
efforts. Everyone in Ohio was watching these events unfold in the months
after the passage of the Indian Removal Act, and any missteps might spark
significant protests from removal opponents. The fact that many of the
Delawares had relatives in other Ohio Indian communities also made the
agent believe that they now would not leave until the Senecas, Shawnees,
and Wyandots left Ohio as well.[24]

The Senecas of Sandusky shared the Delawares' sentiments. On October 15, 1829, just two months after the Delawares had made their marks on
a removal treaty, twelve Seneca leaders sent a communication to President
Andrew Jackson signaling their desire to leave Ohio. "Our agents have
long since told us that there was a good country in the West, and plenty of
game," they stated through their interpreter. "Some of our young chiefs
and warriors have visited Missouri and Arkansas," they added, "and have
returned much pleased with the country." The Senecas showed particular
interest in the lands on which the Western Cherokees were living. Therefore the Senecas requested that the President present a treaty that would
arrange for their removal to a western location adjacent to those Cherokees.[25] Despite this expressed interest, however, federal officials moved
slowly, and as of late May 1830, McElvain had to remind his superiors
in Washington that the Senecas were "anxious to be off." McElvain was
concerned, though, because the Senecas' expectations meant they had
not prepared to stay in Ohio for another year. The agent could only persuade a few to plant corn, and by fall the situation looked even grimmer.
"Since these Indians made up their minds to remove," McElvain warned,
"they have almost totally give up farming & hunting, and they are realy
in a destitute situation for the necessaries of life." Meanwhile, the Senecas
believed that perhaps their request had never made it to Washington and
sent another one in September 1830. This time nineteen Senecas, led by
Comstick, made their marks on another petition to the president. "The
game is destroyed around their [Seneca] lands," the petition declared, "and
their young people are daily learning bad habits from the white people."[26]

Subsequent events, including the actual treaty with the Senecas of Sandusky, were shaped by a number of other developments. James B. Gardiner, the special agent appointed by President Jackson to oversee Ohio
removals, viewed the Seneca negotiations as a crucial precedent. Gardiner
suggested to all treaty commissioners operating in Ohio that the "treaty

and Agreement lately made with the Senecas should be the basis, as far as the circumstances may permit." This was particularly important in relation to the complete removal of the Indians. "The cessions of territory should be *absolute*," Gardiner urged, "without any future reservations, except in particular cases to individuals who may be unable or unwilling to remove." In addition, as John McElvain had insinuated in earlier discussions about the use of force with the Delawares, any difficulties in the Seneca removal or signs of mismanagement "would quickly be spread amongst those tribes who [were] in a fair way to follow the Senecas, provided things [were] properly managed, and thus prevent their removal for years to come." Federal agents knew that they were being watched.[27]

The land cessions in the Seneca treaty were indeed absolute. At the conclusion of a council held in Washington in February 1831, Comstick, Small Cloud Spicer, Seneca Steel, Hard Hickory, and Captain Good Hunter made their marks and consented to the sale of their reserve on the Sandusky River. The opening statement of the accord reads, "The tribe of Seneca Indians, residing on Sandusky River, in the State of Ohio, have earnestly solicited the President of the United States to negotiate with them, for an exchange of the lands, now owned and occupied by them, for lands of the United States, west of the river Mississippi, and for the removal and permanent settlement of said tribe." With this negotiation they surrendered approximately 40,000 acres that had been granted just over a decade earlier in two different treaties. In exchange the Senecas received title to 67,000 acres adjacent to the Cherokee lands west of the Mississippi River. When they returned from their trip to Washington, the Senecas met in council with representatives from the Wyandots and the Lewistown Shawnees and Senecas to discuss the treaty and their plans to move west.[28]

Yet despite the treaties and the letters indicating Delaware and Seneca support for removal, the events of 1831 revealed that perception did not always match the reality. In May of that year the Delawares were still in Ohio, and the federal agents now pinned their hopes on the Senecas. "When they [the Delawares] see the Senecas in motion," Samuel Hamilton told McElvain, "perhaps it will induce them to make a move also." The Seneca removal was not so easily managed, however. Part of the problem was a struggle between McElvain and a subagent named Henry Brish. McElvain actually suspected that Brish had pushed the Seneca chiefs to ask for removal, which was one reason he had a low opinion of subagents in the Ohio Agency who, he claimed, "seem to me to be of less value than any other attached to it." In April 1831 McElvain even attempted to fire Brish. The real issue, however, was that the Senecas had their own ideas about the process and how it should work.[29]

During the spring and summer of 1831 the Senecas exerted their influence over the removal process and muddled the efforts of McElvain and others to dictate affairs. Seneca leaders sent a communication to Secretary of War John Eaton in June requesting payment of $6,000, which had been promised by treaty as an advance on the sale of their lands before they left Ohio. Although the official policy called for payment after removal, Comstick, Small Cloud Spicer, Seneca Steel, Hard Hickory, and Captain Good Hunter declared the need to furnish provisions for their "almost starving families." Rather than have white men point fingers at them as they left, saying "there goes a scoundrel that owes me," the Seneca chiefs also intended to use the funds to pay debts. "We are told too, by the whites," the Seneca chiefs stated, "that they will not let us go unless we pay them, that they will take our property and imprison us—we believe they will." By August McElvain had become frustrated with such requests and delays, as well as with what he termed "the perfect indifference of these people as it respects time." Nevertheless, he finally received a commitment to a date. One party of Senecas moving by land would do so by September 15, and the party moving by water would depart by the end of that month. This division of the emigration was not McElvain's idea. He, like many other federal officials, saw the water route as the most cost-efficient and the easiest means of travel to the West. Once the Indians made their way to the Ohio River, they could reach St. Louis in a matter of days. Yet many of the Senecas refused to travel by water and insisted on a land emigration. McElvain's submission to their wishes had a lot to do with the presence of Wyandots during their conversation. If he pressed the Senecas too hard on this issue, he felt the Wyandots might not agree to any negotiations of their own.[30]

McElvain's problems did not end there as, once again, the Senecas' condition and desires became entangled in personal rivalries. James Gardiner informed new secretary of war Lewis Cass that the Seneca chiefs had personally expressed their displeasure with McElvain. They accused the latter of withholding money and complained that he was forcing himself upon them as a removal conductor. According to Gardiner, the Seneca chiefs also declared, "They will not go under the charge of Col. McElvain.

They say they would rather stay until they are *pushed off* by their Great Father." Gardiner warned Cass that the Wyandots were still watching all of this unfold and would quite possibly refuse to remove should such abuse continue. Gardiner supported Brish, and Brish was utterly opposed to McElvain's meddling. As for McElvain's suggestion that he take a Seneca party by land on September 21, Brish asserted that he was supposed to oversee the sale of chattel property for the next several days and would not be able to leave before then. The deadline set by McElvain for the Seneca removal had already passed.[31]

By mid-November, as both the Senecas and Delawares had commenced their journeys, the Wyandot influence remained. More than two years after first signing a removal treaty, fifty-eight Delawares led by Captain Pipe left Ohio. The small number reflected the fact that approximately twenty Delawares related by blood to the Wyandots "could not be persuaded to leave their friends" and said they would leave when the Wyandots did. Out of the approximately 340 Senecas beginning the relocation, 232 traveled by land and the remainder traveled by water. McElvain was extremely ill, however, and hoped Brish would take the more difficult and longer land route. When Brish refused, McElvain felt obligated to go forward, believing that any further delay would not only keep the Senecas in Ohio but also undermine ongoing efforts to convince the Wyandots to sign a removal treaty. Yet instead of going himself, he left the responsibility in the hands of the Indians' interpreter, and "owing to their tardy movements, high waters & their determination to hunt on their journey he [the interpreter] left them to persue their journey in their own way which was their choice so to do." Writing safely from his office in Columbus, McElvain assured Cass that the Senecas would be fine because they were good hunters and because the government had provided them with tents and other necessities.[32]

For the Senecas, however, the winter of 1831–1832 was an unmitigated disaster and a tragedy of epic proportions. The Senecas traveling by land began their journey well enough, and visited several Indian villages along their route to say goodbye. At times these stops lasted several days, and the Senecas received relatively generous provisions from government officials who did not want perceived stinginess to undermine future removals. But the social early days of the journey soon ended, and in a letter written at a stop in Munseytown, Indiana, Small Cloud Spicer, Seneca John, Wipingstick, Isaac White, John Shye, Jacob Nicely, and Littletown Spicer

informed Superintendent William Clark that circumstances had deteriorated. "We have already encountered much difficulty from bad weather,
sickness, and loss of horses," they reported. They had buried the youngest
child of Wipingstick and the oldest child of Cayuga James, and the death
of eleven horses served to make the journey that much more arduous.
Until the weather improved and allowed them to travel, they had to halt
at the settlements along the White River in Indiana. Their provisions
had run out, and their interpreter, Martin Lane, had no means to support
them. They had turned to Clark because they had no one left to help
them, and they wanted him to pass along a message to their relatives who
had traveled by water. "We hope you have all arrived safe," they said, "and
are enjoying the pleasures of health and comfort."[33]

The 232 Senecas traveling on the steamboat *Ben Franklin* under Brish's
command arrived in St. Louis on November 16. Comstick, Seneca Steel,
Captain Good Hunter, and Hard Hickory headed up this party, and while
the first segment of their journey was difficult, it worsened once they
left the city. Loading all of their belongings onto sixteen wagons, they
departed St. Louis in late November and by mid-December had only
put fifty-five miles behind them. At least three Senecas died and scores
suffered from frostbite. The weather was simply too harsh. Brish made
arrangements for the Senecas to be supplied for the next six months in
their encampment near the town of Troy, Missouri, while he headed east
to check on the party that had stopped in Indiana.[34]

As 1831 drew to a close, the two Seneca emigrant parties were
encamped in Indiana and Missouri, far from their final destination, separated from one another, and hoping to survive the winter months. They
were dependent more on the people in the immediate vicinity than on the
federal government. While the Senecas suffered, William Clark sought to
tie a neat bow on the removal by providing various explanations for the
problems. High food prices because of poor crops the previous fall made
the removal expensive. Bad weather made for another serious obstacle.
Perhaps the biggest problem, according to Clark, was that the Indians had
"been more ungovernable, by far, than any others of this [the St. Louis]
superintendency, and certainly [had], by their own misconduct at times,
very much increased the real difficulties which [had] occurred in their
removal." Back in Ohio, McElvain, describing the condition of the Seneca party on the White River in Indiana, said simply, "If this party have
suffered it is their own fault as they could not be persuaded to remove by

water, or to goe through before next spring." The agent had washed his hands of that particular affair and had turned his attention elsewhere.[35]

The final stages were thus in the hands of Brish. In May 1832 he returned to the encampment at Troy with those Senecas who had spent the winter in Indiana, but their journey had been harsh and they had left behind six individuals who were sick and would "no doubt die in a short time." Sixteen other members of the party traveled by wagon due to illness, and measles struck the Seneca children. In addition, a party of just over forty Senecas who had long resided in Missouri joined the removal, adding to the size and expense of the emigration. By mid-June only the surging springtime waters of the Marais des Cygne River in eastern Kansas stood in the Senecas' path. Although one woman had died and several children were severely sick, Brish was optimistic that the end was in sight. On July 4 the Senecas of Sandusky arrived at the lands set aside for them along the Cowskin River in present-day northeastern Oklahoma. During the last weeks of the removal four more adults and five more children died. While Brish reported that the Senecas were happy with their lands, the agent also acknowledged a brutal reality. "I charge myself with cruelty," he wrote, "in forcing these unfortunate people on at a time when a few days' delay might have prevented some deaths and rendered the sickness of others more light, and have to regret this part of my duty, which . . . has made the task of removing the Senecas excessively unpleasant to me."[36]

The human tragedy of this particular removal is difficult to fathom. Yet it is also surprising that, based on their ongoing concerns about the potential removal of the Wyandots, federal officials allowed the Senecas to suffer to such an extent. As it turned out, the Wyandots knew what had happened. When Brish informed James Gardiner that he had left his emigrant party of Senecas west of St. Louis, his report also carried word that the subagent had encountered William Walker, Jr., and a Wyandot exploring delegation in Missouri. Unaware of what Walker and his colleagues must have learned about the Senecas' experience, Gardiner had high hopes for a Wyandot removal. "It is said they are *highly pleased with the country assigned them*," he wrote to Cass. Because of this initial report of a positive Wyandot response to the western territories, Gardiner was optimistic: "I flatter myself that I should be able, in four or five weeks to present you [Lewis Cass] with a definitive treaty with this sagacious, intelligent, and *crafty* tribe of Indians." The very next day, however, Gardiner's mood shifted. He had now received word that, instead of talking positively about removal, William Walker had declared that the Wyandots "were determined *not to cede*, as they did not like the country 'very well' and were particularly displeased with their neighbors, the whites of Missouri." Gardiner saw dishonesty in this apparent change of heart. He was not willing to give up any hope for a treaty, because he was still confident that the "'pagan' or 'savage party,' (composing full half the nation)" would "*be willing to treat*." And that fact would allow the government to bypass the influence of the influential "Christian party" that included Walker and most other men of mixed descent.[37]

Gardiner's letters provide one entry point into Wyandot affairs, and his reference to the Pagan and Christian parties highlights a critical element of Wyandot history prior to 1832. To the extent that scholars have discussed the Ohio Wyandots in the nineteenth century, the emphasis has largely been on the introduction of Methodism and its impact on the Sandusky communities in the 1820s. The Methodists were not the first missionaries to practice their work among the Wyandots, for the Jesuits had a long history with the Hurons, and a Presbyterian missionary effort was cut short by the War of 1812. Yet in 1816, when the first Methodists came to Sandusky, the Wyandots were at a critical juncture in their history, their community compressed on the diminishing reserves they still had to fight to retain. The growing presence and influence of men of mixed descent within the Wyandot settlements was another factor shaping events. Wyandot society and politics were changing, both in terms of who was involved and who had power. The family headed by William Walker, Sr., became a focal point for the discussion of those changes. It was ultimately a combination of all these factors and the internal workings of the Wyandot community that most affected negotiations with both state and federal governments over removal.[38]

The Wyandot delegation that encountered Henry Brish and the Senecas in early 1832 had journeyed west because of an agreement made with Gardiner the previous fall. Warpole, John Hicks, and other Wyandot leaders pledged, "On the return of said delegation if their report should prove favorable to the country examined, then they, the said Chiefs, will enter into a treaty with the said Gardiner for a cession of the Wyandott lands in Ohio." Having concluded four different removal treaties with other Ohio Indian communities, Gardiner thought the fifth would soon follow. But the delegation's unfavorable report scuttled his dreams. Angry with this perceived betrayal, the agent alleged, "The object [of the delegation's duplicity] was to quiet all anxieties on the part of the tribe, relative to removal, and settle them down into a state of false security and complete subserviency to the few, (white and partly white,) who are the only gainers by their continued residence in Ohio." Gardiner then interrogated members of the delegation to find out why they had chosen to make a negative report. He was convinced that the Wyandots had decided ahead of time to judge against the land and believed that no real exploration had even occurred.[39]

Contrary to Gardiner's belief, however, the Wyandots' assessment was based on a knowledgeable review of circumstances in the West. The delegation had been told to explore land on the northwestern borders of Missouri, and they recognized both that the Sauks and Mesquakies had claimed a part of the lands and that the citizens of Missouri would not welcome the Indians, especially while the politicians spoke "of Indians as 'a nuisance' a 'curse to the states,' etc." In another nod to context, the delegation reported, "Missouri is a slaveholding state, and slaveholders are seldom very friendly to Indians: (See Georgia)." After a lengthy report that touched on everything from climate to local politics, the delegation had their recommendation. "In conclusion," they reported to the Sandusky Wyandots, "your delegation must say, and that in all truth and sincerity, that they are decidedly of opinion that the interests of the nation will not be promoted, nor their condition ameliorated, by a removal from this to the country examined." Instead of removal, then, the delegation stated, "[We] recommend to the Chiefs and nation at large to cease all contention, bickerings and party strifes; settle down & maintain their position in the State of Ohio."[40]

These recommendations made sense but also established difficult goals. To "cease all contention, bickerings and party strifes" required more than just managing the problems created by having a sizeable minority of the Sandusky Wyandots who had converted to Methodism. It also meant resolving the ongoing disputes and tensions that divided four different communities—Sandusky, Big Springs, the Huron River, and Amherstburg. No single Wyandot nation existed, and over the course of the 1830s federal agents targeted those disparate settlements in an effort to gain as much land as possible. This pressure also made it extremely difficult to "settle down & maintain their position in the State of Ohio." Federal agents sought to build on the momentum created by the departure of Delawares, Senecas, and Shawnees and constantly harassed the Wyandots about removal. And when the federal government was not applying pressure, it was the state of Ohio that flirted with extending jurisdiction over Indian lands. Yet the final blow may have been struck by a small party of white men who killed one of the most staunch removal opponents among the Wyandots.

The War of 1812 had created one division within the larger Wyandot population, for the Detroit River villages had allied with Tecumseh and the British while the Ohio Wyandots under Tarhe had hewed to the United States. Yet on the Sandusky River in the war's aftermath, the arrival of Methodist missionaries provided another fracturing element. The legacy of past missionary efforts remained, but in the 1810s growing external pressures exacerbated the impact of those religious outsiders. From the late 1810s throughout the 1820s the Wyandots on the Sandusky and Big Spring Reservations struggled over who should lead their community and the attitudes of those leaders toward Christianity. The Methodist Episcopal Church appointed Reverend James B. Finley to the missionary post at Sandusky in 1821, and within two years he had overseen the construction of three buildings along with the cultivation of approximately eighty acres of land. Finley tried to shape the Wyandots' future by turning them not only toward Christianity, but also toward agricultural pursuits that fit Western norms. However, this was not the only divisive element of his agenda. "I used my influence to persuade the Indians not to sell, but to remain where they were," Finley remembered, "for if they were removed to the base of the Rocky Mountains, or beyond them, the white population would follow them." Finley and the Methodists may have been a disruptive presence, but they also supported the stance against removal.[41]

The first substantial battle of the 1830s occurred because of the Big Springs Treaty, an agreement through which the United States obtained the 16,000-acre reserve secured under the 1817 accord. James Gardiner had informed the Wyandots at Solomonstown and Blanchard's Fork, "In case the Chiefs at Upper Sandusky utterly refused to unite with them in ceding the whole of the Wyandott lands in the United States, the Big Spring Band should have the privilege of concluding a separate treaty for the cession of their own Reservation." In January 1832 he made good on that promise. The opening statement of the Big Springs accord indicates that Wyandot and American sentiments had aligned in this particular negotiation. "WHEREAS the said band of Wyandots," it reads, "have become fully convinced that, whilst they remain in their present situation in the State of Ohio, in the vicinity of a white population, which is continually increasing and crowding around them, they cannot prosper and be happy, and the morals of many of their people will be daily becoming more and more vitiated." They had decided to sell. The first draft of the treaty called for these Wyandots to relocate west of the Mississippi, but they refused those conditions, and consequently that article did not appear in the final document. Instead, the ratified treaty stated that they could "remove to Canada, or to the river Huron in Michigan, where they own a reservation of land, or to any place they may obtain a right or privilege from other Indians to go."[42]

Over the next year the Wyandots battled over the treaty's validity and the unity of their larger community. The treaty listed eight signatories, but accusations flew that several of those who made their mark on the document were recent emigrants from Canada who had "sold this reservation from under" the rest. Although they had no desire to undo the treaty, Henry Jaquis and the twenty-one others listed in a letter addressed to President Jackson stated that a "meddlesome white man (Joseph McCutcheon)" was a part of the problem. This group, presenting themselves as the true representatives of the Big Springs interests, now intended to work closely with the Sandusky Wyandots, who were providing "a seat upon the Grand Reservation" so that they could "live as 'one family.'" This meant in part that the money from the treaty would be put in the hands of the Sandusky chiefs to distribute on the Grand Reserve. Two days after that letter was written, Rouenuas, Bearskin, and the other treaty signatories fired back, arguing that "boys and children" had signed the letter and that witness Thomas Long was an "intruder" who, they said, "is making mischief among us." A month earlier the treaty signatories had asserted, "We have nothing to do with the Indians at Upper Sandusky." As of May, their position had not changed.[43]

Not until December 1832 did the Wyandots resolve their differences. In the presence of agent John McElvain, five of the eight signatories of the Big Springs treaty agreed to live at Sandusky and "bury all their former difficulties & hostilities & enter upon terms of lasting peace and friendship." Glaring in their absence were the marks of Bearskin, Isaac Driver, and Alexander Clark. Those three Wyandots did not sign the December agreement because, according to McElvain, "They have of late removed to Canada, and it is not known whether they would have agreed to it had they been present." McElvain added that not only was Isaac Driver a minor who therefore "had no legal right in the first place to sign" the 1832 treaty, but also Alexander Clark had never resided on the Big Springs Reserve and so had no right or interest in it. Similarly missing from the agreement were the names of Joseph McCutcheon and James Gardiner. The battles of 1832 had shown those two men to be less than trustworthy in the eyes of the Wyandots. William Walker, Jr., hoped that the federal government shared this unfavorable opinion of the two men. "A treaty could have been concluded long since with the chiefs of this tribe," Walker explained to Cass, "had proper persons been selected to negotiate with them." James Gardiner did not fit that description. "The opposition of the Wyandots to removing to the west," Walker continued, "is attributable mainly to the imprudent conduct of Mr. G and likewise to the reprehensible course pursued by Mr. McCutcheon." Just as important, "the difficulties existing between the Big Spring Wyandotts and Solomonstown people could have been long since settled by Col. McElvain had it not been for the interference of Mr. Gardiner & Mr. McCutcheon."[44]

The peace brokered in the December 1832 agreement was temporary, however, and fractures within the Wyandot community did not disappear. Nor did the persistent demands to cede and remove. The badgering came not only from the citizens of Ohio but also from the state legislature. Then–governor of Michigan Territory Lewis Cass had heard rumblings about an attempt by Ohio politicians to extend the state's jurisdiction over the Wyandot reservation lands in early 1825. Cass criticized the tactic, saying, "If this principle can be maintained, all prospects of future usefulness or improvement there are blasted." At that time the territorial governor spoke of improvement and sided with Reverend Finley in his assessment of the situation. Within a decade, however, Cass's opinion shifted into step with citizens and federal officials who believed that the only and best option for Indians was to leave their lands in Ohio and other eastern states.[45]

Some of the rhetoric coming from the mouths of federal agents in Ohio subsequently echoed the national debates over removal and its focus on jurisdiction and citizenship. McElvain told the Wyandots in council during the fall of 1833 that he and other friends of the Wyandots believed "that if they [the Wyandots] still wished to live independant and happy & free that they must remove to a new country." If they were determined to stay, however, they needed to face certain realities. "I stated to them that it was out of the question for them to remain and retain their old, or even their present degraded national character," McElvain explained. The agent therefore advised them that if, despite all the warnings, they chose to stay in Ohio, the Wyandot chiefs should "at once petition to come under the state laws," while at the same time knowing "that they need not expect ever again to be respected & to be clothed with the ancient greatness, etc." At the time that McElvain delivered this message, the state of Ohio had yet to extend jurisdiction over territory either held or ceded by the Indians. According to U.S. District Attorney Noah H. Swayne, however, the "extinguishment of the Indian title has always been considered ipso facto—an extension of the jurisdiction of the state over all their persons and things within the limits of the ceded territory." The question then became, would Ohio take the next step and finally assert jurisdiction over land that had not been ceded?[46]

The *Worcester v. Georgia* ruling declared that only the federal government had jurisdiction over Indian lands, but Governor Robert Lucas of Ohio did not see that decision as a problem. Frustrated by a failed attempt to convince the Wyandots to remove in the fall of 1834, Lucas invoked the possibility of extending state laws over the Grand Reserve. The governor had opened the September council by comparing the Wyandots' rapidly declining situation in Ohio with the fertile landscape and opportunity provided by the western territories. "The President believes," Lucas explained, "that you cannot occupy the position you now hold in Ohio, surrounded as you are by dense settlements of our citizens without subjecting you to the operation of those causes which have everywhere, in such situations, brought destruction upon the Indians." The governor also detailed at great length the treaties and removal measures framing the federal government's approach to the southern tribes as part of his effort to show the efficacy of removal. Speaker Thomas Long responded succinctly to the long-winded effort, stating that while the Wyandots appreciated the "great sincerity and candor" of the governor, they had decided to postpone any decision. When the two parties met again in late October, Wyandot chief Henry Jaquis reported, "The Tribe had come to the conclusion not to sell or dispose of their lands." Another chief named Summondowat elaborated on the Wyandot position, stating, "The prevailing opinion of the nation was adverse to selling, and had always been so expressed whenever they had been together on the subject." Summondowat's response also implied that Lucas had raised the issue of state law during the course of the council. "He [Summondowat] said he was averse, as was the nation," Lucas wrote, "to extending the laws of the State over them. . . . If, however, the state authority, contrary to their wishes, proceeded to accomplish this object, and thereby put them under the law of the State, why, he said, it was a matter beyond their control, and they had only to submit to it when it should take place."[47]

By early 1835, the hypothetical had become real. In his message to the Ohio legislature in December 1834 Governor Lucas discussed extending jurisdiction over the Wyandot lands, and the Wyandots moved swiftly to counter. The chiefs sent McElvain to Columbus in early January, and the agent noted, "This will be something novel in our state, for Indians to act in the capacity of lobby members." For the Wyandots, the situation was more terrifying than novel, and the chiefs were "prodigiously alarmed." Yet McElvain believed that this was a positive development. He declared, "If the laws are extended over them—of which I have no doubt—they then will most certainly conclude a treaty." That confidence had disappeared by the second week of February because the committee charged with discussing extension had written a report deeming such a move to be "inexpedient." The news so disheartened the agent that, rather than continue trying to convince the Wyandots to remove, he resigned his position. Governor Lucas had higher hopes, however, because in late March he heard that the Ohio legislature had "at its late Session ordered the [Wyandot] Reserve to be attached to the civil townships in Crawford County." "I am under the impression," he stated, "that the operation of the law will have considerable effect on the minds of the Indians." Based on his experience in council with the Wyandots, he had every reason to believe that would be true. Any extension of state law, in combination with the pressure of increased white settlement in the region, did not bode well for the Wyandots.[48]

Ohio's legal maneuvers coincided with the growing desires for economic development. Businessmen and state officials targeted the Grand Reserve because of its geographically important location, not solely because it was Indian land. Upper Sandusky had developed into a way station for travelers moving between Lake Erie and the Ohio River, and in the eight years since the completion of the Erie Canal, several of the leading roads passed by the settlement. The size of the Wyandot reservation made Upper Sandusky a natural, even necessary, stop along the route. By 1836, then, it is not surprising that the Mad River and Lake Erie Rail Road petitioned the federal government for a preemption grant to certain

INTRODUCTION.

From his wild covert, (in the visioned Past?)
    The jealous Red-Man sees
The settler's cabin, near; on yonder stream,
The boat fire-driven; far-off, over these,
The spire-lit city:—if to him they seem
    Shadows of pitiless doom that travels fast,
They realize our fathers' eager dream.

—JOHN JAMES PIATT.

Indian and the Approach of the White Man. This illustration and the accompanying words by John James Piatt appeared in an 1880 publication titled *The Biographical Cyclopedia and Portrait Gallery of Distinguished Men, with an Historical Sketch of the State of Ohio, Volume 1.* Courtesy of the Ohio Historical Society.

lands on the reservation. Joseph Vance, who would be elected governor of Ohio in November 1836, was directed by the Mad River board of directors to present that petition to Congress.[49]

Faced with these developments, the Wyandot chiefs chose to appease white Ohioans while simultaneously shoring up their own position. William Walker, Jr., had been elected to assume the role of principal chief for the remaining year of the late Thomas Long's term, and in January 1836 he informed Governor Lucas that the Wyandots wanted to resume negotiations that had been suspended in the fall of 1834. Knowing that the state assembly was in session and that the governor would not be able to travel to Sandusky, the Wyandot council proposed to meet Lucas in Columbus, where they could present "their views and propositions, together with other matters of deep interest to them and the state." The Wyandots had decided to negotiate, but only proposed selling approximately 38,000 acres of land on the eastern side of the reserve. Lucas noted, "[They] appear not at present to be willing to leave the land of their fathers," and the treaty concluded on April 23, 1836, testifies to that fact. It ceded land, but it also designated money made from the land sale to improve the conditions of roads, schools, mills, and other institutions on the Grand Reserve at Upper Sandusky. Rather than arranging for removal, the Wyandots intended to strengthen their infrastructure. For the moment, at least, the federal government appeared willing to accept that stance.[50]

Yet the treaty of 1836 did little to sate the American hunger for Wyandot lands. The unrelenting assault on the Grand Reserve continued, aided in part by fraud and violence. Having received new commissions from the federal government to negotiate a removal treaty in early 1837, the familiar entities of Joseph McCutcheon and Henry Brish expressed confidence that the only opposition to the removal among the Wyandots came from "the whites and the mixtures that live[d] on the Reserve." Another dividing line originated in religion, because the Methodist converts appeared to present the strongest opposition to removal. Success, therefore, might depend on arranging for "a number of individual reserves by the *white* or *Christian party*," which would make no difference with the department, McCutcheon said, "inasmuch as that party conform on all respects to the habits of the white population of the country."[51] Brish and McCutcheon believed their success also depended on handling particular individuals. McCutcheon wrote, "There is probably not any greater haters of the present Administration than the person I have alluded to. William Walker a quarter blood is the Post Master at Upper Sandusky, and I have no doubt but he has done as much against the present Administration as any man in the county of Crawford." The commissioner believed that the chiefs opposed to removal were mere tools in the hands of Walker and his cohort. On the other side stood Warpole and Standing Stone, the chiefs of the "selling party" who favored relocation if it could be arranged. As of late May, McCutcheon asserted, the "principle men of the Selling party are now waiting patiently until you inform Col McElvain, Col. Brish and myself that they are at Liberty to Council freely on the subject of a treaty and removal west without being in fear of the imprisonment gag Laws of the opposition party."[52]

To federal officials, the divisions among the Wyandots became a matter of governing authority and legal jurisdiction. Warpole, Standing Stone, and Porcupine had all been placed in custody by the Wyandot leadership in May 1837. They had allegedly broken a law passed by the Wyandot council in 1832 "prohibiting any individual from attempting to conclude a Treaty with a view of extinguishing their title to the whole or part of their Reservation or remove to the West." McCutcheon and Brish argued that the Wyandot law had no standing, while agent Purdy McElvain asserted that even the 1834 version of the Trade and Intercourse Act did not provide him with the power to interfere in such situations. Yet the U.S. attorney for Ohio, Noah Swayne, disagreed with McElvain and based his position on the wording of the supplementary treaty of 1818. According to Swayne, the "State Laws are entirely sufficient for the protection of the selling party—& they will be promptly enforced, so far as may be necessary for that purpose." By all appearances this pressure had consequences, because on August 1 Purdy McElvain reported, "This [Wyandot] law has been abandoned by the Chiefs and they have left every man to act freely for himself, without any fear of being imprisoned or punished in any manner whatever."[53]

During the course of this debate Brish and McCutcheon pursued their ultimate goal of a treaty. They started by abandoning the traditional council and instead presented the Wyandots with a draft removal treaty similar to that signed by the Senecas of Sandusky in 1831. Then, they altered the method of treaty signing: "The Indians having to secure their crops, we have not thought it advisable to conclude the treaty—but hold it open in order that many who are anxious to remove, but have not yet signed may have an opportunity to do so." Any Wyandot who desired could therefore stop and sign the treaty at his or her convenience. At the end of the first week of August the commissioners declared that most of the fifty signatures they had obtained were of those named in or descended from those named in the schedules of the 1817 treaty. In their eyes, these individuals were the only ones with the right to make decisions in relation to the Wyandot lands.[54]

The entire episode looked suspicious to several Wyandots opposed to negotiations, and they questioned the persistent attempts to obtain the reserve. William Walker, Jr., wrote to Governor Joseph Vance, asking, "[Do] the people of this State positively require our removal to the West?" If they did, then the Wyandots would feel "abandoned by [their] Ohio friends, with whom [they had] so long lived upon terms of intimacy (and on [the Wyandots'] part) ardent friendship." Principal Chief John Barnett and the Wyandot national council also addressed the governor, stating that, based on the commissioners' approach to negotiations, the Wyandots had to assume that they were "going contrary to the wishes of the Government." Brish and McCutcheon, who are labeled "vampires" in this letter, had abandoned the standard protocol of working with the chiefs "after finding that the Council and a large majority of the nation, were opposed to ceding and removing to the West." More to the point, the signatures they had obtained were those of minors and others with no rights to the reservation. Indeed, a government investigation revealed substantial wrongdoing on the part of the commissioners. Mrs. Half-John, a Delaware woman married into the tribe and with no rights to the reservation, said her name appeared on the treaty even though she never attended any of the council sessions. George Williams asserted that he witnessed Henry Warpole and George Solomon sign when they were clearly drunk. Many of the deposed Wyandots mentioned the central role McCutcheon's tavern played in the process. In one example, Thomas Punch stopped by the tavern for a drink, and McCutcheon took him into a separate room to present the possibility of cession and removal.[55]

With all that had transpired, the Wyandot council appealed to Vance to find out if the people of Ohio really did want them to leave. "For," they said, "*we* have never discovered any such disposition." Although Vance did not directly answer this plea, the federal government continued to move forward with a new set of commissioners. Subsequent events revealed that the identities of the commissioners mattered less than the divisions on the Grand Reserve. In August 1838 Warpole and two other Wyandots headed to Washington in an attempt to arrange for removal. Not only did they fail to accomplish that goal, but their attempt also led to another visit to the Wyandot jail. In a brief summation of what must have been a spirited exchange, Purdy McElvain described the events following Warpole's public report on his visit to Washington. After Warpole spoke, McElvain said, "Some discussion took place between the Chiefs and Warpole and his party. Warpole became much excited, drew a knife and defied the nation; there upon the Head Chief ordered their immediate arrest." McElvain gained Warpole's release and concluded that only a separate negotiation with Warpole's party would secure peace. Warpole refused to back down, and along with the support of twenty-eight signatories he petitioned President Martin Van Buren for a treaty that would arrange for both a partial land cession and removal for those Wyandots who desired those terms. A treaty commissioner should talk to the whole Wyandot Nation, it was decided, but "in case of failing in this object to make a treaty with the undersigned portion of this nation at the earliest possible time." Warpole had tried to assert his vision, and despite being imprisoned by his own government and being rejected by federal officials, he continued to advocate for all those who wanted to leave Sandusky. He followed the October petition with a letter in November stating his intent to travel to Washington one more time.[56]

Warpole's advocacy compounded the longstanding external pressures, all of which led the Wyandot council to consent to yet another exploratory expedition west of the Mississippi River. According to treaty commissioner William H. Hunter, "The apprehension of a treaty being made with a portion of the tribe had opened their eyes and made them more favourably disposed to listen to my propositions." Five Wyandots appointed by the national council left Upper Sandusky in June 1839 and returned by the end of July after viewing a wide swath of the western territories and talking to the Cherokees, Senecas, Shawnees, and Delawares who lived there. The Shawnees expressed a willingness to sell a section of land at the eastern side of their reserve south of the Kansas River, stating that they had "a great desire to have their old friends the Wyandots for neighbors once more." This led to a second expedition during which the Wyandots concluded an initial agreement with the Shawnees for the purchase of a two-mile-long strip of land.[57]

With all of the efforts put into council discussions and negotiations, it is telling that an act of unmitigated violence proved to be the final catalyst. Purdy McElvain observed in 1840 that the wild animal population in the Sandusky region was quickly vanishing, which meant that those who still attempted to hunt "almost invariably return[ed] in the spring more impoverished than when they left." Yet the Wyandots continued to hunt in the winter months, and on December 8, 1840, a young Wyandot man on a hunting excursion found the bodies of Summondowat and the chief's sister and brother-in-law. All three were found dead in their hunting camp, and it became clear that several white men whom the Wyandots had welcomed at their campfire had waited until the Indians were asleep and then murdered them. Shortly after this gruesome discovery, a joint group of Indians and non-Indians searched for and found James Lyons and

John Anderson. The stolen property in their possession confirmed their guilt, but Lyons and Anderson never faced trial. They escaped from jail in Henry County three or four weeks after they were first imprisoned, and authorities never tracked them down. The violent deaths of three Wyandots, and the absence of justice in the aftermath, spoke volumes about local attitudes. The murder of Summondowat in particular proved even more devastating. The former chief had been a Christian convert and an outspoken opponent of removal. His murder substantially weakened that faction's resistance.[58]

In 1841 the federal government turned to the familiar and trusted figure of John Johnston. The former head of the Piqua Agency believed he could succeed where others had failed as long as he could secure specific lands in the West for the Wyandots. By all accounts, the Wyandots wanted to live near the Shawnees and Delawares on the Kansas River, and Principal Chief Francis Hicks mentioned that if the federal government's offer of financial support for removal and initial subsistence were not adequate, the chiefs would make up the difference. Yet, as John Armstrong noted, his people would not naively surrender their lands regardless of the money offered. Based on rising speculation in the region, they estimated a just price to be at least five dollars an acre, well above the expenditures made in previous treaties. "Our chiefs are sound, calculating men," Armstrong reminded Commissioner of Indian Affairs T. Hartley Crawford, "and I think nothing less than what they propose will obtain their reservation." In late November 1841 Johnston reported that after a full two days of debate, "the whole male part of the nation being present, it was determined without a division, that the chiefs be authorized and empower to enter into a Treaty for the sale of all their lands to the U.S. and removal of the tribe to the West." Outside of the Grand Reserve, everyone on the local and the national levels hoped the agent was right. Construction undertaken by the Mad River and Lake Erie Railroad had been underway for some time, and the location of the tracks had already increased the value of the Wyandot lands substantially. Johnston was worried that if he waited to press the issue, the Wyandots would hold out for more money and better terms overall. If all went according to plan, Johnston would convene the Wyandot Nation at the end of December.[59]

Despite Johnston's optimism, his negotiations with the Wyandots lasted longer than expected, and he worried about the impact of further delays. Past treaties dogged the discussions. The Wyandots, knowing that the

Senecas and Shawnees from Lewistown were unhappy about aspects of their 1831 treaty, refused to agree to receive annuity payments in the West derived from the interest of the net proceeds of the sale of their lands in Ohio. In addition, Johnston reported, "[The] practices which has prevailed for many years in making Indian treaties in Indiana and Michigan has proved the greatest bar to any thing like a fair arrangement with these people. Extravagant allowances have been made there and private fortunes accumulated by numbers connected with the natives; these things are well known here and have their full weight." The agent grew worried that his efforts might still fall short. Conditions on the reservation continued to worsen, and from Johnston's estimation there were "probably resident on the Reserve four hundred white persons under the guise of renters, croppers, squatters, hired men and women, many of them the most abandoned of their race." There also remained the continued threat of violence and the long shadow of past injustices. "I regret that no funds can be spared to prosecute the murderers of the Chief Summondowot and his family," Johnston confessed. "The local authorities in Ohio I fear will not furnish the means of doing so." More than a year after the murder of the Wyandot chief, the state of Ohio and its citizens continued to show little interest in finding and punishing James Lyons and John Anderson.[60]

On March 17, 1842, Principal Chief Francis Hicks and six other leading men signed the treaty that ceded all Wyandot lands in Ohio and Michigan. Johnston had successfully obtained possession of approximately 114,000 acres of land for the United States. In addition, the Huron River Wyandots had agreed to join their relatives at Upper Sandusky, and the combined parties would travel west to settle on the 148,000 acres the government would provide for them west of the Mississippi River. The treaty allowed use of their improvements in Ohio until April 1, 1844, granting the Wyandots two years to conclude any final business. As of March 1843 the forty-five men, women, and children from the Huron River settlement had sold their log houses, barns, and cattle, and joined their relatives at Sandusky. All those gathered at Upper Sandusky were "desirous to reach their new homes before the inclement season of the fall [came] on, with a vision of enabling the party that [would] go by land." The treaty gave the Wyandots authority over their removal, and the logistics were not easy to organize. As of early June they were "busily employed in collecting in their stock consisting principally of horses, cattle, hogs and [were] disposing of such portions as [would] not justify them in taking west, particularly the two latter kinds of stock." Their preparations also included selling off household furniture and other bulky items too large to move.[61]

When the Wyandots finally began their journey on July 11, 1843, the train of wagons, horses, and people headed south to Cincinnati where they expected to board steamboats bound for St. Louis. "Their final departure was a scene of intense interest to all who witnessed it," Purdy McElvain wrote, "and called for the many expressions of deep feeling, on the part of the Indians, who are leaving the land which has been to them a home for years." The tally, according to government agents, was 664 men, women, and children. Fifty remained behind and planned to remove in the spring of 1844. In a little more than a week they completed the trip to Cincinnati, but they endured constant harassment by liquor peddlers hoping to profit as much as possible from the circumstances. Reverend James Wheeler, the Methodist missionary to the Wyandots since 1838 who traveled west with them, recorded, "The Indians concluded that as they appear to be without law to protect them, (or if they have any, it is of no use,) they would be law unto themselves." Yet even the guards placed around the camp at night failed to prevent the infiltration of alcohol. Tavern keepers in towns along the emigrants' route prepared ahead of time for the Indians' arrival, and Wheeler was astounded at the willingness and desire of Ohio citizens to take advantage of the situation. Some whites pilfered horses from the wagon trains during the night, and others did more unintentional damage. Everyone wanted to see the Indians as they left Ohio, "yet their curiosity was of the kind that promoted them to crowd around the wagons in such a way as to cause the Indians to think that the whites were very poor hands to teach good manners." Local newspapers also reported on the strong emotional reaction to the Wyandots' journey to Cincinnati, and these published reflections showed how the citizens of Ohio had managed to separate themselves from the very causes of the journey. "The interest entertained by our people for the welfare of the Wyandotts," the *Logan Gazette* reported, "was manifested by a strong desire to see them ere they departed." The Wyandots were "just civilized enough to have lost their savage courage," wrote the *Cincinnati Chronicle*. "They go forth on the broad prairies of the west, like sheep among wolves." The phrase "just civilized enough" was more than just a commentary on their way of life. It also applied to their appearance. "From the light complexion of four fifths of the party," the *Chronicle* continued, "we judge that in ten years more, had they remained in Ohio, all traces of the Indian would have disappeared by the process of amalgamation." Left unsaid was the fact that such time would not and could not be allowed.[62]

The situation did not improve once the Wyandots reached Cincinnati. The chiefs contracted with two steamboats, the *Nodaway* and *Republic*, to take them to the mouth of the Kansas River for a total cost of $4,500. Chaos reigned as the Wyandots attempted to load the boats amid throngs of onlookers and whiskey sellers. An old woman and a young child both died within hours of arriving at the docks of the "Queen City," and the deteriorating situation forced the Wyandots to finish loading in the early morning hours of July 20 to avoid the crowds. That night James B. F. Driver, who had been drinking all afternoon, fell off the top deck of the *Republic* and drowned in the Ohio River. Four days out of Cincinnati the boats reached St. Louis, and the Wyandots had a brief and, according to Wheeler, unpleasant meeting with the superintendent of Indian affairs before they boarded a Missouri riverboat headed for the Kansas River. The operator of the *Nodaway* was willing to take the Wyandots' money but was less pleased with his human cargo. He placed in storage all of the carpets that usually decorated the boat cabin's floors and on the last night of the journey forced the Wyandots to sleep on the riverbank instead of on the boat. Families huddled together on grass already wet with evening dew, bringing a miserable end to an already miserable journey.[63]

One final issue remained unresolved. Neither the Wyandots nor the federal government had determined the exact final destination. A small party had left Sandusky in late May to scout the western territory for potential sites, and the Wyandots had agreed to terms with the Delawares. The first article of the accord proclaimed that the "Delaware nation of Indians residing between the Missouri and Kansas Rivers being very anxious to have their Uncles the Wyandotts to settle and reside near them," agreed to a land deal that included the exchange of thirty-nine total sections of land [approximately 30,000 acres] situated between the Missouri and Kansas Rivers, right along the Missouri border. The Wyandots agreed to pay $46,800 over the next ten years. Because this agreement had yet to receive the final approval of the federal government, the Wyandots had to come up with a temporary solution when they reached the western border in late July. The wealthier members of the community, including the Walkers, the Armstrongs, and the Clarks, rented homes in the bustling border town of Westport, Missouri. Most Wyandots, however, built a makeshift settlement on the banks of the Kansas River, about two miles north of where it joined the Missouri River. Harsh conditions, including an outbreak of measles and what Wheeler described as "distressing diarrhea," made things worse. The spread of disease affected the young children especially, and within the first year of their arrival in the West nearly one hundred Wyandots died. By the spring of 1844 the Wyandots finally began to live in more permanent homes and were able to plant crops.[64]

Commissioner of Indian Affairs T. Hartley Crawford assured his colleagues that the removal of the Wyandots benefited everyone involved. "The State of Ohio, in a rising section of it," he proclaimed in his annual report for 1843, "has thus been freed from a population that prevented the settlement of a large body of fine lands, and interposed a serious obstacle, the last of its kind in the State, to the advance of a thrifty district—while the Wyandots are also relieved from white influences that were destructive of any hope of Indian improvement." The removal even provided the people of Ohio with an iconic departing speech in the words of Squire Grey Eyes, a Wyandot Methodist convert who delivered one final address to the Wyandot congregation before they left their homes along the Sandusky River. In words remarkably similar to the speech composed by James Fenimore Cooper to conclude *The Last of the Mohicans*, which had been published less than two decades earlier, Grey Eyes spoke of the Wyandot ancestors they would leave behind. "Soon they shall be forgotten," he intoned, "for the onward march of the strong White Man will not turn aside for the Indians graves." Perhaps more than any other moment, this is the one utilized by those who wrote the histories of Ohio over the course of the twentieth century. The final eloquence of Squire Grey Eyes was seemingly all that remained of not just the Wyandots, but of all Indians who once called Ohio home. The last of the Ohio Indians had departed, and the citizens of that state could now comfortably confine the Indians, whether Wyandots, Senecas, or Delawares, to the past.[65]

5

THE 1833 TREATY OF CHICAGO AND POTAWATOMI REMOVAL

On April 16, 1833, Reverend Joseph Rosati, the Catholic bishop of St. Louis, received a petition signed by forty men then living in a settlement that would be officially organized as the town of Chicago four months later. Asserting, "We count about one hundred Catholics in this town," the petitioners requested that the bishop send them a priest to strengthen and grow their congregation. The very next day Bishop Rosati assigned Father John Mary Irenaeus St. Cyr to serve the needs of that emerging community. Four years later the Catholic residents of Chicago once again petitioned the bishop, this time hoping to retain the services of Father St. Cyr, who had "endeared himself to every member of [the] congregation" during his time in Chicago. Unfortunately for these devoted followers, their second petition failed to change the minds of the church's hierarchy. Father St. Cyr left Chicago under orders in April 1837 and soon thereafter assumed a new post at Quincy, Illinois.[1]

Whatever the story behind this diocesan maneuver might have been, the identities of the petitioners in the two different documents provide insight into a more intriguing development—the transformed social, economic, and political landscape that specifically affected the Potawatomis then residing in the western Great Lakes region. The forty men who signed the 1833 petition included Jean Baptiste Beaubien, Billy Caldwell, Joseph Laframbois, Alexander Robinson, and Pierre Leclerc, each of whom had a strong connection, through either descent or marriage, to the Potawatomi bands of northern Illinois and Indiana, as well as to those of southern Wisconsin. Yet of those five men, only Jean Baptiste Beaubien also signed the 1837 document. In analyzing these two petitions in 1921, religious scholar Joseph J. Thompson observed that they highlight the "distinct metamorphoses in the resident population of Chicago." And as he proposed ideas for future research, Thompson focused on a few questions about these "first families of Chicago" who helped shape the city's founding. He wanted to know "how and when they came to this remote station on civilization's frontier," as well as the nature of their economic pursuits.[2] The answers to these queries cannot be separated from the history of American Indian removal and the transformation of the lower Great Lakes region that sparked and framed it, for Thompson hit on a key element of Potawatomi dispossession and relocation. Removal may have been an overarching federal government policy, but the people involved in the process on the ground made removal their business in both the literal and figurative sense. From both without and within the Potawatomi communities of northern Indiana and Illinois, this business encompassed Indians, government officials, traders, missionaries, and private citizens.

What most influenced the treatment of Potawatomi peoples in the 1830s and 1840s were the complex networks of external entities that saw some manner of benefit in either the presence or absence of Indians. A vast array of persons had particular interests in the debate and reality of removal, and the joining and clashing of those interests facilitated and complicated removals over the course of more than three decades. Consequently, while many of the personalities of early Chicago were in the business of transforming the landscape to conform to their ideas of development and progress, they understood that this same development could not take place without Indians and Indian policies. Once the tribes drained their financial resources, then they no longer had a role to play in the region's growth. From the perspective of non-Indian businessmen and private citizens, the indigenous presence had financial benefits up to a point, and the time at which that usefulness ended differed slightly from place to place depending on the circumstances of the particular localities and the people involved. Yet at every turn economics played a distinct role in removal, and it followed that the Indians who managed that world best were able to at least dull the sharp edges of the policy and the efforts of those who drove it on the local and regional levels.

Within that historical context, the 1833 Treaty of Chicago provides three threads connecting the diverse removal experiences of Potawatomis. First, although the Black Hawk War produced the most direct spark for

Indian removal in the region,[business concerns shaped the process of the Potawatomis' removal most significantly.] Second, through those economic activities we can also see the region's transformation as new frameworks and attitudes replaced the business practices of the past. And because business was as social and political as it was economic, only those able to engage in all facets had the best chance to resist removal. Third, the process and impact of the 1833 accord illustrates that while business was as social and political as it was economic in both the past and the present, the transition occurring at that time ushered in a new kind of society and a new kind of politics. Along the southern shores of Lake Michigan, then, the Indian Removal Act was part of the equation, but it was not the driving force for dispossession and relocation.[Under the circumstances, the removal of the Potawatomis could never have been about one piece of legislation. Nor could it have been about one single relationship.] The Potawatomis' political world was built on autonomous villages, and as a result different Potawatomi bands had very different connections with the people who lived around them, including other Indians, traders, missionaries, and local citizens. Understanding the role of removal in Potawatomi history, then, is built as much on the framework of those multiple relationships as it is on anything else. And those very relationships grew out of the enduring world of the Great Lakes fur trade in particular. Yet the narrative is even more tangled because it is not simply about the fragmentary aspect of Potawatomis within the removal experience. It is also about a fragmented implementation of removal in Michigan, Indiana, and Illinois. From the late 1820s through the 1840s removal was contested far more within a regional and local context than it was in relation to national concerns. On the southern shores of Lake Michigan and its extended watershed, this meant that Indian removal became inextricably linked to the economic development of the region and all that those economics entailed.

To the extent that any one document can capture a complex historical narrative, the Treaty of Chicago has the ability to encompass the diverse facets of Potawatomi removals. Just as William Cronon has used the growth of Chicago to explain the larger environmental history of the region, the 1833 accord can illuminate the diverse history that characterized the decades before and after its creation.[3] Like the railroad tracks that soon defined Chicago's emergence as a mercantile hub of the American Midwest, the treaty was enmeshed in a web built by chronological, economic, political, and social strands, and its conclusion affected the entire western Great Lakes region. Indeed, the treaty represents at once cause, effect, and illustration in the history of Potawatomi removal and the transformation of Indian country during the first half of the nineteenth century. It highlights the multiple networks that came together in that council, from the fur trade world of times past to the real estate speculations of the present, from the religious missionaries and federal agents to the Potawatomi leaders throughout the years.

The name "Chicago" dates back in written history to René-Robert Cavelier, Sieur de La Salle's, use of "*checagou*" to describe a specific portage along Lake Michigan in a 1682 exploration report. His use of that term is most likely indebted to the Miami-Illinois name for the river, *šikaakwa siipiiwi*, which originated from the wild leeks that grew so abundantly on its banks. The French referred to the wild leeks as wild garlic, which is also why some early records speak of the Wild Garlic River.[4] Chicago as a developed town laid out in a grid reflecting notions of private property, however, has its origins in land ordinances written and passed in the 1780s under the authority of the Articles of Confederation. These ordinances forever altered the geography of the American landscape, as anyone flying west of Ohio at 30,000 feet on a clear day can attest. A survey map from 1822 and "A Map of the Town of Chicago," drawn in 1830, reveal the early influences of those ordinances. William Rector drew the 1822 map, and he based his renderings on the survey completed one year earlier by John Walls, who worked for the office of the surveyor general for Illinois and Missouri. The map shows the location of Fort Dearborn but also clearly indicates the sections owned by the Illinois and Michigan Canal Commission. Although the title to much of the surrounding territory of northeastern Illinois remained in the hands of the Potawatomis, the lands targeted for canal development in the 1822 drawing had been obtained for the future state of Illinois by treaty in 1816. The 1830 map, drawn by James Thompson, originated from the next phase of this developmental vision, when the state assembly for Illinois established a commission to do all the work necessary to survey and sell the land to raise money for a canal. Upon its completion, that canal would connect the town of Chicago to the Mississippi River.[5]

Similar to the one-two punch of the Land Ordinance of 1785 and the Northwest Ordinance of 1787, then, the American gaze of development came first, and the specific plans for obtaining all the lands necessary to fulfill that vision came second. Those plans received a healthy jumpstart less than two years after James Thompson first drew his map of Chicago. When Congress passed ["An Act to Enable the President to Extinguish Indian Land Title within the State of Indiana, Illinois, and Territory of Michigan" in the summer of 1832] the origins of that particular legislation were not primarily based in the federal removal legislation.[6] While the calls to extinguish Indian land title were not brand new, the immediate impetus for what became the Treaty of Chicago was the recent violent outbreak of the Black Hawk War. The Black Hawk War is often used as the exemplary event for northern Indian removal, and as such plays the role granted to the Cherokee Trail of Tears in the Southeast. Instead, it was the catalyst for some of the more representative elements of northern removal and the relationships that framed it.

The pursuit of Sauk warrior Black Hawk and a band of Sauks and Mesquakies during the summer of 1832 sparked widespread calls for removal in the 1830s. Both location and recent history shaped Potawatomi attitudes toward the conflict. In the early weeks of the conflict a Potawatomi wkama (leader) named Shabonee did his best to warn non-Indian residents of northern Illinois when it seemed danger might be near. And famed wkama Waubansee, whose village was located about forty miles west of Chicago, led a band of Potawatomi men who served as scouts for General Henry Dodge during his pursuit of the Sauks.[7] Yet even Potawatomi neutrality and friendliness could not weaken the growing anti-Indian sentiment in the western Great Lakes region. [The anti-Indianism was built not only on the pursuit of Black Hawk but also on the brief Ho-Chunk uprising in the lead-mining region of southern Wisconsin five years earlier. Consequently, only a few weeks before Black Hawk's capture in early August 1832, Congress took action to initiate negotiations for removal.]
In early July the Senate considered and passed a bill authorizing three commissioners to purchase Indian lands in Indiana, Illinois, and Michigan Territory. Lewis Cass stated that the overall intention was to "extinguish entirely" Indian land titles, specifically those of the Potawatomis, in each of those three states or territories and "to procure the removal of the tribes now occupying them west of the Mississippi." This commission mirrored the principles of the Indian Removal Act but was specific to the lands in question. Despite the intentions, however, the three agreements that came out of this commission created small reservations spread throughout Illinois, Indiana, and Michigan, which allowed for the continual residence of hundreds of Potawatomis.[8]

In his address to the Illinois General Assembly in December 1832, Governor John Reynolds connected the hostilities of the summer to removal. After summarizing the actions taken against the Sauks, Reynolds advocated the removal of the Potawatomi Indians from Illinois. "When they are permitted to remain intermixed with the white population," Reynolds concluded, "it is almost certain that contests, and collisions will arise, and thereby, both parties be injured." Reynolds and the local Indian agents agreed that removal would benefit both Indians and Americans. Agent Thomas Owen told his superiors in early March 1833 that "there would be but little difficulty in effecting an exchange of lands on fair and reasonable terms" with the Potawatomis of northern Illinois. Michigan territorial governor George Porter affirmed Owen's opinion and proclaimed that an exchange of lands would remove the Indians "from the country in which they caused so much trouble during the past year." And in the fall of 1833 Owen and Porter were two of the three commissioners appointed by the federal government to follow through on this notion.[9]

The treaty negotiated at Chicago in September 1833 was, in its most simplistic form, an agreement that transferred approximately five million acres of land along and near the southern shores of Lake Michigan from the Potawatomi signatories to the United States. This accord arranged for the removal of those signatories within three years, although the second article also encouraged that relocation take place "as soon as conveniently can be done."[10] In terms of the process by which the treaty came to be, the diverse agendas of the individuals and parties involved, and the ultimate impact of its terms, however, the 1833 treaty had implications that reached far beyond such basic statements.

The topic of the Black Hawk War showed up repeatedly in the treaty negotiations at Chicago. Over the course of nearly four weeks, from early September to early October, the three treaty commissioners focused on extinguishing Indian land titles in northern Illinois and southern Michigan. The violence that had concluded with so much bloodshed on the Bad Axe River just over a year earlier was still fresh in the minds of all in attendance. Metea, an Ojibwe wkama, tackled the issue directly on the first full day of discussion and informed the commissioners, "Clouds of war and adversity have passed away and a clear sky and bright sun now shed their beams of peace upon us a happy people." Yet whereas Metea addressed the violence to show that it had passed, the treaty commissioners consistently used the war as a threat, a symbol of what Indian resistance to government desires brought. On September 20, after a Potawatomi wkama named Leopold Pokagon and two other Indians claimed that they did not know what lands the government wanted, Governor Porter showed frustration at what he judged to be feigned ignorance. He reminded all in attendance that President Andrew Jackson was "the greatest war chief" and that when the Sauks had not listened to their Great Father's counsel, he had "treated with them at the Cannon's mouth." Porter was clearly aggravated by the entire proceeding, and as his speech went on, his rhetoric returned to the war and how the Sauks and Mesquakies had "refused to listen to his [Jackson's] wise councils." In case he had not already made his point, Porter reinforced the fact that after the Sauks and Mesquakies "were cut to pieces by the Warriors, he [Jackson] treated them as he pleased." So long as the Indians dropped their act and closed their ears to the "wicked and designing men" around them, Porter believed all would be well. Should they continue to play dumb, however, Porter wanted them to know the type of treatment they should expect to receive.[11]

Porter's "wicked and designing men" came in all shapes and sizes, however, and carried with them an equally diverse set of agendas. Indeed, the Chicago treaty may be as well known for the circus atmosphere its council created as it is for the terms included in its articles. Countless numbers of Indians, traders, and other assorted gawkers who wanted to see, and hoped to benefit from, the federal government's arrangements for the land cession and relocation made it their business to be in the vicinity. There was a tremendous amount of money at stake in the negotiations that transpired over the course of nearly four weeks, and there were myriad stakeholders.

Charles Latrobe happened to witness the events at Chicago, and his observations of the "motley scene" are often cited to showcase the chaos and general shenanigans. This British traveler was somewhat bemused by the affair, and he noted that the "little village was in an uproar from morning to night, and from night to morning." He wrote of "horse-dealers, and horse-stealers,—rogues of every description, white, black, brown, and red—half-breeds, quarter breeds, and men of no breed at all." Latrobe also referenced "the men pursuing Indian claims" as well as the creditors "who know that they have no chance of getting their money, if they do not get it from the Government agents."[12] Peter Vieau, the son of trader Jacques Vieau, remembered a similar scene. His father, then based out of Milwaukee, traveled to Chicago in August 1833 to sell goods to Indians at the council and to settle outstanding debts. Or, as Peter described it in words that echoed Latrobe, to deal with "claims which could only be collected at the time of the government payments, when money was plenty." Vieau mentioned upwards of 6,000 Indians being present in the vicinity of council grounds. His account focused on a couple of colorful anecdotes, one in which his father wrestled an arrogant Potawatomi chief and another in which two young Potawatomi men dueled to the death over the love of a young woman. The environment "had much the appearance of a fair," the man recalled.[13]

Beyond the overly dramatized language and colorful anecdotes, however, these accounts reveal some critical aspects of Potawatomi participation in the process. Latrobe, for example, did not lump all Indians together as a single, unified entity. "The main divisions are the Pottawattomies of the Prairie and those of the Forest," he noted, "and these are subdivided into distinct villages under their several chiefs."[14] It was a reality that made the official heading of the treaty something of a misnomer and the actual negotiation of terms more difficult. The treaty preface states that it is an agreement made between the three American commissioners and the proper representatives of the "United Nation of Chippewa, Ottowa and Potawatamie Indians." Yet the multiple payment schedules and appended agreements tell a different story, as does the background to the appellation of the United Nation. The alliance of the Three Fires—the Potawatomis, Odawas, and Ojibwes—had its origins in a shared western migration and common interests that developed from the sixteenth century forward. To describe them as a nation or a confederacy is not accurate, however, "since the tribe were not permanently united, nor was their occasional unity only political." It is telling, then, that the Indian delegates at the council made it clear to the commissioners that the Indians in attendance did not all share the same relationships or agendas. Leopold Pokagon, who hailed from a village in the St. Joseph River Valley of southwestern Michigan, reminded Owen and his colleagues that not all the Potawatomis were the same, saying, "Some of us are called 'wood Indians' altho we are Potawattomies, and others are called 'Prairie Indians.'" The designation was one that the Potawatomis made government officials recognize, even when those officials hoped to avoid any distinctions that complicated matters. And they were distinctions that in the early nineteenth century were both regional and political. The Prairie Potawatomis were those who inhabited villages in the Illinois River Valley, and they were distinct, to an extent, from the Lake Potawatomis who lived along the southern shores of Lake Michigan.

The Woods Potawatomis, referred to by both Pokagon and Latrobe, were those who resided in northern Indiana and southern Michigan. Even those distinctions did not fully capture the situation, however, as within those geographic configurations were often more specific designations and interests. The Woods Potawatomis, for instance, included those from villages clustered around the St. Joseph River as well as those from the Wabash River drainage. Therefore, rather than the "United Nation," a better, though still imperfect, appellation for those who negotiated the treaty would be the "United Bands."[15]

In short, the council at Chicago was not simply a meeting between a unified group of Potawatomi leaders and representatives of the federal government. It occurred in a much more contested environment in which the government commissioners were only the first named group with an interest in the treaty's outcome. There were also men seeking to capitalize on an Indian treaty and the money that the negotiation represented, and there were the men pushing for the treaty so that they could build a city whose future existence and growth depended on the lands to be ceded. And finally, the Potawatomis in attendance did not all share the same opinions and desires. By the early 1830s Potawatomis throughout the region had made different choices in response to federal, state, and local policies, especially in the context of civilization efforts and treaty negotiations. The consequence of numerous decisions made in the early nineteenth century "was a realignment of villages to form new bands as the interests of these Potawatomi groups changed and their identities diverged according to their approach to acculturation." In Chicago, then, village leaders such as Pokagon from southwestern Michigan approached the treaty council with a very different mindset than his peers who lived in northern Illinois did.[16]

Each group of Potawatomis had selected specific individuals to serve as mediators in the council, and these men reflected a particular transition in leadership and influence within their bands. Ann Durkin Keating writes that by 1832 the Potawatomis "were not interested in volatile warriors" as leaders and instead supported those "who worked well with the Americans."[17] Yet this was not simply about good working relationships. On September 25, nearly two weeks into the council sessions, Pokagon explained, "The Prairie Indians have appointed Joseph Laframboise to assist Caldwell and Robinson" in the negotiations. Laframboise had kinship ties to the Potawatomi communities of northern Illinois and southern

Wisconsin through his Potawatomi mother, Shawwenoqua, and his father, Jean François, who had been a trader operating out of Milwaukee and Chicago. Billy Caldwell and Alexander Robinson, both men of Euro-Indian descent, also had intricate familial and economic connections to the Potawatomi villages of northern Illinois, and the two men left a sizeable imprint on the Chicago negotiations. Perhaps most important, under the authority granted them in council, the marks of Sawkanosh (Caldwell) and Cheecheepinquay (Robinson) appeared on several amendments attached to the final treaty.[18] Caldwell and Robinson were not newcomers, and as Waymichsaygo, a Potawatomi wkama from a Wisconsin village, had asserted earlier in the council proceedings, "They have been raised amongst us." Waymichsaygo also referred to the treaty council at Prairie du Chien held four years earlier when the United Bands of Potawatomis named those two individuals as their chief counselors. In that particular treaty the Potawatomis had agreed to cede land in northwestern Illinois and southern Wisconsin Territory, which did not sit well with all those affected by it. Nevertheless, Caldwell and Robinson retained their influence to the extent that Waymichsaygo could say in open council at Chicago, "So long as they live, they were chosen to manage our business." And even though these designated chief counselors and the federal government's treaty commissioners stated publicly that only the United Bands' wkamek had the authority to make the agreement official, some of the most important negotiating occurred with Robinson and Caldwell, behind closed doors and off the record.[19]

Outside of these public and private council sessions awaited scores of traders who sought payment for all manner of debts and even reparations for damages allegedly incurred during the War of 1812. "These traders seem to have had very little to do with the actual terms of the treaty," Anselm Gerwing observed, "but their work is evident enough in the long list of claims they presented." All told, the treaty called for the distribution of $175,000 to creditors in payments that ranged from as little as $25 to as much as $17,000. In the case of Jacques Vieau, the $2,000 received via this payment schedule made his trip from Milwaukee very worthwhile. Yet the vast schedule of claims and connected stories of fraud prompted the Senate to launch an investigation, which caused unrest among some of Vieau's compatriots.[20] John P. Bourie, who was to receive $3,000, and Francis Comparet, set to receive $5,000, warned Secretary of War Lewis Cass about the consequences of any interference with the business concluded in

Chicago. "Should the Senate reject the Treaty in part on a/c of the Schedule of claims," the two men asserted, "it will very much injure the future prospects of the Government in this the anticipated treaty with Indians in this State which can be brought about by the Traders alone." Bourie expressed similar concerns to Indiana senator John Tipton (formerly an Indian agent) in a letter written the very same day.[21]

Like the petitions received by Bishop Rosati, the traders' economic concerns evident in the payment schedule for the Chicago treaty provide insight into the social elements of that business. Milo Quaife wrote that the treaty "afforded the last, and at the same time the greatest, opportunity at Chicago for individuals to enrich themselves at the expense of the Indians or of the government of the United States."[22] Yet even as it transferred land and money, the treaty also served as the means by which one world began to supplant another that had long operated on a different set of relationships and understandings. A quick perusal of Schedule B, which lists the claims against the United Bands said to be "justly due," provides a mixture of the old and new Chicago worlds coming together. Alongside the aforementioned Jacques Vieau were men with surnames of Kinzie, Burbonnais, and Beaubien, each one long attached to the kinship and economic networks forged in the region during the late eighteenth and early nineteenth centuries.[23] Other names appearing on the list, such as those of the siblings William G. and George W. Ewing, belonged to traders whose interest in the treaty, and in Indian affairs in general, was purely economic. The Ewings, who had first established a trading post at Logansport in 1829, listed their claim at $5,000. From 1829 into the 1840s they viewed Indian affairs as an integral source of revenue, and it was a position that shaped their attitude toward removal and the treaties like those signed in 1833.[24]

The Ewing brothers saw a clear connection between Indian affairs and the financial support of the infrastructure that newcomers to northern Illinois and Indiana wanted and demanded. Removal and the financial interests of traders were seldom, if ever, unrelated, and the Ewings' attitude toward the policy often fluctuated with their economic condition. The revenue stream of Indian annuities and treaty payments could not only provide a safety net for traders like themselves, but it could also support physical development and public works projects. In February 1830, in fact, William Ewing had put this sentiment in clear terms to then–Indian agent John Tipton. Ewing, like many others, was interested in the construction of the Wabash canal in northern Indiana and shared the belief that the Miamis in particular were obstacles and potential dangers to its construction. However, he viewed the removal of those Indians from the state as "impracticable, . . . as their increased annuity [would] be of material benefit in the first settleing of our country." Besides, Ewing added, "There is yet room for all."[25] In the economic attitudes of the Ewings was a good example of what William Cronon meant when he wrote, "The hybrid cultural universe of Indians and Euroamericans that had existed in the Chicago area for decades, was finally to be shattered by different conceptions of property and real estate."[26] George and William Ewing saw economic utility in the Potawatomis and their Miami neighbors, but they also believed that the growth of non-Indian settlements would ultimately eliminate the necessity of depending on and tolerating the Indian presence. By the 1830s Chicago and its vicinity had thus become subject to speculators with a definitive vision of what that city could and should be.

This transition was not, however, one in which a signed treaty and a cession of five million acres resulted in Indians and their relations handing over Chicago to non-Indians. Prior to any removal the treaty first had to complete the ratification process, and a broader conflict over boundaries and valuable lands in the western territories served as the most prominent obstacle to that approval. Though first signed in September 1833, the treaty did not clear the U.S. Senate until February 21, 1835. A variety of circumstances created that substantial delay, but the primary point of contestation revolved around land. Missouri politicians protested the proposed settlement of the Potawatomis on approximately 3,125 square miles (two million acres) of fertile land along the Platte River in the northwestern corner of the state. Their constituents had expressed a desire for that territory at least a year before the treaty council even began and could not believe the commissioners stood ready to hand it over to Indians. Led by the protests of its two Missourian members, the Senate altered the terms of the 1833 accord and approved a modified version that removed the Platte country from consideration as a new Indian home.[27] Caldwell, Robinson, and Laframbois pushed back, passing along their "deepest regret" at the news that the federal government had changed the terms, and asserting, "[The United States government's] interpretation of a Treaty and ours is very different." Yet if the Senate sought to renegotiate, the three representatives of the United Bands were prepared to counter. Their first condition was that the Platte country removal be balanced by "four hundred sections [256,000 acres] of land to be selected by us within the boundaries of the Country ceded" by the Chicago treaty. This request had precedent in prior treaties but failed to gain approval because the government now stood firmly against providing individual land grants in treaties.[28] Caldwell, Robinson, and the United Bands' leaders they spoke for finally assented to the altered accord in early October; they gained in exchange ten thousand dollars to be used for the benefit of the tribe once relocated. Thomas Owen urged his superiors to accept this final proposal, stating that the persistent intrusions onto lands supposedly ceded by the 1833 accord as initially drafted made it possible that military force would have to be used against trespassers. The official ratification and proclamation occurred the following winter.[29]

Even before it was officially ratified, however, the treaty set in motion a human tragedy, exacerbated by an ever-expanding bureaucratic mess. Ratification did not settle the matter of where removed Indians should go once they left northern Illinois, and the years of uncertainty led to tremendous confusion on the part of Indians, government officials west of the Mississippi River, and non-Indian settlers. Potawatomis who had relocated west of the Mississippi River prior to the Chicago accord moved into the Platte country in 1834 upon learning of the initial treaty negotiation. And when approximately 250 members of the United Bands relocated from northern Illinois at the end of 1835 and moved into the Platte country as well, Indian agent Anthony Davis reported in an obvious understatement, "There has been something wrong in emigrating these people." Davis knew that the ratified treaty had taken the Platte country out of the equation, but when he told the Potawatomis they were not in the right place, they informed him, "They know that this is the land they treated for."[30] By the end of 1836 Davis had nearly 1,300 Potawatomis to contend with on land that the federal government had said did not belong to the Indians. That number had increased by three hundred the following March, the same month that President Martin Van Buren officially declared that the Platte country in question was now a part of Missouri. The floodgates opened with this presidential proclamation, and as non-Indians began moving into the region, tensions rose, precipitating yet another removal. Starting in mid-July 1837, by both land and steamboat, nearly 1,500 Potawatomis were moved yet again, under military supervision, from the Platte country to a new home near Council Bluffs.[31]

The Council Bluffs area provided a home to the United Bands even though circumstances soon made it clear that this home would be just as impermanent as their first settlements on the Platte River. By early August the two parties that had traveled by steamboat had arrived and established an encampment approximately two miles north of Bellevue, the site of the Council Bluffs Agency. They still awaited the arrival of the bulk of the United Bands who had started their journey by land in mid-July. Edwin James, their appointed agent, advised that because the landscape was "well adapted to an agricultural and especially a stock-raising people," the government should act quickly to provide the Potawatomis with live-stock of the "most approved and profitable breeds" in addition to the most advanced agricultural tools necessary for cultivation. The United Nation would be challenged, however, by the two general environments James described. The sizeable portion of "marshy ground" comprising the Mis-souri bottom lands, James reported, would "probably make this portion of the country sickly," even as any farming or other improvements would "be very liable to be washed away by changes in the course of the stream." The uplands James described did not sound much better: "There is in general a great want of timber for the purposes of permanent settlement."[32] Less than two months later it appeared that the Potawatomis at Council Bluffs might not need to worry about marshlands, seasonal flooding, or the lack of timber. In a series of discussions with James, delegations of Otoes and Missouris informed the agent that they had "never ceded their right to hunt on the lands recently taken by the authority of the government for the use of the Potowatomies." Therefore, in the same letter in which James reported that Potawatomis from the Platte purchase were still making their way to Council Bluffs, he mentioned the possibility that they might soon have to endure another relocation.[33]

From the summer of 1837 forward, the final destination of removed Potawatomis caused as many problems as the treaties that initiated the process. As the United Bands' experience illustrated, the growing number of interested parties exacerbated the situation immeasurably. Missouri citizens and state officials, intent on keeping their boundaries impermeable to Indians, sought to direct removal parties away from the lands they desired. Federal agents did their best to direct the Potawatomis to suit federal wishes and needs while confronting the influence of missionaries who had their own ideas about what best suited their charges. Traders operating out of Michigan, Indiana, and Illinois also continued to lobby for terms that best suited their financial interests. In the midst of it all, each party of Potawatomis struggled to make, and act on, the decisions that would provide for the safety, security, and prosperity of their people.

Many of the difficulties resisted easy resolutions because the Chicago treaty was no longer the only accord arranging for the removal of Potawatomis from the Great Lakes region. The trouble began well before any arrangements for relocation because numerous traders did their best to obtain as substantial a portion of the Indian annuities as possible. Over a period of six months in 1836 Commissioner Abel C. Pepper negotiated nine different treaties with Potawatomi bands in northern Indiana alone, and each treaty established a two-year deadline for removal. Indian affairs was still considered a valuable economic enterprise in Indiana, and the Treaty of Chicago had not slaked the thirst of men who refused to support any treaty that arranged for removal but did not allow for the proper payment of any and all claims against the Indians. As Agent J. P. Simonton had noted in the summer of 1835, "With regard to the removal of the Indians from this section of country, I have to say that it is almost useless to attempt it in the present state of affairs. Many of the traders are opposed to their removal and some have come out openly and declare that the Indians shall never go west unless their debts are paid." Simonton continued, writing, "[The traders] are selfish and would sacrifice the prosperity of this whole country to secure their private fortunes."[34]

The drama that consumed an annuity payment in the fall of 1836 showcases the economic machine that fueled the competing interests both in and out of the Potawatomi communities in the region and the problems it created for the removal process as a whole. Each one of the treaties that Pepper had negotiated between March and August had included a provision for one final annuity payment to be made before any relocation occurred. Pepper had also made sure that the Potawatomi signatories had agreed to use the proceeds from the sale of their lands to pay any and all valid debts. This final annuity distribution occurred in late September 1836 at the traditional Potawatomi payment grounds on the banks of the Tippecanoe River. Shortly after the payment, however, Pashpoho and eleven other Potawatomi wkamek from the villages on the Wabash River (all but two of whom had signed one or more of the 1836 treaties) wrote to President Andrew Jackson and reported that they had "escaped from the late payment ground in [their] own country under cover and protection of the Troops" who were there to ensure a stable and secure process.

According to the Wabash Potawatomis, they needed protection from the "Catholic and hostile British Indians of the north and their evil advisers, namely a great number of degraded Frenchmen and half bloods who live near to and among the St. Joseph's Indians." If the Wabash Potawatomis were to be believed, they now lived under the threat of a deadly attack by their northern relations who were angry that the Wabash headmen had sold all of their lands.[35]

Whereas the Wabash Potawatomis appeared to argue that their northern relatives had no justification for their anger, the very words they used to describe the events in question implied otherwise. As far as the treaty signatories were concerned, they were following the advice of their Great Father to agree to terms surrendering the sections of land set aside in previous treaties, located in northern Indiana and southern Michigan. Yet once the substance of those cessions was "known to the Catholic Indians who resided on these last sold reserves, and to those St. Josephs and Chicago renegade Indians who had collected on them in great numbers, . . . a great excitement prevailed." This very statement suggests that the reserves were sold out from under those who were residing on them and had the right to make decisions about their land. Thus the news, "Those Indians who opposed us held a council of War and resolved that every one of us who had signed the Treaty should be killed," could not have been all that surprising to the Wabash Potawatomis.[36]

The reports of tension and the threats of violence were one reason why this particular payment received attention from government officials in Washington. Commissioner of Indian Affairs Carey Harris charged John Edmonds with the task of digging into the alleged improprieties and conflicts associated with the annuity payments of September 1836. The investigation commenced in Logansport in mid-June, and Edmonds issued his final report in December 1837. In a fair and measured account that highlighted the intricate webs complicating Indian affairs in the region, Edmonds did his best to describe not just the difficulties that had occurred but also their particular origins. He recognized that the St. Joseph Potawatomis, who had been accused by their Wabash relatives of making threats, had a clear reason for their outrage. Edmonds specifically referenced the intent and decision of Colonel Pepper to purchase all Potawatomi reservation lands in a September 23, 1836, accord, including those reservations originally granted to chiefs who did not give in to the commissioner's requests. Ashkum and Chechawkose were two of those chiefs who had

This watercolor of a Potawatomi couple on a white horse, followed by a man leading a gray horse, was one of many paintings completed by George Winter while the Potawatomis were at Logansport in the summer of 1837, during the investigation of the annuity payments made in 1836. Courtesy of the Tippecanoe County Historical Association, Lafayette, Ind.

refused to sell, and as Edmonds noted, they vehemently "denied the right of the Chiefs of the nation to sell their particular reservations without their consent." This particular conflict was further inflamed by a decision reached at the payment grounds to deny the St. Joseph Potawatomis from receiving any of the annuities as well.[37]

The Edmonds report also attested that the disputes within the Potawatomi community did not fully explain the problems. Traders and their intertwined financial interests and personal relationships carried much of the responsibility for the mess. "The excitement among the white people [at the payment] was produced by a different cause," Edmonds reported. "Almost all of them were claimants against the Indians." Indeed, the very first sign of violence on the payment grounds was not among the Potawatomis but instead "grew out of a personal altercation between Wm. G. Ewing and Alexander Coquillard." It might be argued that the drama that unfolded in September 1836 grew out of the disputes among traders. This meant that the fights between the Wabash and St. Joseph Potawatomis were indications of larger battles between businessmen. Alexis Coquillard, a merchant based in South Bend, pushed the St. Joseph Potawatomis to protest the cessions and annuity restrictions, and the Ewing brothers had facilitated the growth of the substantial debt among the Wabash Potawatomis that made them more willing to sell land for money that might allow them to pay off their creditors. The reality was more complicated, however, especially because the different Potawatomi villages could not be so easily divided between those who traded with Coquillard and those who only did business with Ewings. Nevertheless, the traders, along with their economic and social relationships, had clearly shaped events in the region to fit their agendas, and the Indians suffered the consequences. Edmonds sought to combat those developments by suggesting changes to the government's annuity system in order to weaken the traders' influence, "which is naturally exercised rather for their own benefit than that of the Indians."[38]

Even as Edmonds conducted his investigation, however, the efforts to act on the treaties signed by Pepper in 1836 moved forward. By the summer of 1837 federal officials operating out of the agencies at Chicago and Logansport scrambled to satisfy the terms for removal set by those agreements. The first steps began in mid-July at the council grounds near Keewaunay's Lake, where Pepper, who now held the illustrious title of removal superintendent, did his best to persuade the Potawatomis from the Wabash villages to "delay no longer to accept the offer he [their Great Father] ha[d] been making to [them] for the last two years." More to the point, while the government would not force them to leave, Pepper stated, "Those of you who remain in this country and refuse the good offers of your Great Father will become subject to the Laws of the land." Following Pepper's opening address, Naswaukay spoke for the assembled Wabash Potawatomis and made clear that those Indians living in northern Indiana had not forgotten past agreements and were determined to hold the Americans' feet to the fire. In addition to a direct reference to the Treaty of Greenville, the Potawatomi speaker brought up the numerous times American officials had affirmed the Indian claims to the land. "We recollect all you said," Naswaukay noted. "You spoke on the subject of removal, you said we should not be driven away." Yet the Wabash Potawatomis had another impetus to agree to terms. Since the fallout from the 1836 annuity payment, they had feared retaliation by the St. Joseph Potawatomis and had stayed in the vicinity of Logansport rather than return to their villages. Despite some initial resistance, therefore, two days later the Wabash Potawatomis stated that they would agree to reconvene in one week to discuss the terms of removal.[39]

On August 1 these Potawatomis gathered once more, explaining that while they believed an immediate removal would be detrimental, they would consent to relocation under the terms of the treaty. Naswaukay concluded his talk with a more personal statement reflecting both the loss of land and the ongoing tensions among the Potawatomi bands, saying, "No permanent home is mine. Nothing is left to me but to place myself under the protection of my Great Father." And with those words, he signed the emigrating rolls. Colonel Lewis Sands then informed the Potawatomis that they should move closer to Logansport to get provisions, for the trip west would begin on August 11. Their final destination would not be Council Bluffs but a new agency established by the federal government earlier that year on the Osage River in present-day eastern Kansas. "I believe that most of the Indians that are termed the Wabash Indians would be willing to go to the Osage," agent Anthony L. Davis observed, "[for] they are violently opposed to going up on the north side of the Missouri." That opposition came less from any dislike of Council Bluffs as a place to live than it did from the fear of living on the same lands where the St. Joseph Potawatomis might also relocate.[40]

Yet when the appointed date for the Potawatomi departure arrived, Sands had moved on to coordinate a separate removal, and a new conductor named George Proffit had assumed responsibility for the process. This change did not sit well with the Potawatomis, and only fifty-two consented to the removal that began on August 23. The small party made a rain-soaked journey that lasted longer than it should have because of higher-than-normal river levels and severe illness. The latter even struck Proffit, and he stopped to recuperate in Harmony, Missouri, at the end of September while Naswakay and the other Potawatomis moved forward to complete their journey. Upon their arrival at the Osage River on October 23, however, this particular removal party had somehow managed to avoid losing a single person and even welcomed a newborn baby into their lives. Yet they had left behind a large number of relatives, most of whom had deserted the staging camps near Logansport and returned to villages on the Tippecanoe River. Judge William Polke wrote to Senator John Tipton of this failure, predicting, "From the Circumstances of their Raising no

Corn this year I am apprehensive Difficulties will occur between them and the whites, who have settled on their Reserves." Polke composed his letter in early September, more than a month before Naswakay's party had completed its journey, and he had already been called upon to settle disputes between the Potawatomis who had stayed behind and the whites who had moved onto lands they believed were open for occupation.[41]

Sands, meanwhile, had left Logansport in early August under orders to take over the removal of Potawatomis from Illinois, Wisconsin, and Michigan that had first been assigned to an agent named Gholson Kercheval. Kercheval had been fired for his failure to accomplish the task at hand, which put the pressure on his replacement. Early reports indicated that Sands was responding well to this pressure, and by early September he and his men had reached a camp at Shabona's Grove, seventy miles west of Chicago, and had "30 Waggons loaded with Baggage, Women & children, 200 Indians horse back, and great many travelling on foot." Twenty armed guards kept watch day and night over the Potawatomis to maintain order and prevent any runaways prior to their imminent departure for the West.[42] Despite his early belief that he could persuade more than one thousand Potawatomis to head west under his command, Sands had gathered at the northern Illinois staging ground only 470 individuals. Both his abrasive manner and his refusal to distribute any annuities east of the Mississippi River had driven an even larger number of Indians away from Shabona's Grove, and nearly eight hundred Potawatomis journeyed west to Council Bluffs without any government oversight or assistance. When Sands finally led his removal party out of Illinois, they endured the same rainy conditions that had been experienced by the party led by George Proffit. Upon arrival at the Platte River in Missouri, Sands could only watch as nearly two hundred Potawatomis under the leadership of young wkama Topinebee broke off and headed south to the settlements along the Osage River. This particular band had no interest in living among the United Bands at Council Bluffs.[43]

As of November 1837, then, Potawatomi removal parties had two possible destinations, and a variety of factors and individuals shaped their choices between the two. The settlements at Council Bluffs contained a population of approximately 2,400, including Billy Caldwell, who appeared to have the ear of federal officials and thus a significant amount of influence. Johnston Lykins and Isaac McCoy, two Baptist missionaries hoping to assure further federal funding by gathering all the Potawatomis at the Osage River Agency, saw a conspiracy at work in the attempts to make Council Bluffs the destination of choice. "It appears to me," Lykins wrote, "there is a *secret spring* some where operating to send the Indians to the Bluffs, for I know that Topinabee while pleading to be sent to the osage was threatened with troops." For the time being, the villages on the Osage River had somewhere between 850 and 900 men, women, and children. More than anything, money and the power to make decisions for all Potawatomis in the West appeared to be at stake. The federal government wanted to consolidate the Potawatomis for the sake of bureaucratic efficiency. A single Potawatomi reservation in the West, hopefully one not located in Iowa, would simplify at least one aspect of Indian affairs. The multitude of agents, traders, and missionaries in the West had different ideas based on what they believed was best for both the Potawatomis and their own financial interests. Lykins wrote directly of his "desire to have Putawatomie head quarters on the Osage," and therefore he welcomed any measures that undermined the influence of Caldwell and the Potawatomis living at the Bluffs.[44]

Lykins's concerns about removal destinations encompassed all of the Potawatomis, including those still living in southern Michigan, northern Indiana, and southern Wisconsin. From 1837 to 1840 state and federal officials shared those concerns about western destinations while they did their best to clear those regions of Indian title and an Indian presence. One of the most well-known incidents occurred in the fall of 1838 when Indiana governor David Wallace and Senator John Tipton enlisted one hundred men to round up and force Menominee's band of Potawatomis to move from their homes along the Yellow River to the West. The timing of the march west coincided with the removal of the Cherokee Nation from Georgia, but the context more clearly matched those of other Potawatomi relocations. Menominee had fought hard to invalidate the 1836 treaty that formalized the cession of his reserve, which an 1832 accord had set aside. As he had done in so many other instances, Abel Pepper had managed to gain the x-marks of Potawatomi men on an accord that became a flashpoint for controversy. In this case, despite the protests by the Potawatomis that they had not agreed to any land cessions, shortly after the 1836 treaty was announced Menominee reported, "White people was running through our reservation putting Preemption claims and told us that they were informed by Col. Pepper that our reserve was sold." Menominee could not believe that the federal government would enforce a "false treaty," and his band was determined "to remain upon [their] lands to cultivate them, to become subjects of the Laws of the State and live like white people." By August 1838, however, the treaty had long since been ratified, the two-year deadline for removal had expired, and conflicts between the Yellow River Potawatomis and non-Indian invaders had resulted in arson and assault within the boundaries of the ceded territory.[45]

The journey, later termed the Trail of Death, began on September 4, 1838, at 9:30 in the morning when the Potawatomis left the encampment near Twin Lakes with twenty-six wagons carrying their property and supplies. William Polke, a former judge, had been appointed to oversee the removal, and he maintained an account of the journey. The Indians and their military escort traveled twenty-one miles on day one, a journey that lasted longer than intended because they struggled to find water. Polke's account of the first day ends on a poor note: "Provisions and forage rather scarce and not of the best quality." The record of the second day illustrates a diverse series of events that encapsulate the affair as a whole. When all was said and done, twenty Potawatomis had fled the encampment over-night, fifty-one were left behind because of illness, one child died at the day's end, and another child was born. Water continued to prove scarce. Day after day the removal continued until the Potawatomis finally arrived at the Osage River on Sunday, November 4. Forty-three Potawatomis had died, twenty-eight of them children. The next day, as Polke began settling accounts with all of the men involved in overseeing the removal, a number of Potawatomis gathered at the agency to address the conductors. Although their final destination had reunited them with other Potawato-mis, their words as recorded by Polke reflect their pain. Pepishkay report-edly said "They had been taken from homes affording them plenty, and brought to a desert—a wilderness, and were now to be scattered and left as the husbandmen scatters his seed." The Potawatomis had never met their new agent, Anthony Davis, and did not know if he would fulfill the terms of their treaty. After giving all the necessary assurances, Polke turned east and headed back to Indiana, "every thing having resulted as well and as happily as could have been anticipated by the most sanguine." Few state-ments better represent the disconnect between the federal agent, confident in a job well done, and the Potawatomis, trying to come to terms with the loved ones they had lost and seeking for some kind of reassurance that the federal government had not simply abandoned them on the banks of the Osage River.[46]

Yet just as Polke had turned to the East and eyed a return to his home in Indiana, federal officials received constant reminders from their non-Indian constituents in the Great Lakes region that the removals were incomplete. Illinois, Wisconsin, Indiana, and Michigan continued to contain "a remnant of pottowatomies," reported John Tipton in early January, but he said, "[They] may be speedily removed if proper steps are taken." It was difficult to get an accurate count on just how many Indians had not yet removed, and just as difficult to get a sense of how many actually wanted to move west. Pepper was confident that the Indians would want to remove, especially now that they were "quite convinced at last that they [were] no longer to receive annuity this side of the Mississippi." Agent G. N. Fitch advised from Logansport that any efforts to initiate removal should happen in early summer before the Potawatomis in northern Indiana scattered to go hunting. Samuel Milroy, a subagent for the Miamis, explained that the Potawatomis were willing "to remove as the only means of relieving their distress." On the other extreme, however, Milroy relayed word from Isaac Ketchum in St. Joseph County, Michigan, who believed, "Nothing but an armed force, will move the Indians in Michigan." The agent hoped that such use of force would not be necessary.[47]

Despite all of the letters back and forth, the desired removal did not happen in 1839, and traders once again became critical to the outcome. In early September William Polke accepted the appointment to conduct these operations, a responsibility that required him to travel throughout northern Indiana trying to find the Potawatomis and convince them to gather for relocation to the western territories. One month later he named Pashpoho's village on the Tippecanoe River as the place to assemble, but only seventy Potawatomis answered the call. Polke continually referenced the deplorable conditions of the Potawatomis he found, and he wrote of the devastating presence and impact of alcohol in the villages. His most powerful opponent appeared to be the traders. On October 25 he found out that Pashpoho, along with interpreter Joseph Barron, "had been arrested for debt the evening before, and were in confinement." Polke bailed Pashpoho out, "as without him the emigration must fail." The Logansport traders, however, would not be so easily tamed. The next day Polke learned that they had issued similar calls for debt payment against at least twenty more Potawatomis, and so the conductor made a decision. "I proposed to the Indians," he informed his superiors, "that as their creditors were determined to brake up the emigration, they had better disperse to their hunting camps." In the meantime Polke intended to report back to Washington to obtain a plan of action. The question posed by Samuel Milroy at the end of Polke's report summed up the situation well: "Have they [traders] the right, under the laws to interfere with and brake up an emigration—authorized by the General government—under the pretext of alleged debts due by the Indians?" If they did have that right, then any further removals would be extremely complicated. As it turned out, the trader proving to be the most antagonistic was none other than George W. Ewing.[48]

At the dawn of a new decade federal agents in northern Indiana continued to discuss the possibilities of removal with the Potawatomis who remained and fretted over their inability to compete with the traders and the lies they spread. The federal government had denied the requests of Polke and Milroy to provide provisions to the Potawatomis so that they could be weaned off their dependency on the Ewings and thus avoid the kind of debts that had put Pashpoho in prison. As evidenced by a visit to Milroy from Abram Burnett and a number of other headmen in late January, many of the Potawatomis hoped that the federal government might support their relocation when spring finally arrived. Federal officials had also decided to prepare for any possibilities. Secretary of War Joel Poinsett appointed Brigadier General Hugh Brady to oversee the removals to come, giving him leeway to use any means necessary, including military force, to make it happen. Brady organized two different removals in the second half of 1840. The first consisted primarily of Potawatomis who had expressed a desire to remove, and overt coercion was deemed unnecessary. From June to early August federal agents gathered the bands led by Burnett, Pashpoho, and Checawkose. A total of 524 Potawatomis left their encampment at South Bend in early August and arrived at the Osage River on October 6. A week after that first party left, however, General Brady reported that traders were making last-ditch efforts to keep the remaining Potawatomis in place, telling them that they had "lands, still unsold to the United States" and that they could not be removed. Faced with some Potawatomis who believed these lies and others who dispersed into the woods at the rumor of smallpox-infected troops heading in their direction, Brady took advantage of Poinsett's orders and by late August had 300 armed men combing the lands of northern Indiana and southern Michigan. These efforts extended through September and into October, resulting in a second removal of 439 Potawatomis who arrived at the

Osage River on November 25. According to Brady, no more than twenty of them moved of their free will. "On the contrary," he wrote, "we were compelled to hunt them up, in the woods, and to conduct them to Peru in Illinois, with troops, at which place they were placed on board of a Steam Boat." Similar to Polke more than two years earlier, Brady was content with his accomplishments and only expressed regret that his officers would most likely not be paid enough for their efforts.[49]

The Potawatomi removals that resulted from the Chicago treaty of 1833, and those that followed in the next seven years, illustrate the manner in which federal policies filtered through numerous prisms in the Great Lakes region. Local and state politics and economics mattered, as did the relationships within and between the different Potawatomi bands. It meant that no single removal explained the experience for all Potawatomis, much less all Indians in the Great Lakes region. And just as the focus on 1833–1840 is a restrictive chronology, for not all removals occurred within that time frame, the emphasis on east-to-west relocations is a restrictive geography, for upwards of three thousand Potawatomis avoided forced removal by crossing the border into Canada.[50]

The focus on Potawatomi bands and larger removals also overshadows some of the smaller and subtler aspects of these processes that transformed the landscape of the Old Northwest in the early nineteenth century. Many of the social, political, and economic factors that shaped the band relocations played a role in the less noticeable, but no less complete, removal and relocation of individuals and their families who had hoped to remain a significant part of the new regional development. The life of Madore Beaubien is one example that demonstrates how a more individualized removal played out in the city of Chicago.

Madore Beaubien's family had deep roots in the Great Lakes region. His father, Jean-Baptiste Beaubien, was born in Detroit and descended from a lineage that had begun with the arrival in Canada of French-born René Cuillerier in the 1660s.[51] Madore was born in 1809 in southern Michigan, the product of a marriage between Jean-Baptiste and Manabenaquah, an Odawa woman from the Grand River villages.[52] Jean-Baptiste began working for the American Fur Company in the early nineteenth century and during the first decade spent most of his time in Milwaukee, though he also frequented the settlements around Fort Dearborn on the southern shores of Lake Michigan. In 1816 his superiors permanently transferred him to Chicago.[53] According to Madore, his father often traveled to Chicago, Milwaukee, Green Bay, and Michilimackinac from his new posting. His family usually came with him, though more often than not they would go as far as Milwaukee, where his third wife, Josette Laframboise Beaubien, would keep the children and visit her relatives while Jean-Baptiste continued on his business travels. Madore's mother died in 1812, and his father subsequently married Josette, further entwining the Beaubiens with regional kinship networks.[54]

Just as his father was intricately connected to fur trade economic and kinship networks, so was Madore's life intertwined with the early history of Chicago and the Indian people who lived there. He and his brother Charles both received land grants in the 1821 Treaty of Chicago due to their maternal connections. Ten years later Madore was officially licensed as a merchant in Chicago and had a two-room log house where he sold goods purchased from suppliers in Detroit. In 1833, while thousands of Potawatomis, Odawas, and Ojibwes assembled for a council that would ultimately lead to a cession of five million acres, Madore tied his future to the nascent American town. At a special election held at the house of his uncle Mark, Madore received thirteen votes, enough to earn a position as one of the five trustees of the new town of Chicago.[55]

Despite such signs of acceptance, Madore struggled to find his place in this transforming world. He sought to maintain connections to his Potawatomi family even as he responded to the social and economic demands made by the government civilization policies. One event in particular, an annuity payment held in Chicago in the fall of 1831, provided a stark demonstration of the troubles men like Madore faced. Madore was one of several young men of mixed descent who wrote to Secretary of War Lewis Cass in 1831 about an apparent alteration in the process of annuity payments. "A few of the half blood, though they did not vote nor pay taxes, did not receive their part of the annuity paid to the Indians," the young men explained to Cass. "Even those that were quarter Indian received their portion because they were dressed like Indians. The Agent said to some of us if we did not vote nor pay the taxes we should draw like the rest. But after we got there he observed we were not entitled to draw because we wore our dress as the Whites." The scenario described by Madore and his peers raises a number of fascinating questions and issues regarding how the scene played out and what the exact line between dressing White and dressing Indian would have been. But the young men had more to say. "We inquired of the principal Chief and he said of course you may draw for you are Indians as much as ourselves." So what did it mean for all involved to be part Potawatomi and part other? "Your Excellency well knows the immalgamation is powerful," the letter goes on. "Nearly one half of the potawatomies is part blood. Then according to the Agent of Chicago I must lose my right because I follow his mode of dress. And this is paying us well for trying to live in the civilized mode."[56]

The phrase "to live in the civilized mode" indicates the manner in which the young men had absorbed the policy language of the day, but Madore did not simply believe that his change of clothing made the only difference. His family was already well connected in the growing town, and not only because of the fur trade. Jean-Baptiste, his father, had not depended solely on his career as a trader, but had made wise land purchases as well. In 1812, even before the American Fur Company permanently transferred him to Chicago, Jean-Baptiste had purchased a log cabin built on the grounds of Fort Dearborn on the southern banks of the Chicago River. Five years later he made a more substantial acquisition, buying the house of a former contractor that was located just south of the fort. This meant that Jean-Baptiste Beaubien owned land in what would become the centerpiece of real estate speculation over the next decade. He was also a prominent member of the local community, having been appointed justice of the peace in 1825. Thinking of the future, Jean Baptiste wanted his sons to receive a Westernized education. Consequently Madore and his brother attended the Carey Mission School run by the Baptists in the St. Joseph River Valley, and Madore also spent four years at the Hamilton Baptist Theological Institute in New York.[57]

Madore became the ultimate representation of the transformation of Chicago—the personification of the city's past, which would be not allowed to remain in its present. Yet it is not because Madore did not want to stay. He enlisted in one of the militia companies formed in the Chicago area during the months of the Black Hawk War, though it is not clear that he saw much service beyond standing watch over the settlement's environs. While he received money in the 1833 Chicago treaty as a Potawatomi, he also received payments from the proceedings as a creditor. And in 1835 he married a white woman from Pennsylvania named Mary Boyer, the younger sister of his business partner at the time, Valentine Boyer. Three years later, however, Madore found himself very much in debt to his father-in-law, John K. Boyer. To make matters worse, his wife had left him and would officially divorce him five years later. Whereas he had once been near the peak of Chicago society, he appeared to represent the colorful past, which was expected to give way to a more progressive present. Mary remarried in 1843, living the rest of her life as the wife of Laurin Palmer Hilliard, a merchant who first arrived in the city from New York in 1836. Madore, however, received a different treatment. "The people of Chicago have forgotten old Beaubien," he lamented in 1882. "They don't remember that old Beaubien ever did anything for them." Just as important, at the time he criticized the poor memories of Chicagoans, Madore lived hundreds of miles to the west in the small town of Silver Lake, Kansas.[58]

Madore Beaubien had left Chicago in 1840 and moved west of the Mississippi River to live among the Potawatomis who had settled near Council Bluffs. Jacqueline Peterson has asserted that Madore "cast his fate" with the Potawatomis. According to Virgil Beaubien, his great-grandfather Madore left Chicago in 1840 because his "Indian blood got the best of him."[59] At the very least it can be said that among the Potawatomis Madore found the influence and success that had eluded him in the new Chicago. In 1845 federal officials visited the Potawatomi agencies at Council Bluffs and the Osage River seeking land cessions as well as the consolidation of the disparate Potawatomi communities onto one reservation. Madore served as an interpreter during the councils held over the course of several weeks in November and December 1845 at Council Bluffs, and his name appeared on the treaty of 1846 that brought the Potawatomis from the Osage River and Council Bluffs to a single reservation in Kansas. In 1854 he married Theresa Laframboise, and in 1861 Madore signed the treaty that was instrumental in the formation of how they are known today: the Prairie Band of Potawatomis and the Citizen Potawatomi Nation. He was also one of six men comprising the Potawatomi Business Committee, a group formed in 1861 "to transact all business between the Potawatomi Indians and the government of the U.S."[60]

Madore's departure from Chicago in 1840 did not separate him completely from his past or from his family, however. His brother Charles moved to Council Bluffs with his wife and three children in 1844. Their half-brother Alexander, whose mother was Josette Laframboise Beaubien, stayed in Chicago and became a policeman. Jean-Baptiste also remained in the vicinity of Chicago, taking up residence in Napierville. Despite the distance from his son, Jean-Baptiste never stopped offering advice about using treaty negotiations as a source of financial support. Indeed, Madore and his father exchanged letters prior to the 1846 Potawatomi treaty, discussing the possibility of getting the Beaubien name on the list of valid creditors to be paid out of any monies provided. Jean-Baptiste remained in Napierville until his death in 1863, and Madore died twenty years later in Kansas.[61]

As seen through the lens of Madore Beaubien's life, the Chicago Treaty of 1833 signaled a transformation that was about far more than just land, and it was not simply about dispossessing one community of people and replacing it with another. The treaty and all that it represented removed people who had demonstrated a distinct interest in building a community and coexisting with the new emigrants to the region. Yet whereas the founding of the first Catholic church in Chicago would be cause for celebration in writing the city's history, the men who had helped found it would not receive the same treatment. If anything, in fact, their departure was a victory proclaimed less than a decade after the treaty had been signed and ratified. That particular sentiment comes through in the words of Joseph Balestier, who declared in a speech before the Chicago Lyceum in January 1840, "The miserable race of men have been superseded by a population distinguished for its intelligence and enterprise." Balestier lauded all that Chicago had become in just a few years and the promise it already showed. In the process, he highlighted the people and the places that could no longer be seen and who no longer obstructed the vision that he and many others shared. In 1840, of course, his words could be applied not just to Chicago but also to the Great Lakes region as a whole.[62]

Yet even as the 1833 treaty proved to be a catalyst for this transition "from a first Chicago, set in an Indian country, to a new one soon firmly in the hands of American settlers," it also contained terms that facilitated an ongoing Potawatomi presence in the lower Great Lakes region. Most notably, Pokagon's band did not have to remove west of the Mississippi River. Instead, they successfully requested, "on account of their religious creed, permission to remove to the northern part of the peninsula of Michigan."[63] That provision was an amendment to the original treaty, and its importance went far beyond avoiding removal because that evasion reflected not only contemporary circumstances but also a specific approach taken over time by that Potawatomi community. Leopold Pokagon had welcomed Reverend Isaac McCoy and his civilization efforts in the 1820s, but he discarded the Baptist missionary when McCoy became a strong proponent of removal. The wkama then requested to have a Catholic priest come among his people, one who would rescue them from the "American minister [who] wished to draw [them] to his religion."[64] Yet religious affiliations did not alone define this community or their approach to the changing world around them. The coalescence and maintenance of Pokagon's band also originated out of an ongoing response to external pressures. This included their adaptation to the construction of the Michigan Road and their relationships with their non-Indian neighbors. Overall, the Pokagon band's strategy in the first half of the nineteenth century was an illustration of how, "depending on the quality of their relationship with state and local officials, entire Native communities managed to survive intact and unremoved."[65] For the Pokagon band, the 1833 treaty served as one more step on a long journey to secure their home in southern Michigan.

The Pokagon band's desire and ability to avoid removal had diverse specific origins, but were also more broadly based in a particular geographic location and an enduring willingness to adapt. Benjamin Secunda places Pokagon, and the St. Joseph River Valley Potawatomi villages, at the epicenter of the "adaptive resistance movement" that was grounded in Potawatomi autonomy at the village level, and he saw its initial fluorescence in the aftermath of the nativist movements of the early nineteenth century. Most important, though, is that the language of the 1833 treaty indicates not the power of religion, but instead the manner in which cooperation with the Catholic church represented one facet of that broader approach. Examination of archaeological evidence in northern Indiana and southern Michigan has been particularly effective in demonstrating this fact and has led scholars to suggest that "ideological and religious stances are most successful when coupled with effective economic strategies." The material evidence examined in various surveys reveals the ongoing effort at Pokagon's village to shift the foundation of the band's subsistence and economy to one reliant more on domesticated animals and agriculture than on traditional lifeways. Yet the adoption of such practices was not the only evidence of such an attitude.[66]

Also crucial to the Pokagon band's adaptive resistance was their willingness and desire not only to accommodate but also to welcome the changes brought by the Michigan Road. The state of Indiana wanted to connect Lake Michigan to the Ohio River, and the desire for a north-south road from the lake to Indianapolis sparked the inclusion of a targeted land cession in an 1826 treaty with the Potawatomis. It took the better part of eight years to secure the land and complete construction of the road, but during that time the Potawatomi villages closest to the new route, including Pokagon's village, had easier access to the people and goods that traveled along that path. Their response to the ongoing development of the region provided a cohesive identity to the Potawatomis in those villages who had chosen to adapt. This collective identity was evident in the conflict at the annuity payment of 1836, for though the documents speak about the hostile northern Indian villages or the Catholic Indians, the split among the Potawatomis might best be described as one centered on the villages oriented toward the Michigan Road.[67]

Therefore the language of the Chicago treaty that focused on religion misrepresented the crucial aspects of the Pokagon band's resistance. Similarly, religion did not provide the practical elements that allowed for their continued presence, either. Instead, the practical means to hold on to land came about in part through the terms of two different treaties. In an 1832 treaty signed at Tippecanoe, both Pokagon and his wife had each received one section of land in addition to the lands set aside for Pokagon's band as a whole. Then, in Schedule A of the 1833 Chicago accord, Pokagon received a total of $2,000 because the policy regarding reservations had changed. "In furtherance of the policy of the Government to remove these Indians West of the Mississippi," George Porter, one of the commissioners, later explained, "[We] refused to grant reservations of land, although they were greatly preferred, but agreed, in lieu thereof, that a part of the consideration money should be apportioned among such individuals, as the Indians chose to designate." That 1833 treaty payment, as well as money obtained from the sale of the sections of land from the 1832 treaty, enabled Pokagon to make a definitive purchase between 1836 and 1838. The Chicago accord permitted his band to avoid removal, but it also called for the Potawatomis to do so by joining their Odawa relatives at L'Arbre Croche in northern Michigan. Land cessions in an 1836 treaty with the Odawas in Michigan made such a move more difficult even as the pressure to leave their ceded lands near Niles, Michigan, increased. Instead of moving from one unstable position to another, Pokagon bought at least seven hundred acres of land in the Silver Creek township of Michigan, approximately thirty miles northwest of South Bend, Indiana. The title to the land was in Pokagon's name and was not recorded as an Indian reserve.[68]

The timing of the purchase was extremely important, as was the relationship Pokagon developed with the surrounding citizens. Pokagon's land in Silver Creek became a place of refuge during the terrifying years of the late 1830s. Having a title to the land was not enough, however, a fact that became clear when Brigadier General Hugh Brady sent armed men to force the Potawatomis west of the Mississippi River in the summer and fall of 1840. Knowing that the general would come calling and that he needed external assistance, Pokagon engaged the services of the state's legal system. More specifically, Pokagon explained his band's circumstances to Epaphroditus Ransom, who had been a circuit judge for the western part of the state and now served as an associate justice on the Michigan Supreme Court. The wkama wanted to obtain the judge's legal opinion "in reference to their emigration" so that the Potawatomis could properly address the forces arrayed against them. Ransom met approximately 150 Potawatomis near their village at Silver Creek, and because General Brady happened to be in the vicinity, he had the ability to talk to the judge about his decision. "The Judge informed me," General Brady reported, "that in the event of their applying to him, he should feel bound to relieve them by Habeus Corpus, from any forcible effort, made to emigrate them." As a result the general backed off and did not press the issue. The grounds for this legal opinion came largely through the land Pokagon had purchased, which according to what the register of the Kalamazoo land office told Brady, was somewhere in the neighborhood of 1,200–1,300 acres. At the time Brady listed only 106 individuals from thirteen families who would be staying behind on the purchased lands.[69]

The number of Potawatomis living on the lands purchased in the Silver Creek township fluctuated in the years that followed, as did the security of their status as landowners in the state. Throughout the 1840s the Pokagon band showed up briefly in the annual reports of the commissioner of Indian affairs. In 1847 acting superintendent of Indian affairs William Richmond reported from Detroit, "The Pottowatomies at Pokagon are under the care of the Catholic missionary and teachers and are generally sober and peaceful. With the exception of the prevalence of the small-pox during the last winter among a few of the bands, they have generally enjoyed good health, more especially when they have refrained from intoxicating drinks." One year later, little appeared to have changed. "Those of them at Pokagon village," Richmond observed, "are under the teachings of the Catholics, who have erected a church and school house, and have labored assiduously for their improvement in civilized manners and pursuits." Perhaps more important, in the years after Leopold Pokagon's death in 1841, the members of his family and band had to fight to maintain their land and had to petition Congress to receive the annuities owed through prior treaties.[70]

The experience of Pokagon's band demonstrates the tangled interests and outcomes of the 1833 Chicago treaty as well as the numerous intersections of economics, society, and politics in the lives of Potawatomis during the first four decades of the nineteenth century. At first glance it also appears to provide an instance of victory over the powerful forces that called for removal. The Pokagon band's struggles to hold on to their lands and protect their community in Michigan from the 1840s on, however, serve as a reminder that Judge Ransom's legal opinion did not guarantee anything. Decades passed before the Potawatomi community near Dowagiac had good reason to believe that they would not be forced west of the Mississippi River to join the thousands who had traveled there in the 1830s.

6

MICHIGAN ANISHINABEK
IN THE REMOVAL AGE

A very telling exchange occurred in Detroit on the morning of July 28, 1855. On one side was Commissioner of Indian Affairs George Manypenny. He was one of two treaty commissioners appointed to talk to delegations representing Odawa and Ojibwe bands in Michigan who had been party to a treaty signed in March 1836.[1] On the other side was Macaadupenase, a young Odawa man known more familiarly as Andrew Blackbird. Their discussion occurred on the third day of a larger council, and it made clear that the Indians and the American officials still had some work to do before coming to an agreement. A key and unsurprising point of contention was based on what some of the Indians had expected from this council and what Manypenny and his fellow commissioner Henry Gilbert had been authorized to offer. The commissioners had the responsibility of discovering what lands the different Odawa and Ojibwe bands wanted to reserve from sale so that they might select permanent homes within the boundaries of Michigan. From the American perspective, this was a time-sensitive issue, for as the non-Indian population of the state grew, the amount of available public lands decreased proportionately. But the pressure placed on the Indians to select land on a short timetable raised a host of questions. On that morning of July 28, Macaadupenase stated that he did not think the commissioners understood what the Anishinabek wanted, and he laid out his concerns regarding the offers made.[2]

The main issue revolved around the land. As Macaadupenase stated, "Our white brethren tell us that if we do not settle upon these lands at

once, you will take them back." This was something different from the
lands that the Indians had purchased from the government separately, for
they understood, "We can keep the land we buy, do what we please with
it, give it to our children or relations when we die." That was landholding the way the whites did it and, theoretically, the practice that whites
wanted the Indians to adopt. But what Macaadupenase now heard about
the plots to be selected under the auspices of a new treaty sounded different. "We are displeased that we cannot hold this land in the same way,"
he explained. "It seems as if you hold the land by a big string ready to
pull it from us." Manypenny quickly replied to what he saw as an obvious
misunderstanding. "Now this idea that the land will be pulled from under
you originates either in error, or in something I cannot comprehend," the
commissioner of Indian affairs declared. He sought to put the minds of
the gathered Odawas and Ojibwes to rest. "You shall have good strong
papers, so that your children may inherit your lands." With that statement
the morning session came to an end. Three days later those gathered in
Detroit signed a treaty that withdrew thousands of acres of public lands
from sale so that the Odawas and Ojibwes could select sites to call home.
Two days after that the same two commissioners signed a similar treaty
with the Saginaw Ojibwes of Michigan.[3]

Manypenny's response to Macaadupenase's concerns on the morning
of July 28 says a great deal about the American government's perspective. Most revealing is the commissioner's admission that the origin of the
Indians' anxiety was possibly something that he could not comprehend.
The Americans either refused or were unable to understand the fears faced
by hundreds of Odawa and Ojibwe families during the first half of the
nineteenth century. Indeed, for the bands represented at that council in
Detroit along with the Saginaw Ojibwes, the two treaties signed within
days of each other in the summer of 1855 had very important and clear
meanings. These treaties represented the hope of eliminating decades of
uncertainty and nearly two decades of removal threats that had always
loomed overhead. One of the Sault Ste. Marie Ojibwe headmen, Shawanah, explained that he and his people had approached the treaty council
fearfully, unsure of what its clouds might bring. "Now we find that it is
not full of storms; but only casts a pleasant shade," he said. "We are satisfied with what is done." While neither the accord that Shawanah signed
nor the one signed by the Saginaws would ever provide the pleasant shade
anticipated, the treaties initially appeared to resolve many of the concerns

that had exacerbated the Indians' struggles to remain in Michigan in the mid-nineteenth century.[4]

The sentiments expressed by Macaadupenase in his exchange with Manypenny have not been lost in the passage of time. In *Diba Jimooyung, Telling Our Story: A History of the Saginaw Ojibwe Anishinabek*, the Saginaws assert, ["The darkest days our Anishinabe ancestors ever faced were those between 1837 and 1855."] The book's discussion of the early nineteenth century provides particular insights into the decades-long pressures placed on the Saginaw Ojibwes' ancestors and their lands by government agents and private citizens.[5] In contrast to the experiences of so many other Indian tribes in the Great Lakes region, the Saginaws were not forced to leave their homes for new lands west of the Mississippi River. Instead, just as the federal government had seemingly arranged their removal with a series of treaties ratified in the summer of 1838, the nationwide economic downturn that had begun in 1837 altered the trajectory of Indian affairs in Michigan. The subsequent decreased demand for land, caused largely by the drastic decline in available credit and bank failures, resulted in a similar decrease in the demands for the removal of the Saginaw Ojibwes and their Indian neighbors at both the local and national levels.[6] Yet this turn of events and the evasion of removal did not lead to security. The removal treaties and their terms did not disappear, and their existence created a tremendous amount of anxiety and uncertainty. For nearly two decades the Saginaws, like their Odawa and Ojibwe neighbors throughout the Lower Peninsula especially, lived under dark clouds reminding them that removal always remained a possibility.

The statement made in *Diba Jimooyung* therefore cautions anyone making historical assessments of American Indian removal in general. The evasion of a forced relocation west of the Mississippi did not necessarily equal success or peace of mind. It did not indicate that the struggle had ended. This truth was very apparent in the experiences of the numerous Anishinabe bands that called the Lower Peninsula of Michigan home. The history of Indian removal—or the history of attempts to remove Indians—in Michigan is interwoven with specific elements of geography and chronology. Michigan's location undoubtedly influenced the manner in which national trends shaped Indian affairs in the region, especially from the 1830s to the 1850s. Just as important, the timing of key national events such as economic busts, presidential elections, and rapid advances in western expansion all affected the abilities of the Saginaws and others

[handwritten margin note: Panic of 1837's impact]

to maintain a presence in the state. The local context mattered in Michigan, but at times it seemed that the national context mattered even more. As a result, the territory that served as a home for Lewis Cass, one of the strongest supporters of Indian removal from the 1820s through the 1830s, became a state in which many Indian tribes found it possible to avoid the deportations suffered by so many of their Native neighbors.

Yet the actions these Anishinabek took in response to the changing world around them also laid crucial foundations for the remainder of the nineteenth century and beyond. As long as Indian tribes and bands wanted to remain a coherent community in a place they could call home, their struggles with local, state, and national interests would never cease. Successful resistance to removal was thus also very much about Anishinabe determination and action. It never meant that the battle was over, but simply that the Anishinabek had to continue to find ways to hold on to land and avoid removal until attitudes changed around them. Their strategies incorporated a wide network of economic, political, and social relationships that intersected with events and people outside of their own communities. As a result, the Anishinabek were very much a factor, not an abstract presence, in the state and its early development.[7] This chapter, then, is not simply about what enabled the Anishinabek in Michigan to avoid removal, but instead it is about what happened once they had weathered the first storm. As the experience of Odawas and Ojibwes makes clear, the desire for Indian lands endured well beyond the 1830s. The dark clouds were never absent from the skies above the Lower Peninsula of Michigan, and the fear and uncertainty of the mid-1800s thus laid a foundation for the struggles of the decades and centuries that followed. Removal had been avoided, but the Anishinabek of Michigan still had to protect their sovereignty and cultural cohesiveness.

This story begins with the treaty negotiations that occurred over the course of two years beginning in March 1836. By July 1838 the United States government had used a series of accords to gain land cessions from the majority of Odawa and Ojibwe bands residing in the Lower Peninsula of Michigan and established a loose framework for their removal from the state. These treaties were signed at a point in time when federal and state officials were already comfortable with the use of force to dispossess and relocate Potawatomis from northern Illinois and Indiana. Each accord included the general phrasing that appeared in the March 1836 treaty with the Odawas and Ojibwes: "As soon as the said Indians desire it, a deputation shall be sent to the southwest of the Missouri River, there to select a suitable place for the final settlement of said Indians." As for the section of land selected by that exploratory delegation, "the United States [would] forever guaranty and secure to said Indians" that portion of the western territory. Yet while this statement put into place the legal foundations for removals intended to echo those of the Cherokees, Choctaws, Potawatomis, and others, the Michigan experience did not follow suit. There would not be a Trail of Tears or Trail of Death for the Odawas and Ojibwes. With the exception of the fifty-one Swan Creek and Black River Ojibwes who removed in 1839 and those who made new homes on Canadian soil, these Anishinabek would remain residents of Michigan.[8]

Scholar Theodore J. Karaminski asserts that the Treaty of Washington, signed by the Odawas and Ojibwes in March 1836, "was the most important agreement the Indian peoples of western and northern Michigan ever made with the United States." That distinction comes from the fact that it "both set the stage for their potential removal from Michigan and at the same time was the basis for their eventual persistence in the state." James M. McClurken refers to the treaty in somewhat different terms. "Instead of a firm commitment ending the removal threat," he writes, "they received only legislative ambivalence." Similar assessments could be made for the treaties signed by the Swan Creek and Black River Ojibwes and the Saginaw Ojibwes around the same time. It is true that the very accords that were initially intended to clear Michigan lands for American settlers failed to do so, and even as those treaties provided a foundation for the Indians' "eventual persistence," that eventuality was a long time coming. In every case it would take at least one more treaty to move forward on that timeline.[9]

The push for land cessions in the Lower Peninsula of Michigan during the late 1830s came primarily from two interconnected developments—the growing population of the region and the drive for statehood. In the federal census of 1830 the population of Michigan Territory was 31,639, but the territorial boundaries extended as far west as the Mississippi River, and the northern boundary cut through Lake Superior. Four years later the population within the Lower Peninsula alone registered 85,856. The non-Indian population of Michigan Territory had been rising at small increments for years, largely because of the difficulty of reaching the region. The construction of the Erie Canal and the rise of steamboat traffic on

Lake Erie altered that reality, as did the rising financial prosperity of easterners who saw great possibilities in the real estate north of Ohio and Indiana. Yet the population explosion that occurred between 1830 and 1834 ultimately had one major catalyst: the financial world of credit created by Andrew Jackson's war on the U.S. Bank. By vetoing the renewal of the U.S. Bank's charter and removing federal government deposits from that institution, Jackson altered the financial landscape of the nation. Most relevant to this discussion, the elimination of the U.S. Bank encouraged the formation of state banks through which loans and credit flowed freely in the mid-1830s. In Michigan alone, nearly forty-nine banks were organized beginning in 1837. Paper money flooded the market at a rate that far outpaced the hard currency available.[10]

This widespread availability of credit, along with a series of general preemption acts passed by Congress in the early 1830s, fueled a land rush that made Michigan Territory "the scene of the greatest speculation" in the Old Northwest. Wealthy easterners in particular "saw in the public lands in Michigan and elsewhere in the West a profitable form of investment for surplus capital." Even with all the long-distance speculation, however, the number of actual residents also dramatically increased, and by 1835 that population had already adopted a constitution and formed a state government. Statehood would not come until 1837, a delay that occurred almost exclusively because of the boundary dispute with Ohio over what was known as the Toledo Strip. In the mid-1830s, then, Michigan was at the heart of a booming national economy built on an extraordinary amount of land speculation. It was only natural that there was an increase in demands to extinguish Indian land ownership in order to open up more lands for sale. Such regional developments provided a critical context for the treaties signed between 1836 and 1838 with the Odawa and Ojibwe bands of Michigan.[11]

The mindset of the Anishinabe bands in Michigan during the late 1830s reflected a different set of circumstances. Simultaneous, and undoubtedly connected, to the influx of non-Indians into the region, the Odawas living along the Grand River suffered a smallpox epidemic in the fall of 1835. Although no records indicate the mortality rate, entire villages were abandoned as men, women, and children sought to escape the deadly outbreak. The winter of 1835–1836 had also brought exceedingly harsh weather conditions that devastated the wild game populations of the Lower Peninsula, the deer in particular. Heading into the spring of 1836,

smallpox & poor hunting seasons

then, these conditions, along with an ongoing need for cash to pay off trade debts, seemingly made the possibility of land cessions more likely. Despite these circumstances, there were differences of opinion regarding the proper approach to the American influx. In December 1835 Secretary of War Lewis Cass authorized Henry Schoolcraft to hold a council with the Odawa and Ojibwe bands living on lands from the Grand River to Sault Ste. Marie. The Indians from that vast amount of territory did not agree on the proper response to the government's proposals. With some exceptions, the southern Odawas along the Grand River did not want to sell, but the Odawas and Ojibwes living on the Upper Peninsula were more inclined to consent to land cessions.[12]

For the Saginaw Ojibwes the treaty negotiations in 1837 occurred under similarly stressful conditions. Smallpox ravaged their villages in the summer of that year. A man named Peyton Morgan called for immediate relief for the Indians, reporting, "There are scarcely well ones enough to take care of the sick & starving—some eight or ten died in the neighbour-hood of Green Point while they were petitioning the White People for relief." Morgan painted a dire picture of the circumstances among the Saginaws. "They fled panic stricken to their Reservations," he wrote, "where I understand they are dying daily. Whole families have been carried off within a few days of each other." One year later Schoolcraft reported that the death toll from smallpox reached 354, including 106 men, 107 women, and 141 children. The remaining Saginaw popula-tion was just under one thousand, which meant that when Schoolcraft sought land cessions from the Saginaws, they were in the midst of an epi-demic that ultimately claimed the lives of more than 25 percent of their population.[13]

This demographic disaster led some Saginaws to leave Michigan, not for the territories west of the Mississippi River, but for northern climes. In the summer of 1838 at least two hundred Saginaws contacted their subagent and "registered their names for emigration to upper Canada." Schoolcraft expressed some concerns about the creation of a sizeable Indian colony on the Canadian side of the northern border. A portion of the Swan Creek and Black River Ojibwes also opted for a Canadian relocation over a west-ern one, though their destination was a mission run by Wesleyans near Port Sarnia. Overall, it was a situation that Schoolcraft wanted the federal government to monitor closely, especially because of the historical con-nections between many of these Indians and the British. "All the tribes and bands who were actors in the disastrous scenes of 1812–'14 are still there," Schoolcraft was quick to note.[14]

Of all the treaties negotiated during that period of time, the one signed by the Swan Creek and Black River Ojibwes involved both the smallest population and the smallest cession of land. As it so happened, it also led to the only actual removal from Michigan. The Swan Creek and Black River Ojibwes lived on four different reservations established by a treaty signed at Detroit in 1807. These reservations encompassed little more than eight thousand total acres, but many, especially those who coveted the white pine trees that covered the landscape, deemed that land to be extremely valuable. As a result, the relatively small population of three hundred or so Indians felt a great deal of pressure to cede these reservations and remove. At the forefront of the ensuing negotiations was a man known as Eshtono-quot (also called Frances Macoonse). He became the spokesman for the Swan Creek and Black River bands seeking relocation.[15]

Two years before the treaty Eshtonoquot and other headmen sent word to the federal government that they wanted to exchange their lands in Michigan for a new home elsewhere. Commissioner of Indian Affairs Elbert Herring had responded cautiously, saying that only Congress had the power to grant their request, and they would do it "if good reason be shown for such a measure." Herring kept the lines of communication open but did not make any promises. In the spring of 1836, however, a delegation of four Ojibwe headmen, including Eshtonoquot, negotiated and signed a treaty in Washington. With this accord they surrendered all 8,320 acres of land contained in their four reservations and accepted an equal amount of land to be selected either "west of the Mississippi or northwest of St. Anthony's Falls." Four months later a delegation from the Swan Creek and Black River bands explored territories west of the Mississippi River. Because of government pressure the Ojibwes first explored lands along the Osage River under the guidance of Reverend Isaac McCoy. McCoy, now living in Westport, Missouri, on the border with Indian Territory, continued to support removal by assisting in the location of removed Indians in the western lands.[16]

Yet nothing about removal would be straightforward. When the delegation returned to Michigan, Eshtonoquot expressed general unhappiness with what they had seen. "The principal objection to the lands that they have examined seems to be the scarcity of timber and consequently of game," reported their conductor, Albert Smith, who took issue with their assessment. Eshtonoquot seemed "anxious to see the Lands near the falls of St. Anthony on the St. Peters which he seem[ed] to think [were] promised to him." Smith's phrasing foreshadowed the changing government attitude toward the notion of relocation to the northern territories. According to Commissioner of Indian Affairs T. Hartley Crawford, "No location could be found for them northwest of the Falls of St. Anthony, in which they would not be exposed to collisions with the Sioux." Federal officials had unofficially decreed that the only option for removal would be to the territories just west of the Missouri border. Yet the 1836 treaty had not specified the particulars for removal, which meant that it was still necessary for the federal government to arrange for such simple but critical details as funding the relocation. These arrangements became exceedingly important by early 1839 because the ceded lands had sold: "The purchasers were entitled to the possession, and a compliance with their reasonable expectation would leave the Indians homeless." Because the land sales and white encroachment had already disrupted the Swan Creek and Black River communities, a number of these Ojibwes had crossed the border into Canada by the spring of 1839.[17]

Two years after the treaty had been signed, and even as it looked like the federal government had come to terms with the Indians regarding their removal to a reservation on the Osage River in eastern Kansas, the small community of Swan Creek and Black River Ojibwes was scattered. Albert Smith, the same man who had led the exploratory expedition two years earlier, was appointed as the official conductor for the removal, which as of September 1839 had not yet happened. He gathered those interested in removal at an encampment near Swan Creek, but the Ojibwes refused to leave until they received their annuity payments for 1839. On September 13 they were still waiting. "I regret to state," Smith wrote, "that the party have become dissatisfied by this long delay and are leaving us occasionally." This dissatisfaction caused more Indians to travel to Canada. Consequently Smith informed his superiors, "The whole number at present upon which I can rely for the trip amount to sixty persons." Those sixty, led by Eshtonoquot, negotiated an additional compact designating that the Swan Creek and Black River annuities would only be paid to those who relocated to the Indian Territory and that the annuity distribution would only occur in that western location. Following a trip that occurred primarily via steamboats, fifty-one members of those bands arrived at their new home on the Osage River at the end of October. This small group struggled to obtain the necessary supplies to survive their first winter and complained that the government did not live up to its side of the bargain. Through their relocation Eshtonoquot and the fifty Ojibwes had taken a different path than their relatives, and their struggles would be different than those occurring in Michigan.[18]

A chief concern of federal officials, however, was what happened to those who stayed behind. According to government estimates at the end of 1841, nearly two hundred Swan Creek and Black River Ojibwes remained east of the Mississippi. Approximately 108 lived near the Black River while an equal number had crossed the St. Clair River into Canada and joined a colony of British Methodists. "A few of those who have remained on our side have bought farms and are determined to become citizens," acting superintendent of Indian affairs Robert Stuart reported. "The residue wander about, doing little good, and must ere long be removed somewhere." These two categories of Indians had Stuart considering two different solutions. One solution built on what he considered to be a growing sentiment about Indians in Michigan. "Petitions to the State Legislature are, I understand, in a course of preparation," he wrote, "claiming for such as procure farms the right of citizenship, and deprecating any effort to have them at present removed, as many are making rapid progress toward civilization, &c." But for those Indians who had not shown similar signs of "progress," Stuart asserted that the federal government would "have to extend its bountiful aid to them ere long, else many of them must perish."[19]

In the six years since they had signed the treaty arranging for the cession of their reservations in 1836, the Swan Creek and Black River Ojibwes had separated into at least three different communities. There were those who had removed to Indian Territory under the terms of the treaty and those who had moved to Canada. The third community, encompassing approximately one hundred individuals, had purchased land from the United States government and lived together in the vicinity of Fort Gratiot and the Black River in eastern Michigan. Robert Stuart wrote, "They have attached themselves to the Methodist mission, and most of them have become industrious, temperate, and apparently truly religious." Yet even those living among the Methodists had several complaints, most notably about the fulfillment of the terms of their treaty.[20]

Consistent talk of treaty councils and land cessions in the 1830s forced other Michigan Anishinabe communities to respond to federal and state pressure as well. Toward the end of January 1836 the Odawa headmen of the Grand River bands worked with Reverend Leonard Slater, the Baptist missionary who had been stationed at the Thomas Mission at Grand Rapids since the spring of 1828, to compose a letter to President Andrew Jackson. In unambiguous terms they rejected the idea of a treaty: "We hear that you would make a treaty for our land. We refuse to go, it is too hard for us. We tried to remain on our land here and not sell it. . . . When we die we expect our bodies to rest on this land." The representatives for the eight Odawa villages in the region also rejected the basic arguments put forth, favoring removal. "We have not a mind to remove to a distant land our children would suffer," they explained. "You say we shall see prosperity and be in health if we remove. We have knowledge of the country you offer us, our eyes have seen it, and our feet have trode on it." Neither a proposed treaty nor the notion of removal had the support of the Odawas. This was not a newly declared position. Rather it repeated and affirmed a sentiment of long standing among the Odawa leaders in northern Michigan. Nearly two years earlier the Odawas had held a council at Grand Rapids that included the bands from Grand River and L'Arbre Croche. Over the course of ceremonies and discussions held during a single day, the representatives of these Odawa bands had resolved to never cede and never leave their lands.[21]

Yet two months later, in the city of Washington, six Odawas from the Grand River villages were among those who put their marks on a treaty that surrendered all of their territory and created reservations that the Indians could live on for only five more years. The treaty illustrated well the effective strategies of the federal government. First, the treaty discussions were held in Washington, an approach that forced Native leaders to negotiate on unfamiliar ground and away from their people. Second, American officials manipulated the circumstances. Indeed, as a close examination of the situation reveals, the participation of the Grand River Odawas was at odds with the true intentions and desires of their leadership. The statement drafted by the Grand River Odawas in January 1836 spoke to the fact that they had heard about the efforts to negotiate a treaty. However, they had also learned that a delegation of L'Arbre Croche Odawas intended to travel to Washington to negotiate. Rather than risk the possibility of those Odawas signing away all of their land, the Grand River leadership took action. In an effort to have a voice in the council and prevent the possibility of a land cession, they did not send a delegation of prominent headmen. Instead, "they selected for all the members of the

Reps. were not chiefs

delegation, excepting one, such men as were not chiefs, and who consequently were incompetent to treat." This delegation, comprised of Wabi Windego, Megiss Ininee, Nabun Ageezhig, Winnimissagee, Mukutaysee, and Wasaw Bequm, as their names were recorded on the treaty, carried with them the statement drawn up by their leaders. Leonard Slater accompanied the Odawas to Washington because the Grand River headmen back in Michigan believed the missionary would protect their interests.[22]

Despite all the safeguards put into place by the Grand River Odawas, the terms of the treaty signed in March 1836 ceded their territory and initiated procedures for removal. The route to that conclusion was crooked and implicated numerous parties. All told, twenty-four different Odawa and Ojibwe delegates assembled at the Masonic Hall in Washington to discuss potential land cessions. Such negotiations were not a new experience for all involved, which meant in part that each individual came to the meeting with particular expectations. Commissioner Henry Schoolcraft, for example, felt confident that the Ojibwes from Sault Ste. Marie would favor proposed cessions, a confidence built on the fact that the leader of that delegation, Waishkee, was his wife's uncle. Marriage relations similarly influenced the stance presented by the Grand River Odawa delegation over the course of the negotiations. A trader present in the Masonic Hall named Rix Robinson was married to a woman named Sebequay, who was the sister of Nabunageezhick, one of the Grand River representatives. *marriage influencing negotiations* Although anything Robinson did occurred off the record, he was most likely one of the parties who shaped the final consent of the Grand River delegation to a treaty. The majority of such intrigue occurred during the days when the council was not officially in session and the secretary was not recording conversations. Schoolcraft opened the council on March 15 by summarizing the manner in which both Odawas and Ojibwes had proposed land cessions to the government in the previous years. He now intended to give the delegates time to discuss the matter, and an Ojibwe spokesman named Ogemagigido stated that they would need three days.[23]

When the council resumed on Friday, March 18, a young Odawa man from L'Arbre Croche named Augustus Hamlin informed those assembled about what had occurred during the recess. Outside parties had influence over the wkamek who had opened the council on March 18, he declared. The words coming out of their mouths were not theirs, he said, "but the words of white man who wanted reservations" and who "dictated to them what to say." Hamlin did not call out any individuals by name, but asserted that the Indians "were constantly beset by individuals and disturbed in their private councils." These men advised the Indians to keep saying no until they could get as much money as possible. Hamlin was confident that the Indians wanted "to dispose of their lands and derive present benefit." Whether or not Hamlin's speech was the tipping point is arguable, but after another recess of several days, the Indians returned to the council and expressed a willingness to sell their lands. Megis Ininne from Grand River gave his consent, "provided his great Father would give them reservations as would benefit them and their children." He also wanted Rix Robinson to review the treaty to make sure it was properly written. As of March 28, then, Schoolcraft managed to obtain the consent of representatives from not only Grand River and L'Arbre Croche, but also from Odawa and Ojibwe delegates from Sault Ste. Marie, Michilimackinac, Maskigo, and Grand Traverse. The Anishinabek in attendance appeared content with a treaty that created reservations, provided sizeable cash distributions, and did not call for removal. All Reverend Isaac McCoy could say about the final agreement was, ["To my extreme grief and mortification, the treaty was concluded and signed by the very delegation that was sent to Washington to *prevent* it."[24]]

Although that statement might initially make it seem that McCoy was unhappy with the way in which Schoolcraft had managed to undermine the efforts of the Grand River Odawas, such was not the case. By 1836 the Baptist missionary was a passionate and notable advocate for removal, and he was mortified that the agreement indicated that the Indians could remain in Michigan on small reserves. On this point he was at odds with his colleague, Leonard Slater, who as McCoy noted, "had never concurred with" him in the idea of "securing to the Indians a permanent home in the West." The terms of the treaty gave Slater the ability to serve the Grand River Odawas according to his own determination. The ninth article contained provisions for payments to mixed-descent members of the Odawa and Ojibwe communities on the Grand River and named Slater as the trustee for what would amount to be a payment of $6,400 to Chiminoquat. The Baptist missionary took that money and purchased land on which approximately 140 Odawas then settled. He fully intended for those who belonged to his mission community to have a permanent home in Michigan. Such efforts were critical because the treaty as signed by the Odawas in March did not contain the same language as the treaty that was finally ratified. The U.S. Senate altered the terms by which the

Odawas and Ojibwes could remain on the Michigan lands. Simply put, the reservations created from the ceded lands would not be permanent. Instead, the Indians could only remain on them for a period of five years following treaty ratification. McCoy acted in response to what he viewed as untenable treaty terms and lobbied the secretary of war as well as members of the Committee on Indian Affairs. According to Schoolcraft, the senators, and especially Hugh White, the chairman of the Committee on Indian Affairs, may have also taken the opportunity to decrease the potential patronage power of the Jacksonian Democrats. No more Indian reservations in Michigan meant no more appointments for agents, blacksmiths, farmers, and the like. In this particular case, it also meant the Odawas and Ojibwes had the right to live on the reservations designated in the treaty only until May of 1841. Thus, through McCoy's efforts and some backroom political deals, the treaty of 1836 with the Odawas and Ojibwes supported, rather than opposed, the push for removal that was occurring throughout the eastern half of the continent.[25]

The treaty negotiations with the Saginaw Ojibwes illustrate the same trends, though it took a total of three different treaties to establish the final terms. The first step in these negotiations occurred in May 1836 when a delegation of Saginaws arrived in Washington. Among other points, Secretary of War Lewis Cass advised Schoolcraft to "take care that a sufficient fund [was] reserved to provide for their removal." Yet following his negotiations with the Saginaws, Schoolcraft once again had a treaty that found disfavor in the Senate. The statement on record stated, "The Senate do *not* advise and consent to the ratification of the Treaty between the United States and the Saganaw Bands of Chippewa Indians," concluded on May 24. Months later, Commissioner of Indian Affairs Carey Harris did not have any explanations for the failure of the treaty to pass muster. "I have no certain information of the causes of the rejection by the Senate of the treaty made by you with these Indians the last winter," the commissioner wrote to Schoolcraft, "but presume, as you were here, you are sufficiently aware of them to enable you to avoid the objectionable stipulations."[26]

A comparison of the unratified treaty and the agreement finally made in January 1837 provides some possible reasons for that initial rejection. The opposition could not have come from the types of arguments that McCoy raised against the treaty that the Odawas and Ojibwes had signed in March 1836. Schoolcraft had learned his lesson and given the Saginaws only three years on their reserves before they had to leave. Both the unratified and ratified documents contained specific descriptions of removal, so the Senate could not have strenuously objected to any measure in that regard, either. However, the May treaty did provide more substantial support for the continued employment of blacksmiths and farmers to assist the Indians during their remaining time in Michigan, while the final version asserted simply, "The President is authorized to direct the discontinuance of the stated farmers should he deem proper." Schoolcraft once again blamed Hugh White's attack on Jacksonian patronage. More than the support of farmers, however, the specific financial elements of the accords may have been the primary source of opposition. Schoolcraft's treaty of May 1836 established in writing that $100,000 from the sale of the 102,400 ceded acres would be invested in state stock for the benefit of the Saginaw Ojibwes. The treaty negotiated in Detroit in January 1837 did not make a specific commitment beyond stating, "After deducting therefrom the sums hereinafter set apart, for specified objects, together with all other sums, justly chargeable to this fund, the balance shall be invested, under the direction of the President, in some public stock, and the interest thereof shall be annually paid to the said tribe." Specific monies were set aside for other expenses, including goods, provisions, and support for schools.[27]

While the revised treaty was initially signed in January 1837, it was not officially proclaimed until July 2, 1838, and its ratification was announced in conjunction with two additional treaties with the Saginaws, signed in December 1837 and January 1838, respectively. The fact was that despite all of the efforts made by Schoolcraft, the treaty signed in January 1837 had still faced an uphill battle in the Senate. One sticking point came in the sixth article, which stated that the federal government would acquire "a location for them at such place, west of the Mississippi, and southwest of the Missouri, as the legislation of Congress may indicate." The treaty never made it out of the Committee on Indian Affairs because of that vague language. The phrasing of the sixth article could also be interpreted, as Commissioner Harris observed, "to bind the United States to give them this land, which, being in addition to the entire nett proceeds would amount to a two fold payment for the lands ceded." When Harris wrote to Schoolcraft in the fall of 1837, the time seemed right to approach the Saginaws once more to correct the latest criticism. A delegation had visited the lands just west of the Missouri border to see what lands were available for their relocation. Isaac McCoy had shown them sites along the

Proclamation of 1836 treaty

headwaters of the Osage River, and reports indicated that the Ojibwes were pleased with what they saw.[28]

Schoolcraft successfully negotiated yet another treaty with the Saginaws, this time meeting with a delegation along the Flint River in Michigan. As he reported to his superiors in Washington, he had responded to the Senate's wishes. "All the objections to the former treaty have, I believe, been obviated," Schoolcraft noted, "but this has not been effected without encountering the usual obstacles to negociations with a people who are prone to take advice of interested individuals." One of the biggest problems had been that, following the return of the exploratory party, the Saginaws had become less favorable toward the idea of removal. Schoolcraft, however, had managed to persuade them of the advantages of securing western territory while the federal government still had the ability to do so. Reluctantly, then, the Saginaws consented to a treaty in December 1837 that provided a new home on the Osage River and prohibited any relocation to territory immediately west of Lake Superior.[29]

One more issue remained, and it revolved around the ceded lands and the money to be obtained from their sale. The sixth article of the December 1837 accord prohibited the practice of preemption on the lands ceded by the Saginaws. Schoolcraft deemed this a critical statement because preemption "would materially diminish their fund, and prove a boon, not from the government, but from the Indians, which the latter never designed." This protection of Saginaw interests was furthered by the negotiation of the third and final compact that made up the triple-treaty package finally ratified by the Senate in the summer of 1838. This time the negotiations occurred at the behest of the Saginaws, who were rightfully anxious about the possible ways in which they could lose money during the public sales of the ceded lands. The Saginaw leadership was particularly alarmed with the manner in which buyer collusion might keep the prices down during the course of the sales. Schoolcraft admitted they had a just concern, and therefore the agreement signed in January 1838 established a system intended to address that very issue. For the first two years of the sale, the minimum price would be set at five dollars per acre. After two years had passed, the minimum price would decrease to $2.50 until the five-year term for the Saginaws had expired. Five years after the ratification of the treaty, any unsold lands would then sell at no less than seventy-five cents per acre. Schoolcraft had consulted with the General Land Office for an assessment of the land's value and had been

informed that the acreage could sell at eight dollars per acre. The opening value of five dollars was therefore "deemed to be moderate as the
minimum price."[30]

Yet in the years that followed, the problem that arose was one that
neither the Saginaws nor the federal government had anticipated. The
land did not sell. [Schoolcraft noted in his annual report of 1839, "[The]
survey of the ceded lands in Michigan is now in the process of execution,
and it is probable that they will be put in market in all the year 1840." As
1840 drew to a close, however, no money from land sales was available.]
The Saginaw treaties had fallen victim to the economic downturn whose
effects had now reached Michigan. As of the spring of 1841 the ceded
lands had not even been fully surveyed or brought onto market. Schoolcraft recognized that it was fortunate that the lands had not been put up
for sale at a time when prices were falling. He also happily pointed out that
the minimum prices set by the January 1838 treaty ensured a "handsome
surplus" once the lands went on the market. Nevertheless, the delayed
sales also complicated matters because of the very terms set by that January 1838 accord. The first land sales began under presidential declaration
on September 6, 1841, more than three years after the ratification of the
treaty. This meant that if the treaties were followed to the letter, the five-
dollar minimum price had officially expired before the lands even went up
for sale, and the rock-bottom seventy-five-cent price would kick in starting September 1843. The economic downturn therefore had the potential
to immediately undermine the terms put in place to protect the economic
interests of the Saginaws. John Moore, the acting commissioner for the
General Land Office in Detroit, asked for advice about how to handle this
unforeseen problem.[31]

These developments did not occur without the knowledge of the Saginaw Ojibwes, and unsurprisingly, they responded strongly to the possibility that the seventy-five-cent-per-acre price would commence as early as
the summer of 1843. The situation was problematic in every aspect. "This
would not only be ruinous to us," the letter signed by twenty-one different headmen explained, "but it would prevent the United states receiving
back the heavy advances already made to us." The blame for this situation
fell heavily on the failures related to the enactment of the three different Saginaw accords. More specifically, the delayed survey of the ceded
lands and the subsequent delay in opening up the sales meant that a "great
injustice ha[d] been done to [their] interest by the Government." The

consequences of the federal government's failings were clear. "Had due diligence been exercised in this respect," the chiefs continued, "ample proof can be adduced that our lands might all have been sold at more than an average of $5 per acre; whereas they will hardly sell now at any price." The Saginaw leadership wrote to President John Tyler to request his support for a postponement in the public sales of the lands ceded in their treaties. Based on Michigan's current economy, the Saginaws believed that a delay of several years would be necessary before prices might stabilize enough to do justice to all interested parties, their people in particular. Commissioner of Indian Affairs T. Hartley Crawford shared their belief, arguing forcefully, "[The] interests of the Indians and the United States demand a postponement of the sale, and I respectfully suggest that measure be immediately adopted to prevent those interests from being sacrificed." Crawford sent his letter in the summer of 1843, fully intending to halt any movement toward instituting the seventy-five-cent price point.[32]

The Tyler administration did not take immediate action on these requests, however, and the land sales coming out of the three Saginaw treaties continued to flounder. James Piper, the acting commissioner for the General Land Office, reported in early 1847, "The aggregate quantity of land sold within the cession of the Chippewas of Saginaw, in Michigan, to the 31st of December last appears to be Five thousand Six hundred and ten acres and ninety seven hundredths." In short, fewer than 6,000 acres of land had been sold out of the 102,000 acres ceded nearly ten years earlier. Yet it was not just about the number of acres, it was also about the financial consequences of such dismal sales. According to Piper, the lands had sold for a total of $18,405.78. Piper did not go into further detail, but that amounted to an average price of $3.28 per acre.[33]

Finally, in the spring of 1848 Congress passed a bill targeting the Saginaw lands. Senate Bill 197 was titled, "To provide for the sale of lands purchased by the United States from the Saginaw tribe of Chippewa Indians, in the State of Michigan." The legislation declared that any of the land ceded by the treaty of January 14, 1837, and remaining unsold should "be offered for sale and sold as other public lands at the land offices of the proper districts as soon as practicable." To protect the interests of the Saginaw Ojibwes, Congress assured the Indians that the act should "not be construed so as to deprive said Indians of any surplus of the proceeds of said lands, if any should exist, after reimbursing the United States" for expenditures and advances made over the previous decade. Perhaps the land issue would finally be resolved.[34]

Indian and non-Indian residents of Michigan simultaneously tackled the issue on the state and local levels. The Saginaw Ojibwe petition sent to President Tyler in 1842 made up only one part of their strategy. As of November of that same year they had also purchased somewhere between 1,200 and 1,500 acres of land through the General Land Office and had expressed a desire to participate in Michigan society as farmers and citizens. Within two years the government agents stationed in Michigan viewed the Saginaw position as a reflection of the shifting government policy. "Each band have more or less land which they have purchased," reported Andrew McReynolds, the subagent for the Saginaw Agency, "and which they in part cultivate. And here let me observe, that their purchases are chiefly Government lands, and in the remote parts of the country, so well suited to their habits, and yet so objectionable to the white settlers." In Michigan, at least, by the mid-1840s the driving push for removal had begun to fade. As long as the Indians remained on lands that the white citizens did not desire, then it appeared that their presence would be tolerated, if not welcomed. This became very evident when federal officials raised the possibility of relocating the Saginaw subagency. McReynolds did not think it was a good idea, in part because he and other white residents agreed, "The Town of Saginaw has been sustained by and lives upon, but little else than Indian business for the last twenty years." According to McReynolds, the white population of the region was still just below nine hundred souls, and the scattered settlements of the ten different bands of Saginaws did not represent an imposition on the countryside or the potential prosperity of its non-Indian inhabitants.[35]

The land purchases made by the Saginaws were not unique. Starting in the mid-1830s such purchases had become a tried-and-true strategy used by Anishinabe communities throughout Michigan. The manner in which those purchases occurred differed according to the circumstances, however. The general approach was for the Indians to use money from their annuities, a strategy that partially explains why wkamek sought to have annuities paid out in cash rather than goods. Joseph Wakazoo, an Odawa wkama from Allegan County, first sent a petition to Congress in the spring of 1836 asking for permission to purchase land in Michigan Territory. The petition came in the month after the 1836 Treaty of Washington. Wakazoo was clearly interested in holding on to land on the Lower Peninsula in the aftermath of that accord, but the actual purchase took time and involved a number of outside parties. During the course of his efforts, Wakazoo received assistance from the Western Michigan Society to Benefit the Indians, an organization established in 1837 that espoused the civilizing mission of previous decades more than it did the removal policy of the 1830s. With the support of this organization, as well as a successful appeal to Congregationalist missionary George Smith, Wakazoo and the other leading men of his band finally completed the purchase of 1,200 acres on the Black River in the spring of 1839. Similarly, two other Odawa wka-mek, Muckatosha and Megisinini, spent nearly $1,200 to purchase enough land to support the subsistence needs of their people. The big difference for them was that the mediator of their purchase was Richard Godfroy, a local trader who held the official title to the lands purchased. Therefore, though the seventy-eight members of Muckatosha's and Megisinini's bands had a measure of security, their residence was dependent on Godfroy and his fidelity to the Indians' interests.[36]

Because these lands were not reserves made by treaty but instead private property held by official deed, this ownership had an impact on Odawa and Ojibwe attitudes. Judge John R. Kellogg, a member of the Western Michigan Society to Benefit the Indians, wrote to Schoolcraft that Joseph Wakazoo and his band now felt that a "new relation" existed because of the purchase. "They say they will conform to our laws," he wrote. "I am sure they will be protected as good citizens," Kellogg added.[37]

Such talk of citizenship peppered discussions of the Indians' circum-stances in the 1840s, and it was a conversation held among all parties with an interest in Michigan, from the local to the federal level. In the fall of 1844 acting superintendent of Indian affairs Robert Stuart included in his annual report a petition signed by sixty-one different Odawas and Ojibwes. The petition, addressed to President Tyler, approached the ongoing effort among many Indian communities in Michigan to obtain both permanent residence in the state and "ultimately the rights and privileges of American citizens." The L'Arbre Croche Odawas had seen a previous message on the topic meet success in the Michigan legislature only to have it lost among other priorities within the Michigan congres-sional delegation at the national level. This petition to Tyler reflected the next attempt to persuade the federal government to take action, and their reasoning rested on a number of factors—they had a small population, cultivated the soil, and lived in houses similar to the whites. In addition, many had intermarried with the white population of Michigan. Finally, while the land in question was not "well adapted to the advanced culture of the white men" because of the severe weather conditions, they said, the Indians could make it suit their needs. All they wanted was "to die on the soil" where they had "always lived and to leave it as an inheritance to [their] children." Stuart hoped that the president and Congress would listen to their words and grant their wishes because "nearly half their number [stood] so high in the scale of moral and social virtues as would render them worthy and valuable members of any community," and granting them citizenship would only motivate them to make even more progress.[38]

[The Anishinabek wanted to own land and gain citizenship as a means to achieve the most important goal—maintaining a permanent residence in Michigan.] Some of their prominent supporters viewed permanent residence as part of the larger goal of civilizing the Indians. Leonard Slater, the Baptist missionary who worked hard to keep his colony of Odawas safe from removal in the 1840s, was as cheered by the success of those Indians attached to missions as he was disheartened by the degradation of those who had shunned the Christian settlements. Yet Slater also blamed the difficulties of the missionary undertaking on the fact that the Indians were consistently deprived of their dignity through the limits placed on their independence. "In our civil code," Slater asserted, "we refuse them the privileges of American citizens. We have quenched their council fires, and deny them an elective franchise." When Slater assessed the status of the Anishinabe residents of Michigan in the 1840s, he saw problems caused as much by policy as by anything else. In his mind, the federal government needed to end the uncertainty. "To elevate their character, one or two things must be done," Slater argued. "Either remove them west of the Mississippi, and give them the same independence with other prosperous tribes, or, for the last resort, secure to them the privileges of citizenship within the States."[39]

It always came back to the uncertainty that neither state nor federal actions had alleviated. Reverend Peter Dougherty, a Presbyterian missionary who had arrived in 1838 at Grand Traverse, echoed Slater's arguments in the fall of 1847. Dougherty believed the time had finally come for questions about the Indians' status in Michigan to be decided. "Becoming uneasy lest they may have to leave here," he reported to Superintendent of Indian Affairs William Richmond, "[the Odawas at Grand Traverse] are beginning to make purchases, here and there, at distant points, which will scatter them into such small bands that it will almost be impossible to collect them into schools and meetings for improvement." Like Slater, Dougherty had his own agenda for keeping the Indians in one place.[40]

The Odawas living near the Old Wing Mission on the Black River in Allegan County were also beginning to move to new lands during the late 1840s. In 1846, led by Reverend Albertus C. Van Raalte, a small group of fewer than fifty Dutch immigrants established a colony on Black Lake, only a few miles northwest of the mission. By the spring of 1847 more than 1,500 Dutch men, women, and children joined that initial group. Within a short period of time the Odawas' crops suffered damages from the roaming cattle and pigs brought in by these immigrants, and in the summer of 1847 smallpox spread from the Dutch settlements into the Odawa homes. In December Peter Wakazoo addressed these and other problems in a letter to William Richmond. He desired a timely and complete annuity payment so that the Black River Odawas could purchase lands at a new settlement located further north. "We don't wish to own land merely one hour," Wakazoo explained, "but to own it always, so that we may always have a home." One month later the Odawas met in council with Reverend George Smith and discussed plans for moving later that year. The move required a tremendous amount of work, especially because the Odawas would need to sell their land in Allegan County before they could move to their new home along the shore of Lake Michigan on the Leelanau Peninsula. The Indians purchased this land in July 1848 at the Ionia land office, but at the time still had more than three-quarters of their former homes to sell. That land was spread out. Indeed, based on the tax assessment records of 1847 for Manlius Township, twenty-four different Odawas owned a total of 656 acres of land, and they needed to pass through an inordinate number of hoops to sell it. In fact, the Michigan state legislature had to pass specific bills permitting the sale of Odawa lands in Allegan County, and those sales could not occur without the consent and approval of both George Smith and the probate judge for the county. By the summer of 1849, however, the Black River Band of Odawas under Peter Wakazoo had relocated, at which point the Carp River and Cat Head Odawa bands joined them. Yet despite the seeming security of new lands purchased in the northern reaches, away from the hotspots of non-Indian settlement, the shadows remained. The mere rumor and threat of removal west of the Mississippi River still had power. As late as 1850 a Catholic missionary from the Little Traverse still coerced baptisms by threatening those who resisted his ministrations with removal to the West.[41]

Under the dark clouds of ongoing threats and uncertainty, citizenship continued to present an appealing path to stability and security. The state of Michigan took the first official step to bring the Indians into the fold in the new state constitution adopted in 1850. This decision to revise the original governing document came primarily out of the political dialogue of the Jacksonian era, and it is therefore not surprising that the one hundred delegates who met in Lansing in the summer of 1850 discussed voting rights. Yet they had also been lobbied by what is only listed in the record as "sundry civilized Indians" who petitioned for "the rights of American citizenship." In the final version, in fact, article 7 read in part, "Every civilized male inhabitant of Indian descent, a native of the United States and not a member of any tribe, shall be an elector and entitled to vote." Ratifying a constitution that included this provision was an important step, though every word and phrase could be dissected for meaning, beginning with "civilized male inhabitant of Indian descent." It could be argued that the phrasing, which was proposed by delegate William Norman McLeod, was intended to target the men of mixed descent, whom McLeod asserted were "white to all intents and purposes." Though his proposal clearly referred to Indians of mixed French and Indian descent, alluding to the métis population of the Upper Peninsula in particular, the phrasing in the constitution would apply to all. Yet it would still leave open to debate the designation of "civilized" as well as what it would mean to not be "a member of any tribe."[42]

Then, in April 1851 the state legislature of Michigan drafted and adopted a joint resolution directed at the federal government, requesting the government "to make such arrangements for said Indians as they may desire for their permanent location in the northern part" of Michigan. As far as the state legislators were concerned, the Anishinabek were "a civil, well disposed, peaceable and orderly people," and for several years had "made great advancement in the agricultural and mechanical arts," and many of them wished to remain in Michigan, "to become civilized," and to share the "social, political, and religious privileges" of U.S. citizens. This resolution, following on the heels of the new state constitution, heralded the new attitude of Americans toward the presence of Indians in their midst. Yet the reference to permanent lands specifically in the northern reaches of the state also clarified that attitude. As of 1850 Michigan had a population

of 397,654, but the five most populous counties—Jackson, Leenaw, Oak-
land, Washtenaw, and Wayne—were those surrounding the Detroit area,
and they contained nearly 40 percent of the state's total population. Then
there were other regions just a bit further north, such as those encompassed
by Huron, Tuscola, Saginaw, and Midland counties, all surrounding Saginaw Bay, which had a total population in 1850 of 3,175. [Even further
north, in counties like Michilimackinac, the non-Indian population was
just as small. Michigan would welcome the Indians to stay, as long as they
made their homes in the portions of the state that remained undesirable to
its non-Indian residents.[43]]

At the beginning of the 1850s, then, it appeared that the Indian and
non-Indian inhabitants of Michigan had reached an understanding that
would allow them to coexist. Questions remained, however, about the
true permanence of the Anishinabe presence and the extent to which
the federal government would support this mutual understanding. The
Saginaws in particular became increasingly unhappy and concerned with
that uncertainty. Ohsahwahbon, a Saginaw wkama, wanted answers from
the government about the status of the Saginaw lands and payments. He
had been elected by a council of all of the Saginaw wkamek to find out
what money had been advanced to them and how much of the land had
been sold in the ten-plus years since they had signed their treaties in the
late 1830s. "He wants to propose to the Government," missionary George
Bradley reported, "to take the unsold lands, under those treaties above
mentioned and pay the Indians the minimum price and after the Expenses
of Govt are paid let the Indians have the balance deposited in some way to
their best interest in agriculture and schools." The Saginaws did not want
to sit back and wait for what the government might grant them, and they
worried about the future security and safety of their children and the generations to come. In a separate missive Bradley wrote, "The chiefs and old
men come and ask the question, what they shall do to help their children
to a permanent home, say they shall die soon and they would like to see
their children have a permanent home." For those Saginaw leaders who
had sought to navigate their people through the previous three decades
and more, the time had come to focus on what they could provide or
ensure for their children.[44]

All signs pointed to the need for a new assessment of Indian lives
and lands in the state, and while the residents of Michigan had come to
terms with this, it appeared that the federal government still needed some

convincing. In the Senate, the Committee on Indian Affairs was told to explore who might "consummate such measures as may be necessary for their permanent settlement in the country" where they then lived. Meanwhile, missionary George Bradley continued to push for a consideration of the Saginaws in particular. They had been cultivating land in eight or nine different locations near Saginaw Bay, but in his mind their future depended on relocation to permanent homes established further away from growing white settlements. "In my opinion," he informed Lewis Cass, "the best policy is to colonize them give them a territory of land say 6 miles square somewhere in the Northern part of this Lower peninsula, say in North of what we call Cass River." Bradley advocated for permanency through lands held in fee simple that the Indians could not sell to any white man. In addition he emphasized the need for the federal government to provide, once and for all, some semblance of reassurance to the nearly 1,400 Saginaw Ojibwes who lived with an ever-present feeling of doom. "They are as you know opposed to going west of the Mississippi," Bradley explained. "They fear if they say anything to the Government it will force them away so they are literally in bondage through fear."[45]

That fear and insecurity were common among the missionary reports of the early 1850s in Michigan. In September 1853 Peter Lefevre, the Catholic bishop stationed in Detroit, summarized the efforts of the various Catholic missions and schools throughout Michigan, including Mackinaw, Little Traverse, Point St. Ignace, Middletown, and Cross Village. He noted that while Odawas and Ojibwes had shown progress in "industry, morality, and religion," they were still hindered in their progress due to the "despair of ever obtaining a permanent location for themselves and their posterity, where they [would] not be importuned to emigrate and give place to the white man." He also asserted that the relatively poor condition of the Indians resulted largely from "the insecurity of property, and the very uncertain and unsettled condition in which they live[d]."[46]

Based on the reports from his various agents and his own beliefs, then, Henry Gilbert encouraged the federal government to change its ways: "I deem it important not only that the policy of removal should be abandoned but that such a determination on the part of the United States should be communicated to them in an official forum." Once more the talk turned to eliminating fear. "They can then acquire lands & make settlements & improvements unmolested by the fear of being driven from their homes which has paralyzed their energies & thwarted the labors & efforts of missionaries & teachers for several years."[47] Gilbert then moved from encouraging removal to outlining specific recommendations for the next steps that should be taken by the federal government in Michigan. His suggestions began with a common refrain, to "set apart certain tracts of public lands in Michigan in locations suitable for the Indians & as far removed from white settlements as possible." The land would be held by the head of the family, but the Indians would not be allowed to sell it. "All the land embraced within the tract set apart should be withdrawn from sale & no white person should be permitted to locate or live among them, except teachers, traders, & mechanics specially authorized by rules & regulations to be prescribed by the State Government." Gilbert was thoroughly convinced of the efficacy of his particular ideas. He viewed his plan as the only one that provided for some sort of future for the Anishinabek who continued to reside in the state. If nothing was done to secure permanent homes that would give them greater motivation to provide for the subsistence, he insisted, the Anishinabek would "be turned over to the State in the condition of paupers" and would "be from year to year a continual source of annoyance to her citizens & expense to her treasury." Action had to be taken soon, for the available public lands would not be available for long.[48]

The Saginaws knew of these developments and hoped that the federal government would take action. In a council with missionary George Smith held in the fall of 1854, they made a specific request and stated that the federal government could simply take the entire county of Isabella off the market so that the Indians could then use their annuity moneys to purchase the lands and form a permanent settlement. "The Indians fully understand the terms on which we propose to settle them," Smith reported, "and we have given them no encouragement to hope for any thing from the Genl Govt and in view of this heartily concur as far as we have been able to consult them."[49]

By the end of 1854 the federal government began to address the expressed interests of the Indians and the missionaries. On December 20, 1854, John Wilson of the General Land Office in Michigan informed Secretary of the Interior Robert McClelland that he had received from the commissioner of Indian affairs a letter "recommending, for the reasons stated, the withdrawal from market and reservation for Indian purposes the lands in Isabella County, Michigan, or so much thereof as may be

deemed expedient." That recommendation became reality the following year when President Franklin Pierce issued an executive order with-
drawing from public sale the lands mentioned in McClelland's letter. The
executive order was brief and to the point, and its reference to McClelland's missive meant that lands within both Isabella and the newly formed
Emmet counties in Michigan would be withdrawn for the purpose of
establishing the residencies of various Odawa and Ojibwe bands.[50]

The executive order laid the foundation for a substantial attempt to
address the concerns of the Odawas and Ojibwes throughout Michigan.
In June 1855 Henry Gilbert received orders to gather together representatives of the Odawas and Ojibwes who had been party to the 1836 Treaty
of Washington. He suggested that he also invite a delegation of Saginaws
to come to Detroit around the same time so that a treaty could be signed
with them. "Their matters are in a very unsettled & unsatisfactory state,"
Gilbert explained, "and they & all who are connected with them are
extremely anxious to have them arranged." Some of that dissatisfaction
continued to grow from the disappointing land sales established by the
treaties of the late 1830s. As of June 20, 1855, the General Land Office
had recorded land sale revenues of $96,202.08. Yet in the fourteen years
of those sales the office had also recorded charges against the Saginaws of
$96,257.72. Not only had less than one-third of the Saginaw land cessions
been sold, but also, fourteen years into the deal, the Saginaws were in the
red by $55.64.[51]

The parties gathered in Detroit at the end of July. First into the negotiations were the Odawas and Ojibwes who had been party to the 1836
treaty. The two appointed commissioners, Henry Gilbert and George
Manypenny, represented the regional and national interests in American
Indian affairs. Manypenny in particular wanted to start the negotiations
with a clean slate, and he addressed the concerns raised by two distinct delegations of Odawas and Ojibwes who had visited Washington the previous
winter. Most important, Manypenny wanted the assembled Indians to
know that there were no unresolved issues nor was there unspent money
from previous treaties. While he was willing to correct any errors of the
past, Manypenny stressed, "The great thing for you now is to look to the
future." Assagon, the first wkama to speak, commented that the Indians
had those very intentions. The Indians came to the council to secure the
future for the succeeding generations even as they sought to correct any
problems from the past. "For ourselves, we do not wish, or hope, what is

Picture of Naugechegumme (or Nauke-Chig-Um-Ie), a Saginaw leader who signed the 1837 Detroit treaty, the 1855 Treaty of Detroit, and the 1864 treaty that established the Isabella Reservation. Courtesy of the Bentley Historical Library, University of Michigan.

not our due," he noted, "& we rely upon you, our father for what is ours. . . . We are now acting for our children."[52]

The treaty council lasted from July 25 to July 31, and in the last recorded comment before the treaty was signed, Oshawwanah stated, "I will sign your treaty; but I do not want to go West of the Mississippi. I trust to your justice that this treaty is all that it is explained to be." The treaty did withdraw unsold public lands from sale throughout Michigan's Upper and Lower Peninsulas, "for the benefit of said Indians as hereinafter provided," and made no mention of removal. As Paybahmesay stated, "When we started here, were like travellers on a log. We knew not when we might fall off, or where the end of it was; but we find we have not fallen off, or reached the end of it. Instead of darkness we find a bright light." A mere two days later the Saginaws signed a treaty that appeared to provide the same kind of brightness. The federal government had surrendered its notions of removal and had negotiated a treaty furnishing not only land but also "all such articles as may be necessary and useful for them in removing to the homes herein provided, and getting permanently settled thereon." A lot had changed in the nearly two decades since the last treaties had been signed by these various bands of Indians in Michigan.[53]

The government and the nation had now turned their attention further west. For the Anishinabek in Michigan this presented an opportunity to establish a measure of security that had so long eluded their communities. Yet it did not free them from fear or anxiety, for well into the twentieth century the Native inhabitants of Michigan had to struggle to maintain the lands they had fought for during the nineteenth century. In the mid-1850s it also did not mean that the attitude of the American public had necessarily changed. Instead, the temporary security granted to Michigan's Anishinabe populations through treaties in the 1850s indicated that the focal point of western expansion had shifted. The Old Northwest and the fertile soils of the Southeast no longer drew the eyes of speculators as they once had. The new target had become the grasslands of the newly minted Kansas Territory, the open range of Indian Territory and Texas, and the territories that lay beyond them.

7

THE AMERICAN ERA IS A REMOVAL ERA

"Not long ago," Annie Young Bumberry commented, "our Agent told us that we should return to our former ways and customs and I asked him how he expected us to do it when the white men had for so many years been educating us out of our former ways and customs until now the old ways and customs were forgotten or only partially remembered by the very old people." Bumberry did not provide an exact date for that conversation with the agent, but she brought up this topic in early November 1937, at a time when Commissioner of Indian Affairs John Collier had instituted policies that sought to shift the trajectory of Indian affairs in the United States. Within the context of Collier's Indian New Deal, American Indian individuals and tribes were encouraged to return to traditional cultural practices, a reversal of more than a century of intrusive efforts to civilize and assimilate the indigenous populations of the country. Yet as the fifty-nine-year-old Seneca woman explained, the problem was not isolated to the loss of language or culture. Even as Collier's administration officially halted allotment and proposed the possibility of restoring Indian lands, dispossession remained an issue. For example, Quakers had set up a mission among the Senecas in the Indian Territory before Bumberry had been born in 1878, and they built their meetinghouse on land set aside for the tribe. "Somehow the Friends have been given a deed to the property," Bumberry reported, "and now we are told that it is theirs and now they are building a new parsonage there. Our Council house and property was sold to a white man and destroyed." More than one hundred years after Congress passed legislation formalizing the patterns of dispossession and relocation that had become customary practice, systematic land loss and removal continued in earnest.[1]

The removal treaties signed in the 1830s and 1840s consistently used the word "permanent" to describe the lands to be reserved for Indians west of the Mississippi River. In the 1831 treaty negotiated with the Shawnees then living at Wapakoneta in Ohio, for instance, the accord spoke of the Indians' desire "to obtain a more permanent and advantageous home for themselves and their posterity." Yet few things in the second half of the nineteenth century were less permanent than lands reserved for Indians in the territories that would become the states of Texas, Oklahoma, and Kansas. Removal as an era and as a policy may have been equated with eastern Indians relocating west, but the dispossession and all-out assault on Indian lands and lives did not abide by any such boundaries. Both thematically and chronologically this pattern in Indian affairs parallels the warning contained in statements made by famed abolitionist Frederick Douglass on May 10, 1865, to the American Anti-Slavery Society. The society's members had gathered in Boston to contemplate their future now that the Civil War had ended and slavery had been abolished. Indeed, what was an anti-slavery organization to do now that the Thirteenth Amendment had seemingly provided the end for which so many had struggled? Douglass did his best to make sure that no one present strained a muscle patting his neighbor on the back and specifically warned that slavery would not be dead until black men were given the right to vote. The new amendment may have prohibited enslavement, but it would not protect against "unfriendly legislation" in any state of the Union that might seek to constrain the rights of the newly freed men and women. "It [slavery] has been called by a great many names," Douglass proclaimed, "and it will call itself by yet another name; and you and I and all of us had better wait and see what new form this old monster will assume, in what new skin this old snake will come forth." Reconstruction and its aftermath proved Douglass to be prophetic, and during those same decades in the late nineteenth century the federal government waged war against Indians throughout the American West, instituted an allotment policy that decimated Indian landholdings, and supported boarding schools that launched an assault on Indian children.[2]

In 1854 the Committee on Indian Affairs in the House of Representatives issued a report that in part contained a eulogy for the removal policy. Although it had "seemed wise and humane" when adopted, the relocation of Indians west of the Mississippi River had failed to accomplish its goals, largely because of the unanticipated speed and power of American expansion. "Enlightened philanthropy now suggests an abandonment of our former system," the congressmen wrote, "and the institution of a new one which will alienate the Indian from the precarious fortunes of the chase, and attach him to the more stable and happy pursuits of agriculture." The report's authors acted as if they had come upon something new, when in fact little in the rhetoric had changed. Removal did not end; it merely resurfaced in decade after decade, taking on a different form or policy name each time. Indeed, it could be said that policy suggestions, made by members of the government-appointed Peace Commission in their report to Congress in January 1868, merely "amounted to a variation on removal with special attention paid to the civilizing mission." The pressure on Indian lands persisted, as did the all-encompassing assault on Indian peoples and cultures. And because territorial outlets for physical relocation were limited by the passage of time and the reach of the non-Indian population, the federal government's emphasis turned to increased efforts to destroy tribalism, eliminate culture, and silence language. Native communities who had already endured multiple removals over the course of the eighteenth and nineteenth centuries never received a respite and continued to fight for a permanent home.[3]

The Shawnee and Delaware bands that had sought refuge in Mexico during the early nineteenth century did not have to move to become residents of the Republic of Texas following the brief war for independence in 1836. Twenty-three years later, in the summer of 1859, American officials forcibly removed these communities, along with hundreds of Caddos and Wichitas, from the Brazos Agency in the northern part of what had become the state of Texas. Their escorts, the Second Cavalry of the U.S. Army, were not just present to keep the Indians in line but also for protection, as Texans in the vicinity had indicated in previous years, months, and even weeks their willingness and desire to attack and kill the Indians living on the Brazos River. The violent context of this removal was only the latest in a near-constant effort to eliminate the Indians from the region since the moment Anglo-Americans first arrived on the scene. The Delawares and Shawnees were a relatively small part of this targeted population, but an examination of their experience illuminates the intersections of powerful expansionist desires, weak federal authority, inter-Indian relationships, and decreasing land bases that made life for eastern

Indians exceedingly difficult and dangerous west of the Mississippi River during the mid-nineteenth century.[4]

From the 1830s to the end of the 1850s these southern Delawares and Shawnees lived at the crossroads of numerous expansionist waves and ruling powers—specifically Mexico, Texas, the United States, and the Comanches. As a result they constantly had to deal with the consequences of the turbulent political transitions and the accompanying violence that engulfed the region as the different entities struggled to dictate affairs and bound the landscape. The soldiers of the Lone Star Republic defeated Mexican troops at the Battle of San Jacinto in the spring of 1836, but just more than a month before that military victory, the provisional government of Texas had signed a treaty with the Indian tribes who had been living in the region for more than a decade. Delawares, Shawnees, Kickapoos, and Cherokees were only four of the communities represented in the negotiations that resolved to provide a new territory in which all the tribes would reside. In the parlance of the Texas government, the Cherokees and affiliated bands would surrender their former land grants in the eastern part of the republic and move to territory encompassing more than one million acres, which was bounded on the north by the Sabine River, the south by the San Antonio Road, the east by the Angelina River, and the west by the Neches River. The problem was that although the treaty was officially signed in February 1836, the Texas senate refused to ratify it once the war for independence had ended. There were substantial differences of opinion between President Sam Houston, who advocated for peaceful and just relations with these immigrant communities, and the Texas congress, which saw all Indians, and not just Comanches, as a problem. At a session convened in early October 1837, the members of the Standing Committee on Indian Affairs in the Texas senate declared that they not only viewed the treaty signed in February 1836 as invalid but also believed that Indians not indigenous to Texas did not have any rights to the land, regardless of any prior arrangements with Mexico. In addition, they believed that many of the tribes were "the most savage and ruthless of [their] frontier enemies ever since and even at the very date of the signing of [the] Treaty," and said, "No part of said tribes have been our friends in War." In the conclusion of its report, the Texas senate asserted that the "Northern tribes of Indians," a category that included the Delawares and Shawnees then living in Texas, were "properly under the superintendence and direction of the Govt. of the U.S. of America." President Houston's ideas for an Indian policy based on peaceful negotiation and reserved lands were subsequently swept away, a move that set the stage for much of the violence that followed.[5]

In the years that Texas remained an independent republic, the Delawares, Shawnees, and their neighbors lived an unstable existence, knowing that most of the republic's leading figures and their constituents wanted them removed from the region, if not simply killed. President Mirabeau Lamar, who had succeeded Houston in November 1838, assumed his new responsibilities set on removing the Indian presence from Texas, and "adopted a policy of ethnic cleansing almost from the first day he came into office." Convinced that the Cherokees under Chief Bowles were working surreptitiously with the Mexicans to raid Texas settlements, Lamar sought to force the Cherokees from Texas in the spring of 1839. He then informed the affiliated Indians that they would not suffer the same fate as long as they distanced themselves from their Cherokee neighbors. Lamar simultaneously communicated to other prominent Texans that he desired the "ultimate removal of all other emigrant Tribes now residing in Texas," and wanted to make sure that anyone dealing with the friendly Shawnees and Delawares would "be careful to excite no hopes on their part, of being eventually allowed to identify themselves with the Country, or to claim any right in the Soil." That position was followed up two months later by a treaty signed with the Shawnees stating that the Indians would "return from whence they came and depart in peace from their brethren and the territory of Texas." These removal efforts occurred even as the Lamar administration used military force and subterfuge to wage war, against the Comanches in particular. This approach was epitomized by what was known as the Council House Massacre of Penateka Comanches in San Antonio on March 19, 1840.[6]

When Sam Houston returned to the presidency in December 1841, the situation changed yet again, for the returning executive asserted that Lamar's Indian policy had failed. Initially it also appeared to indicate that the push for removal might have run its course. At a council held at Tehuacana Creek in March 1843, the Texas commissioners told the assembled Delawares, Shawnees, Caddos, and others that the republic desired peace with all Indians. The Texans stated that they wanted an end to war and promised that they would "give [their] red brothers a country to live in, in Texas." Pierce Butler, a representative from the United States at the council, stated that the American government also had a serious interest in ending the conflict in Texas and urged the assembled Indians to be "men in *real earnest*." Roasting Ear, one of three Delaware chiefs present, was the first Native leader to respond to these statements, and he expressed his pleasure with the proposals. He also reminded the Texans that peace would be not only mutually beneficial but also mutually dependent. "Prevent your young men from committing depredations and I will do the same," he asserted. Linney, the Shawnee chief, supported Roasting Ear and noted that he and his Delaware colleague stood ready to "act as mediators in Concert with [the] commissioners." That session ended with a plan to hold a grand council with all of the Indians of Texas. If all went according to Houston's design, the immigrant Indians would stay in Texas and provide an effective buffer between the growing population of Texans and the still-powerful Comanches whose range extended from the Texas panhandle to south of the Rio Grande.[7]

Overall, however, two issues complicated the situation for the Delawares and Shawnees in Texas during the 1840s, especially after annexation in 1845. First, Texans maintained an overwhelming desire to eliminate Indians from within the boundaries of the state, although they did not always agree about whether elimination meant extermination or relocation. That attitude and the subsequent actions taken by citizens and the notorious Texas Rangers exacerbated the problematic fact that the federal government did not have a clear and effective approach to the diverse indigenous populations of the region. The second issue that continued to complicate the Delawares' and Shawnees' relationship with Texas was that while these northern Indian communities were not the Comanches, their fate was more often than not tied to the prevailing attitudes toward the Comanches and other tribes that were deemed hostile to white settlements. In the end, whether viewed as buffers or as equally dangerous as their Comanche neighbors, the Delawares and Shawnees were clearly not citizens. Therefore Texans believed that these Indians did not deserve the better lands that were still available in the state.[8]

Throughout the 1840s the Shawnees and Delawares who appear in the records are described as both mediators and instigators. At some points the Delawares appeared to fulfill the grandfatherly role that they held for so long in the inter-Indian affairs east of the Mississippi. At a council held in May 1844 Delaware chief St. Louis assumed that familiar status when he addressed the Wacos and Tawakonis in attendance as grandchildren before he scolded them for stealing. From this authoritative position based on kinship terms and alliance with the Texans, St. Louis said he was tired of talk and told the assembled Indians, "If you love your young men, women and children assist your chiefs to make peace between these red and white people." By 1845, in fact, the Delawares were deemed indispensable to the efforts of the Texas government in their negotiations with different Comanche bands in the region. This meant that any potential conflicts between the Delawares and Comanches had dangerous repercussions, a circumstance evident in April 1845 when a small Delaware hunting party allegedly attacked and killed three Comanches on the San Marcos River. When the Comanches declared their desire for revenge, Thomas G. Western, the superintendent of Indian affairs for Texas, warned his superiors that an eruption of violence between the two would be catastrophic. "The Delaware are, as it were, the connecting link between us and the Comanche," he explained, "and it is important at this juncture that the best understanding should exist between them." Delaware men, especially John Conner, Jim Shaw, and Jack Harry, were indeed integral components of most efforts to negotiate with the Comanches in the 1840s. If Texas officials wanted to bring a Comanche band in for a council, they sent a small party of Delawares to deliver the message.[9]

Despite the services rendered by these individuals, state officials forced the Delawares further west in the late 1840s to accommodate the needs and demands of the thousands of Anglo-Americans moving into the region. These officials not only wanted to make more land available to whites but also wanted to separate the Indians from merchants eager to sell them alcohol, among other goods, so they pushed the Delawares out of settlements, such as the one established on Bosque Creek, and relocated them once more. These "immigrant" or "northern" Indian groups, as they were often described, presented a unique problem, especially because of their established relationship with the state and former republic. Former president of Texas David Burnet described these Indians in September 1847 as "intruders" who had garnered a measure of rights to occupancy through a treaty signed in 1844. "That they are tenants without title, and hold only at the will of the government, does not divest them of a recognized right of residence, to which they naturally attach a right of soil," Burnet stated. "Their peaceable removal, which the tranquility of the State will soon require, is practicable only by the Federal Government." He did not say so directly, but Burnet's statement implied that Texans might not actually be capable of peaceful negotiations. Robert Neighbors, a Texas

Portrait of Wy-A-Wa-Qua-Cum-An or Waiawakwakumau ("Tramping Everywhere"), who was called Jack Harry, in partial Native dress, March 1898. Courtesy of the National Anthropological Archives, Smithsonian Institution, gn-00814a.

Indian agent from 1845 to 1847, saw clear evidence of that problem when Anglo newcomers took matters into their own hands and undermined his efforts to demarcate the line between Indian and non-Indian settlements. The Delawares and Shawnees in west Texas, whose total population was listed at 650 in 1849, struggled to hold on to a precarious existence as state officials continued to debate this particular problem.[10]

No manner of action, military or otherwise, brought satisfaction to the dominant forces, and by the early 1850s Texans sought an alternative solution. The answer appeared to come in the reservation policy instituted by the federal government that emphasized bounded portions of territory, allowing for government supervision as well as opportunities to experiment with different methods of assimilating Indians throughout the West. For the governor of Texas it meant something else. Yes, a set-aside section of land was necessary to separate the Indians from the citizens of his state. However, such reservations should not be permanent and clearly should not interfere with other, more important interests. In written remarks to the Texas legislature in November 1853, Governor Peter H. Bell requested that the legislators give the government the authority to designate a section of the state for "temporary occupation" by Indians, "which [would] not conflict with existing private claims, nor any contemplated route for the Pacific Railroad." Perhaps most important, any resolution in this regard should stipulate "that the district so occupied [should] revert to the State so soon as the General Government [would] be able to effect more permanent arrangements for the final disposition of the Indian tribes in Texas." In short, the reservation policy would provide a means for maintaining peace until Texas could finally relocate the Indians to a more suitable location.[11]

This reservation policy did not bring peace, and it had a very short life in Texas. Under the auspices of legislation passed by the state legislature in February 1854, agents created two reservations totaling nearly 18,000 acres. The reservation on the Brazos River south of Fort Belknap is where the Shawnees and Delawares settled alongside bands of Caddos, Wichitas, and Tonkawas. By specifically designating what would be Indian lands, the new policy created the impression that Indians had no claim or right to any other territory in Texas. In other words, those Indians not living on one of the created reserves, primarily Comanches, Kiowas, and Lipan Apaches, had no rights to reside anywhere else in the state, and their mere presence indicated hostile intentions. Yet fewer than three years into the new reservation policy, Texans did not simply target Indians living off the reserves as hostile. Even as agents reported on the progress toward civilization made by Indians on the Brazos Reserve, and as military officials recruited Delaware and Shawnee scouts for campaigns against the Comanches, the growing non-Indian population of west Texas eyed the reservation lands with desire. A leading voice against the reservations,

John Baylor, had actually been assigned to oversee the reservation on the Clear Fork, which was then assigned to the northern Comanches. By 1858 Baylor publicly criticized the reservations and publicized the depredations allegedly committed by the reserve Indians. He greatly exaggerated, and at times fabricated, but he had an audience in west Texas eager to believe his narrative. His passion was so great that even when he learned that the government planned to remove the reserve Indians from the state, he argued that they should still be killed rather than placed in a new location from which they might launch even more raids.[12]

In the spring of 1859 "extermination rather than removal" was demanded in Texas. The removal of the reserve Indians from the Brazos River, including the Shawnees and Delawares, therefore took place with a federal military escort positioned to prevent Texans led by Baylor from killing the Indians. Although Baylor did lead an attack on the Brazos Agency on May 23, his disorganized force of nearly three hundred men was scattered by reserve Indians and federal soldiers, who had been sparked into action when they saw the Texans brutally kill an elderly Indian man and woman. Two months later Shawnees and Delawares were part of a train of more than 1,400 Indians whom federal agents escorted north of the Red River to new homes at the recently created Wichita Agency. This agency was established within a portion of Indian Territory leased by the federal government from the Chickasaws and Choctaws, and it allowed the Texas Indians to establish homes along the Washita and Canadian Rivers. Their residency in Texas had not lasted beyond four decades.[13]

Even as the Texas Indians moved north into Indian Territory, former neighbors and relatives from the Great Lakes region relocated south into Indian Territory from Kansas. Both the Kansas-Nebraska Act and the treaties signed in the mid-1850s providing for allotment played key roles in this particular development. Growing largely out of the desire to build a railroad along a central route cutting across the Great Plains, the Kansas-Nebraska Act unleashed a furious assault on Indian lands that had been secured by the removal treaties of the 1830s and 1840s. No reservation was immune to the onslaught, and the different tribal communities faced a series of critical decisions connected to not only their lands but also their very existence as sovereign entities. The Wyandots who had removed to Kansas from Ohio in 1843 signed a treaty with the United States government in 1855 that not only allotted their reserve but also stated that upon ratification of the accord, the Wyandots' "relations with the United States as an Indian tribe" would be "dissolved and terminated." Within a few years of the treaty's ratification, Wyandots had begun to leave Kansas and head south. "Much of their land was being sold for taxes and purchased by white settlers, the matter of taxes not being understood from their treaties," Leander Zane related. "Then, too, the railroad building to the Pacific and the influx of white settlers made the Wyandottes see that they would soon lose their tribal relations." With the options for other lands in Kansas limited, if not nonexistent, Wyandot leaders turned to the Senecas living on the Cowskin River in the northeastern corner of Indian Territory. The Senecas accepted the Wyandots, Zane stated, "because the Wyandottes had given the Senecas a home when the Senecas were driven from their home near the Great Lakes." As of 1858 more than two hundred Wyandots had left Kansas and moved to live near the Senecas. Although a final agreement took several years to take shape, the two nations also made arrangements for the Wyandots to purchase land from the Senecas on which their people could live. Yet not all the Wyandots moved south, and at the dawn of the 1860s the community had split between those who had left and those who had remained in Kansas, taken individual pieces of property, and started down the path to American citizenship per the 1855 treaty. Thus the 1855 treaty, and the choices made by individual Wyandots in its aftermath, divided the community by more than just geography, for by the end of 1862 the traditionalist Wyandots had established a tribal council to lead the community that had not chosen allotment and the dissolution of tribal relations. Although the treaty Wyandots continued to function under their Executive Council into the early 1870s, they had become known as the Citizens Party. For many, including the federal government, the Wyandots in Indian Territory led by Tauromee now held the legitimate council for the Wyandots as a tribal nation.[14]

The Wyandot story is not unique among the tribes living on lands that were incorporated into Kansas Territory. The Shawnees and Delawares residing along the Kansas River just west of the Missouri border signed treaties in 1854 that ceded sizeable portions of their respective reserves and set in motion processes that led to allotment and dispossession. The Kickapoos, Potawatomis, and their Kansas neighbors signed similar agreements in the 1850s and early 1860s. All of these accords reflected the tremendous pressure placed on the land that had originally been set aside as permanent homes for the Indians who were removed from the eastern half of the continent. They first struggled to counter the onrush of settlers who moved into the territory and suffered during the years of violence and unrest that defined Bleeding Kansas. Although Benjamin Robinson, agent for the Delawares, reported that opening Kansas Territory to American citizens had not proven disastrous, as of September 1855 he still had to admit, "[The Delawares in particular] have witnessed enough to shake their confidence in the laws which govern the white, or perhaps I should say civilized race." Proslavery and antislavery forces had turned the region into a battleground. They did not spare the Indian residents, yet they still found time to trespass on the Delaware reserve and cut down valuable stands of timber. In report after report sent to Washington from Kansas Territory, agents described the manner in which Potawatomis, Kickapoos, Delawares, Shawnees, and Wyandots were striving to make a life in the midst of the turmoil. Missionaries wrote about their school operations and the progress made by the children in attendance. Yet the underlying problem remained, and Robinson reported in September 1857 that it continued to be "exceedingly difficult to protect the extensive territory of these people [Delawares] from the inroads of their white neighbors."[15]

In a foreshadowing of the Dawes Act of 1887 and an indication that the experience of the Choctaws in the 1830s may have been either forgotten or ignored, American officials turned to allotment as a means of handling the circumstances in Kansas Territory. In some instances, including that involving the Delaware leaders who pushed for land in severalty and signed a treaty in 1860, some Indians also saw individual property ownership as the only remaining option to preserve and protect a land base in the region. Yet anyone, non–Indian and Indian alike, who believed that allotment might prove beneficial to Indians was wrong. It instead proved devastating to the integrity of tribal lands and communities, largely because both allotment and the absence of federal protections provided openings for manipulation and corruption by outsiders intent on obtaining land in Kansas. Railroad companies were perhaps the most notorious private interests that capitalized on the practice. The Leavenworth, Pawnee, and Western Railroad's inclusion in two 1861 treaties, with the Delawares and Potawatomis respectively, provides only a brief glimpse into the political and economic relationships that facilitated the transfer of Indian lands. A vast web of individual and business connections made up these "Indian rings," which secured the transfer of vast amounts of land and money within a relatively short period of time.[16]

Just as devastating, however, were the property taxes that local govern-ments in Kansas levied on Indian allotments as a means of both gaining revenue and establishing liens. Even before the admission of Kansas into the Union, some town councils in the territory assessed property and attempted to collect taxes from Indians living on allotted lands within the established town boundaries. Such was the case in the spring of 1859 when Shawnees owning land within the settlement named Shawneetown received a tax bill totaling $500. The Shawnee council and the lawyers who advised them questioned whether the allotted lands were subject to taxation, but the legal question was not fully addressed or answered until well into the 1860s. In 1867 the U.S. Supreme Court ruled in the case of *The Kansas Indians* that as long as the federal government recognized the "national character" of the Indians who held the allotted lands, "they [were] under the protection of treaties and the laws of Congress, and their property [was] withdrawn from the operation of State laws." This ruling at the federal level represented a legal victory for the Shawnees, Weas, and Miamis, all of whom had signed treaties instituting allotment. But for all of the plaintiffs, as well as those Indians not a part of the litigation, the ruling arrived too late to undo the substantial land loss due to forfeiture that had occurred in the years prior to the Supreme Court's decision. By the fall of 1866 a substantial portion of the Wyandot allotments in Kansas had been "sold to the whites for taxes and debts," and those whites had "stripped it of the timber, which, in many instances, was more valuable than the land itself."[17]

Still, the relentless encroachment of non-Indian settlers and the power-ful economic blows of property taxes were not the only external forces disrupting Indian landholding and lives in Kansas and Indian Territory during the 1860s. Border violence, which defined the Civil War for the region, also undermined the ability of Indians to not just survive but also maintain their lands and homes. Indians from Kansas served in the war with distinction, and the enlistment of 170 out of the 201 eligible Delaware men is rightfully touted as an unmatched community engage-ment in the war. For the Delawares who did not enlist, and for all others living along the Missouri-Kansas border in the first half of the 1860s, however, the raids by Confederate forces from Missouri, Arkansas, and Indian Territory proved incredibly destructive. More than anything, the war made fear and uncertainty a daily reality and resulted in the loss of property. In the fall of 1862 agent James Abbot reported, "The Wyandots and Shawnees are suffering materially from the bushwackers, who are operating on the border of Kansas, from Missouri, and many of the finest horses owned by these tribes have been stolen and driven off, and their losses cannot fall short of eight thousand dollars during the last year." Illustrating that Confederate bushwhackers were not the only instruments of destruction, another agent reported that the Kickapoos' "stock of horses and ponies [had] nearly all been 'jayhawked' from them during the past season." Indian Territory proved to be just as dangerous, especially because Confederate emissaries invested so heavily in their relationship with the southern tribes, promising the Indians more than the U.S. federal government ever had to support the Confederate States of America in their battle against the Union. Divisions within the Creeks, Cherokees, and Seminoles in particular led to violence that radiated out from their lands and engulfed neighboring communities. Consequently, more than seven thousand Indians, including the Wyandots who had only recently moved onto Seneca lands, fled Indian Territory and sought refuge at different points in central and eastern Kansas, where they depended on the hospitality of other Indians and provisions supplied by the federal government.[18]

The maelstrom of events in Kansas predictably led federal officials to discuss the possibility, and later the inevitability, of removal. In his contribution to the annual report of the commissioner of Indian Affairs in 1856, Superintendent Alfred Cuming described Kansas Territory as the final stop for those tribes removed from the eastern half of the continent. "Beyond this point they cannot well be driven," Cuming wrote, "as there is no longer any outlet for them." Six years later Commissioner of Indian Affairs William Dole had decided that the situation in Kansas had declined to the extent that the time had come for the federal government to find an outlet that had not seemed possible in previous years. His eyes, like those of the Wyandots in the late 1850s, turned south to Indian Territory. A plan for the removal of Indians from Kansas had also been the subject of congressional discussions. Senators James Lane and Samuel Pomeroy had secured wording in Congress' annual Indian affairs appropriations bill in 1863 that authorized the president to negotiate with Indians in Kansas, "providing for the extinction of their titles to lands held in common within said State, and for the removal of such Indians of said tribes as [held] their lands in common to suitable localities." The very next paragraph of the legislation, which authorized parallel negotiations for land with tribes in Indian Territory, made it clear where the federal government hoped to find a final destination. This legislation was followed two years later by the proposal, but not the passage, of Senate Bill 459, which provided "clear insight into one direction of federal Indian policy at the moment: increasing the political, social, geographic, and economic confinement of Indian people."[19]

The removals of Indians from Kansas to Indian Territory ultimately occurred under a diverse set of arrangements, from the negotiations between Wyandots and Senecas in the late 1850s to treaties signed by the Delawares in 1866 and the Potawatomis in 1867. The Senate rejected six different Shawnee treaties in the 1860s, until finally the Shawnees moved onto Cherokee lands following a series of negotiations that ended in an official agreement between the two tribes in June 1869. Similar to past experiences, however, none of these arrangements fully encapsulated the ongoing fractures within different communities. Decisions made to take allotments had split tribes along numerous lines, so that even while many Wyandots, Shawnees, and Delawares traveled south, others remained in Kansas on their allotments. Under the terms of the allotment treaties, those who chose private property had also taken a path toward American citizenship, and that choice shaped their future relations with relatives who had not done the same. The 1867 treaty that provided lands for the Wyandots out of the former Seneca reserve also granted power to the so-called Indian Party to decide which, if any, of those Wyandots who had chosen allotment might be allowed to regain their membership in the tribe. As for the Shawnees and Delawares who moved onto Cherokee lands, their arrangements set the stage for a battle, lasting more than a century, to retain their political and cultural integrity within the boundaries of the Cherokee Nation.[20]

Many stories of these removals from Kansas to Indian Territory in the 1860s and 1870s are captured in interviews gathered in the Indian-Pioneer Papers collection, and in every interview there is an initial sense of ordinariness to the anecdotes that each individual chooses to tell. By the 1930s those men and women living in the state of Oklahoma had houses, jobs, families, and sometimes tales about fateful encounters with outlaws made famous in the myths of the Wild West. Yet a closer look at the transcripts and the accounts contained within the collection reveals the memory and the pure relentless power of the removal and dispossession that framed the lives of Indian men and women during the late nineteenth and early twentieth centuries in the territory that became Oklahoma. Some of the memories are clearer than others, some of the stories are more vivid, but each individual has a personal experience that illustrates the obstacles they had faced in the past and continued to face in the 1930s. Each man and woman interviewed has a story of how they got to Oklahoma, why they were living there, and what family histories they carried. After reading enough of these interviews, it is impossible to avoid the combined impact of those experiences and the ways in which their lives connected the nineteenth century to the twentieth. Their personal histories also make it impossible to deny the continuous thread of government policies centered on dispossession and removal.

By the 1870s federal officials viewed Indian Territory as the repository for any and all Indians that civilian or military officials decided should be relocated from their present homes. Those Indians who had removed from Kansas as children remembered decades later when government soldiers brought Poncas, Nez Perces, and Modocs to the region. William Long recollects, "[The Poncas], were brought here from the western part of this state as prisoners of war," and the Modocs arrived by train from Oregon several years later. The Nez Perces, forcibly removed to Indian Territory following the capture of Chief Joseph in 1877, were not there so long, according to Long. Dave Geboe, who had a strong visceral reaction to the physical appearance of the Modocs upon their arrival in 1873, also remembered how the Indians from the Pacific Northwest struggled to deal with the severe environmental differences in their new home, stating quite simply, "They died like sheep." Cora Hayman, the daughter of two Modocs who died so soon after their arrival in Indian Territory, was the only member of that original group of 152 Modocs the army had relocated to Indian Territory who was still living in Oklahoma by 1937. Others had left and returned to Oregon, though most who had come to Indian Territory now resided in a cemetery that had quickly filled during the first years of residence on the southern plains.[21]

All Indian residents of the territory came under fire from the next phase of federal policy in the 1880s. According to a story related by Lola Jane Chouteau, a Shawnee resident of Vinita, Oklahoma, when her grandfather Benjamin "saw allotment coming on," he often informed his son, "The Government is after you boys now, and will not let up until they get your land." The General Allotment Act of 1887 and later, more targeted legislation had a clear impact on Indian lands and lives. Eliza Journeycake Minshall "owned a mile square between Centralia and Mills but had to surrender all except eighty acres for herself and allotments for her

The headstone of Shepline Smith, one of the fifty-five Modocs who died in the six years following the removal of 154 Modoc men, women, and children to Indian Territory in 1873. The Modoc cemetery in which Shepline rests is in Ottawa County, Oklahoma. Photo by author.

David Geboe.   Miami. J.

Portrait of David Geboe or Goodbault ("Mixed Blood"). Courtesy of the National Anthropological Archives, Smithsonian Institution, gn-00797.

children." Henry Armstrong was a Delaware Indian, the son of Arthur Armstrong and Nancy Ketchum-Armstrong, and he had been born in 1870, only three years after his family moved into Indian Territory from Kansas to live among the Cherokees. His father served on the Cherokee council in the 1890s, and Henry remembered the passion with which Arthur had opposed allotment coming to Cherokee lands, and thus to its Delaware occupants as well. Speaking to an assembled crowd, Arthur had warned that any restrictions on sales "would be lifted in a few years, and the Indians would soon sell their land and in a few years they would be penniless." Under the terms of the Curtis Act in 1898, the federal government instituted allotment among the Cherokees and others who had initially received exceptions under the terms of the Dawes Act. According to Henry Armstrong, "Out of the eight hundred Delawares who received allotments, there are only about two hundred who have their homes now." Not all the stories are of lands lost, however. Jake Longtail, who had moved to Indian Territory around 1871 with other Shawnees, still maintained his hundred-acre allotment in 1938. Katie Day, who along with her Delaware family took allotments among the Cherokees, was also one of the fortunate ones who had retained her eighty-acre allotment south of Bartlesville.[22]

A similar mixture of loss and preservation is evident in the ways in which the men and women interviewed in the collection reference the elements of their cultures that had or had not survived removals and other federal policies. Interviewer James Carseloway mentions at the beginning of his transcript that he hesitated to interview Jake Longtail because the ninety-year-old Shawnee man did not speak English very well. Jake, for all of his pride in his own ability to hold on to and work his land, was less optimistic about his own people's ability to maintain their language and tribal identity. "The Shawnee Tribe of Indians, be play out pretty fast now," he says, before noting all of the prominent individuals who had died in the years since they had moved to Indian Territory. Sarah Longbone, who had been raised by her Eastern Shawnee grandparents, speaks about numerous cultural traditions, dances in particular, that the Eastern Shawnees had maintained and that she enjoyed attending. Her own experiences simultaneously reflected changes in other cultural practices. "We were married in the old Indian way," she says of her first marriage, in 1909 to Daniel DuShane, another Eastern Shawnee. Sarah remarried in 1930, a year after Daniel died in a car accident. Of this marriage to Jack Longbone, a Delaware, she simply says, "This time we were just married like other people." David DuShane, Jr., makes note of the influence of external forces, asserting that "since Congress ruled against the Indian marriage and adoption customs that they have ceased to hold any of their old tribal ceremonies and that these rites and ceremonies [were] being fast forgotten by the Indians themselves." Meanwhile, Ruth Parks, who comments on the fact that Delaware children often went away to school at Carlisle, Haskell, or Chilocco, states, "There will in time to come be lost forever the language of the Delawares." Yet she also mentions that certain dances had "been perpetuated through the years" and were "enjoyed to the utmost for various reasons." These discussions of cultural practices, and their persistence or absence, are a reflection of numerous factors. Each man and woman interviewed presents a unique perspective and experience, meaning that an assertion about a loss of culture may just as well reflect that individual's personal involvement with his or her community. It is just as likely that some individuals had no intention of sharing information that outsiders had no right to know.[23]

There is less ambiguity, however, in the consistent references to burial grounds. Time and time again, the men and women interviewed describe cemeteries that were no longer accessible or had been destroyed. It is a devastating illustration of one more way in which Indians continued to be physically removed from the landscape, even after their final breath. James Carseloway wrote a brief account of a Shawnee man named Jonathan Blackfeather and described how the Blackfeathers had all passed away. Seeking more information about their burials, Carseloway learned that "the tomb stones had all been removed . . . and that plows were being run over the graves, so that they could not be located." As of 1937 the cemetery was part of a farm operated by a man named Gene Rogers. A Seneca woman, Eva Spicer Whitetree Nichols, similarly comments on the altered landscape around her in northeastern Oklahoma, including the longhouse that had been destroyed when "some white people bought the place," and the stomp grounds that had been turned into farmland. She ends, however, with a mention of the old Wyandotte cemetery. "I am told that a man by the name of Hollis bought this land," Eva says, "and had all the markers and stones piled up, and ploughed it up, saying he didn't have any use for it."[24]

In 1998 former assistant chief of the Delaware Tribe of Indians Michael Pace noted in reference to the removal of his ancestors, "We don't really understand that today, how much those people suffered. We don't understand how they truly felt because we have not experienced those things." Both the sentiment and the logic of his statements cannot be challenged. Yet Pace did not end his comments on that note. "I cannot really be like those people," he continued, "but what I can do today is to honor the legacy that they have given to me and to remember their suffering and remember their hardships and to remember that what they did they actually did for us to preserve their history, to preserve their legacy, to preserve their culture." It is with those words in mind that this chapter, and the book, ends in the manner it does.[25]

Despite what we want to make of notions of an objective historical truth, it is an author's choice to decide where and how to end the particular story he or she is telling. In a history of Indian removal, should the narrative end on a note of cultural persistence with an eye toward the future? Or should the story of cemeteries destroyed in 1930s Oklahoma frame the final scene? After a great deal of thought I initially chose the latter course, not because I see the narrative of American Indian history solely as one of declension, but because the attempts to eliminate Indian property and presence in the United States over the course of more than two hundred years have been so powerful and unrelenting that the weight of that assault should not be ignored or forgotten. Nor can those efforts be viewed as patterns of a past world or way of life. Indian tribes remain as sovereign entities in Oklahoma, Michigan, Kansas, and throughout the United States, and their political and economic strength in the early twenty-first century is unprecedented in many instances. It is a testament, as Michael Pace notes, to the strength of their ancestors and to those in the present who fight to preserve and protect that legacy. Yet even for the most populous and powerful Indian nations, political and legal challenges to land, culture, and sovereignty are never distant.

That fact brings us full circle to Annie Bumberry, the Seneca woman whose stories began this final chapter. Annie was born on the stomp ground near Elk River, where her parents lived, in northeastern Oklahoma. In November 1937 she observed, "The only property which the Seneca Tribe has left is the east half of the forty acres located at the Basset Springs near Turkey Ford on the Elk River. Here we have our Long House or a cemetery and here we hold our tribal councils, our feasts, etc." At the end of the interview, Annie talks about the home where she then lived, a five-room house she had inherited from her grandmother. "I do not know how long I can stay here," Annie says, "as I am told that the water from the Grand River dam will come up to the top of the doors." The Grand River Dam was part of a larger project pushed by Oklahoma state officials in the mid-1930s aimed at converting the waters of the Grand River into hydroelectric power. The completion of three different dams by 1940 created a body of water known as Grand Lake, or the Lake of the Cherokees. As it so happens, if you enter the search terms "Elk River Oklahoma" into the Google search engine and then click on the map provided, the red dot signifies a location in the middle of the Neosho River right where it meets the Grand Lake. The Seneca-Cayugas were one of several Indian communities whose tribal lands are submerged beneath the waters of that lake.[26] Minnie Thompson, a Seneca-Cayuga woman speaking in 1970, remembers the days before the dam came, a time when folks could just go and swim in the Elk River near Turkey Ford. All that had changed with the Grand River Dam. "I just get sick of it sometimes," the eighty-year-old woman states. "Nothing but boats on the lake." She did not even want to think about the future and worried about what it meant for the younger generations. "Just be an Indian with no country. Nowhere to go."[27]

AFTERWORD

Shortly after I finished my first draft of the concluding chapter of this book, I spent several days in northeastern Oklahoma. On the last day of my trip, I was invited to visit the Seneca-Cayuga longhouse and ceremonial grounds in Ottawa County. It was late spring, and the camps on the grounds were empty, waiting for the weeks to come when hundreds of men, women, and children would gather together to share stories and food when they were not taking part in the ceremonies that brought them to this place. On one side of the grounds a chain-link fence separated the camps from a road, and on the other side of the road were bluffs overlooking Grand Lake. Standing at that fence, I could see the waters of the lake and noticed a speedboat racing away in the distance. Under those very waters rest the homes of Annie Bumberry and other Seneca-Cayugas, all of which had been condemned in order to clear the way for the construction of the dam. At the bottom of the lake are the ceremonial grounds established by the Seneca-Cayugas following their removal from Ohio in 1832. It is a powerful symbol of loss that reaches back several centuries. And yet I took in that view while standing within the very grounds that give force and life to the Seneca-Cayugas who continue to perform their ceremonies, maintain their community, and teach their children in the present.

My visit to the Seneca-Cayuga ceremonial grounds forced me to reconsider the manner in which I had decided to conclude my narrative. On the one hand, it would be unfortunate to end on Minnie Thompson's words because of the dire picture she paints of her people's future. The hard work of present-day Seneca-Cayuga leaders to engage their people and maintain their ceremonial calendar testifies to the vibrant presence of their nation in northeastern Oklahoma. On the other hand, it would be disingenuous to pretend that Minnie and her prophecy are outliers and that the late twentieth century was more about Native American resurgence than about the persistent forces of settler colonialism in the United States. More than two centuries of American policies and more than four centuries of European colonization cannot be swept aside by making the statement that Indians are still here.

Instead, perhaps it is best to end by remembering that American Indian tribes, bands, nations, families, and individuals continue to shape the lives of their communities and are becoming more engaged in taking control of the manner in which their stories are told and their ancestors are treated. The evolving relationship between the federally recognized tribes, whose histories intertwine with the lands that became the state of Ohio, and the Ohio History Connection (formerly the Ohio Historical Society) represents a particularly cogent example of this trend. Events described within this book created a relative vacuum within Ohio and the other states carved out of the Old Northwest Territory. From the mid-nineteenth century to the present the removed tribes focused on their struggles in Kansas, Oklahoma, and elsewhere, and thus did not have the time or the resources to respond to or counter the narrative constructed by Midwestern pioneers about the former Indian inhabitants. Now the descendants of the Shawnees, Delawares, Seneca-Cayugas, Wyandots and others who were removed in the 1800s are declaring their need to have a prominent say in the content and style of the stories told about the past and present. In addition, Oklahoma-based tribes are now more resolute in their efforts to use federal policies like the Native American Graves Protection and Repatriation Act (NAGPRA) to assert control over the proper treatment of human remains and material artifacts stored in museums or uncovered on construction sites throughout the lands where they once made their home.

The actions taken and the statements made by these sovereign nations do not exist in a society in which settler colonialism has disappeared or even faded, but the circumstances of the twenty-first century are different than those of the nineteenth. The relationship between American Indian nations and the United States has never consisted of a one-sided conversation. In the twenty-first century, however, the members and leaders of these sovereign nations are in a better position to make people listen to what they are saying.

NOTES

ABBREVIATIONS USED IN THE NOTES

1855 Proceedings	Proceedings of a council with the Chippewas and Ottawas of Michigan held at the city of Detroit, by the Hon. George W. Manypeny [*sic*] and Henry C. Gilbert, Commissioners of the United States, July 25, 1855, Records of the U.S. Court of Claims, National Archives and Records Administration, Washington, D.C., Record Group 123, Docket 27978.
ARCIA	Office of Indian Affairs, Annual Reports of the Commissioner of Indian Affairs, Documents Relating to Indian Affairs, University of Wisconsin Digital Collections, http://uwdc.library.wisc.edu/collections/History/IndianTreatiesMicro.
ASPIA	*American State Papers, Documents, Legislative and Executive, of the Congress of the United States, Class II, Indian Affairs*, ed. Matthew St. Clair Clarke and Walter Lowrie (Washington, D.C.: Gales and Seaton, 1832). *A Century of Lawmaking for a New Nation.*
MPHC	Michigan Pioneer and Historical Collections, Michigan State University Library.
OIA-LR	Record Group 75 M234, Letters Received by the Office of Indian Affairs, 1824–1881, National Archives and Records Administration, Washington, D.C.
OIA-LS	Record Group 75 M21, Letters Sent by the Office of Indian Affairs, 1824–1881, National Archives and Records Administration, Washington, D.C.

OIA-M1   Record Group 75 M1, Records of the Michigan Superinten-
          dency, 1824–1851. National Archives and Records Admin-
          istration, Washington, D.C.

DRNRUT   Record Group 75 T494, Documents Relating to the Nego-
          tiation of Ratified and Unratified Treaties with Various
          Indian Tribes, 1801–1869, National Archives and Records
          Administration, Documents Relating to Indian Affairs,
          University of Wisconsin Digital Collections, http://uwdc
          .library.wisc.edu/collections/History/IndianTreatiesMicro.

SD 512   Senate Document 512, *U.S. Serial Set, A Century of Law-
          making for a New Nation: U.S. Congressional Documents and
          Debates, 1774–1875*, Library of Congress, memory.loc.gov
          /ammem/amlaw/lwsslink.html#anchor23

TDC-GLOVE Tribal Documents Collection, Great Lakes and Ohio Val-
          ley Ethnohistory Collection, Glenn A. Black Laboratory of
          Archaeology, Indiana University.

TPUS   *The Territorial Papers of the United States*, ed. Clarence Edward
          Carter and John Porter Bloom (Washington, D.C.: U.S.
          Government Printing Office, 1934–1975).

USSL   *U.S. Statutes at Large, A Century of Lawmaking for a New Nation*,
          Library of Congress, memory.loc.gov/ammem/amlaw
          /lwsl.html.

INTRODUCTION

1. Richard Graham to William Clark, April 4, 1827, OIA-LR, roll 300.

2. Journal in Randall L. Buchman, *A Sorrowful Journey* (Defiance, Ohio: Defiance College Press, 2007), 46.

3. J. J. Abert to General George Gibson, November 18, 1832, SD 512, Serial No. 245, 399–400.

4. Dwight L. Smith, ed., "Journal of an Emigrating Party of Pottawattomie Indians, 1838," *Indiana Magazine of History* 21 (December 1925): 318.

5. Ibid., 317–19.

6. Scott Richard Lyons, *X-Marks: Native Signatures of Assent* (Minneapolis: University of Minnesota Press, 2010), 8. An overview can be found in James Taylor Carson, "Ethnogeography and the Native American Past," *Ethnohistory* 49 (Fall 2002): 769–88.

7. Lyons, *X-Marks*, 8.

8. James Joseph Buss, *Winning the West with Words: Language and Conquest in the Lower Great Lakes* (Norman: University of Oklahoma Press, 2011), 6.

9. James A. Henretta, Rebecca Edwards, and Robert O. Self, *America's History*, 7th ed. (New York: Bedford/St. Martin's, 2011), 318.

10. James L. Roark et al., *Understanding the American Promise: A Brief History* (New York: Bedford/St. Martin's, 2011), 1:288.

11. Daniel Walker Howe, *What Hath God Wrought: The Transformation of America, 1815–1848* (New York: Oxford University Press, 2007), 342.

12. Grant Foreman, *Indian Removal: The Emigration of the Five Civilized Tribes of Indians* (Norman: University of Oklahoma Press, 1932), 13. It bears mention, of course, that not all textbooks have followed this trend. Not surprisingly, two of the better textbook treatments of the topic can be found in Frederick Hoxie, R. David Edmunds, and Neal Salisbury, *The People: A History of Native America* (New York: Cengage Learning, 2007); Colin G. Calloway, *First Peoples: A Documentary Survey of American Indian History*, 4th ed. (New York: Bedford/St. Martin's, 2012).

13. Grant Foreman, *Last Trek of the Indians* (Chicago: University of Chicago Press, 1946), 14.

14. John P. Bowes, *Exiles and Pioneers: Eastern Indians in the Trans-Mississippi West* (New York: Cambridge University Press, 2007); Grant Foreman, *The Five Civilized Tribes* (Norman: University of Oklahoma Press, 1934); Grant Foreman, *Advancing the Frontier, 1830–1860* (Norman: University of Oklahoma Press, 1933); Gloria Jahoda, *The Trail of Tears: The Story of American Indian Removals, 1813–1855* (New York: Wings Books, 1995).

15. Theda Perdue and Michael D. Green, *The Cherokee Nation and the Trail of Tears* (New York: Penguin, 2007), xiv–xv.

16. Howe, *What Hath God Wrought*, 421.

17. A very brief bibliography of this historiography on southeastern removal includes Foreman, *Indian Removal;* William L. Anderson, ed., *Cherokee Removal: Before and After* (Athens: University of Georgia Press, 1991); John Ehle, *Trail of Tears: The Rise and Fall of the Cherokee Nation* (New York: Anchor Doubleday, 1997); Theda Perdue and Michael D. Green, eds., *The Cherokee Removal: A Brief History with Documents* (New York: Bedford/St. Martin's, 1995); Michael D. Green, *The Politics of Indian Removal: Creek Government and Society in Crisis* (Lincoln: University of Nebraska Press, 1982); Amanda L. Paige, Fuller L. Bumpers, Daniel F. Littlefield, Jr., *Chickasaw Removal* (Norman: University of Oklahoma Press, 2010); Arthur H. DeRosier, Jr., *The Removal of the Choctaw Indians* (Knoxville: University of Tennessee Press, 1981); Mary Young, "The Exercise of Sovereignty in Cherokee Georgia," *Journal of the Early Republic* 10 (Spring 1990): 43–63; Jill Norgren, *The Cherokee Cases: Two Landmark Federal Decisions in the Fight for Sovereignty* (Norman: University of Oklahoma Press, 2004).

18. "drift" in Robert Remini, *Andrew Jackson and His Indian Wars* (New York: Penguin, 2002), 279–81; "recognition" in Lucy Maddox, *Removals: Nineteenth Century American Literature and the Politics of Indian Affairs* (New York: Oxford University Press, 1991), 16–17.

19. John A. Andrew III, *From Revivals to Removal: Jeremiah Evarts, the Cherokee Nation, and the Search for the Soul of America* (Athens: University of Georgia Press, 1992), 176; Mary Hershberger, "Mobilizing Women, Anticipating Abolition: The Struggle against Indian Removal in the 1830s," *Journal of American History* 86

(June 1999): 14–40; Fred Rolater, "The American Indian and the Origin of the Second American Party System," *Wisconsin Magazine of History* 76 (Spring 1993): 180–203; Ronald N. Satz, *American Indian Policy in the Jacksonian Era* (Norman: University of Oklahoma Press, 2002), 39–63.

20. Recent discussions of the field illustrate the impact of this scholarship on the study of colonial America, the American West, and the twentieth century especially. See Ned Blackhawk, "Look How Far We've Come: How American Indian History Changed the Study of American History in the 1990s," *Organization of American Historians Magazine of History* 19 (November 2005): 13–17; Nicolas G. Rosenthal, "Beyond the New Indian History: Recent Trends in the Historiography on the Native Peoples of North America," *History Compass* 4 (2006): 962–74; John Wunder, "Native American History, Ethnohistory, and Context," *Ethnohistory* 54 (Fall 2007): 591–604; R. David Edmunds, "Blazing New Trails or Burning Bridges: Native American History Comes of Age," *Western Historical Quarterly* 39 (Spring 2008): 4–15. For a few examples of the transformative books I mean, see Richard White, *The Middle Ground: Indians, Empires, and Republics in the Great Lakes Region, 1650–1815* (New York: Cambridge University Press, 1991); Pekka Hämäläinen, *The Comanche Empire* (New Haven, Conn.: Yale University Press, 2009); Colin G. Calloway, *One Vast Winter Count: The Native American West before Lewis and Clark* (Lincoln: University of Nebraska Press, 2003). For examples of the Cherokee historiography, see note 17 above.

21. A short list of the books that have made it impossible to write about colonial North America without a Native perspective includes R. White, *Middle Ground*; Jane T. Merritt, *At the Crossroads: Indians and Empires on a Mid-Atlantic Frontier, 1700–1763* (Chapel Hill: University of North Carolina Press, 2003); James H. Merrell, *The Indians' New World: Catawbas and Their Neighbors from European Contact through the Era of Removal* (New York, 1991); James H. Merrell, *Into the American Woods: Negotiators on the Pennsylvania Frontier* (New York: Norton, 1999); Alan Gallay, *The Indian Slave Trade: The Rise of the English Empire in the American South, 1670–1717* (New Haven, Conn.: Yale University Press, 2002); Kathleen DuVal, *The Native Ground: Indians and Colonists in the Heart of the Continent* (Philadelphia: University of Pennsylvania Press, 2007); Daniel H. Usner, Jr., *Indians, Settlers, and Slaves in a Frontier Exchange Economy: The Lower Mississippi Valley before 1783* (Chapel Hill: University of North Carolina Press, 1992); James F. Brooks, *Captives and Cousins: Slavery, Kinship, and Community in the Southwest Borderlands* (Chapel Hill: University of North Carolina Press, 2002); Juliana Barr, *Peace Came in the Form of a Woman: Indians and Spaniards in the Texas Borderlands* (Chapel Hill: University of North Carolina Press, 2007).

22. R. David Edmunds, "'A Watchful Safeguard to Our Habitations': Black Hoof and the Loyal Shawnees," in *Native Americans and the Early Republic*, ed. Frederick Hoxie, Ronald Hoffman, and Peter J. Albert (Charlottesville: University of Virginia Press, 1999), 162–99; John P. Bowes, "The Gnaddenhutten Effect: Moravian Converts and the Search for Safety in the Canadian Borderlands," *Michigan Historical Review* 34 (Spring 2008): 101–17.

23. Stephen Warren, *The Worlds the Shawnees Made: Migration and Violence in Early America* (Chapel Hill: University of North Carolina Press, 2013), 228.

24. John P. Bowes, "Shawnee Geography and the Tennessee Corridor in the Seventeenth and Eighteenth Centuries," in *Before the Volunteer State: New Thoughts on Early Tennessee History, 1540–1800*, ed. Kristofer Ray (Knoxville: University of Tennessee Press, 2015), 83–105; Bowes, "Gnaddenhutten Effect."

25. For the connection of the eighteenth century to the nineteenth century among the Creeks and Choctaws, see Green, *Politics of Indian Removal*; Claudio Saunt, *A New Order of Things: Property, Power, and the Transformation of the Creek Indians, 1733–1816* (New York: Cambridge University Press, 1999); Greg O'Brien, *Choctaws in a Revolutionary Age, 1750–1830* (Lincoln: University of Nebraska Press, 2005). Examinations of continuities in the removal and postremoval eras can be seen in William McLoughlin, *After the Trail of Tears: The Cherokees' Struggle for Sovereignty, 1839–1880* (Chapel Hill: University of North Carolina Press, 1994); David La Vere, *Contrary Neighbors: Southern Plains and Removed Indians in Indian Territory* (Norman: University of Oklahoma Press, 2001); Andrew Denson, *Demanding the Cherokee Nation: Indian Autonomy and American Culture, 1830–1900* (Lincoln: University of Nebraska Press, 2004); Clara Sue Kidwell, *The Choctaws in Oklahoma: From Tribe to Nation, 1855–1970* (Norman: University of Oklahoma Press, 2008); Wendy St. Jean, *Remaining Chickasaw in Indian Territory, 1830s–1907* (Tuscaloosa: University of Alabama Press, 2011).

26. The topic of slavery has been an especially valuable avenue of inquiry leading to a more inclusive and continuous narrative that incorporates experiences before, during, and after removal. It should not be surprising, of course, that the inclusion of slavery into the discussion does not shift the discussion outside of the southern context. See Tiya Miles, *Ties That Bind: The Story of an Afro-Cherokee Family in Slavery and Freedom* (Berkeley: University of California Press, 2006); Tiya Miles and Sharon Patricia Holland, eds., *Crossing Waters, Crossing Worlds: The African Diaspora in Indian Country* (Durham, N.C.: Duke University Press, 2006); Celia E. Naylor, *African Cherokees in Indian Territory: From Chattel to Citizens* (Chapel Hill: University of North Carolina Press, 2008); Kevin Mulroy, *The Seminole Freedmen: A History* (Norman: University of Oklahoma Press, 2007). Reviews of the larger historiography of American Indian history and its relative impact on broader narratives can be seen in Claudio Saunt, "Go West: Mapping Early American Historiography," *William and Mary Quarterly* 65 (October 2008): 745–78; Daniel Richter, "Whose Indian History?" *William and Mary Quarterly* 50 (1993): 379–93; Rosenthal, "Beyond the New Indian History."

27. Kerry A. Trask, *Black Hawk and the Battle for the Heart of America* (New York: Henry Holt, 2006); Patrick J. Jung, *The Black Hawk War of 1832* (Norman: University of Oklahoma Press, 2008); John W. Hall, *Uncommon Defense: Indian Allies in the Black Hawk War* (Cambridge, Mass.: Harvard University Press, 2009). Monographs focused on the postremoval experiences of Indians from the Great Lakes include Craig Miner and William Unrau, *The End of Indian Kansas: A Study in Cultural Revolution, 1854–1871* (Lawrence: University Press of Kansas,

1990); Joseph Herring, *The Enduring Indians of Kansas: A Century and a Half of Acculturation* (Lawrence: University Press of Kansas, 1990); William E. Unrau, *The Rise and Fall of Indian Country, 1825–1855* (Lawrence: University Press of Kansas, 2007).

28. "despite" in Ethan Davis, "An Administrative Trail of Tears: Indian Removal," *American Journal of Legal History* 50 (January 2010): 53; "to emigrate" in Message from the President of the United States, December 8, 1829, *Journal of the Senate, A Century of Lawmaking for a New Nation*, Library of Congress, 21st Cong., 1st Sess., 5–22.

29. Patrick Griffin, *American Leviathan: Empire, Nation, and Revolutionary Frontier* (New York: Hill and Wang, 2008); David Andrew Nichols, *Red Gentlemen and White Savages: Indians, Federalists, and the Search for Order on the American Frontier* (Charlottesville: University of Virginia Press, 2008).

30. Patrick Wolfe, "Settler Colonialism and the Elimination of the Native," *Journal of Genocide Research* 8 (December 2006): 388; Gary Clayton Anderson, *Ethnic Cleansing and the Indian: The Crime That Should Haunt America* (Norman: University of Oklahoma Press, 2014). Other examples include Walter Hixson, *American Settler Colonialism: A History* (New York: Palgrave Macmillan, 2013); Lisa Ford, *Settler Sovereignty: Jurisdiction and Indigenous People in America and Australia, 1788–1836* (Cambridge, Mass.: Harvard University Press, 2010); Bethel Saler, *The Settlers' Empire: Colonialism and State Formation in America's Old Northwest* (Philadelphia: University of Pennsylvania Press, 2015).

31. Kevin Bruyneel, *The Third Space of Sovereignty: The Postcolonial Politics of U.S.–Indigenous Relations* (Minneapolis: University of Minnesota Press, 2007), 50.

32. Lyons, *X-Marks*, 3. Although the term "adaptive resistance" may have its origins elsewhere, credit for my understanding and use of it within the removal context goes to George Ironstrack.

1. Violence and Removal from Little Turtle to Black Hawk

1. John Knight, John Slover, and William Crawford, *Indian Atrocities, Narratives of the Perils and Sufferings of Dr. Knight and John Slover* (Cincinnati: U. P. James, 1867), 22–25; Consul W. Butterfield, *An Historical Account of the Expedition against Sandusky under Col. William Crawford in 1782* (Cincinnati: Robert Clarke, 1873), 379–92.

2. Knight, Slover, and Crawford, *Indian Atrocities*, 5–6.

3. Samuel C. Stambaugh to Winfield Scott, August 13, 1832, in Ellen M. Whitney, comp. and ed., *The Black Hawk War 1831–1832* (Springfield: Illinois State Historical Library, 1973), vol. 2, bk. 1, 996.

4. Declaration of Independence; Memorial of citizens of Shelbyville, Illinois, July 10, 1832, OIA-LR, roll 132. Although the quotation refers to "Winnebago Indians," I will use "Ho-Chunk" outside of any direct quotes because that is the preferred name in the present day.

5. Colin G. Calloway, *The American Revolution in Indian Country: Crisis and Diversity in Native American Communities* (New York: Cambridge University Press, 1995), 289–91.

6. Calloway, *American Revolution in Indian Country*; Alan Taylor, *The Divided Ground: Indians, Settlers, and the Northern Borderland of the American Revolution* (New York: Alfred A. Knopf, 2006).

7. Randolph Downes, *Council Fires on the Upper Ohio* (Pittsburgh: University of Pittsburgh Press, 1969), 287–88.

8. Neville Craig, ed., *The Olden Time: A Monthly Publication Devoted to the Preservation of Documents and Other Authentic Information*, reprint (Cincinnati: Robert Clarke, 1876), 2:424–26; emphasis in original.

9. Treaty of Fort Stanwix of 1784, *Indian Affairs: Laws and Treaties*, ed. and comp. Charles A. Kappler (Washington, D.C.: U.S. Government Printing Office, 1904), 2:273–77, 5–6; Treaty of Fort Stanwix of 1768, E. B. O'Callaghan, ed., *Documents Relative to the Colonial History of the State of New York* (Albany, N.Y.: Weed, Parsons, 1857), 8:135–37; "spoke" in R. White, *Middle Ground*, 351; "Brother" in Craig, *Olden Time*, 2:522; "expressed" and "doctrine" in Report of the Secretary of War: Indian Affairs, May 2, 1788, *TPUS*, 2:103–104.

10. "foundered" in R. White, *Middle Ground*, 417; Taylor, *Divided Ground*, 238–40; "Indians," "be taken," and "finances" in Report of H. Knox, Secretary of War, to the President of the United States, June 15, 1789, *ASPIA*, 1:13.

11. Speech of the United Indian Nations, *ASPIA*, 1:3–4.

12. "Indians" in Judge Innes to Secretary of War, July 7, 1790, *ASPIA*, 1:38; Hamtramck to Harmar, August 31, 1788, in Gayle Thornbrough, ed., *Outpost on the Wabash* (Indianapolis: Indiana State Historical Society, 1957), 114–17; "mortifying" in Hamtramck to Harmar, July 29, 1789, Thornbrough, *Outpost on the Wabash*, 182; other attacks by Kentuckians north of the Ohio River in the 1780s discussed in Downes, *Council Fires*, 278–79; 298–99, 311–13.

13. R. White, *Middle Ground*, 448–68; Colin G. Calloway, *The Victory with No Name: The Native American Defeat of the First American Army* (New York: Oxford University Press, 2014); Treaty of Greenville, *Indian Affairs*, 2:39–45.

14. R. White, *Middle Ground*, 470–72; "assure" in Henry Knox to Governor St. Clair, August 23, 1790, *ASPIA*, 1:98.

15. "probable" in Instructions to Commissioners from Henry Knox, April 26, 1793, *ASPIA*, 1:342; Colonel McKee to Major of Brigade Littlehales, April 11, 1793, ibid., 1:343; additional communications from the commissioners to McKee and agents in Detroit, ibid., 1:345–46; Reginald Horsman, "The British Indian Department and the Abortive Treaty of Lower Sandusky, 1793," *Ohio Historical Quarterly* 70 (July 1961): 189–213.

16. "unfounded" in Commissioners to Governor Simcoe, June 7, 1793, *ASPIA*, 1:347; "jealousy" in Simcoe to the Commissioners, June 7, 1793, ibid., 1:347; for the motivations and agenda of Simcoe, see Taylor, *Divided Ground*, 268–70.

17. Journal of Commissioners, *ASPIA*, 1:349.

18. Ibid., 1:349; Minutes of a Council with the Indians, in E. A. Cruikshank, ed., *The Correspondence of Lieutenant Governor John Graves Simcoe* (Toronto: Toronto Historical Society, 1923), 1:377. *ASPIA* includes a brief summary of the exchange between Brant and Simcoe but notes that they received it from Simcoe's secretary on July 10, 1793. See *ASPIA*, 1:351.

19. Journal of Commissioners, *ASPIA*, 1:349–51; Minutes of a Council with the Indians, in Cruikshank, *Simcoe*, 1:377–82.

20. "seriously" in Record of Council at Captain Elliot's, *ASPIA*, 1:352; Alan Taylor provides another explanation for the movement of the commissioners through Detroit, namely the notion of using the "backdoor" and not the war-paths. See Taylor, *Divided Ground*, 268, 278.

21. "impossible" in Record of Council at Captain Elliot's, *ASPIA*, 1:353.

22. "sorry" in ibid., 1:354.

23. Statement to the Commissioners of the United States, ibid., 1:356–57.

24. "trust" in ibid., 1:357; Commissioners to Major General Wayne, August 23, 1793, ibid., 1:359; "Indians" in Commissioners to Henry Knox, August 21, 1793, ibid., 1:359–60.

25. Minutes of treaty council at Greenville, *ASPIA*, 1:564–82; Buss, *Winning the West*, 17–27; text of Jay's Treaty in *American State Papers, Documents, Legislative and Executive, of the Congress of the United States, Class I, Foreign Affairs*, ed. Matthew St. Clair Clarke and Walter Lowrie (Washington, D.C.: Gales and Seaton, 1833), 1:520–25.

26. Minutes of treaty council at Greenville, *ASPIA*, 1:572–73.

27. "to use" in Buss, *Winning the West*, 20–25; Tarhe quotes in *ASPIA*, 1:575, 580.

28. New Corn's quote in *ASPIA*, 1:580.

29. Timothy D. Willig, *Restoring the Chain of Friendship: British Policy and the Indians of the Great Lakes, 1783–1815* (Lincoln: University of Nebraska Press, 2008), 54–58, 91–102.

30. C. A. Weslager, *The Delaware Indians: A History* (New Brunswick, N.J.: Rutgers University Press, 1972), 330–33; Helen Hornbeck Tanner, *Atlas of Great Lakes Indian History* (Norman: University of Oklahoma Press, 1987), 100–101; R. David Edmunds, *The Shawnee Prophet* (Lincoln: University of Nebraska Press, 1985), 17–27; Edmunds, "'Watchful Safeguard,'"162–99.

31. Edmunds, *Shawnee Prophet*, 28–39; John Sugden, "Early Pan-Indianism; Tecumseh's Tour of the Indian Country," *American Indian Quarterly* 10 (Fall 1986): 273–304; John Sugden, "Tecumseh's Travels Revisited," *Indiana Magazine of History* 96 (June 2000): 151–68.

32. Adam Jortner takes to task the accepted narrative of Harrison's challenge and the Shawnee Prophet's miracle in *The Gods of Prophetstown: The Battle of Tippecanoe and the Holy War for the American Frontier* (New York: Oxford University Press, 2011), 3–14; Edmunds, *Shawnee Prophet*, 47–48; "fear" in Harrison to Secretary of War, July 11, 1807, Logan Esarey, ed., *Messages and Letters of William*

Henry Harrison (Indianapolis: Indiana Historical Society, 1922), 1:223–24; "British" in William Wells to Harrison, August 20, 1807, Esarey, *William Henry Harrison*, 1:242.

33. "lift" in The Prophet to Harrison, June 24, 1808, Esarey, *William Henry Harrison*, 1:292; "given" in Harrison to the Prophet, n.d., ibid., 1:293; "no doubt" in Harrison to Secretary of War, April 25, 1810, ibid., 1:418.

34. Stephen Warren, *The Shawnees and Their Neighbors, 1795–1870* (Urbana: University of Illinois Press, 2005), 36–42; Jortner, *Gods of Prophetstown*, 172–85; Sugden, "Early Pan-Indianism"; "You must" in Proceedings of a Private Meeting with the Shawenoes, March 25, 1808, MPHC, 25:242; "push forwards" in Indian Speech, November 15, 1810, MPHC, 25:276; Matthew Elliott to William Claus, November 16, 1810, MPHC, 25:277.

35. Reginald Horsman, *Expansion and American Indian Policy, 1783–1812* (Norman: University of Oklahoma Press, 1992), 166–68; Edmunds, *Shawnee Prophet*, 92–93; discussion of Tenskwatawa, Tecumseh, and the sacred elements of the movement in Gregory Evans Dowd, *A Spirited Resistance: The North American Indian Struggle for Unity, 1745–1815* (Baltimore: Johns Hopkins University Press, 1993), 139–47.

36. Harrison to Secretary of War, July 5, 1809, Esarey, *William Henry Harrison*, 1:349–55; "all" in Snelling to Harrison, November 20, 1811, ibid., 1:644; Harrison to Secretary of War, December 4, 1811, ibid., 1:656; "hostile" in Jackson to Harrison, November 28, 1811, ibid., 1:665. For other testaments to a continued alliance between the British and Indians, see William Wells to Secretary of War, February 10, 1812, ibid., 2:21–22; B. F. Stickney to Governor Hull, May 25, 1812, ibid., 2:53–55.

37. Information about aspects of Wyandot history in the region can be found in Tanner, *Atlas*, 40–41, 57–62, 80–83, 87–91, 102; R. White, *Middle Ground*, 433–48; Bowes, *Exiles and Pioneers*, 163–64.

38. William E. Connelley, ed., "The Provisional Government of Nebraska Territory and the Journals of William Walker," *Proceedings and Collections of the Nebraska State Historical Society, Second Series* 3 (1899): 5–14; "Notes on Wyandot and Gen. William Walker," Frontier Wars MSS, Draper Manuscript Collection, State Historical Society of Wisconsin, 11U13; Tanner, *Atlas*, 101–106.

39. Frontier Wars MSS, 11U13–14, 1–2.

40. The details of John Walker's escape are provided by his younger brother in a series of exchanges with Lyman Draper. Less is known about the manner in which William Walker broke free. See Frontier Wars MSS, 11U14, 3–8, 72–73; Benjamin Stickney to William Henry Harrison, April 7, 1813, quoted in Gayle Thornbrough, ed., *Letterbook of the Indian Agency at Fort Wayne* (Indianapolis: Indiana Historical Society, 1961), 195n89.

41. David Curtis Skaggs, *The Battle of Lake Erie and Its Aftermath: A Reassessment* (Kent, Ohio: Kent State University Press, 2013).

42. Because the commissioners relied on a template, most of these treaties have the same wording. Examples can be found in *Indian Affairs*, 2:110–12, 116–19;

"among" in A. J. Dallas to Richard Graham, July 14, 1815, *TPUS*, 17:198–200; "British" in Richard Graham to Secretary of War, July 8, 1816, *TPUS*, 17:359–61.

43. "invited" in Ninian Edwards to the Secretary of State, March 3, 1816, *TPUS*, 17:308–10; Ninian Edwards to the Secretary of War, March 20, 1816, ibid., 17:318–19; "having" in Ninian Edwards to the Secretary of War, November 18, 1816, ibid., 17:430–37.

44. "nine" in Governor Cass to the Secretary of War, August 3, 1819, ibid., 10:852–55; "efficient" in Secretary of War to Governor Cass, February 11, 1822, ibid., 11:224–25; Governor Cass to the Secretary of War, with enclosures, June 27, 1823, ibid., 11:375–80.

45. "Young" in Wyandott Chiefs at Sandusky to John Johnston, February 6, 1816, Huron 1816, TDC-GLOVE; Return of Indians Dependent on the Post of Amherstburg 15th August 1816, MPHC, 16:523–25.

46. "exaggerated" in Governor Cass to the Acting Secretary of War, July 2, 1815, *TPUS*, 10:556–57; "mode" in Governor Cass to the Secretary of War, December 15, 1815, ibid., 10:611–12; "tract" in Governor Cass to the Secretary of War, July 30, 1816, ibid., 10:661–63.

47. Willig, *Restoring the Chain*; "costly" and "hoisted" in Henry Rowe School-craft, *Narrative Journal of Travels through the Northwestern Regions of the United States* (Albany, N.Y.: E. and E. Hosford, 1821), 136–38; Michael Witgen, *An Infinity of Nations: How the Native New World Shaped Early America* (Philadelphia: University of Pennsylvania Press, 2013), 338–44.

48. Bowyer quoted in Jedidiah Morse, *A Report to the Secretary of War of the United States, on Indian Affairs, Comprising a Narrative of a Tour Performed in the Summer of 1820. . . .* (New Haven: S. Converse, 1822), 40–42, 53–54; Governor Cass to the Secretary of War, October 26, 1821, *TPUS*, 11:156–57.

49. "perfectly" in Governor Cass to the Secretary of War, April 17, 1818, *TPUS*, 11:744–46; for military actions in Florida, see Howe, *What Hath God Wrought*, 97–107.

50. Edmunds, *Shawnee Prophet*, 142–64.

51. Trask, *Black Hawk*; Jung, *Black Hawk War*.

52. Richard H. Bell to Alexander Macomb, August 16, 1831, *TPUS*, 12:332–35.

53. Hall, *Uncommon Defense*; Lucy Eldersveld Murphy, *A Gathering of Rivers: Indians, Métis, and Mining in the Western Great Lakes, 1737–1832* (Lincoln: University of Nebraska Press, 2004).

54. "been" and "that" in William Clark to Edmund P. Gaines, May 28, 1831, Whitney, *Black Hawk War*, vol. 2, bk. 1, 16–17; Articles of Agreement and Capitulation between the United States and the Sauk and Fox, June 30, 1831, ibid., vol. 2, bk. 1, 85–88.

55. "arguments" in Paul L. Chouteau to William Clark, June 27, 1831, ibid., vol. 2, bk. 1, 78–79; "Indians" in John Reynolds to the Secretary of War, July 7, 1831, ibid., vol. 2, bk. 1, 104–105.

56. "that" in Richard M. Young, Benjamin Mills, and James M. Strode to John Reynolds, April 20, 1832, ibid., vol. 2, bk. 1, 288–89; John Reynolds:

Proclamation, May 15, 1832, ibid., vol. 2, bk. 1, 373–74; Thomas J. V. Owen to George B. Porter, May 18, 1832, ibid., vol. 2, bk. 1, 383–84; Thomas J. V. Owen to the Public, June 5, 1832, ibid., vol. 2, bk. 1, 527–28.

57. George A. McCall to Archibald McCall, June 17, 1831, ibid., vol. 2, bk. 1, 55–58.

58. "The faithless" in William Clark to Lewis Cass, June 8, 1832, ibid., vol. 2, bk. 1, 549–50; "some individuals" in Joseph M. Street to Henry Atkinson, August 5, 1832, ibid., vol. 2, bk. 2, 939–41. Other examples can be seen in Joseph M. Street to William Clark, May 21, 1832, ibid., vol. 2, bk. 1, 401–403; Lewis Cass to Winfield Scott, September 4, 1832, ibid., vol. 2, bk. 2, 1104–105.

59. R. David Edmunds, *The Potawatomis: Keepers of the Fire* (Norman: University of Oklahoma Press, 1978), 186–88.

60. Thomas V. Owen to Steven T. Mason, May 3, 1832, OIA-LR, roll 132; Thomas J. V. Owen to John Reynolds, May 12, 1832, Whitney, *Black Hawk War*, vol. 2, bk. 1, 365; "persuade" in Thomas V. Owen to George Porter, May 18, 1832, OIA-LR, roll 132; "leave" in Thomas V. Owen to Stephen T. Mason, June 3, 1832, OIA-LR, roll 132; Tanner, *Atlas*, 151–53.

61. Edmunds, *Potawatomis*, 235–37; "received" in Donald Jackson, ed., *Black Hawk: An Autobiography* (Urbana: University of Illinois Press, 1955), 121–23; Tanner, *Atlas*, 140.

62. Jackson, *Black Hawk*, 105–106; "Their" in Edmund P. Gaines to Roger Jones, June 1831, in Whitney, *Black Hawk War*, vol. 2, bk. 1, 47–51.

63. John Bliss to Henry Atkinson, April 6, 1832, in Whitney, *Black Hawk War*, vol. 2, bk. 1, 227–28; John Bliss to Henry Atkinson, April 9, 1832, ibid., vol. 2, bk. 1, 239; "saukees" in Journal of Henry Gratiot, ibid., vol. 2, bk. 2, 1302–303; Henry Gratiot to Henry Atkinson, April 27, 1832, ibid., vol. 2, bk. 1, 318.

64. Gideon Low to Winfield Scott, September 3, 1832, ibid., vol. 2, bk. 2, 1100–101; Minutes of Examination of Prisoners, ibid., vol. 2, bk. 2, 1028–37.

65. Taimah and Apenose to William Clark, July 22, 1832, ibid., vol. 2, bk. 2, 852–54.

2. The Rhetoric of Removal and the Evolution of Government Policy

1. "An Ordinance for the Government of the Territory of the United States North West of the River Ohio," in *Journals of the Continental Congress, 1774–1789, A Century of Lawmaking for a New Nation*, 32:334–43.

2. Joel W. Martin, *Sacred Revolt: The Muskogees' Struggle for a New World* (Boston: Beacon Press, 1991), 87–113; Lyons, *X-Marks*.

3. Horsman, *Expansion*; Satz, *American Indian Policy*; Francis Paul Prucha, *The Great Father: The United States Government and the American Indians* (Lincoln: University of Nebraska Press, 1984); Anthony F. C. Wallace, *Jefferson and the Indians: The Tragic Fate of the First Americans* (Cambridge, Mass.: Harvard University Press, 1999).

4. Henry Knox to George Washington, June 15, 1789, *ASPIA*, 1:12–14; all quotes in Henry Knox to George Washington, July 7, 1789, ibid., 1:52–54.

5. This process is examined particularly well in Saler, *Settlers' Empire*, 41–82.

6. Knox to Washington, July 7, 1789, *ASPIA*, 1:54.

7. "originally" in Prucha, *Great Father*, 1:89–90; different versions of the Trade and Intercourse Acts include "An Act to regulate trade and intercourse with the Indian tribes," July 22, 1790, *USSL*, ch. 33, 2 Stat. 137; "An Act to regulate Trade and Intercourse with the Indian Tribes," March 1, 1793, *USSL*, ch. 19, 2 Stat. 329. See also Nichols, *Red Gentlemen and White Savages*.

8. Thomas Jefferson to William Henry Harrison, February 27, 1803, in Francis Paul Prucha, ed., *Documents of United States Indian Policy* (Lincoln: University of Nebraska Press, 2000), 22.

9. Robert M. Owens, *Mr. Jefferson's Hammer: William Henry Harrison and the Origins of American Indian Policy* (Norman: University of Oklahoma Press, 2007); Wallace, *Jefferson and the Indians*, 206–40.

10. Reginald Horsman, "The Indian Policy of an 'Empire for Liberty,'" in *Native Americans and the Early Republic*, ed. Frederick E. Hoxie, Ronald Hoffman, and Peter J. Albert (Charlottesville: University Press of Virginia, 1999), 55.

11. "clear" in *Annals of Congress, A Century of Lawmaking for a New Nation*, Library of Congress, 3rd Cong., 2nd Sess., 1276; "An Act making provision for the purpose of trade with the Indians," March 3, 1795, *USSL*, ch. 51, 1 Stat. 443; "western" in "An Act for establishing Trading Houses with the Indian Tribes," April 18, 1796, *USSL*, ch. 13, 1 Stat. 452.

12. Prucha, *Great Father*, 1:115–34; Royal B. Way, "The United States Factory System for Trading with the Indians, 1796–1822," *Mississippi Valley Historical Review* 6 (September 1919): 220–35; "factory" in Herman J. Viola, *Thomas L. McKenney, Architect of America's Early Indian Policy: 1816–1830* (Chicago: Swallow Press, 1974), 6–11.

13. Thomas L. McKenney to Henry Johnson, December 27, 1821, *ASPIA*, 2:260–64.

14. Benton speech in *Annals of Congress*, Senate, 17th Cong., 1st Sess., 235–36, 317–31; Abolition of the Indian Trading Houses, Communicated to the House of Representatives, May 25, 1824, *ASPIA*, 2:513–22; Abolition of the Indian Trading Houses, Communicated to the House of Representatives, January 21, 1825, *ASPIA*, 2:531–41.

15. *Annals of Congress*, House of Representatives, 15th Cong., 2nd Sess., 546, 1432, 1435; *Annals of Congress*, Senate, 15th Cong., 2nd Sess., 273.

16. "An Act making provision for the civilization of the Indian tribes adjoining the frontier settlements," March 3, 1819, *USSL*, ch. 85, 3 Stat. 516–17.

17. Exchange of Lands with the Indians, Communicated to the Senate, January 9, 1817, *ASPIA*, 2:123–24.

18. John C. Calhoun to James Monroe, January 24, 1825, ibid., 2:544.

19. "would" in James Monroe to the Senate of the United States, January 27, 1825, ibid., 2:542; "enlightened" in John C. Calhoun to James Monroe, January 24, 1825, ibid., 2:544; Thomas L. McKenney to John C. Calhoun, January 10, 1825, ibid., 2:544–45.

20. Perdue and Green, *Cherokee Nation*, 66.

21. *Cherokee Phoenix*, February 21, 1828.

22. Wilson Lumpkin, *The Removal of the Cherokee Indians from Georgia* (New York: Dodd, Mead, 1907), 1:43.

23. "arms" in John Eaton to the Cherokees, April 18, 1829, Prucha, *Documents*, 44–47; "emigrate" in Message from the President of the United States, December 8, 1829, *Journal of the Senate*, 21st Cong., 1st. Sess., 5–22.

24. Hershberger, "Mobilizing Women," 14–40; Andrew, *From Revivals to Removal*, 180–98; Petition from Amherst College, *Journal of the House of Representatives, A Century of Lawmaking for a New Nation*, 21st Cong., 1st Sess., 353; records of other submitted petitions can be found in the *Journal of the House of Representatives*, 21st Cong., 1st Sess., 261–62, 296–97, 317–18, 321–22, 382–83, 416, 448, 474–75; Jeremiah Evarts, *Cherokee Removal: The William Penn Essays and Other Writings*, ed. Francis Paul Prucha (Knoxville: University of Tennessee Press, 1981), 94.

25. Isaac McCoy, *Remarks on the Practicability of Indian Reform, Embracing Their Colonization* (New York: Gray and Bunce, 1829), 39.

26. Lewis Cass, "Documents and Proceedings Relating to the Formation and Progress of a Board in the City of New York, for the Emigration, Preservation, and Improvement of the Aborigines of America," *North American Review* 30 (January 1830): 102.

27. "Removal of Indians," House of Representatives Reports of Committees, *U.S. Serial Set*, 21st Cong., 1st sess., No. 200, Report No. 227, 3, 5.

28. Ibid., 8.

29. *Register of Debates, A Century of Lawmaking for a New Nation*, Library of Congress, House of Representatives, 21st Cong., 1st Sess., 1070.

30. *Register of Debates*, Senate, 21st Cong., 1st Sess., 383; *Register of Debates*, House of Representatives, 21st Cong., 1st Sess., 1135–36.

31. *Register of Debates*, Senate, 21st Cong., 1st Sess., 309–20, 381; Message from the President of the United States, December 8, 1829, *Journal of the Senate*, 21st Cong., 1st Sess., 5–22; Frelinghuysen's amendment found in *Journal of the Senate*, 21st Cong., 1st Sess., 266–68.

32. *Register of Debates*, Senate, 21st Cong., 1st Sess., 364.

33. Ibid., 383; *Register of Debates*, House of Representatives, 21st Congress, 1st Sess., 1135–36.

34. *Register of Debates*, House of Representatives, 21st Cong, 1st Sess., 1032–33.

35. Tim Alan Garrison, *The Legal Ideology of Removal: The Southern Judiciary and the Sovereignty of Native American Nations* (Athens: University of Georgia Press, 2009), 6.

36. *Worcester v. Georgia* decision as published in Norgren, *Cherokee Cases*, 183.

37. Garrison, *Legal Ideology of Removal*, 5.

38. *Register of Debates*, House of Representatives, 21st Cong., 1st Sess., 1014; Rolater, "American Indian," 180–203; Satz, *American Indian Policy*, 27–31; Alfred A. Cave, "Abuse of Power: Andrew Jackson and the Indian Removal

Act of 1830," *The Historian* 65 (December 2003): 1330–53; "Cherokee" in Mark Rifkin, *Manifesting America: The Imperial Construction of U.S. National Space* (New York: Oxford University Press, 2009), 39.

39. R. White, *Middle Ground*; Richard White, "Creative Misunderstandings and New Understandings," *William and Mary Quarterly* 63 (January 2006): 9–14.

40. Message, December 4, 1832, in Dorothy Riker and Gayle Thornbrough, eds., *Messages and Papers Relating to the Administration of Noah Noble, Governor of Indiana 1831–1837* (Indianapolis: Indiana Historical Bureau, 1958), 140.

41. Vine Deloria, Jr., "Self-Determination and the Concept of Sovereignty," in *Native American Sovereignty*, ed. John R. Wunder (New York: Routledge, 1999), 122, 123.

42. "Proceedings, Potawatomi and Miami Treaty Negotiations, September 30–October 23, 1826," in Nellie Armstrong Robertson and Dorothy Riker, comps. and eds., *John Tipton Papers* (Indianapolis: Indiana Historical Society, 1942), 1:579–80.

43. Ibid., 1:580–81.

44. Ibid., 1:582–84; I use here his name in the Myaamia language, but Meehcikilita's name in the council record is written as "Legro." It should be written as "Le Gros," and he is the same Le Gros interviewed by Charles Trowbridge in 1824 and 1825. See Vernon Kinietz, ed., *Meearmeear Traditions* (Ann Arbor: University of Michigan Press, 1938), 1–5.

45. "Proceedings," in Robertson and Riker, *John Tipton Papers*, 1:584–86; Miami Treaty of 1818, *Indian Affairs*, 2:171–74.

46. Potawatomi Treaty of 1826, *Indian Affairs*, 2:273–77; Miami Treaty of 1826, ibid., 2:278–81; "Proceedings," in Robertson and Riker, *John Tipton Papers*, 1:590.

47. G. B. Porter to Lewis Cass, August 23, 1833, OIA-LR, roll 416.

48. Council with the Miamis, October 1833, ibid.

49. Joint Memorial of the Legislature of the State of Indiana to the President of the United States, January 6, 1834, OIA-LR, roll 354; John B. Richardville to Lewis Cass, February 12, 1834, ibid.

50. Lewis Cass to William Marshall, July 12, 1834, "Ratified Treaty No. 192, Documents Relating to the Negotiation of the Treaty of October 23, 1834, with the Miami Indians," DRNRUT; William Marshall to Lewis Cass, September 22, 1834, ibid.; Lewis Cass to William Marshall, October 24, 1834, ibid.; original Miami treaty, October 23, 1834, ibid.; "fraction" and "influx" in William Marshall to Lewis Cass, October 23, 1834, ibid.

51. Talk at a Council Held at the Forks of the Wabash on the 29th of April, 1836, OIA-LR, roll 355; Miinciniikia's name is written as "Meangenequagh" in the council record; "some" in "Tipton to the People of Indiana," ca. July 4, 1836, Robertson and Riker, *John Tipton Papers*, 3:297–99.

52. *Indian Affairs*, 2:425–28, 519–24; Abel C. Pepper to T. Hartley Crawford, November 6, 1838, "Ratified Treaty No. 234, Documents Relating to

the Negotiation of the Treaty of November 6, 1838, with the Miami Indians," DRNRUT.

53. "habits" in Samuel Milroy to T. Hartley Crawford, 1840, ARCIA, 1840, 351; Treaty of 1834 and Treaty of 1838, *Indian Affairs*, 2:425–28, 519–24; Samuel Milroy to T. Hartley Crawford, June 8, 1839, OIA-LR, roll 356; Samuel Milroy to T. Hartley Crawford, August 18, 1839, OIA-LR, roll 361; Treaty of 1840, *Indian Affairs*, 2:531–34;William Wilkins to T. Hartley Crawford, May 4, 1844, OIA-LR, roll 418.

54. Treaty of 1838, *Indian Affairs*, 2:519–24; "one" in John Tipton to John H. Eaton, April 5, 1831, Robertson and Riker, *John Tipton Papers*, 2:400; "sale" in Samuel Milroy to T. Hartley Crawford, August 10, 1840, OIA-LR, roll 357; "Lafontaine" in Allen Hamilton to T. Hartley Crawford, June 10, 1844, OIA-LR, roll 418; "permit" in Francis Lafontaine to Joseph Sinclair, December 1845, OIA-LR, roll 418.

55. Treaty of 1838, *Indian Affairs*, 2:519–24; list of Miamis permitted to remain in Indiana by joint resolution of Congress for the benefit of Frances Slocum and her children and grandchildren, approved March 3, 1845, OIA-LR, roll 418; Martha Bennett Phelps, *Frances Slocum: The Lost Sister of Wyoming* (Wilkes-Barre, Pa.: privately published, 1916), 138–44.

56. Susan Sleeper-Smith, *Indian Women and French Men: Rethinking Cultural Encounter in the Western Great Lakes* (Amherst: University of Massachusetts Press, 2001), 116–40. Sleeper-Smith discusses in more depth than I do here this strategy of "hiding in plain view" to examine the ways the Miamis retained land. Her ideas, and mine as well, are also indebted to the work of O'Brien. See Jean O'Brien, *Dispossession by Degrees: Indian Land and Identity in Natick, Massachusetts, 1650–1790* (New York: Cambridge University Press, 1997); Sarah E. Cooke and Rachel B. Ramadhyani, eds., *Indians and a Changing Frontier: The Art of George Winter* (Indianapolis: Indiana Historical Society/Tippecanoe County Historical Society, 1993); James Joseph Buss, "'They Found and Left Her an Indian': Gender, Race, and the Whitening of Young Bear," *Frontiers: A Journal of Women Studies* 29 (2008): 6–12.

57. Robert A. Trennert, *Indian Traders on the Middle Border: The House of Ewing, 1827–1854* (Lincoln: University of Nebraska Press, 1981), 83–84, 102–104; "disposed," "fear," and "for" in Thomas Dowling to William Wilkins, July 30, 1844, OIA-LR, roll 418; "would" in Joseph Sinclair to William Medill, August 19, 1846, OIA-LR, roll 418; Bert Anson, "Chief Francis Lafontaine and the Miami Emigration from Indiana," *Indiana Magazine of History* 60 (September 1964): 256–57.

58. "hottest" in Joseph Sinclair to William Medill, June 1, 1846, OIA-LR, roll 418; "could" in Joseph Sinclair to William Medill, August 19, 1846, ibid.; Joseph Sinclair to William Medill, October 1, 1846, ibid.; list of Miami Indians mustered at Peru, Indiana, and who commenced their emigration on the 6th day of October A.D. 1846, ibid.; Joseph Sinclair to William Medill, November 1, 1846, ibid.; Joseph Sinclair to William Medill, November 11, 1846, ibid. Sinclair

did his best to explain in his letter how the muster roll at departure was smaller than the number who arrived in Kansas City despite the deaths that had occurred on the journey. Alexis Coquillard to the Secretary of War, May 4, 1848, ibid. For more on the removal, see George Strack et al., *myaamiaki aancihsaaciki: A Cultural Exploration of the Myaamia Removal Route* (Miami, Okla.: Miami Tribe of Oklahoma, 2011).

59. "Journal of the Proceedings at the Treaty Held with the Miami Indians, September 10–25, 1832," in Carole M. Allen et al., eds., "The Man in the Middle—Chief J. B. Richardville," *Indiana Historian: Exploring Indiana History* (November 1993): 9.

3. The Delaware Diaspora in and out of the Early American Republic

1. "I think" in James W. Brown and Rita Kohn, eds., *Long Journey Home: Oral Histories of Contemporary Delaware Indians* (Bloomington: Indiana University Press, 2007), 374; "Being" in ibid., xv.

2. Ives Goddard, "The Delaware," in *Handbook of North American Indians*, ed. Bruce Trigger (Washington, D.C.: Smithsonian Institution, 1978), 15:213–39; village locations from map 16 in Tanner, *Atlas*, 80.

3. Lawrence Henry Gipson, ed., *The Moravian Indian Mission on White River: Diaries and Letters, May 5, 1799, to November 12, 1806* (Indianapolis: Indiana Historical Society, 1938), 67–70; Earl P. Olmstead, *Blackcoats among the Delaware: David Zeisberger on the Ohio Frontier* (Kent, Ohio: Kent State University Press, 1991), 15, 27; Louise Phelps Kellogg, ed., *Frontier Retreat on the Upper Ohio, 1779–1781* (Madison: State Historical Society of Wisconsin, 1917), 376–78; Tanner, *Atlas*, 80–83.

4. Goddard, "Delaware," 15:213, 222–23; Weslager, *Delaware Indians*, 296–316. For a broader perspective of American Indian participation in the American Revolution, see Calloway, *American Revolution in Indian Country*.

5. "Two" in Eugene F. Bliss, ed., *The Diary of David Zeisberger: A Moravian Missionary Among the Indians of Ohio* (Cincinnati: Robert Clarke, 1885), 1:4; Weslager, *Delaware Indians*, 282–322; Dowd, *Spirited Resistance*, 65–83; "family" and "where" in John Heckewelder, *A Narrative of the Mission of the United Brethren among the Delaware and Mohegan Indians, from Its Commencement, in the Year 1740, to the Close of the Year 1808* (Philadelphia: M'Carty and Davis, 1820; reprint, New York: Arno, 1971), 219.

6. Heckewelder, *Narrative of the Mission*, 267–312; Bliss, *David Zeisberger*, 1:9–74; R. White, *Middle Ground*, 387–96; the site of Captives Town can be seen in Tanner, *Atlas*, 80.

7. Bliss, *David Zeisberger*, 1:78–82; "killed" in Heckewelder, *Narrative of the Mission*, 309–17.

8. Bliss, *David Zeisberger*, 1:83.

9. Ibid., 1:86–87, 103–105, 112, 147–48.

10. Ibid., 1:164–65, 256.

11. Ibid., 1:279–332, 335, 340, 2:238–39.

12. "how" and "help" in ibid., 2:150–52, 188; *ASPIA*, 1:489; Helen Hornbeck Tanner, "The Glaize in 1792: A Composite Indian Community," *Ethnohistory* 25 (Winter 1978): 15–39; Dowd, *Spirited Resistance*, 103–109.

13. Bliss, *David Zeisberger*, 2:241, 251–60.

14. Public Library of Fort Wayne and Allen County, ed., *General Harmar's Campaign* (Fort Wayne, Ind.: Library, 1954), 1–2; H. W. Beckwith, *History of Fountain County* (Chicago: H. H. Hill and N. Iddings, 1881), 172–73; William Henry Smith, ed., *The St. Clair Papers* (Cincinnati: Robert Clarke, 1882), 2:251–62; *ASPIA*, 1:582; *Indian Affairs*, 2:273–77, 39–45.

15. Tanner, *Atlas*, 72, 85, 88; Public Library of Fort Wayne and Allen County, *General Harmar's Campaign*, 1–2; Milo M. Quaife, ed., "A Narrative of Life on the Old Frontier," *Proceedings of the State Historical Society of Wisconsin* (1914): 226; George R. Wilson and Gayle Thornbrough, *The Buffalo Trace* (Indianapolis: Indiana Historical Society, 1946), 188, 211; Charles N. Thompson, *Sons of the Wilderness: John and William Conner* (Indianapolis: Indiana Historical Society, 1937), 42.

16. Weslager, *Delaware Indians*, 332–33; for more on government Indian policy and land acquisition under Jefferson, see Wallace, *Jefferson and the Indians*; Owens, *Mr. Jefferson's Hammer*.

17. Kinietz, *Meearmeear Traditions*, 10–11; *ASPIA*, 1:570; William H. Keating, *Narrative of an Expedition to the Source of St. Peter's River, Lake Winnepeek, Lake of the Woods, etc., Performed in the Year 1823* (Philadelphia: H. C. Carey and I. Lea, 1826), 1:92.

18. William Henry Harrison to Henry Dearborn, March 3, 1803, Esarey, *William Henry Harrison*, 1:76–84; Roger James Ferguson, "The White River Indiana Delawares: An Ethnohistoric Synthesis, 1795–1867" (Ed.D. dissertation, Ball State University, 1972), 48; Tanner, *Atlas*, 88; Treaty of 1804, *Indian Affairs*, 2:70–73.

19. A perfect example of Harrison's treaty-negotiating style is seen in the Treaty of 1804 with the Sauk and Fox, in which Harrison obtained a sizeable land cession from four Sauk men who did not have the authority to cede it. See John P. Bowes, *Black Hawk and the War of 1832: Removal in the North* (New York: Chelsea House, 2007); "instrument" in Delaware Indians to William Wells, March 30, 1805, Esarey, *William Henry Harrison*, 1:117–18; "Friend" in William Patterson to William Wells, April 5, 1805, Esarey, *William Henry Harrison*, 1:121–23.

20. "false" in Secretary of War to Governor Harrison, May 24, 1805, *TPUS*, 7:287–88; "had" in Governor Harrison to the President, August 29, 1805, ibid., 7:301–302; Treaty of 1805, *Indian Affairs*, 2:80–82; "told" in Gipson, *Moravian Indian Mission*, 378–79.

21. Ferguson, "White River Indiana Delawares," 52–56; Daniel P. Barr, "Odyssey's End: The Battle of Lake Erie and the Failure of the Delaware Indian Struggle for Autonomy," in *The Battle of Lake Erie and Its Aftermath: A Reassessment*, ed. David Curtis Skaggs (Kent, Ohio: Kent State University Press, 2013), 106–107; "Delawares" in Harrison to the Secretary of War, August 10, 1805,

Esarey, *William Henry Harrison*, 1:180–81; "move" in Gipson, *Moravian Indian Mission*, 378–79.

22. "firm" and "twelve" in Louis Houck, ed., *The Spanish Regime in Missouri* (Chicago: R. R. Donnelley and Sons, 1909), 1:209–10, 292; Lorimier's notes appear in his journal, in ibid., 2:87–99; "therefore" in Linda Sabathy-Judd, ed. and trans., *Moravians in Upper Canada: The Diary of the Indian Mission of Fairfield on the Thames, 1792–1813* (Toronto: Champlain Society, 1999), 66–67; Bowes, *Exiles and Pioneers*, 25–32.

23. Bowes, *Exiles and Pioneers*, 33–35; "they" in Gipson, *Moravian Indian Mission*, 267–68.

24. Gipson, *Moravian Indian Mission*, 385.

25. Edmunds, *Shawnee Prophet* 34–41; "Schawanos" in Gipson, *Moravian Indian Mission*, 392.

26. "reported," "already," and "live" in Gipson, *Moravian Indian Mission*, 192, 194, 333; 361–62; Alfred A. Cave, "The Failure of the Shawnee Prophet's Witch-Hunt," *Ethnohistory* 42 (Summer 1995), 445–75; Barr, "Odyssey's End," 110–16; Edmunds, *Shawnee Prophet*, 42–48.

27. Jay Miller, "The 1806 Purge among the Indiana Delaware: Sorcery, Gender, Boundaries, and Legitimacy," *Ethnohistory* 41 (Spring 1994): 245–66; Jay Miller, "Old Religion among the Delawares: The Gamwing (Big House Rite)," *Ethnohistory* 44 (Winter 1997): 113–34; Gipson, *Moravian Indian Mission*, 415, 417; Treaty of 1804, *Indian Affairs*, 2:70–72.

28. Draper interview quoted in Miller, "The 1806 Purge," 261; "the Prophet" and "took" in Gipson, *Moravian Indian Mission*, 420, 444–45, 452–53; Miller, "Old Religion," 113–34.

29. Harrison to the Secretary of War, July 11, 1807, Esarey, *William Henry Harrison*, 1:222–25; "can" in Harrison to the Secretary of War, January 27, 1808, ibid., 1:281.

30. "no longer" in Governor Meriwether Lewis to Secretary of War, July 1, 1808, *TPUS*, 14:196–203; Delaware Chiefs to Harrison, September 9, 1808, Esarey, *William Henry Harrison*, 1:303–304; Treaty of 1808, *Indian Affairs*, 2:95–99; "send" in Jefferson to Delawares, December 1808, Esarey, *William Henry Harrison*, 1:330–32; Kathleen DuVal, "Debating Identity, Sovereignty, and Civilization: The Arkansas Valley after the Louisiana Purchase," *Journal of the Early Republic* 26 (Spring 2006): 25–58.

31. "neither" in Deposition of Thomas Jefferson, December 21, 1808, Thornbrough, *Letterbook of the Indian Agency*, 53–54; "climax" in Andrew R. L. Cayton, *Frontier Indiana* (Bloomington: Indiana University Press, 1996), 215; Treaty of 1809, *Indian Affairs*, 2:101–103; Robert M. Owens, "Jeffersonian Benevolence on the Ground: The Indian Land Cession Treaties of William Henry Harrison," *Journal of the Early Republic* 22 (Autumn 2002): 428–33.

32. "always" in Journal of the Proceedings at the Indian Treaty at Fort Wayne and Vincennes September 1 to October 27, 1809, Esarey, *William Henry Harrison*, 1:373; "facilitate" in Harrison to the Secretary of War, November 3, 1809, ibid., 1:388–89.

33. "but" in Tecumseh's Speech to Governor Harrison, August 20, 1810, ibid., 1:466; Edmunds, *Shawnee Prophet*, 80–81; Dowd, *Spirited Resistance*, 139–47; "having" in Harrison to the Secretary of War, June 26, 1810, Esarey, *William Henry Harrison*, 1:435. For other references to Delawares working with and for Harrison, see Harrison to the Secretary of War, June 14, 1810, Esarey, *William Henry Harrison*, 1:427; Harrison to the Secretary of War, October 13, 1811, Esarey, *William Henry Harrison*, 1:599–603.

34. Speeches of Indians at Miassassinway, May 15, 1812, Esarey, *William Henry Harrison*, 2:50–53.

35. The diplomatic efforts of American agents are discussed in detail in Karim M. Tiro, "The View from Piqua Agency: The War of 1812, the White River Delawares, and the Origins of Indian Removal," *Journal of the Early Republic* 35 (Spring 2015): 30–37; "have" in Harrison to Campbell, November 25, 1812, Esarey, *William Henry Harrison*, 2:228–31; "their" in Harrison to the Secretary of War, March 27, 1813, Esarey, *William Henry Harrison*, 2:400–404; John Johnston to the Secretary of War, August 3, 1813, Esarey, *William Henry Harrison*, 2:509; Ferguson, "White River Indiana Delawares," 90–92.

36. Sabathy-Judd, *Moravians in Upper Canada*, 191, 195–96, 274, 281.

37. "everything" in ibid., 337; Reginald Horsman, "British Indian Policy in the Northwest, 1807–1812," *Mississippi Valley Historical Review* 45 (June 1958): 51–66.

38. Sabathy-Judd, *Moravians in Upper Canada*, 358, 376; Gipson, *Moravian Indian Mission*, 412–18; Edmunds, *Shawnee Prophet*, 97–98; Horsman, "British Indian Policy," 54–58.

39. Sabathy-Judd, *Moravians in Upper Canada*, 481–82, 486, 488–89.

40. Ibid., 495, 504–506, 513–20; R. David Edmunds, *Tecumseh and the Quest for Indian Leadership* (New York: Pearson Longman, 2007), 194–212.

41. Sabathy-Judd, *Moravians in Upper Canada*, 506–11.

42. "elegantly" in Journal of the Proceedings of the Commissioners Plenipotentiary, Appointed on Behalf of the United States of America, to Treat with the Northwestern Tribes of Indians, *ASPIA*, 1:828; "associated" in *Indian Affairs*, 2:105–106, 117–19; "many" in Harrison and Graham to Secretary of War Crawford, September 9, 1815, *ASPIA*, 2:16.

43. Ferguson, "White River Indiana Delawares," 92; Treaty of 1818, *Indian Affairs*, 2:170–71; two Johnston letters regarding the 1818 treaty negotiations reprinted in Richard Calmit Adams, *A Delaware Indian Legend and the Story of Their Troubles* (Washington, D.C., 1899), 41–45; "white" in Isaac McCoy, *History of Baptist Indian Missions* (Washington, D.C.: William H. Morrison, 1840), 52–53; Tiro, "View from Piqua Agency," 48–50.

44. "Arkansas" in S. Charles Bolton, "Jeffersonian Indian Removal and the Emergence of Arkansas Territory," *Arkansas Historical Quarterly* 62 (Autumn 2003): 253; "As" in Governor James Miller to Secretary of War Calhoun, February 11, 1820, *TPUS*, 19:145–46.

45. "requiring" in Proclamation of Governor Meriwether Lewis, April 6, 1809, *TPUS* 14:261; "that" in William Clark to President Madison, April 10,

1811, ibid., 14:445–46; "unsettled" in Resolution of Territorial Assembly of Missouri, January 22, 1816, ibid., 15:105–107; Resolutions of the Missouri Territorial Assembly, January 24, 1817, ibid., 15:234–36; John Mack Faragher, "'More Motley than Mackinaw': From Ethnic Mixing to Ethnic Cleansing on the Frontier of the Lower Missouri, 1783–1833," in *Contact Points: American Frontiers from the Mohawk Valley to the Mississippi, 1750–1830*, ed. Andrew R. L. Cayton and Fredrika J. Teute (Chapel Hill: University of North Carolina Press, 1998), 304–26.

46. The Delaware abandonment of the Cape Girardeau lands is mentioned in the 1825 treaty with the Shawnees in *Indian Affairs*, 2:262; Report of J. M. Peck and J. E. Welch in *American Baptist Magazine and Missionary Intelligencer*, July 1818; Chart of Indian Tribes, August 24, 1817, *TPUS*, 15:305; statement of former Spanish commandant, June 5, 1816, *TPUS*, 15:178–80; Secretary of War to Governor William Clark, May 8, 1818, *TPUS*, 15:390–91.

47. "they" in Stephen H. Long to Thomas A. Smith, January 30, 1818, *TPUS*, 19:4–10; *Indian Affairs*, 2:140–45; Chart of Indian Tribes, August 24, 1817, *TPUS*, 15:305. One overview of this conflict is in Grant Foreman, *Indians and Pioneers: The Story of the American Southwest Before 1830* (Norman: University of Oklahoma Press, 1930), 63–79.

48. Lynn Morrow, "Trader William Gillis and Delaware Migration in Southern Missouri," *Missouri Historical Review* 75 (January 1981): 147–67; George E. Lankford, "Shawnee Convergence: Immigrant Indians in the Ozarks," *Arkansas Historical Quarterly* 58 (Winter 1999): 398; Bowes, *Exiles and Pioneers*, 130–33; "number" in Delaware Indians to William Clark, February 29, 1824, OIA-LR, roll 300; Weslager, *Delaware Indians*, 363–69; Richard S. Grimes, "The Early Years of the Delaware Indian Experience in Kansas Territory, 1830–1845," *Journal of the West* 41 (Winter 2002): 73–75.

49. *Indian Affairs*, 2:304–305; H. Allen Anderson, "The Delaware and Shawnee Indians and the Republic of Texas, 1820–1845," *Southwestern Historical Quarterly* 94 (October 1990): 231–60.

50. "place" in Shawnee Petition to Alcalde of San Antonio, October 29, 1824, Grant Foreman Collection, Oklahoma State Historical Society, folder 12, box 36; Establishment of "Old" Miller County, Arkansas Territory, ibid., folder 6, box 26; David G. Burnet et al. to Gen. Bustamente, July 2, 1827, in Eugene Barker, ed., *The Austin Papers* (Washington, D.C.: American Historical Association, 1924), 2:1667–71; H. Anderson, "Delaware and Shawnee Indians," 233–41.

51. "appears" in George Gray to the Secretary of War, June 13, 1827, *TPUS*, 20:479–81; "all" in Citizens of Miller County to Governor Izard, March 20, 1828, ibid., 20:629–30; J. G. W. Pierson to Governor Izard, March 22, 1828, ibid., 20:632; "Saying" and "agreed" in Wharton Rector to Governor Izard, May 8, 1828, ibid., 20:677; "Indians" in Capt. Russel B. Hyde to Adj. Genl. Col. R. Jones, November 17, 1828, ibid., 20:784–85.

52. Gary Clayton Anderson, *The Conquest of Texas: Ethnic Cleansing in the Promised Land, 1820–1875* (Norman: University of Oklahoma Press, 2005), 30,

45–47, 72; all quotations in Burnet et al. to Bustamente, Barker, *Austin Papers*, 2:1667–71; emphasis in original.

53. Affidavit of John C. Morrison, Barker, *Austin Papers*, 2:1574–75; Stephen F. Austin to the Cherokees, April 24, 1826, ibid., 2:1307–309; Burnet et al. to Bustamente, ibid., 2:1667–71; G. Anderson, *Conquest of Texas*, 62–65. The topic of the Delawares in Texas is explored in more depth in chapter 7 of this book.

54. William Anderson to Cass, September 22, 1831, OIA-LR, roll 300.

55. Articles of Agreement, November 8, 1823, OIA-LR, roll 601; Darryl K. Stonefish, *Moraviantown Delaware History* (Thamesville, Ont.: Moravian Research Office, 1995), 23–25; Weslager, *Delaware Indians*, 298, 334; Sabathy-Judd, *Moravians in Upper Canada*, 107; Bliss, *David Zeisberger*, 1:419–20.

56. The Delaware experience in Kansas following removal is discussed in Bowes, *Exiles and Pioneers*, 89–151, 187–201. For relocations in Texas and Kansas, see also chapter 7 of this book.

4. SANDUSKY RIVER REMOVALS

1. Treaty of Peace and Amity, between His Britannic Majesty and the United States of America, Dec. 24, 1814, *USSL*, 8 Stat. 218.

2. "happened" in Andrew R. L. Cayton, *Ohio: The History of a People* (Columbus: Ohio State University Press, 2002), 16; R. Douglas Hurt, *The Ohio Frontier: Crucible of the Old Northwest, 1720–1830* (Bloomington: Indiana University Press, 1996), 143–78. This process and the colonial forces at work are discussed in depth in Saler, *Settlers' Empire*, 41–82.

3. Excerpted in *Weekly Recorder*, October 23, 1818.

4. Consul W. Butterfield, *History of Seneca County* (Sandusky, Ohio: D. Campbell and Sons, 1848), 73–75; Lucy Elliot Keeler, "Old Fort Sandoski of 1745 and the 'Sandusky Country,'" *Ohio Archaeological and Historical Society Publications* 17 (October 1908): 361–66.

5. Keeler, "Old Fort Sandoski," 369; Sallie Cotter Andrews, "Timeline of Wyandot History," Wyandotte Nation of Oklahoma website, accessed October 28, 2011, http://wyandotte-nation.org/culture/history/timeline/1534-1842/.

6. James Smith, *An Account of the Remarkable Occurrences in the Life of Colonel James Smith. . . .* (Lexington, Ky.: John Bradford, 1799), 44; Montresor's journal quoted in Keeler, "Old Fort Sandoski," 390–95; "Transactions with Indians at Sandusky," Haldimand Papers, MPHC, 20:174–83; Homer Everett, *History of Sandusky County, Ohio* (Cleveland: H. Z. Williams, 1882), 15–17.

7. "About" in John Johnston to Charles Cist, October 22, 1847, Seneca 1829–present, TDC-GLOVE; "many" in William Henry Harrison and John Graham to W. H. Crawford, September 9, 1815, *ASPIA*, 2:16–17; William Sturtevant, "Oklahoma Seneca-Cayuga," in *Handbook of North American Indians*, ed. Bruce Trigger (Washington, D.C.: Smithsonian Institution, 1978), 15:537–38; A Table Shewing the State of Indians in Ohio in October, 1819, by John Johnston, Seneca 1818–1819, TDC-GLOVE; the villages can be found on map 25 in Tanner, *Atlas*,

134; Treaty of 1817, *Indian Affairs*, 2:145–55. The present-day Seneca-Cayuga Nation of Oklahoma is in part descended from these Ohio communities, and the Seneca-Cayuga designation is a clear reflection of the Cayuga population that became more prominent before and after removal.

8. "bad situation" in John R. Walker to Lewis Cass, June 6, 1818, Seneca 1818–1819, TDC-GLOVE; Lewis Cass to John R. Walker, June 7, 1818, ibid.; "go" in An Abstract Exhibiting the Number of Indians in the Piqua Agency, Ohio, November 1829, OIA-LR, roll 669. Although federal officials continued to refer to this community as Senecas, the majority of the population was ultimately comprised of Cayugas. I also primarily refer to them as Senecas in this chapter for consistency with the records upon which I rely.

9. Tanner, *Atlas*, 81; "his" in Memorial and Petition of Montgomery Montour, December 26, 1806, *ASPIA*, 1:744; Henry Dearborn to John Boyle, January 8, 1807, *ASPIA*, 1:744; Act of March 3, 1807, *USSL*, ch. 49, 2 Stat. 448; Treaty of 1817, *Indian Affairs*, 2:145–55.

10. Excerpt from "Autobiography of Abraham Luckenbach, Moravian Missionary," in Lower Sandusky 1810–1814, Rutherford B. Hayes Papers, Rutherford B. Hayes Presidential Library, Fremont, Ohio; Paul Butler to Governor Return J. Meigs, August 24, 1812, ibid.; "hope" in Tarhee's Speech at Lower Sandusky, August 13, 1812, ibid.

11. "Wyandottes" in excerpt from "Autobiography of Abraham Luckenbach, Moravian Missionary," ibid.; "To add" in Elizabeth Whitaker to William Henry Harrison, January 5, 1813, ibid.; Larry L. Nelson, *Fort Meigs: War of 1812 Battleground* (Columbus: Ohio Historical Society, 1999); several essays on the battle and its impact can be found in Skaggs, *Battle of Lake Erie*.

12. "severe" and "we" in Petition to Governor Return J. Meigs, December 21, 1813, Lower Sandusky 1810–1814, Rutherford B. Hayes Papers; "was by" in Thomas L. Hawkins to [?], May 24, 1815, Lower Sandusky 1815–1824, Rutherford B. Hayes Papers; Thomas L. Hawkins to William Crayton, January 24, 1816, Lower Sandusky 1815–1824, Rutherford B. Hayes Papers.

13. Treaty of 1815, *Indian Affairs*, 2:117–19; "it will" and "employed" in Records of Treaty Council at Spring Wells, *ASPIA*, 2:17–25; "Good" in William Henry Harrison and John Graham to W. H. Crawford, September 9, 1815, *ASPIA*, 2:16–17.

14. "commanding" in "James Madison, IV President of the United States, 1809–1817: Proclamation 22—Ordering Unauthorized Persons to Remove from the Public Lands, December 12, 1815," by Gerhard Peters and John T. Woolley, *The American Presidency Project*, accessed July 7, 2012, www.presidency.ucsb.edu /ws/index.php?pid=65888; "It is" in Thomas L. Hawkins to William Crayton, January 24, 1816, Lower Sandusky 1815–1824, Rutherford B. Hayes Papers.

15. "held" in Duncan MacArthur to George Graham, January 20, 1816, Huron 1816, TDC-GLOVE; "negotiations" in George Graham to Lewis Cass, March 23, 1817, *ASPIA*, 2:136; George Graham to Lewis Cass and Duncan McArthur, May 19, 1817, *ASPIA*, 2:137.

16. "they" in William Walker to Cass, May 27, 1817, in Huron 1817, TDC-GLOVE; "determined" in John Johnston to Lewis Cass, June 23, 1817, ibid; John Johnston to Lewis Cass, June 13, 1817, ibid.

17. "I learn" in John Johnston to Lewis Cass, June 13, 1817, in Huron 1817, ibid.; biographical information on Elizabeth Whitaker found in folder 1, Whitaker, James and Elizabeth—Local History Misc. MSS, Rutherford B. Hayes Presidential Library; "returned" in Elizabeth Whitaker to Lewis Cass, June 14, 1817, Huron 1817, TDC-GLOVE.

18. "their Father" and "it was" in Elizabeth Whitaker to Lewis Cass, July 6, 1817, Huron 1817, TDC-GLOVE; Elizabeth Whitaker to General William Henry Harrison, January 5, 1813, Lower Sandusky 1810–1814, Rutherford B. Hayes Papers; Treaty of 1817, *Indian Affairs*, 2:145–55; John Johnston to Lewis Cass, June 26, 1817, Huron 1817, TDC-GLOVE. Elizabeth Whitaker received 1,200 acres of land in the 1817 treaty.

19. "by" and "as" in Lewis Cass and Duncan McArthur to George Graham, September 30, 1817, *ASPIA*, 2:138–39; Treaty of 1817, *Indian Affairs*, 2:145–55.

20. "undertaken" in John Johnston to Lewis Cass, November 5, 1817, Huron 1817, TDC-GLOVE; "several" in Treaty of 1818, *Indian Affairs*, 2:162–63; "received" in Lewis Cass and Duncan McArthur to John C. Calhoun, September 18, 1818, *ASPIA*, 2:177.

21. County information in Lower Sandusky 1815–1824, Rutherford B. Hayes Papers; "Historical Census Browser," University of Virginia Library, accessed July 16, 2010, http://mapserver.lib.virginia.edu/; "Our" in Tall Man et al. to President James Monroe, February 17, 1824, Seneca 1822–1828, TDC-GLOVE.

22. "character" in John Johnston to Lewis Cass, June 8, 1819, Huron 1818–1820, TDC-GLOVE; "under" in John Johnston to Lewis Cass, September 8, 1820, Seneca 1820–1821, ibid.; "nothing" in John Johnston to Thos. L. McKenney, July 18, 1825, OIA-LR, roll 669; "general" in James Montgomery to John Johnston, February 1, 1827, OIA-LR, roll 669; "more" in John McElvain to Thomas McKenney, August 14, 1830, OIA-LR, roll 669.

23. "we" in Capt. Pipe et al. to the President of the United States, September 3, 1828, OIA-LR, roll 669; "messenger" in John Johnston to John Eaton, March 12, 1829, ibid.; "almost" in John McElvain to Thos. L. McKenney, June 22, 1829, ibid.; "anxious" in John McElvain to T. S. McKenney, July 19, 1829, ibid.; both Delaware treaties signed in 1829 can be found in *Indian Affairs*, 2:303–305; an abstract exhibiting the number of Indians in the Piqua Agency, Ohio, OIA-LR, roll 669.

24. "bear" in John McElvain to T. L. McKenney, May 27, 1830, OIA-LR, roll 669; "halt" in John McElvain to Thos. L. McKenney, August 14, 1830, Correspondence on the Emigration of Indians, 1831–1833, SD 512, Serial No. 245, 86–87; "useless" in John McElvain to Col. S.S. Hamilton, September 20, 1830, SD 512, Serial No. 245, 119–22.

25. Seneca Chiefs of Ohio to President of the United States, October 15, 1829, ARCIA, 185.

26. "anxious" in John McElvain to Thomas McKenney, May 27, 1830, OIA-LR, roll 669; "Since" in John McElvain to Col. S. S. Hamilton, September 25, 1830, ibid.; "The game" in Seneca Petition to President Andrew Jackson, September 22, 1830, ibid.

27. List of Suggestions by J. B. Gardiner, May 4, 1831, OIA-LR, roll 601; "quickly" in John McElvain to Lewis Cass, August 28, 1831, ibid.

28. Treaty of 1831, *Indian Affairs*, 2:325–27; Treaty of 1817, ibid., 145–55; Treaty of 1818, ibid., 162–63; Henry C. Brish to John Eaton, May 4, 1831, SD 512, Serial No. 245, 443–44.

29. "When" in Samuel Hamilton to John McElvain, May 12, 1831, SD 512, Serial No. 245, 288–89; John McElvain to Col. S. S. Hamilton, February 10, 1831, OIA-LR, roll 601; Memorial of Citizens of Seneca County, Ohio, January 31, 1831, OIA-LR, roll 601; "seem" in John McElvain to the Secretary of War, February 2, 1831, OIA-LR, roll 601; John McElvain to H. C. Brish, April 23, 1831, OIA-LR, roll 601.

30. "almost," "there," and "We" in Comstick et al. to John H. Eaton, June 7, 1831, OIA-LR, 603; "perfect" in John McElvain to Lewis Cass, August, 28, 1831, OIA-LR, roll 601.

31. "they" in J. B. Gardiner to Lewis Cass, September 7, 1831, OIA-LR, roll 601; Henry C. Brish to Col. Samuel S. Hamilton, September 20, 1831, ibid.

32. John McElvain to Lewis Cass, November 15, 1831, ibid.

33. John McElvain to Lewis Cass, December 8, 1831, ibid.; "We" in Seneca Chiefs to William Clark, December 10, 1831, SD 512, Serial No. 246, 9–10.

34. William Clark to Elbert Herring, December 20, 1831, SD 512, Serial No. 245, 722–23; Henry Brish to William Clark, November 16, 1831, ibid., 725; Henry Brish to William Clark, December 13, 1831, ibid., 725–26.

35. Henry Brish to William Clark, December 14, 1831, ibid., 724; William Clark to Elbert Herring, December 20, 1831, ibid., 722–23; "been" in William Clark to the Secretary of War, August, 13, 1832, SD 512, Serial No. 246, 427–28; "If" in John McElvain to Col. S. S. Hamilton, February 21, 1832, OIA-LR, roll 601.

36. "no doubt" in Henry Brish to William Clark, May 8, 1832, SD 512, Serial No. 248, 116; Henry Brish to William Clark, May 16, 1832, ibid., 117; Henry Brish to William Clark, June 12, 1832, ibid., 117; "I charge" in Henry Brish to William Clark, July 12, 1832, ibid., 118–20.

37. "It" and "I flatter" in J. B. Gardiner to Lewis Cass, January 4, 1832, SD 512, Serial No. 246, 8; "were" in James B. Gardiner to Lewis Cass, January 5, 1832, OIA-LR, roll 603.

38. Martin W. Walsh, "The 'Heathen Party': Methodist Observation of the Ohio Wyandot," *American Indian Quarterly* (Spring 1992): 189–211; Robert E. Smith, "The Clash of Leadership at the Grand Reserve: The Wyandot Subagency and the Methodist Mission, 1820–24," *Ohio History* 89 (Spring 1980): 181–205; Emil Schlup, "The Wyandot Mission," *Ohio Archaeological and Historical Society*

Publications 15 (1906): 163–81; for discussion of Walkers, see Bowes, *Exiles and Pioneers*, chapter 5.

39. "On" in Agreement between Wyandot Chiefs and James Gardiner, October 19, 1831, OIA-LR, roll 603; James Washington et al. to the Chiefs of the Wyandot Nation, December 15, 1831, ibid.; "object" in James Gardiner to Lewis Cass, January 28, 1832, ibid.; depositions of Henry Brish, George Williams, Silas Armstrong, and others connected to the delegation can be found in ibid., frames 65–79.

40. Quotations from report in J. Orin Oliphant, ed., "The Report of the Wyandot Exploring Delegation, 1831," *Kansas Historical Quarterly* 14 (August 1947): 248–62; for more on the Platte Purchase lands visited by the Wyandots, see R. David Edmunds, "Potawatomis in the Platte Country: An Indian Removal Incomplete," *Missouri Historical Review* 68 (July 1974): 375–92.

41. Details of this struggle can be found in Walsh, "'Heathen Party'"; Shannon Bontrager, "'From a Nation of Drunkards We Have Become a Sober People': The Wyandot Experience in the Ohio Valley during the Early Republic," *Journal of the Early Republic* 32 (Winter 2012): 603–32; "I used" in James B. Finley, *The History of the Wyandott Mission at Upper Sandusky, Ohio* (Cincinnati: J. F. Wright and L. Swormstedt, 1840), 306.

42. "in case" in James Gardiner to Lewis Cass, January 28, 1832, Oliphant, "Wyandot Exploring Delegation," 258–62; Treaty of 1832, *Indian Affairs*, 2:339–41.

43. "sold" in Henry Jaquis et al. to President Andrew Jackson, May 22, 1832, OIA-LR, roll 601; "boys" in Roennuas et al. to President Andrew Jackson, May 24, 1832, ibid.; "we have" in Big Spring Wyandots to Lewis Cass, April 6, 1832, ibid.

44. "bury" in Agreement of Wyandots at Big Spring Reservation, December 3, 1832, OIA-LR, roll 601; "treaty" in Wm. Walker to Hon. Lewis Cass, November 28, 1832, ibid.; for more relating to the back-and-forth accusations in 1832, see Ronuness et al. to James Gardiner, February 4, 1832, ibid.; Warpole et al. to James Gardiner, February 4, 1832, ibid.; Roenuness et al. to Lewis Cass, February 20, 1832, ibid.; Agreement between the Big Spring Party and Solomonstown Party of Wyandot Indians, July 21, 1832, ibid.; Aaron Welch et al. to the Secretary of War, August 3, 1832, ibid.; Ronuenass et al. to Lewis Cass, September 11, 1832, ibid.

45. "if" in Lewis Cass to Thomas McKenney, October 27, 1825, OIA-LR, roll 419; for an example of Cass's writing, see Cass, "Documents and Proceedings," 62–121; John T. Fierst, "Rationalizing Removal: Anti-Indianism in Lewis Cass's North American Review Essays," *Michigan Historical Review* 36 (Fall 2010): 1–36.

46. "that if" in John McElvain to the Secretary of War, September 10, 1833, OIA-LR, roll 601; "extinguishment" in N. H. Swayne to John McElvain, October 19, 1833, ibid.; John McElvain to Elbert Herring, December 8, 1834, ibid.

47. John McElvain to Elbert Herring, December 8, 1834, OIA-LR, roll 601; "President" and "great" in record of the Wyandot council, included in Robert Lucas to Lewis Cass, March 22, 1835, ibid.; "Tribe" and "prevailing" in Dwight L. Smith, ed., "An Unsuccessful Negotiation for Removal of the Wyandot Indians from Ohio, 1834," *Ohio Archaeological and Historical Quarterly* 58 (July 1949): 305–31.

48. "This" in John McElvain to Elbert Herring, January 31, 1835, OIA-LR, roll 601; John McElvain to Elbert Herring, February 10, 1835, ibid.; "at its" in Robert Lucas to Lewis Cass, March 24, 1835, ibid. Governor Lucas also mentions the legislation passed by the Ohio General Assembly in February 1834 in Robert Lucas, *Message of the Governor of Ohio at the Second Session of the Thirty-Third General Assembly, June 8, 1835* (Columbus, Ohio: James B. Gardiner, 1835).

49. John McElvain to Elbert Herring, May 20, 1833, OIA-LR, roll 601; W. Kermin [?] to Lewis Cass, February 2, 1836, ibid.; Joseph Vance to Lewis Cass, January 18, 1836, ibid.

50. "their views" in Wm. Walker to Robert Lucas, January 13, 1836, "Ratified Treaty No. 206, Documents Relating to the Negotiation of the Treaty of April 23, 1836, with the Wyandot Indians," DRNRUT; "appear" in Robert Lucas to Andrew Jackson, January 20, 1836, ibid; Robert Lucas to Lewis Cass, March 28, 1836, ibid.; Treaty of 1836, *Indian Affairs*, 2:460–61.

51. "whites" in Joseph McCutcheon to C. A. Harris, February 2, 1837, OIA-LR, roll 601; "number" in H. C. Brish and Joseph McCutcheon to C. A. Harris, May 2, 1837, ibid.

52. Joseph McCutcheon to C. A. Harris, May 31, 1837, OIA-LR, roll 601.

53. "prohibiting" in A Law against Ceding Lands to the United States, March 1832, OIA-LR, roll 601; Henry C. Brish and Joseph McCutcheon to Purdy McElvain, May 11, 1837, ibid.; Purdy McElvain to Henry C. Brish and Joseph McCutcheon, May 12, 1837, ibid.; "State" in N. H. Swayne to C. A. Harris, June 28, 1837, ibid.; "this law" in Purdy McElvain to C. A. Harris, August 1, 1837, ibid.

54. Henry C. Brish and Joseph McCutcheon to C. A. Harris, August 6, 1837, OIA-LR, roll 601.

55. "whether" and "abandoned" in Wm. Walker to Joseph Vance, July 9, 1837, OIA-LR, roll 601; "going" and "after" in John Barnett et al. to Joseph Vance, July 29, 1837, ibid.; depositions of Mrs. Half-John, George Williams, and others in ibid.

56. "for" in John Barnett et al. to Joseph Vance, July 29, 1837, ibid.; "some" in Purdy McElvain to C. A. Harris, September 27, 1838, ibid.; Robert E. Smith, "The Wyandot Exploring Expedition of 1839," *Chronicles of Oklahoma* 55 (Fall 1977): 282–92; "in case" in Warpole et al. to President of the U.S., October 23, 1838, OIA-LR, roll 601; Warpole et al. to William H. Hunter, November 3, 1838, OIA-LR, roll 601.

57. "apprehension" in W. H. Hunter to T. Hartley Crawford, May 7, 1839, OIA-LR, roll 602; R. Smith, "Wyandot Exploring Expedition," 286–91; "a

great" in Richard Cummins to T. Hartley Crawford, February 13, 1839, OIA-LR, roll 301.

58. "almost" in Purdy McElvain, September 30, 1840, OIA-LR, roll 602; Statement of William Walker, February 21, 1842, ibid.; John Johnston, *Recollections of Sixty Years* (Dayton, Ohio: John Henry Patterson, 1915), 24–25.

59. R. Smith, "Wyandot Exploring Expedition," 291; John Johnston to T. Hartley Crawford, May 11, 1841, OIA-LR, roll 602; "Our chiefs" in John M. Armstrong to T. Hartley Crawford, June 21, 1841, OIA-LR, roll 602; John M. Armstrong to John Johnston, July 8, 1841, OIA-LR, roll 602; "whole" in John Johnston to T. Hartley Crawford, November 29, 1841, OIA-LR, roll 602.

60. "practices" in John Johnston to T. Hartley Crawford, February 9, 1842, OIA-LR, roll 602; Seneca and Shawnee Treaty of 1831, *Indian Affairs*, 2:327–31; "probably" and "regret" in John Johnston to T. Hartley Crawford, March 14, 1842, OIA-LR, roll 602.

61. Treaty of 1842, *Indian Affairs*, 2:534–37; Assent to 1842 Treaty by Huron River Wyandots, April 5, 1842, OIA-LR, roll 602; Carl G. Klopfenstein, "The Removal of the Wyandots from Ohio," *Ohio Historical Quarterly* 66 (April 1957): 119–36; William Lee to Robert Stuart, December 14, 1842, OIA-LR, roll 602; "desirous" in Purdy McElvain to T. Hartley Crawford, March 3, 1843, OIA-LR, roll 952; "busily" in Purdy McElvain to T. Hartley Crawford, June 1, 1843, OIA-LR, roll 602.

62. "Their" in Purdy McElvain to T. Hartley Crawford, July 12, 1843, OIA-LR, roll 952; ARCIA, 1843, 262; "Indians concluded" in "Cincinnati: A Journal Account by Rev. Wheeler," Wyandotte Nation of Oklahoma website, accessed July 21, 2014, www.wyandotte-nation.org/culture/history/wheeler-memoirs /upper-sandusky-to-cincinnati/; newspaper excerpts quoted in "Indians," *Niles National Register*, August 26, 1843.

63. "Cincinnati," Wyandotte Nation of Oklahoma website; Rev. James Wheeler to Brother Elliott, July 28, 1843, "St. Louis," Wyandotte Nation of Oklahoma website, accessed July 21, 2014, www.wyandotte-nation.org/culture /history/wheeler-memoirs/from-st-louis-to-kansas/; "Lucy B. Armstrong's Account of Travel from St. Louis to Kansas on the Missouri Riverboat Nodaway," Wyandot Nation of Kansas website, accessed July 21, 2014, www.wyandot .org/lucyriv.htm.

64. Purdy McElvain to T. Hartley Crawford, June 1, 1843, OIA-LR, roll 602; "Delaware" in Wyandot Land Purchase Agreement with Delaware Indians, December 14, 1843, OIA-LR, roll 302; "distressing" in Reverend James Wheeler to Rev. E. R. Ames, September 30, 1843, "Letters from the Indian Missions in Kansas," *Collections of the Kansas State Historical Society* 16 (1923–1925): 268; "Lucy B. Armstrong's Account," Wyandot Nation of Kansas website; Frederick A. Norwood, "Strangers in a Strange Land: Removal of the Wyandot Indians," *Methodist History* 13 (April 1975): 45–60; Klopfenstein, "Removal of the Wyandots," 136.

65. ARCIA, 1843, 262; "Soon" in "Farewell: The Wyandot's Last Ohio Church Service July 9, 1843," Wyandotte Nation of Oklahoma website, accessed

July 21, 2014, www.wyandotte-nation.org/culture/history/general-history /farewell-beloved-land/; James Fenimore Cooper, *Last of the Mohicans* (New York: Bantam, 1981), 374; Buss, *Winning the West*, 73–96.

5. The 1833 Treaty of Chicago and Potawatomi Removal

1. "we count" in Gilbert J. Garraghan, "Early Catholicity in Chicago," *Illinois Catholic Historical Review* 1 (October 1918), 147–48; "endeared" in Gilbert J. Garraghan, *The Catholic Church in Chicago, 1673–1871: An Historical Sketch* (Chicago: Loyola University Press, 1921), 94–97.

2. Joseph J. Thompson, "The First Catholics in and about Chicago," *Illinois Catholic Historical Review* 3 (January 1921): 231–40.

3. William Cronon, *Nature's Metropolis: Chicago and the Great West* (New York: W. W. Norton, 1991).

4. Michael McCafferty, "A Fresh Look at the Place Name Chicago," *Journal of the Illinois State Historical Society* 96 (Summer 2003): 116–17; e-mail from George Ironstrack, September 9, 2014.

5. Robert A. Holland, *Chicago in Maps, 1612 to 2002* (New York: Rizzoli International, 2005), 50–53; Treaty of 1816, *Indian Affairs*, 2:132–33; Illinois map in Indian Land Cessions in the United States, 1784–1894, *U.S. Serial Set*, No. 4015, *A Century of Lawmaking for a New Nation*, accessed December 18, 2013, http://memory.loc.gov/ammem/amlaw/lwss-ilc.html.

6. "An Act to Enable the President to Extinguish Indian Land Title within the States of Indiana, Illinois, and Territory of Michigan," July 9, 1832, *USSL*, ch. 175, 4 Stat. 564.

7. Thomas V. Owen to George Porter, May 18, 1832, OIA-LR, roll 132; Captain John Hoyan to Lewis Cass, May 25, 1832, ibid.; Thomas V. Owen to Elbert Herring, May 12, 1832, ibid.; J. N. Bourassa, "The Life of Wah-bahn-se: The Warrior Chief of the Pottawatamies," *Kansas Historical Quarterly* 38 (Summer 1972): 138; Hall, *Uncommon Defense*, 132; Jung, *Black Hawk War*. The Black Hawk War is covered more comprehensively in chapter 1.

8. Bowes, *Exiles and Pioneers*, 63–72; Edmunds, *Potawatomis*, 240–47; James A. Clifton, *The Prairie People: Continuity and Change in Potawatomi Indian Culture, 1665–1965* (Iowa City: University of Iowa Press, 1998), 234–38; Murphy, *Gathering of Rivers*; for consideration of the land title bill in Senate, see *Journal of the Senate*, 22nd Cong., 1st Sess., 432; "extinguish" in Lewis Cass to Jonathan Jennings, John Davis, and Mearks Crume, July 14, 1832, "Ratified treaty no. 172, documents relating to the negotiation of the treaty of October 20, 1832, with the Potawatomi of the Prairie Indians and the Kankakee Indians," DRNRUT; *Indian Affairs*, 2:353–55, 367–70, 372–75. Also see the discussion of the Black Hawk War in chapter 1.

9. "When" in John Reynolds: Message to Both Houses of the Illinois General Assembly, December 4, 1832, Whitney, *Black Hawk War*, vol. 2, bk. 1, 218–22;

"there" in Thomas Owen to Elbert Herring, March 5, 1833, OIA-LR, roll 132; "from" in George Porter to Elbert Herring, March 16, 1833, OIA-LR, roll 132.

10. *Indian Affairs,* 2:402–15.

11. All quotations in September 14 and September 20, 1833, Journal of Proceedings, "Ratified treaty no. 189, documents relating to the negotiation of the treaty of September 26, 1833, with the United Chippewa, Ottawa, and Potawatomi Indians," DRNRUT.

12. Charles Joseph Latrobe, *The Rambler in North America, 1832–1833* (New York: Harper and Brothers, 1835), 2:152–53.

13. Reuben Gold Thwaites, ed., "Narrative of Peter J. Vieau," *Collections of the State Historical Society of Wisconsin* 15 (1900): 460–63.

14. Latrobe, *Rambler in North America,* 2:150.

15. "United" in *Indian Affairs,* 2:402–15; "since" in Donald L. Fixico, "The Alliance of the Three Fires in Trade and War, 1630–1812," *Michigan Historical Review* 20 (Fall 1994): 10; Journal of Proceedings, "Ratified treaty no. 189, documents relating to the negotiation of the treaty of September 26, 1833, with the United Chippewa, Ottawa, and Potawatomi Indians," DRNRUT; Thomas G. Conway, "Potawatomi Politics," *Journal of the Illinois State Historical Society* 65 (1972): 398–400; David A. Baerris, "The Band Affiliation of Potawatomi Treaty Signatories," online at Great Lakes and Ohio Valley Ethnohistory Collection, Glenn A. Black Laboratory of Archaeology, Indiana University (removed from site).

16. W. Benjamin Secunda, "In the Shadow of the Wings of Eagles: The Effects of Removal on the Unremoved Potawatomi" (Ph.D. dissertation, Notre Dame University, 2008), 437.

17. Ann Durkin Keating, *Rising Up From Indian Country: The Battle of Fort Dearborn and the Birth of Chicago* (Chicago: University of Chicago Press, 2012), 227.

18. Journal of Proceedings, "Ratified treaty no. 189, documents relating to the negotiation of the treaty of September 26 1833, with the United Chippewa, Ottawa, and Potawatomi Indians," DRNRUT; *Indian Affairs,* 2:402–15.

19. Treaty of 1829, *Indian Affairs,* 2:297–300; Bowes, *Exiles and Pioneers,* 60–63; Journal of Proceedings, "Ratified treaty no. 189, documents relating to the negotiation of the treaty of September 26, 1833, with the United Chippewa, Ottawa, and Potawatomi Indians," DRNRUT.

20. "These" in Anselm J. Gerwing, "The Chicago Indian Treaty of 1833," *Journal of the Illinois State Historical Society* 57 (Spring 1964): 117–42; Edmunds, *Potawatomis,* 247–50; one example of the charges of fraud can be found in Milo M. Quaife, ed., "The Chicago Treaty of 1833," *Wisconsin Magazine of History* 1 (March 1918): 287–303.

21. "Should" in John Bourie and Francis Comparet to Lewis Cass, February 1, 1834, OIA-LR, roll 132; John B. Boure to John Tipton, February 1, 1834, in Robertson and Riker, *John Tipton Papers,* 3:16–17; for the economic power of

traders in the region, see Trennert, *Indian Traders*; Robert A. Trennert, Jr., "The Business of Indian Removal: Deporting the Potawatomi from Wisconsin, 1851," *Wisconsin Magazine of History* 63 (Autumn 1979): 36–50.

22. Milo M. Quaife, *Chicago and the Old Northwest, 1673–1835* (Chicago: University of Chicago Press, 1913), 353.

23. *Indian Affairs*, 2:406–409; John D. Haeger, "The American Fur Company and the Chicago of 1812–1835," *Journal of the Illinois Historical Society* 61 (Summer 1968): 117–39.

24. See Trennert, *Indian Traders*.

25. William G. Ewing to John Tipton, February 3, 1830, Robertson and Riker, *John Tipton Papers*, 2:244–46.

26. Cronon, *Nature's Metropolis*, 29.

27. Edmunds, "Potawatomis in the Platte Country," 375–92.

28. Billy Caldwell to Thomas Owen, August 4, 1834, included in Thomas Owen to Lewis Cass, August 22, 1834, OIA-LR, roll 132.

29. B. Caldwell et al. to Thomas Owen, October 1, 1834, ibid.; Thomas Owen to Lewis Cass, October 3, 1834, ibid.

30. Anthony L. Davis to John Tipton, January 19, 1836, Robertson and Riker, *John Tipton Papers*, 3:208; Edmunds, "Potawatomis in the Platte Country," 382–92; Clifton, *Prairie People*, 287–93.

31. Quarterly Muster Roll of Chicago Agency Putawatomie Indians Subsisted on the North Side of the Missouri River near Fort Leavenworth West of the Mississippi River under the Direction of Anthony L. Davis Asst. Agt. in the Quarter Ending 31st December 1836, OIA-LR, roll 300.

32. Edwin James to William Clark, August 11, 1837, OIA-LR, roll 215.

33. Edwin James to Gen. Wm. Clark, September 25, 1837, OIA-LR, roll 751.

34. *Indian Affairs*, 2:450–72; J. P. Simonton to [?], July 22, 1835, OIA-LR, roll 355.

35. *Indian Affairs*, 2:450, 457–59, 462–63; statement of Pashpoho et al., September 22, 1836, OIA-LR, roll 356; R. David Edmunds, "'Designing Men, Seeking a Fortune': Indian Traders and the Potawatomi Claims Payment of 1836," *Indiana Magazine of History* 77 (June 1981): 109–22; Pashpoho et al. to Andrew Jackson, n.d., OIA-LR, roll 355.

36. Pashpoho et al. to Andrew Jackson, n.d., OIA-LR, roll 355.

37. J. W. Edmonds, *Report of J. W. Edmonds, United States Commissioner, upon the Disturbance at the Potawatomie Payment, September 1836* (New York: Scatcherd and Adams, 1837), 3, 8.

38. Edmunds, "'Designing Men, Seeking a Fortune,'" 109–22; "grew," "excitement," and "exercised" in Edmonds, *Report of J. W. Edmonds*, 5, 9, 18; Secunda, "In the Shadow," 567–78.

39. Council with Potawatomis, July 21–July 23, 1837, OIA-LR, roll 361.

40. Council with Potawatomis, August 1, 1837, ibid.; "believe" from Anthony L. Davis to John Tipton, February 8, 1837, Robertson and Riker, *John Tipton Papers*, 3:362.

41. Journal of Emigration, August 20, 1837–September 20, 1837, OIA-LR, roll 361; George H. Proffit to Col. A. C. Pepper, October 27, 1837, OIA-LR, roll 356; A. C. Pepper to C. A. Harris, November 18, 1837, OIA-LR, roll 361; "from" in William Polke to John Tipton, September 11, 1837, Robertson and Riker, *John Tipton Papers*, 3:435–36.

42. John B. Duret to John Tipton, September 6, 1837, Robertson and Riker, *John Tipton Papers*, 3:433.

43. Edmunds, *Potawatomis*, 261–63; Isaac McCoy to John Tipton, November 16, 1837, Robertson and Riker, *John Tipton Papers*, 3:458–59; Johnston Lykins to John Tipton, November 17, 1837, ibid., 3:459–62.

44. Johnston Lykins to John Tipton, November 17, 1837, ibid., 3:461 (italics in original).

45. *Indian Affairs*, 2:462–63; Menomi et al. to Lewis Cass, November 12, 1836, OIA-LR, roll 355; Bowes, *Exiles and Pioneers*, 72–77.

46. All quotes in D. Smith, "Journal of an Emigrating Party," 315–36.

47. "remnant" in John Tipton to T. Hartley Crawford, January 2, 1839, Robertson and Riker, *John Tipton Papers*, 3:791; "quite" in A. C. Pepper to T. Hartley Crawford, April 25, 1839, OIA-LR, roll 356; G. N. Fitch to Samuel Milroy, June 21, 1839, OIA-LR, roll 356; "remove" and "nothing" in Samuel Milroy to William Polke, October 23, 1839, Dwight L. Smith, ed., "The Attempted Potawatomi Emigration of 1839," *Indiana Magazine of History* 45 (March 1949): 65–66.

48. "had" and "I" in Journal of Proceedings in Collecting Indians for Emigration, October 31, 1839, OIA-LR, roll 361; "Have" in Samuel Milroy to T. Hartley Crawford, June 8, 1839, OIA-LR, roll 356; other letters related to these events can be found D. Smith, "Attempted Potawatomi Emigration," 51–80.

49. William Polke to Samuel Milroy, January 14, 1840, D. Smith, "Attempted Potawatomi Emigration," 76–77; Samuel Milroy to William Polke, February 1, 1840, ibid., 78–79; Edmunds, *Potawatomis*, 269–71; Anthony L. Davis to T. Hartley Crawford, October 8, 1840, OIA-LR, roll 361; "lands" in Brig. Gen. Brady to T. Hartley Crawford, August 24, 1840, OIA-LR, roll 361; "On the contrary" in H. Brady to Thomas Hartley Crawford, December 29, 1840, OIA-LR, roll 361.

50. James A. Clifton, *A Place of Refuge for All Time: Migration of the American Potawatomi into Upper Canada, 1830–1850* (Ottawa: National Museums of Canada, 1975), 33–34; Phil Bellfy, *Three Fires Unity: The Anishnaabeg of the Lake Huron Borderlands* (Lincoln: University of Nebraska Press, 2011), 97–99.

51. Frank G. Beaubien, "The Beaubiens of Chicago," *Illinois Catholic Historical Review* 2 (July 1919): 96–105.

52. Genealogy folder, Beaubien Family Collection, Citizen Potawatomi Nation Cultural Heritage Center.

53. Reuben Gold Thwaites, ed., "American Fur Company Employees—1818–1819," *Collections of the State Historical Society of Wisconsin* 12 (1892): 169; Reuben Gold Thwaites, ed., "American Fur Company Invoices—1821–1822," *Collections of the State Historical Society of Wisconsin* 11 (1888): 375; Jacqueline

Peterson, "Goodbye, Madore Beaubien: The Americanization of Early Chicago Society," *Chicago History* 9 (1980): 106.

54. Affidavit of Madore Beaubien, January 28, 1878, and Affidavit of Jean B. Letendere, December 21, 1877, in Henry Higgins Hurlbut, *Chicago Antiquities: Comprising Original Items and Relations, Letters, Extracts, and Notes Pertaining to Early Chicago* (Chicago: Fergus Printing, 1881), 313–21; A. Keating, *Rising Up from Indian Country*, 67–68; Peterson, "Goodbye, Madore Beaubien," 107.

55. *Indian Affairs*, 2:199; Alfred Theodore Andreas, *History of Chicago* (Chicago: A. T. Andreas, 1884) 1:175.

56. Joseph Bourassa et al. to Lewis Cass, October 8, 1831, OIA-LR, 132.

57. Jacqueline Peterson, "'Wild' Chicago: The Formation and Destruction of a Multi-racial Community on the Midwestern Frontier, 1816–1837," in *The Ethnic Frontier: Essays in the History of Group Survival in Chicago and the Midwest*, ed. Melvin G. Holli and Peter d'A. Jones (Grand Rapids, Mich.: William B. Erdman, 1977), 52–56; Carl B. Roden, "The Beaubien Claim," *Journal of the Illinois State Historical Society* 42 (June 1949): 147–66; McCoy, *History of Baptist Indian Missions*, 269–72.

58. John Moses and Joseph Kirkland, *History of Chicago* (Chicago: Munsell, 1895), 1:88–89, 615; *Indian Affairs*, 2:405–407; Petersen, "Goodbye, Madore Beaubien," 110–11; Andreas, *History of Chicago*, 1:107; Madore Beaubien interview in Beaubien, "Beaubiens of Chicago," 353.

59. "cast" in Petersen, "Goodbye, Madore Beaubien," 111; "Indian" in Priscilla Mullin Sherrard, *People of the Place of the Fire* (n.p.: privately published, 1975), 144.

60. Journal of a Council with Potawatomis, November 1845, DRNRUT, roll 4; *Indian Affairs*, 2:557–60, 824–28; "transact" in Bowes, *Exiles and Pioneers*, 244–50.

61. J. B. Beaubien to Medore Beaubien, February 21, 1846, Beaubien Family Collection, Family History Folder; *Indian Affairs*, 2:557–60; R. B. Mitchell to unknown, June 6, 1844, ibid.; John Kelley, "1822 Chicago, from Tales of an 1822 Chicagoan: Some Memoirs of the Late Alexander Beaubien," *Journal of the Illinois State Historical Society* 14 (October 1921–January 1922): 407–12.

62. Joseph N. Balestier, *The Annals of Chicago: A Lecture Delivered before the Chicago Lyceum, January 21, 1840*, 2nd ed. (Chicago: Fergus Printing, 1876), 22.

63. "from" in A. Keating, *Rising Up from Indian Country*, 234; "on account" in *Indian Affairs*, 2:413.

64. *Annales de la Propogation de la Foi* (Paris: La Librairie Ecclésiastique de Rusand, 1830), 4:546.

65. Secunda, "In the Shadow," 444–67, 540.

66. Ibid. 261–63, 278, 443–47; "ideological" in Mark Schurr, Terrance J. Martin, and W. Ben Secunda, "How the Pokagon Band Avoided Removal: Archaeological Evidence from the Faunal Assemblage of the Pokagon Village Site (20BE13)," *Midcontinental Journal of Archaeology* 31 (Spring 2006): 160; Elizabeth

Bollwerk, "Controlling Acculturation: A Potawatomi Strategy for Avoiding Removal," *Midcontinental Journal of Archaeology* 31 (Spring 2006): 117–41.

67. Juanita Hunter, "The Indians and the Michigan Road," *Indiana Magazine of History* 83 (September 1987): 244–66; W. Ben Secunda, "To Cede or Seed? Risk and Identity among the Woodland Potawatomi during the Removal Period," *Midcontinental Journal of Archaeology* 31 (Spring 2006): 67.

68. "refused" in Gov. George Porter to Andrew Jackson, December 15, 1833, OIA-LR, roll 421; *Indian Affairs*, 2:372–75, 413; Cecilia Bain Buechner, "The Pokagons," *Indiana Historical Society Publications* 10 (1933): 312; James A. Clifton, *The Pokagons, 1683–1983: Catholic Potawatomi of the St. Joseph River Valley* (Lanham, Md.: University Press of America, 1984), 69–70; Howard S. Rogers, *History of Cass County, from 1825 to 1875* (Cassopolis, Mich.: W. H. Mansfield, 1875), 167–69. The actual number of acres comprising the original purchase is reported differently in multiple sources.

69. A. D. P. Van Buren, "Sketches, Reminiscences, and Anecdotes of the Old Members of the Calhoun and Kalamazoo County Bars," MPHC, 11:290–291; "The Judge" in Brig. Gen. Brady to T. Hartley Crawford, August 24, 1840, OIA-LR, roll 361.

70. Population numbers can be found in charts of "Supplementary Memorial of Certain Indians Residing in Michigan and Indiana," House of Representatives Miscellaneous Documents, No. 137, 42nd Cong., 2nd Sess., *U.S. Serial Set*, No. 1526, 14; "the Pottowatomies" in Wm. Richmond to Wm. Medill, November 20, 1847, ARCIA 1847, 86; "Those" in Wm. Richmond to William Medill, November 6, 1848, ARCIA 1848, 550; Clifton, *Pokagons*, 73–80; Buechner, "Pokagons," 313–15.

6. Michigan Anishinabek in the Removal Age

1. Outside of document quotations or titles from documents, I will use "Anishinabe" (singular), "Anishinabek" (plural), or "Ojibwe" instead of "Chippewa." My reasoning for this comes in part from the explanation provided by the Saginaw Ojibwes who explain that "Chippewa" is a title applied by Americans in the mid-nineteenth century and is not the name they call themselves. "Ojibwe" is used when it is deemed necessary to make distinct references among Anishinabek, including Odawas and Potawatomis. See Charmaine M. Benz, ed., *Diba Jimoonyung, Telling Our Story: A History of the Saginaw Ojibwe Anishinabek* (Mt. Pleasant, Mich.: Saginaw Chippewa Indian Tribe, 2005), 1.

2. 1855 Proceedings; Andrew J. Blackbird, *History of the Ottawa and Chippewa Indians of Michigan* (Ypsilanti, Mich.: Ypsilantian Job Printing, 1887), 61–63; Theodore J. Karamanski, *Blackbird's Song: Andrew J. Blackbird and the Odawa People* (East Lansing: Michigan State University Press, 2012), 146.

3. 1855 Proceedings; *Indian Affairs*, 2:450–56, 725–31, 733–35.

4. 1855 Proceedings.

5. Benz, *Diba Jimoonyung*, 48.

6. Charles Cleland in particular examines the development of these local and national trends, noting that even commissioners of Indian affairs from the 1840s through the 1850s—Charles Mix, Luke Lea, and George Manypenny—"rejected not only removal but also the racism and paternalism" of men like Lewis Cass and Henry Schoolcraft, who had been so influential in Michigan's Indian affairs in previous decades. See Charles Cleland, *Rites of Conquest: The History and Culture of Michigan's Native Americans* (Ann Arbor: University of Michigan Press, 1992), (181, 223, 229, 234.)

7. This idea runs clear and strong in the scholarship of James M. McClurken, who has written primarily about different Odawa communities. See James M. McClurken, *Our People, Our Journey: The Little River Band of Ottawa Indians* (East Lansing: Michigan State University Press, 2009); James M. McClurken, "Ottawa Adaptive Strategies to Indian Removal," *Michigan Historical Review* 12 (Spring 1986); James M. McClurken, "We Wish To Be Civilized: Ottawa-American Political Contests on the Michigan Frontier (Volumes I and II)" (Ph.D. diss., Michigan State University, 1988); other studies that touch on this history of removal and persistence in the Lower Peninsula of Michigan include Elizabeth A. Neumeyer, "Indian Removal in Michigan, 1833–1855" (M.A. thesis, Central Michigan University, 1968); James Z. Schwartz, *Conflict on the Michigan Frontier: Yankee and Borderland Cultures, 1815–1840* (DeKalb: Northern Illinois University Press, 2009); Deborah A. Rosen, *American Indians and State Law: Sovereignty, Race, and Citizenship, 1790–1880* (Lincoln: University of Nebraska Press, 2009).

8. *Indian Affairs*, 2:453.

9. "was" and "both" in Karaminski, *Blackbird's Song*, 78; "Instead" in McClurken, "We Wish To Be Civilized," 189.

10. Willis Frederick Dunbar, *Michigan: A History of the Wolverine State* (Grand Rapids, Mich.: William Eerdmans, 1965), 272, 303, 322–24.

11. "scene" and "saw" in Malcolm Rohrbough, *The Land Office Business: The Settlement and Administration of American Public Lands, 1789–1837* (New York: Oxford University Press, 1968), 202–19, 241, 247; Dunbar, *Michigan*, 301, 316–17.

12. McClurken, "We Wish To Be Civilized," 178, 198.

13. "there are" and "they fled" in Peyton Morgan to Henry Schoolcraft, August 12, 1837, OIA-M1, roll 43; Report of Henry Schoolcraft, December 1838, ARCIA 1838, 480.

14. "registered" and "All" in Henry Schoolcraft to T. Hartley Crawford, February 26, 1839, OIA-LR, roll 745; Report of Henry Schoolcraft, December 1838, ARCIA 1838, 480; Report of Henry Schoolcraft, September 30, 1839, ARCIA 1839, 476–82.

15. *Indian Affairs*, 2:92–95.

16. "if good" in Elbert Herring to Francis Maconse and others, October 25, 1834, OIA-LS, roll 14; "west" in *Indian Affairs*, 2:461–62; Isaac McCoy to Esh-tonoquet, September 8, 1837, OIA-M1, roll 43; Neumeyer, "Indian Removal in Michigan," 34.

17. "principal" in Albert J. Smith to Henry Schoolcraft, October 2, 1837, OIA-M1, roll 43; "location" in T. Hartley Crawford to J. R. Poinsett, January 23, 1839, Senate Document No. 155, 25th Cong., 3rd Sess., *U.S. Serial Set*, No. 340, 2; "purchasers" in T. Hartley Crawford to Secretary of War Joel Poinsett, November 25, 1839, ARCIA 1839, 327–48.

18. "regret" in Albert J. Smith to T. Hartley Crawford, September 13, 1839, OIA-LR, roll 427; Articles of a Compact Made at Detroit in the State of Michigan . . . , September 23, 1839, OIA-LR, roll 423; Neumeyer, "Indian Removal in Michigan," 39–43; for the postremoval experience of the Swan Creek and Black River Chippewa Indians, see Herring, *Enduring Indians of Kansas*, 58–69.

19. Robert Stuart to T. Hartley Crawford, October 18, 1841, ARCIA 1841, 323–26.

20. Robert Stuart to T. Hartley Crawford, October 28, 1842, ARCIA 1842, 400–403.

21. All quotations in Ottawa Chiefs of Grand River to President Andrew Jackson, January 27, 1836, OIA-LR, roll 422; McClurken, *Our People, Our Journey*, 27–29.

22. Treaty of 1836, *Indian Affairs*, 2:450–56; "they selected" in McCoy, *History of Baptist Indian Missions*, 494.

23. Records of a Treaty Concluded with the Ottawa and Chippewa Nations, at Washington, D.C., March 28, 1836, Papers of Henry Rowe Schoolcraft, Library of Congress, Washington, D.C.; George H. White, "Sketch of the Life of Hon. Rix Robinson, A Pioneer of Western Michigan," MPHC, 11:193–94; McClurken, "We Wish To Be Civilized," 180–89; Karamanski, *Blackbird's Song*, 78–90.

24. Hamlin's speech and "provided" in Records of a Treaty Concluded with the Ottawa and Chippewa Nations, at Washington, D.C., March 28, 1836, Papers of Henry Rowe Schoolcraft; Treaty of 1836, *Indian Affairs*, 2:450–56; "to my extreme" in McCoy, *History of Baptist Indian Missions*, 495.

25. "had never" in McCoy, *History of Baptist Indian Missions*, 496–97; Henry R. Schoolcraft, *Personal Memoirs of a Residence of Thirty Years with the Indian Tribes of the American Frontiers* (Philadelphia: Lippincott, Grambo, 1851), 538; *Indian Affairs*, 2:453.

26. "take care" in Lewis Cass to Henry Schoolcraft, May 17, 1836, OIA-LS, roll 18; "the Senate" in Resolution in the Senate of the U.S., June 8, 1836, "Documents Relating to the Negotiation of an Unratified Treaty of May 24, 1836, with the Saginaw Band of Chippewa Indians," DRNRUT; "I have" in C. A. Harris to Henry Schoolcraft, September 30, 1836, OIA-LS, roll 19.

27. "Articles of a Treaty, Made and Concluded at Washington in the District of Columbia between the United States of America, by their Commissioner, Henry R. Schoolcraft, and the Saganaw bands of the Chippewa Nation," in Documents Relating to the Negotiation of an Unratified Treaty of May 24, 1836, with the Saginaw Band of Chippewa Indians, DRNRUT; Schoolcraft, *Personal Memoirs*, 538, 553; *Indian Affairs*, 2:482–86.

28. *Indian Affairs*, 2:482–86, 501–502, 516–17; Lucius Lyon to Henry Schoolcraft, March 3, 1837, OIA-M1, roll 42; "bind" in C. A. Harris to Henry Schoolcraft, October 3, 1837, OIA-M1, roll 43; Isaac McCoy to Saginaw Chiefs, September 6, 1837, OIA-M1, roll 43.

29. Henry Schoolcraft to C. A. Harris, December 23, 1837, OIA-M1, roll 37; *Indian Affairs*, 2:501–502.

30. *Indian Affairs*, 2:501–502; 516–17; "would" in Henry Schoolcraft to C. A. Harris, December 23, 1837, OIA-M1, roll 37; "deemed" in Henry Schoolcraft to C. A. Harris, January 31, 1838, in Ratified Treaty No. 231, Documents Relating to the Negotiation of the Treaty of January 23, 1838, with the Saginaw Band of Chippewa Indians, DRNRUT.

31. "survey" in Report of Henry Schoolcraft, September 30, 1839, ARCIA 1839, 476–82; Report of Henry Schoolcraft, November 28, 1840, ARCIA 1840, 228–32; "handsome" in Henry Schoolcraft to T. Hartley Crawford, April 14, 1841, OIA-LR, roll 746; John Moore, Acting Commissioner of the General Land Office, to T. Hartley Crawford, November 11, 1841, OIA-LR, roll 746.

32. "This," "great," and "had" in Chiefs and Headmen of Chippewa Indians of Saganaw to President of the USA, November 4, 1842, OIA-LR, roll 425; "interests" in T. Hartley Crawford to Thomas H. Blake, Commissioner General Land Office, August 18, 1843, ARCIA 1843, 306.

33. James H. Piper to William Medill, January 14, 1847, OIA-LR, roll 426.

34. "To provide for the sale of lands purchased by the United States from the Saginaw tribe of Chippewa Indians, in the State of Michigan," Senate Bill 197, 30th Cong., 1st Sess., *Bills and Resolutions, A Century of Lawmaking for a New Nation*.

35. Robert Stuart to T. Hartley Crawford, November 7, 1842, OIA-LR, roll 425; "Each band" in Andrew T. McReynolds to Robert Stuart, October 30, 1844, ARCIA 1844, 180–82; "Town" in Andrew T. McReynolds to T. Hartley Crawford, June 30, 1845, OIA-LR, roll 746.

36. McClurken, "We Wish To Be Civilized," 212–16; Etta Smith Wilson, "Life and Work of the Late Rev. George N. Smith, A Pioneer Missionary," MPHC, 30:199; J. R. Kellogg to H. R. Schoolcraft, May 28, 1839, Robert P. Swieranga and William Van Appledorn, eds., *Old Wing Mission: Cultural Interchange as Chronicled by George and Arvilla Smith in their Work with Chief Wakazoo's Ottawa Band on the West Michigan Frontier* (Grand Rapids, Mich.: Eerdmans Publishing, 2008), 496–97.

37. J. R. Kellogg to H. R. Schoolcraft, May 28, 1839, Swieranga and Van Appledorn, *Old Wing Mission*, 496–97.

38. "To the President of the United States of America . . . ," ARCIA 1844, 179–80; "nearly" in Robert Stuart to T. Hartley Crawford, October 10, 1844, ibid., 178–79.

39. Rev. Leonard Slater to William Richmond, September 30, 1846, ARCIA 1846, 121–23.

40. Peter Dougherty to William Richmond, September 16, 1847, ARCIA 1847, 188.

41. Swierenga and Van Appledorn, *Old Wing Mission*, 42–52; George Smith to Wm. A. Richmond, August 31, 1847, ibid., 585–86; "We don't" in Peter Wakazoo to Wm. A. Richmond, December 3, 1847, ibid., 589–90; George Smith to Wm. A. Richmond, July 16, 1848, ibid., 602–603; Real Estate Tax Assessment for the Township of Manlius, Allegan County, 1847, ibid., 298–99; Acts of Legislature of the State of Michigan, (1849), ibid., 607–608; George N. Smith to C. P. Babcock, August 28, 1849, ibid 611–13; Geo. N. Smith to C. P. Babcock, October 9, 1850, ibid., 616–17.

42. Dunbar, *Michigan*, 424–26; Rosen, *American Indians and State Law*, 134–35; "sundry" and "white" in *Report of the Proceedings and Debates in the Convention to Revise the Constitution of the State of Michigan, 1850* (Lansing, Mich.: R. W. Ingals, 1850), 93, 420; the revised constitution of 1850 is found on pages xxiii–xliii. The fact that the petition was referred to the committee on the government and judicial policy of the Upper Peninsula suggests that this was the origin of the petition.

43. "to make" in Joint Resolution Relative to the Ottawa and Chippewa Indians, *Acts of the Legislature of the State of Michigan Passed at the Annual and Extra Sessions of 1851*, 258–59; 1850 Census for Michigan, Historical Census Browser, University of Virginia Library, accessed February 22, 2013, http://mapserver.lib.virginia.edu/php.

44. "He wants" in George Bradley to Babcock, Secretary of Indian Affairs, May 17, 1850, OIA-M1, roll 64: 197; "the chiefs" in George Bradley to Lewis Cass, December 14, 1852, OIA-LR, roll 403.

45. "consummate" in Senate Resolution, April 6, 1852, OIA-LR, roll 403; all other quotations in George Bradley to Lewis Cass, December 14, 1852, ibid.

46. Peter Lefevre to H. C. Gilbert, September 8, 1853, ARCIA 1853, 46–48.

47. Henry Gilbert to George Manypenny, December 10, 1853, OIA-LR, roll 404.

48. Henry Gilbert to George Manypenny, March 6, 1854, ibid.

49. George Smith and P. G. Johnson to McClelland, Secretary of the Interior, November 8, 1854, OIA-LR, roll 787.

50. "recommending" in John Wilson to McClelland, December 20, 1854, *Indian Affairs*, 1:846; Executive Order of Franklin Pierce, May 14, 1855, ibid., 1:847.

51. "Their" in Henry Gilbert to George Manypenny, June 9, 1855, OIA-LR, roll 404; Acting Commissioner of General Land Office George Whitney to Acting Commissioner of Indian Affairs Charles Mix, July 13, 1855, OIA-LR roll 168.

52. 1855 Proceedings.

53. 1855 Proceedings; *Indian Affairs*, 2:725–31, 733–35.

7. The American Era Is a Removal Era

1. Interview with Annie Young Bumberry, Indian-Pioneer Papers Collection, Western History Collections, University of Oklahoma; Lawrence C. Kelly, *The*

Assault on Assimilation: John Collier and the Origins of Indian Policy Reform (Albuquerque: University of New Mexico Press, 1983).

2. "to obtain" in Treaty of 1831, *Indian Affairs*, 2:331–34; "unfriendly" and "It" in Phillip S. Foner, ed., *The Life and Writings of Frederick Douglass* (New York: International Publishers, 1955), 4:15–16.

3. "Terms of Treaties Hereafter To Be Made with Certain Tribes of Indians," April 7, 1854, House of Representatives Reports of Committees, Report No. 132, 33rd Cong., 1st Sess., *U.S. Serial Set*, No. 743, 2; "amounted" in Denson, *Demanding the Cherokee Nation*, 93.

4. Anderson, *Conquest of Texas*, 318–21; LaVere, *Contrary Neighbors*, 162–65.

5. Hämäläinen, *Comanche Empire*; Brian Delay, *War of a Thousand Deserts: Indian Raids and the U.S.–Mexican War* (New Haven, Conn.: Yale University Press, 2009); Duane Kendall Hale, *Peacemakers on the Frontier: A History of the Delaware Tribe of Western Oklahoma* (Anadarko: Delaware Tribe of Western Oklahoma Press, 1987), 15–20; "Copy of the Treaty between Texas and the Indians," in Richard C. Adams, *A Brief Sketch of the Sabine Land Cession in Texas* (Washington, D.C.: John Byrne, 1901), 13, 18–22; all quotations in "Report of Standing Committee on Indian Affairs," Dorman H. Winfrey, ed., *The Indian Papers of Texas and the Southwest, 1825–1916* (College Station: Texas State Historical Association, 1995), 1:25–28; G. Anderson, *Conquest of Texas*, 153–71.

6. "adopted" in G. Anderson, *Conquest of Texas*, 172, 181–84; M. B. Lamar to Chief Bowles of the Cherokees, May 26, 1839, Winfrey, *Indian Papers of Texas*, 1:61–66; M. B. Lamar to Linney, the Shawnee, May, 1839, Winfrey, *Indian Papers of Texas*, 1:66–67; "ultimate" in Letter from M. B. Lamar to David G. Burnet, Albert Sidney Johnston, Thomas J. Rusk, I. W. Burton, and James S. Mayfield, June 27, 1839, Winfrey, *Indian Papers of Texas*, 1: 67–70; "return" in Treaty between Texas and the Shawnee Indians, August 2, 1839, Winfrey, *Indian Papers of Texas*, 1:80–81.

7. Minutes of Indian Council at Tehuacana Creek, March 28, 1843, Winfrey, *Indian Papers of Texas*, 1:149–63.

8. G. Anderson, *Conquest of Texas*, 238.

9. No. 26, Minutes of a Council at Tehuacana Creek, Winfrey, *Indian Papers of Texas*, 2:32; "if you" in No. 28, Minutes of Treaty Council at Tehuacana Creek, ibid., 2:43; Thomas G. Western to Robert S. Neighbors, April 9, 1845, ibid., 2:216; "The Delaware" in Thomas G. Western to Benjamin Sloat and L. H. Williams, April 9, 1845, ibid., 2:217–18; accounts describing payments for services to John Conner, Jim Shaw, and Jack Harry can be found in ibid., 2:134–41.

10. Anderson, *Conquest of Texas*, 215–16, 222–24; all quotations in D. G. Burnet to Henry Schoolcraft, September 29, 1847, Winfrey, *Indian Papers of Texas*, 3:98.

11. G. Anderson, *Conquest of Texas*, 255–56; "temporary" in Governor's Message, November 9, 1853, *Journal of the Senate of the State of Texas: Fifth Legislature* (Austin: J. W. Hampton, 1853), 20.

12. G. Anderson, *Conquest of Texas*, 256–63, 305–17; LaVere, *Contrary Neighbors*, 162–65.

13. "extermination" in G. Anderson, *Conquest of Texas*, 319–22; LaVere, *Contrary Neighbors*, 149–50, 164–65.

14. "relations" in Treaty of 1855, *Indian Affairs*, 2:677–81; "Much" and "because" in interview with Leander Zane, Indian-Pioneer Papers Collection; Minutes of Wyandotte Council, February 23, 1858, September 15, 1858, September 13, 1859, Indian Files—Wyandot, box 6; Bowes, *Exiles and Pioneers*, 178–84, 201–18.

15. *Indian Affairs*, 2:614–26, 634–36, 824–28; "have" in B. F. Robinson to Colonel A. Cuming, September 21, 1855, ARCIA 1855, 91–92; "exceedingly" in B. F. Robinson to John Haverty, September 14, 1857, ARCIA 1857, 166. More in-depth examinations of events in Kansas Territory related to the impact of American expansion into Kansas Territory in the 1850s can be found in Bowes, *Exiles and Pioneers*, 187–254; Miner and Unrau, *End of Indian Kansas*.

16. Mary Young, *Redskins, Ruffleshirts, and Rednecks: Indian Allotments in Alabama and Mississippi, 1830–1860* (Norman: University of Oklahoma Press, 1961); Bowes, *Exiles and Pioneers*, 194–200; *Indian Affairs*, 2:814–28; Unrau and Miner, *End of Indian Kansas*, 55–80.

17. Glick, Barlett, and Glick to Commissioner of Indian Affairs, May 7, 1859, OIA-LR, roll 810; "national" in *In Re: Kansas Indians*, 72 U.S. 737 (1866); John W. Ragsdale, "The Dispossession of the Kansas Shawnee," *University of Missouri-Kansas Law Review* 58 (Winter 1990): 209–56; "sold" in Thomas Murphy to D. N. Cooley, October 6, 1866, ARCIA 1866, 245–46; examples of property tax assessments in Abstract from the Records of the County Treasurer's Office Showing the Taxes Due Wyandott County, Kansas, by the Shawnee Indians Holding their Lands in Severalty From 1860 to 1865 Inclusive, OIA-LR, roll 814, frames 1109–15; Bowes, *Exiles and Pioneers*, 231–37.

18. "the Wyandots" in James B. Abbot to Colonel F. B. Branch, September 15, 1862, ARCIA 1862, 112; "stock" in C. B. Keith to H. B. Branch, September 25, 1862, ibid., 115; the impact of and participation in the Civil War on Indians in Kansas in Laurence M. Hauptman, *Between Two Fires: American Indians in the Civil War* (New York: Free Press Paperbacks, 1995); Arrell Morgan Gibson, "Native Americans and the Civil War," *American Indian Quarterly* 9 (Autumn 1985): 385–410; Troy Smith, "Nations Colliding: The Civil War Comes to Indian Territory," *Civil War History* 59 (Summer 2013): 279–319.

19. "Beyond" in A. Cuming to George Manypenny, September 25, 1856, ARCIA 1856, 73; Report of the Commissioner of Indian Affairs, November 26, 1862, ARCIA 1862, 24; "providing" in Act of March 3, 1863, *USSL*, ch. 99, 12 Stat. 793; "clear" in C. Joseph Genetin-Pilawa, *Crooked Paths to Allotment: The Fight over Federal Indian Policy after the Civil War* (Chapel Hill: University of North Carolina Press, 2012), 60; discussion of the bill in the Senate in *Congressional Globe, A Century of Lawmaking for a New Nation*, Senate, 38th Cong, 2nd Sess., 1021–22.

20. *Indian Affairs*, 2:937–42, 960–69, 970–74; Articles of Agreement between the Shawnee and Cherokee Indians, June 7, 1869, OIA-LR, roll 817; Brice Obermeyer, *Delaware Tribe in a Cherokee Nation* (Lincoln: University of Nebraska Press, 2009).

21. "[The Poncas] were" in interview with William Long of Commerce, Indian-Pioneer Papers Collection; "They died" in interview with Dave Geboe, ibid.; interview with Mrs. Cora Hayman, ibid. For overviews of the removals of the Nez Perces, Poncas, and Modocs, respectively, see Elliott West, *The Last Indian War: The Nez Perce Story* (New York: Oxford University Press, 2009), 283–304; David J. Wishart, *An Unspeakable Sadness: The Dispossession of the Nebraska Indians* (Lincoln: University of Nebraska Press, 1994), 202–16; Keith A. Murray, *The Modocs and Their War* (Norman: University of Oklahoma Press, 1976), 310–17.

22. "saw" in interview with Lola Jane Chouteau, Indian-Pioneer Papers Collection; "owned" in interview with Eliza Journeycake Minshall, ibid.; "would" and "out" in interview with Henry Armstrong, ibid.; interview with Jake Longtail of Vinita, ibid.; interview with Katie Day, ibid.

23. "The Shawnee" in interview with Jake Longtail of Vinita, ibid.; "We were" and "This time" in interview with Sarah Longbone, ibid.; "since" in interview with David Dushane, Jr., ibid.; "there will" in interview with Miss Ruth Parks, ibid.

24. "the tomb" in Jonathan Blackfeather, Deceased, ibid.; "some" and "I am" in interview with Eva Spicer Whitetree Nichols, ibid.

25. Michael Pace interview in Brown and Kohn, *Long Journey Home*, 256.

26. In 1937, in the very first article of their new constitution, the Seneca-Cayuga Nation of Oklahoma declared that what had sometimes been referred to as the "Seneca Tribe" would now go by "Seneca-Cayuga Nation." In part, this official designation recognizes the fact that the composition of the community from the late 1700s to the 1900s was as much, if not more, Cayuga as Seneca. For the sake of consistency with the documentary record, I have used "Seneca" when discussing the community until the point in history at which that official designation changed.

27. "The only" and "I do not" in interview with Annie Young Bumberry, Indian-Pioneer Papers Collection; Laurence M. Hauptman, *The Iroquois and the New Deal* (Syracuse: Syracuse University Press, 1988), 103–105; "I just" in interview with Minnie Thompson, Seneca, Doris Duke Collection, Western History Collection, University of Oklahoma.

BIBLIOGRAPHY

MANUSCRIPT MATERIALS AND COLLECTIONS

Beaubien Family Collection. Citizen Potawatomi Nation Cultural Heritage Center. Shawnee, Oklahoma.

Documents Relating to Indian Affairs. University of Wisconsin Digital Collections. http://uwdc.library.wisc.edu/collections/History/IndianTreatiesMicro.

Record Group 75 T494. Documents Relating to the Negotiation of Ratified and Unratified Treaties with Various Indian Tribes, 1801–1869. National Archives and Records Collection.

Office of Indian Affairs, Annual Reports of the Commissioner of Indian Affairs.

Foreman, Grant, Collection. Oklahoma State Historical Society. Oklahoma City, Oklahoma.

Frontier Wars Manuscripts. Draper Manuscript Collection. State Historical Society of Wisconsin.

Great Lakes and Ohio Valley Ethnohistory Collection. Glenn A. Black Laboratory of Archaeology. Indiana University.

Indian Claims Commission Collection.

Tribal Documents Collection.

Hayes, Rutherford B., Papers. Rutherford B. Hayes Presidential Library. Fremont, Ohio.

Lower Sandusky, 1810–1814.

Lower Sandusky, 1815–1824.

Indian Files. Kansas State Historical Society. Lawrence, Kansas.

Michigan Pioneer and Historical Collections. Michigan State University Library.

Schoolcraft, Henry Rowe, Papers. Library of Congress. Washington, D.C.

Western History Collection. University of Oklahoma.

Duke, Doris, Collection. http://digital.libraries.ou.edu/whc/duke/.

Indian-Pioneer Papers Collection. http://digital.libraries.ou.edu/whc/pioneer/.

GOVERNMENT PUBLICATIONS

*A Century of Lawmaking for a New Nation: U.S. Congressional Documents and Debates,
1774–1875.* Library of Congress. http://memory.loc.gov/ammem/amlaw/.

*American State Papers, Documents, Legislative and Executive, of the Congress of the
United States, Class I, Foreign Affairs.* Edited by Matthew St. Clair Clarke and
Walter Lowrie. 6 vols. Washington, D.C.: Gales and Seaton, 1833.

*American State Papers, Documents, Legislative and Executive, of the Congress of the
United States, Class II, Indian Affairs.* Edited by Matthew St. Clair Clarke and
Walter Lowrie. 2 vols. Washington, D.C.: Gales and Seaton, 1832.

Annals of Congress.

Bills and Resolutions.

Congressional Globe.

Journal of the House of Representatives.

Journal of the Senate.

Journals of the Continental Congress 1774–1789.

Register of Debates.

U.S. Serial Set.

U.S. Statutes at Large.

*Acts of the Legislature of the State of Michigan Passed at the Annual and Extra Sessions of
1851.* Lansing, Mich.: R. W. Ingals, 1851.

Indian Affairs: Laws and Treaties. Compiled and edited by Charles A. Kappler. 7
vols. Washington, D.C.: U.S. Government Printing Office, 1904.

Journal of the Senate of the State of Texas: Fifth Legislature. Austin, Tex.: J. W. Hampton, 1853.

National Archives and Records Administration, Washington, D.C.

Record Group 75 M1. Records of the Michigan Superintendency, 1824–1851.

Record Group 75 M21. Letters Sent by the Office of Indian Affairs, 1824–1881.

Record Group 75 M234. Letters Received by the Office of Indian Affairs,
1824–1881.

Roll 132. Chicago Agency, 1824–1837.

Roll 168. Chippewa Agency Emigration, 1850–1859; and Chippewa Agency
Reserves, 1853–1855.

Roll 215. Council Bluffs Agency, 1836–1857.

Rolls 300–302. Fort Leavenworth Agency, 1824–1851.

Rolls 354–57. Indiana Agency, 1824–1850.

Roll 361. Indiana Agency Emigration, 1833–1849; and Indiana Agency
Reserves, 1836–1850.

Rolls 403–404. Mackinac Agency, 1828–1880.

Roll 416. Miami Agency, 1824–1841; 1846–1850.

Roll 418. Miami Agency Emigration, 1842–1853.

Rolls 419–26. Michigan Superintendency, 1824–1851.

Rolls 601–602. Ohio Agency, 1831–1843.

Roll 603. Ohio Agency Emigration, 1831–1839; and Ohio Agency Reserves,
1834–1843.

Roll 669. Pima Agency, 1859–1861; and Piqua Agency, 1824–1830.

Rolls 745–46. Saginaw Agency, 1824–1850.

Roll 751. St. Louis Superintendency, 1824–1851.

Roll 787. Schools, 1824–1873.

Rolls 810, 814, 817. Shawnee Agency, 1855–1876.

Roll 952. Wyandot Agency Emigration, 1839-1851; and Wyandot Agency Reserves, 1845-1863.

Record Group 123. Records of the U.S. Court of Claims, 1835–1984.

Report of the Proceedings and Debates in the Convention to Revise the Constitution of the State of Michigan, 1850. Lansing, Mich.: R. W. Ingals, 1850.

The Territorial Papers of the United States. Edited by Clarence Edward Carter and John Porter Bloom. 28 vols. Washington, D.C.: U.S. Government Printing Office, 1934–1975.

BOOKS AND ARTICLES

Adams, Richard Calmit. *A Brief Sketch of the Sabine Land Cession in Texas.* Washington, D.C.: John Byrne, 1901.

———. *A Delaware Indian Legend and the Story of Their Troubles.* Washington, D.C., 1899.

Allen, Carole M., Janine Beckley, Paula Bongen, Alan Conant, Dani B. Pfaff, and Virginia Ternening, eds. "The Man in the Middle—Chief J. B. Richardville." *The Indiana Historian: Exploring Indiana History* (November 1993): 1–15.

Anderson, Gary Clayton. *The Conquest of Texas: Ethnic Cleansing in the Promised Land, 1820–1875.* Norman: University of Oklahoma Press, 2005.

———. *Ethnic Cleansing and the Indian: The Crime That Should Haunt America.* Norman: University of Oklahoma Press, 2014.

Anderson, H. Allen. "The Delaware and Shawnee Indians and the Republic of Texas, 1820–1845." *Southwestern Historical Quarterly* 94 (October 1990): 231–60.

Anderson, William L., ed. *Cherokee Removal: Before and After.* Athens: University of Georgia Press, 1991.

Andreas, Alfred Theodore. *History of Chicago.* 3 vols. Chicago, 1884.

Andrew, John A., III. *From Revivals to Removal: Jeremiah Evarts, the Cherokee Nation, and the Search for the Soul of America.* Athens: University of Georgia Press, 1992.

Annales de la Propogation de la Foi. Paris: La Librairie Ecclésiastique de Rusand, 1830.

Anson, Bert. "Chief Francis Lafontaine and the Miami Emigration from Indiana." *Indiana Magazine of History* 60 (September 1964): 241–68.

Balestier, Joseph N. *The Annals of Chicago: A Lecture Delivered before the Chicago Lyceum, January 21, 1840.* 2nd ed. Chicago: Fergus Printing, 1876.

Barker, Eugene, ed. *The Austin Papers.* 2 vols. Washington, D.C.: American Historical Association, 1924.

Barr, Daniel P. "Odyssey's End: The Battle of Lake Erie and the Failure of the Delaware Indian Struggle for Autonomy." In *The Battle of Lake Erie and Its Aftermath: A Reassessment*, edited by David Curtis Skaggs, 101–25. Kent, Ohio: Kent State University Press, 2013.

Barr, Juliana. *Peace Came in the Form of a Woman: Indians and Spaniards in the Texas Borderlands.* Chapel Hill: University of North Carolina Press, 2007.

Beaubien, Frank G. "The Beaubiens of Chicago." *Illinois Catholic Historical Review* 2 (July 1919): 96–105.

Beckwith, H. W. *History of Fountain County.* Chicago: H. H. Hill and N. Iddings, 1881.

Bellfy, Phil. *Three Fires Unity: The Anishnaabeg of the Lake Huron Borderlands.* Lincoln: University of Nebraska Press, 2011.

Benz, Charmaine M., ed. *Diba Jimoonyung, Telling Our Story: A History of the Saginaw Ojibwe Anishinabek.* Mt. Pleasant, Mich.: Saginaw Chippewa Indian Tribe, 2005.

Berry, Kate A., and Melissa A. Rinehart. "A Legacy of Forced Migration: The Removal of the Miami Tribe in 1846." *International Journal of Population Geography* 60 (March/April 2003): 93–112.

Blackbird, Andrew J. *History of the Ottawa and Chippewa Indians of Michigan.* Ypsilanti, Mich.: Ypsilantian Job Printing House, 1887.

Blackhawk, Ned. "Look How Far We've Come: How American Indian History Changed the Study of American History in the 1990s." *Organization of American Historians Magazine of History* 19 (November 2005): 13–17.

Bliss, Eugene F., ed. *The Diary of David Zeisberger: A Moravian Missionary among the Indians of Ohio.* 2 vols. Cincinnati: Robert Clarke, 1885.

Bollwerk, Elizabeth. "Controlling Acculturation: A Potawatomi Strategy for Avoiding Removal." *Midcontinental Journal of Archaeology* 31 (Spring 2006): 117–41.

Bolton, S. Charles. "Jeffersonian Indian Removal and the Emergence of Arkansas Territory." *Arkansas Historical Quarterly* 62 (Autumn 2003): 253–71.

Bontrager, Shannon. "'From a Nation of Drunkards We Have Become a Sober People': The Wyandot Experience in the Ohio Valley during the Early Republic." *Journal of the Early Republic* 32 (Winter 2012): 603–32.

Bourassa, J. N. "The Life of Wah-bahn-se: The Warrior Chief of the Pottawatamies." *Kansas Historical Quarterly* 38 (Summer 1972): 132–43.

Bowes, John P. *Black Hawk and the War of 1832: Removal in the North.* New York: Chelsea House, 2007.

———. *Exiles and Pioneers: Eastern Indians in the Trans-Mississippi West.* New York: Cambridge University Press, 2007.

———. "The Gnaddenhutten Effect: Moravian Converts and the Search for Safety in the Canadian Borderlands." *Michigan Historical Review* 34 (Spring 2008): 101–17.

———. "Shawnee Geography and the Tennessee Corridor in the Seventeenth and Eighteenth Centuries." In *Before the Volunteer State: New Thoughts on*

Early Tennessee History, 1540–1800, edited by Kristofer Ray, 83–105. Knoxville: University of Tennessee Press, 2015.

Brooks, James F. *Captives and Cousins: Slavery, Kinship, and Community in the Southwest Borderlands*. Chapel Hill: University of North Carolina Press, 2002.

Brown, James W., and Rita Kohn, eds. *Long Journey Home: Oral Histories of Contemporary Delaware Indians*. Bloomington: Indiana University Press, 2007.

Bruyneel, Kevin. *The Third Space of Sovereignty: The Postcolonial Politics of U.S.–Indigenous Relations*. Minneapolis: University of Minnesota Press, 2007.

Buchman, Randall L. *A Sorrowful Journey*. Defiance, Ohio: Defiance College Press, 2007.

Buechner, Cecilia Bain. "The Pokagons." *Indiana Historical Society Publications* 10 (1933): 279–340.

Buss, James Joseph. "'They Found and Left Her an Indian': Gender, Race, and the Whitening of Young Bear." *Frontiers: A Journal of Women Studies* 29 (2008): 6–12.

———. *Winning the West with Words: Language and Conquest in the Lower Great Lakes*. Norman: University of Oklahoma Press, 2011.

Butterfield, Consul W. *An Historical Account of the Expedition against Sandusky under Col. William Crawford in 1782*. Cincinnati: Robert Clarke, 1873.

———. *History of Seneca County*. Sandusky, Ohio: D. Campbell, 1848.

Calloway, Colin G. *The American Revolution in Indian Country: Crisis and Diversity in Native American Communities*. New York: Cambridge University Press, 1995.

———. *Crown and Calumet: British-Indian Relations, 1783–1815*. Norman: University of Oklahoma Press, 1987.

———. *First Peoples: A Documentary Survey of American Indian History*. 4th ed. New York: Bedford/St. Martin's, 2012.

———. *One Vast Winter Count: The Native American West before Lewis and Clark*. Lincoln: University of Nebraska Press, 2003.

———. *The Victory with No Name: The Native American Defeat of the First American Army*. New York: Oxford University Press, 2014.

Carson, James Taylor. "Ethnogeography and the Native American Past." *Ethnohistory* 49 (Fall 2002): 769–88.

Cass, Lewis. "Documents and Proceedings Relating to the Formation and Progress of a Board in the City of New York, for the Emigration, Preservation, and Improvement of the Aborigines of America." *North American Review* 30 (January 1830): 62–121.

Cave, Alfred A. "Abuse of Power: Andrew Jackson and the Indian Removal Act of 1830." *The Historian* 65 (December 2003): 1330–53.

———. "The Failure of the Shawnee Prophet's Witch-Hunt." *Ethnohistory* 42 (Summer 1995): 445–75.

Cayton, Andrew R. L. *Frontier Indiana*. Bloomington: Indiana University Press, 1996.

————. *Ohio: The History of a People.* Columbus: Ohio State University Press, 2002.

Cleland, Charles. *Rites of Conquest: The History and Culture of Michigan's Native Americans.* Ann Arbor: University of Michigan Press, 1992.

Clifton, James A. *A Place of Refuge for All Time: Migration of the American Potawatomi into Upper Canada, 1830–1850.* Ottawa: National Museums of Canada, 1975.

————. *The Pokagons, 1683–1983: Catholic Potawatomi of the St. Joseph River Valley.* Lanham, Md.: University Press of America, 1984.

————. *The Prairie People: Continuity and Change in Potawatomi Indian Culture, 1665–1965.* Revised ed. Iowa City: University of Iowa Press, 1998.

Connelley, William E., ed. "The Provisional Government of Nebraska Territory and the Journals of William Walker." *Proceedings and Collections of the Nebraska State Historical Society, Second Series* 3 (1899).

Conway, Thomas G. "Potawatomi Politics." *Journal of the Illinois State Historical Society* 65 (1972): 395–418.

Cooke, Sarah E., and Rachel B. Ramadhyani, eds. *Indians and a Changing Frontier: The Art of George Winter.* Indianapolis: Indiana Historical Society/Tippecanoe County Historical Society, 1993.

Cooper, James Fenimore. *Last of the Mohicans.* New York: Bantam, 1981.

Craig, Neville, ed. *The Olden Time: A Monthly Publication Devoted to the Preservation of Documents and Other Authentic Information.* 2 vols. Cincinnati: Robert Clarke, 1876.

Cronon, William. *Nature's Metropolis: Chicago and the Great West.* New York: W. W. Norton, 1991.

Cruikshank, E. A., ed. *The Correspondence of Lieutenant Governor John Graves Simcoe.* 4 vols. Toronto: Toronto Historical Society, 1923.

Davis, Ethan. "An Administrative Trail of Tears: Indian Removal." *American Journal of Legal History* 50 (January 2010): 49–100.

Delay, Brian. *War of a Thousand Deserts: Indian Raids and the U.S.–Mexican War.* New Haven: Yale University Press, 2009.

Deloria, Vine, Jr. "Self-Determination and the Concept of Sovereignty." In *Native American Sovereignty*, edited by John R. Wunder, 118–24. New York: Routledge, 1999.

Denson, Andrew. *Demanding the Cherokee Nation: Indian Autonomy and American Culture, 1830–1900.* Lincoln: University of Nebraska Press, 2004.

DeRosier, Arthur J., Jr. *The Removal of the Choctaw Indians.* Knoxville: University of Tennessee Press, 1981.

Dowd, Gregory Evans. *A Spirited Resistance: The North American Indian Struggle for Unity, 1745–1815.* Baltimore: Johns Hopkins University Press, 1993.

Downes, Randolph. *Council Fires on the Upper Ohio.* Pittsburgh: University of Pittsburgh Press, 1969.

Dunbar, Willis Frederick. *Michigan: A History of the Wolverine State.* Grand Rapids, Mich.: William Eerdmans, 1965.

DuVal, Kathleen. "Debating Identity, Sovereignty, and Civilization: The Arkansas Valley after the Louisiana Purchase." *Journal of the Early Republic* 26 (Spring 2006): 25–58.

———. *The Native Ground: Indians and Colonists in the Heart of the Continent.* Philadelphia: University of Pennsylvania Press, 2007.

Edmonds, J. W. *Report of J. W. Edmonds, United States Commissioner, upon the Disturbance at the Potawatomie Payment, September, 1836.* New York: Scatcherd and Adams, 1837.

Edmunds, R. David. "Blazing New Trails or Burning Bridges: Native American History Comes of Age." *Western Historical Quarterly* 39 (Spring 2008): 4–15.

———. "'Designing Men, Seeking a Fortune': Indian Traders and the Potawatomi Claims Payment of 1836." *Indiana Magazine of History* 77 (June 1981): 109–22.

———. *The Potawatomis: Keepers of the Fire.* Norman: University of Oklahoma Press, 1978.

———. "Potawatomis in the Platte Country: An Indian Removal Incomplete." *Missouri Historical Review* 68 (July 1974): 375–92.

———. *The Shawnee Prophet.* Lincoln: University of Nebraska Press, 1985.

———. *Tecumseh and the Quest for Indian Leadership.* New York: Pearson Longman, 2007.

———. "'A Watchful Safeguard to Our Habitations': Black Hoof and the Loyal Shawnees." In *Native Americans and the Early Republic,* edited by Frederick Hoxie, Ronald Hoffman, and Peter J. Albert, 162–199. Charlottesville: University of Virginia Press, 1999.

Edmunds, R. David, Frederick Hoxie, and Neal Salisbury. *The People: A History of Native America.* New York: Cengage Learning, 2007.

Ehle, John. *Trail of Tears: The Rise and Fall of the Cherokee Nation.* New York: Anchor Doubleday, 1997.

Esarey, Logan, ed. *Messages and Letters of William Henry Harrison.* Indianapolis: Indiana Historical Society, 1922.

Evarts, Jeremiah. *Cherokee Removal: The William Penn Essays and Other Writings.* Edited by Francis Paul Prucha. Knoxville: University of Tennessee Press, 1981.

Everett, Homer. *History of Sandusky County, Ohio.* Cleveland: H. Z. Williams, 1882.

Faragher, John Mack. "'More Motley than Mackinaw': From Ethnic Mixing to Ethnic Cleansing on the Frontier of the Lower Missouri, 1783–1833." In *Contact Points: American Frontiers from the Mohawk Valley to the Mississippi, 1750–1830,* edited by Andrew R. L. Cayton and Fredrika J. Teute, 304–26. Chapel Hill: University of North Carolina Press, 1998.

Ferguson, Roger James. "The White River Indiana Delawares: An Ethnohistoric Synthesis, 1795–1867." Ed.D. dissertation, Ball State University, 1972.

Fierst, John T. "Rationalizing Removal: Anti-Indianism in Lewis Cass's North American Review Essays." *Michigan Historical Review* 36 (Fall 2010): 1–36.

Finley, James B. *The History of the Wyandott Mission at Upper Sandusky, Ohio*. Cincinnati: J. F. Wright and L. Swormstedt, 1840.

Fixico, Donald L. "The Alliance of the Three Fires in Trade and War, 1630–1812." *Michigan Historical Review* 20 (Fall 1994): 1–23.

Foner, Philip, ed. *The Life and Writings of Frederick Douglass*. 4 vols. New York: International Publishers, 1955.

Ford, Lisa. *Settler Sovereignty: Jurisdiction and Indigenous People in America and Australia, 1788–1836*. Cambridge, Mass.: Harvard University Press, 2010.

Foreman, Grant. *Advancing the Frontier, 1830–1860*. Norman: University of Oklahoma Press, 1933.

———. *The Five Civilized Tribes*. Norman: University of Oklahoma Press, 1934.

———. *Indian Removal: The Emigration of the Five Civilized Tribes of Indians*. Norman: University of Oklahoma Press, 1932.

———. *Indians and Pioneers: The Story of the American Southwest before 1830*. Norman: University of Oklahoma Press, 1930.

———. *Last Trek of the Indians*. Chicago: University of Chicago Press, 1946.

Gallay, Alan. *The Indian Slave Trade: The Rise of the English Empire in the American South, 1670–1717*. New Haven, Conn.: Yale University Press, 2002.

Garraghan, Gilbert J. *The Catholic Church in Chicago, 1673–1871: An Historical Sketch*. Chicago: Loyola University Press, 1921.

———. "Early Catholicity in Chicago, 1673–1843." *Illinois Catholic Historical Review* 1 (October 1918): 8–28.

Garrison, Tim Alan. *The Legal Ideology of Removal: The Southern Judiciary and the Sovereignty of Native American Nations*. Athens: University of Georgia Press, 2009.

Genetin-Pilawa, C. Joseph. *Crooked Paths to Allotment: The Fight over Federal Indian Policy after the Civil War*. Chapel Hill: University of North Carolina Press, 2012.

Gerwing, Anselm J. "The Chicago Indian Treaty of 1833." *Journal of the Illinois State Historical Society* 57 (Spring 1964): 117–42.

Gibson, Arrell Morgan. "Native Americans and the Civil War." *American Indian Quarterly* 9 (Autumn 1985): 385–410.

Gipson, Lawrence Henry, ed. *The Moravian Indian Mission on White River: Diaries and Letters, May 5, 1799, to November 12, 1806*. Indianapolis: Indiana Historical Society, 1938.

Goddard, Ives. "The Delaware." In *Handbook of North American Indians*, edited by Bruce Trigger, 15:213–39. Washington, D.C.: Smithsonian Institution, 1978.

Green, Michael D. *The Politics of Indian Removal: Creek Government and Society in Crisis*. Lincoln: University of Nebraska Press, 1982.

Griffin, Patrick. *American Leviathan: Empire, Nation, and Revolutionary Frontier*. New York: Hill and Wang, 2008.

Grimes, Richard S. "The Early Years of the Delaware Indian Experience in Kansas Territory, 1830–1845." *Journal of the West* 41 (Winter 2002): 73–82.

Haeger, John D. "The American Fur Company and the Chicago of 1812–1835." *Journal of the Illinois Historical Society* 61 (Summer 1968): 117–39.

Hale, Duane Kendall. *Peacemakers on the Frontier: A History of the Delaware Tribe of Western Oklahoma*. Anadarko, Okla.: Delaware Tribe of Western Oklahoma Press, 1987.

Hall, John W. *Uncommon Defense: Indian Allies in the Black Hawk War*. Cambridge, Mass.: Harvard University Press, 2009.

Hämäläinen, Pekka. *The Comanche Empire*. New Haven, Conn.: Yale University Press, 2009.

Hauptman, Laurence M. *Between Two Fires: American Indians in the Civil War*. New York: Free Press Paperbacks, 1995.

———. *The Iroquois and the New Deal*. Syracuse, N.Y.: Syracuse University Press, 1988.

Heckewelder, John. *A Narrative of the Mission of the United Brethren among the Delaware and Mohegan Indians, from Its Commencement, in the Year 1740, to the Close of the Year 1808*. Philadelphia: M'Carty and Davis, 1820. Reprint, New York: Arno, 1971.

Henretta, James, Rebecca Edwards, and Robert O. Self. *America's History*. 7th Ed. New York: Bedford/St. Martin's, 2011.

Herring, Joseph. *The Enduring Indians of Kansas: A Century and a Half of Acculturation*. Lawrence: University Press of Kansas, 1990.

Hershberger, Mary. "Mobilizing Women, Anticipating Abolition: The Struggle against Indian Removal in the 1830s." *Journal of American History* 86 (June 1999): 14–40.

Hixson, Walter. *American Settler Colonialism: A History*. New York: Palgrave Macmillan, 2013.

Holland, Robert A. *Chicago in Maps, 1612 to 2002*. New York: Rizzoli International, 2005.

Horsman, Reginald. "The British Indian Department and the Abortive Treaty of Lower Sandusky, 1793." *Ohio Historical Quarterly* 70 (July 1961): 189–213.

———. "British Indian Policy in the Northwest, 1807–1812." *Mississippi Valley Historical Review* 45 (June 1958): 51–66.

———. *Expansion and American Indian Policy, 1783–1812*. Norman: University of Oklahoma Press, 1992.

———. "The Indian Policy of an 'Empire for Liberty.'" In *Native Americans and the Early Republic*, edited by Frederick Hoxie, Ronald Hoffman, and Peter J. Albert, 37–61. Charlottesville: University of Virginia Press, 1999.

Houck, Louis, ed. *The Spanish Regime in Missouri*. 2 vols. Chicago: R. R. Donnelley and Sons, 1909.

Howe, Daniel Walker. *What Hath God Wrought: The Transformation of America, 1815–1848*. New York: Oxford University Press, 2007.

Hunter, Juanita. "The Indians and the Michigan Road." *Indiana Magazine of History* 83 (September 1987): 244–66.

Hurlbut, Henry Higgins. *Chicago Antiquities: Comprising Original Items and Relations, Letters, Extracts, and Notes Pertaining to Early Chicago.* Chicago: Fergus Printing, 1881.

Hurt, R. Douglas. *The Ohio Frontier: Crucible of the Old Northwest, 1720–1830.* Bloomington: Indiana University Press, 1996.

Jackson, Donald, ed. *Black Hawk: An Autobiography.* Urbana: University of Illinois Press, 1955.

Jahoda, Gloria. *The Trail of Tears: The Story of American Indian Removals, 1813–1855.* New York: Wings Books, 1995.

Johnston, John. *Recollections of Sixty Years.* Dayton, Ohio: John Henry Patterson, 1915.

Jortner, Adam. *The Gods of Prophetstown: The Battle of Tippecanoe and the Holy War for the American Frontier.* New York: Oxford University Press, 2011.

Jung, Patrick J. *The Black Hawk War of 1832.* Norman: University of Oklahoma Press, 2008.

Karamanski, Theodore J. *Blackbird's Song: Andrew J. Blackbird and the Odawa People.* East Lansing: Michigan State University Press, 2012.

Keating, Ann Durkin. *Rising Up from Indian Country: The Battle of Fort Dearborn and the Birth of Chicago.* Chicago: University of Chicago Press, 2012.

Keating, William H. *Narrative of an Expedition to the Source of St. Peter's River, Lake Winnepeek, Lake of the Woods, etc., Performed in the Year 1823.* 2 vols. Philadelphia: H. C. Carey and I. Lea, 1826.

Keeler, Lucy Elliot. "Old Fort Sandoski of 1745 and the 'Sandusky Country.'" *Ohio Archaeological and Historical Society Publications* 17 (October 1908): 356–430.

Kelley, John. "1822 Chicago, from Tales of an 1822 Chicagoan: Some Memoirs of the Late Alexander Beaubien." *Journal of the Illinois State Historical Society* 14 (October 1921—January 1922): 407–12.

Kellogg, Louise Phelps, ed. *Frontier Retreat on the Upper Ohio, 1779–1781.* Madison: State Historical Society of Wisconsin, 1917.

Kelly, Lawrence C. *The Assault on Assimilation: John Collier and the Origins of Indian Policy Reform.* Albuquerque: University of New Mexico Press, 1983.

Kidwell, Clara Sue. *The Choctaws in Oklahoma: From Tribe to Nation, 1855–1970.* Norman: University of Oklahoma Press, 2008.

Kinietz, Vernon, ed. *Meearmeear Traditions.* Ann Arbor: University of Michigan Press, 1938.

Klopfenstein, Carl G. "The Removal of the Wyandots from Ohio." *Ohio Historical Quarterly* 66 (April 1957): 119–36.

Knight, John, John Slover, and William Crawford. *Indian Atrocities, Narratives of the Perils and Sufferings of Dr. Knight and John Slover.* Cincinnati: U. P. James, 1867.

Lankford, George E. "Shawnee Convergence: Immigrant Indians in the Ozarks." *Arkansas Historical Quarterly* 58 (Winter 1999): 390–413.

Latrobe, Charles Joseph. *The Rambler in North America, 1832–1833.* 2 vols. New York: Harper, 1835.

La Vere, David. *Contrary Neighbors: Southern Plains and Removed Indians in Indian Territory.* Norman: University of Oklahoma Press, 2001.

"Letters from the Indian Missions in Kansas." *Collections of the Kansas State Historical Society* 16 (1923–1925): 227–72.

Lucas, Robert. *Message of the Governor of Ohio at the Second Session of the Thirty-Third General Assembly, June 8, 1835.* Columbus, Ohio: James B. Gardiner, 1835.

Lumpkin, Wilson. *The Removal of the Cherokee Indians from Georgia.* 2 vols. New York: Dodd, Mead, 1907.

Lyons, Scott Richard. *X-Marks: Native Signatures of Assent.* Minneapolis: University of Minnesota Press, 2010.

Maddox, Lucy. *Removals: Nineteenth Century American Literature and the Politics of Indian Affairs.* New York: Oxford University Press, 1991.

Martin, Joel W. *Sacred Revolt: The Muskogees' Struggle for a New World.* Boston: Beacon Press, 1991.

McCafferty, Michael. "A Fresh Look at the Place Name Chicago." *Journal of the Illinois State Historical Society* 96 (Summer 2003): 116–29.

McClurken, James M. "Ottawa Adaptive Strategies to Indian Removal." *Michigan Historical Review* 12 (Spring 1986): 29–55.

———. *Our People, Our Journey: The Little River Band of Ottawa Indians.* East Lansing: Michigan State University Press, 2009.

———. "We Wish To Be Civilized: Ottawa-American Political Contests on the Michigan Frontier (Volumes I and II)." Ph.D. dissertation, Michigan State University, 1988.

McCoy, Isaac. *History of Baptist Indian Missions.* Washington, D.C.: William H. Morrison, 1840.

———. *Remarks on the Practicability of Indian Reform, Embracing Their Colonization.* New York: Gray and Bunce, 1829.

McLoughlin, William. *After the Trail of Tears: The Cherokees' Struggle for Sovereignty, 1839–1880.* Chapel Hill: University of North Carolina Press, 1994.

Merrell, James H. *The Indians' New World: Catawbas and Their Neighbors from European Contact through the Era of Removal.* New York: W. W. Norton, 1989.

———. *Into the American Woods: Negotiators on the Pennsylvania Frontier.* New York: W. W. Norton, 1999.

Merritt, Jane T. *At the Crossroads: Indians and Empires on a Mid-Atlantic Frontier, 1700–1763.* Chapel Hill: University of North Carolina Press, 2003.

Miles, Tiya. *Ties That Bind: The Story of an Afro-Cherokee Family in Slavery and Freedom.* Berkeley: University of California Press, 2006.

Miles, Tiya, and Sharon Patricia Holland, eds. *Crossing Waters, Crossing Worlds: The African Diaspora in Indian Country.* Durham, N.C.: Duke University Press, 2006.

Miller, Jay. "The 1806 Purge among the Indiana Delaware: Sorcery, Gender, Boundaries, and Legitimacy." *Ethnohistory* 41 (Spring 1994): 245–66.

———. "Old Religion among the Delawares: The Gamwing (Big House Rite)." *Ethnohistory* 44 (Winter 1997): 113–34.

Miner, Craig, and William Unrau. *The End of Indian Kansas: A Study in Cultural Revolution, 1854–1871.* Lawrence: University Press of Kansas, 1990.

Morrow, Lynn. "Trader William Gillis and Delaware Migration in Southern Missouri." *Missouri Historical Review* 75 (January 1981): 147–67.

Morse, Jedidiah. *A Report to the Secretary of War of the United States, on Indian Affairs, Comprising a Narrative of a Tour Performed in the Summer of 1820. . . .* New Haven: S. Converse, 1822.

Moses, John, and Joseph Kirkland. *History of Chicago.* 2 vols. Chicago: Munsell, 1895.

Mulroy, Kevin. *The Seminole Freedmen: A History.* Norman: University of Oklahoma Press, 2007.

Murphy, Lucy Eldersveld. *A Gathering of Rivers: Indians, Metis, and Mining in the Western Great Lakes, 1737–1832.* Lincoln: University of Nebraska Press, 2004.

Murray, Keith A. *The Modocs and Their War.* Norman: University of Oklahoma Press, 1976.

Naylor, Celia E. *African Cherokees in Indian Territory: From Chattel to Citizens.* Chapel Hill: University of North Carolina Press, 2008.

Nelson, Larry L. *Fort Meigs: War of 1812 Battleground.* Columbus: Ohio Historical Society, 1999.

Neumeyer, Elizabeth A. "Indian Removal in Michigan, 1833–1855." M.A. thesis, Central Michigan University, 1968.

Nichols, David Andrew. *Red Gentlemen and White Savages: Indians, Federalists, and the Search for Order on the American Frontier.* Charlottesville: University of Virginia Press, 2008.

Norgren, Jill. *The Cherokee Cases: Two Landmark Federal Decisions in the Fight for Sovereignty.* Norman: University of Oklahoma Press, 2004.

Norwood, Frederick A. "Strangers in a Strange Land: Removal of the Wyandot Indians." *Methodist History* 13 (April 1975): 45–60.

Obermeyer, Brice. *Delaware Tribe in a Cherokee Nation.* Lincoln: University of Nebraska Press, 2009.

O'Brien, Greg. *Choctaws in a Revolutionary Age, 1750–1830.* Lincoln: University of Nebraska Press, 2005.

O'Brien, Jean. *Dispossession by Degrees: Indian Land and Identity in Natick, Massachusetts, 1650–1790.* New York: Cambridge University Press, 1997.

O'Callaghan, E. B., ed. *Documents Relative to the Colonial History of the State of New York.* Albany, N.Y.: Weed, Parsons, 1857.

Oliphant, J. Orin, ed. "The Report of the Wyandot Exploring Delegation, 1831." *Kansas Historical Quarterly* 14 (August 1947): 248–62.

Olmstead, Earl P. *Blackcoats among the Delaware: David Zeisberger on the Ohio Frontier.* Kent, Ohio: Kent State University Press, 1991.

Owens, Robert M. "Jeffersonian Benevolence on the Ground: The Indian Land Cession Treaties of William Henry Harrison." *Journal of the Early Republic* 22 (Autumn 2002): 405–35.

————. *Mr. Jefferson's Hammer: William Henry Harrison and the Origins of American Indian Policy.* Norman: University of Oklahoma Press, 2007.

Paige, Amanda L., Fuller L. Bumpers, and Daniel F. Littlefield, Jr. *Chickasaw Removal.* Norman: University of Oklahoma Press, 2010.

Perdue, Theda, and Michael D. Green. *The Cherokee Nation and the Trail of Tears.* New York: Penguin, 2007.

————, eds. *The Cherokee Removal: A Brief History with Documents.* New York: Bedford/St. Martins, 1995.

Peterson, Jacqueline. "Goodbye, Madore Beaubien: The Americanization of Early Chicago Society." *Chicago History* 9 (1980): 98–111.

————. "'Wild' Chicago: The Formation and Destruction of a Multi-racial Community on the Midwestern Frontier, 1816–1837." In *The Ethnic Frontier: Essays in the History of Group Survival in Chicago and the Midwest,* edited by Melvin G. Holli and Peter d'A. Jones, 26–71. Grand Rapids, Mi.: William B. Eerdmans, 1977.

Phelps, Martha Bennett. *Frances Slocum: The Lost Sister of Wyoming.* Wilkes-Barre, Pa.: privately published, 1916.

Prucha, Francis Paul, ed. *Documents of United States Indian Policy.* Lincoln: University of Nebraska Press, 2000.

————. *The Great Father: The United States Government and the American Indians.* 2 vols. Lincoln: University of Nebraska Press, 1984.

Public Library of Fort Wayne and Allen County, ed. *General Harmar's Campaign.* Fort Wayne, Ind.: Library, 1954.

Quaife, Milo M. *Chicago and the Old Northwest, 1673–1835.* Chicago: University of Chicago Press, 1913.

————, ed. "The Chicago Treaty of 1833." *Wisconsin Magazine of History* 1 (March 1918): 287–303.

————, ed. "A Narrative of Life on the Old Frontier." *Proceedings of the State Historical Society of Wisconsin* (1914): 208–61.

Ragsdale, John W. "The Dispossession of the Kansas Shawnee." *University of Missouri-Kansas Law Review* 58 (Winter 1990): 209–56.

Remini, Robert. *Andrew Jackson and His Indian Wars.* New York: Penguin, 2002.

Richter, Daniel. "Whose Indian History?" *William and Mary Quarterly* 50 (1993): 379–93.

Rifkin, Mark. *Manifesting America: The Imperial Construction of U.S. National Space.* New York: Oxford University Press, 2009.

Riker, Dorothy, and Gayle Thornbrough, eds. *Messages and Papers Relating to the Administration of Noah Noble, Governor of Indiana 1831–1837.* Indianapolis: Indiana Historical Bureau, 1958.

Roark, James L., Patricia Cline Cohen, Susan M. Hartmann, Alan Lawson, Michael P. Johnson, and Sarah Stage. *Understanding the American Promise: A Brief History.* Vol. 1, *To 1877.* New York: Bedford/St. Martin's, 2011.

Robertson, Nellie Armstrong, and Dorothy Riker, comps. and eds. *John Tipton Papers.* 3 vols. Indianapolis: Indiana Historical Society, 1942.

Roden, Carl B. "The Beaubien Claim." *Journal of the Illinois State Historical Society* 42 (June 1949): 147–66.

Rogers, Howard S. *History of Cass County, from 1825 to 1875.* Cassopolis, Mich.: W. H. Mansfield, 1875.

Rohrbough, Malcolm. *The Land Office Business: The Settlement and Administration of American Public Lands, 1789–1837.* New York: Oxford University Press, 1968.

Rolater, Fred S. "The American Indian and the Origin of the Second American Party System." *Wisconsin Magazine of History,* 76 (Spring 1993): 180–203.

Rosen, Deborah A. *American Indians and State Law: Sovereignty, Race, and Citizenship, 1790–1880.* Lincoln: University of Nebraska Press, 2009.

Rosenthal, Nicolas G. "Beyond the New Indian History: Recent Trends in the Historiography on the Native Peoples of North America." *History Compass* 4 (2006): 962–74.

Sabathy-Judd, Linda, ed. and trans. *Moravians in Upper Canada: The Diary of the Indian Mission of Fairfield on the Thames, 1792–1813.* Toronto: Champlain Society, 1999.

Saler, Bethel. *The Settlers' Empire: Colonialism and State Formation in America's Old Northwest.* Philadelphia: University of Pennsylvania Press, 2015.

Satz, Ronald N. *American Indian Policy in the Jacksonian Era.* Norman: University of Oklahoma Press, 2002.

Saunt, Claudio. "Go West: Mapping Early American Historiography." *William and Mary Quarterly* 65 (October 2008): 745–78.

———. *A New Order of Things: Property, Power, and the Transformation of the Creek Indians, 1733–1816.* New York: Cambridge University Press, 1999.

Schlup, Emil. "The Wyandot Mission." *Ohio Archaeological and Historical Society Publications* 15 (1906): 163–81.

Schoolcraft, Henry R. *Narrative Journal of Travels through the Northwestern Regions of the United States.* Albany, N.Y.: E. and E. Hosford, 1821.

———. *Personal Memoirs of a Residence of Thirty Years with the Indian Tribes of the American Frontiers.* Philadelphia: Lippincott, Grambo, 1851.

Schurr, Terrance J. Martin, and W. Ben Secunda. "How the Pokagon Band Avoided Removal: Archaeological Evidence from the Faunal Assemblage of the Pokagon Village Site (20BE13)." *Midcontinental Journal of Archaeology* 31 (Spring 2006): 143–63.

Schwartz, James Z. *Conflict on the Michigan Frontier: Yankee and Borderland Cultures, 1815–1840.* DeKalb: Northern Illinois University Press, 2009.

Secunda, W. Benjamin. "In the Shadow of the Wings of Eagles: The Effects of Removal on the Unremoved Potawatomi." Ph.D. dissertation, Notre Dame University, 2008.

———. "To Cede or Seed? Risk and Identity among the Woodland Potawatomi during the Removal Period." *Midcontinental Journal of Archaeology* 31 (Spring 2006): 57–88.

Sherrard, Priscilla Mullin. *People of the Place of the Fire.* N.p.: privately published, 1975.

Skaggs, David Curtis. *The Battle of Lake Erie and Its Aftermath: A Reassessment.* Kent, Ohio: Kent State University Press, 2013.

Sleeper-Smith, Susan. *Indian Women and French Men: Rethinking Cultural Encounter in the Western Great Lakes.* Amherst: University of Massachusetts Press, 2001.

Smith, Dwight L., ed. "The Attempted Potawatomi Emigration of 1839." *Indiana Magazine of History* 45 (March 1949): 51–80.

———, ed. "Journal of an Emigrating Party of Pottawattomie Indians, 1838." *Indiana Magazine of History* 21 (December 1925): 315–36.

———, ed. "An Unsuccessful Negotiation for Removal of the Wyandot Indians from Ohio, 1834." *Ohio Archaeological and Historical Quarterly* 58 (July 1949): 305–31.

Smith, James. *An Account of the Remarkable Occurrences in the Life of Colonel James Smith.* Lexington, Ky.: John Bradford, 1799.

Smith, Robert E. "The Clash of Leadership at the Grand Reserve: The Wyandot Subagency and the Methodist Mission, 1820–24." *Ohio History* 89 (Spring 1980): 181–205.

———. "The Wyandot Exploring Expedition of 1839." *Chronicles of Oklahoma* 55 (Fall 1977): 282–92.

Smith, Troy. "Nations Colliding: The Civil War Comes to Indian Territory." *Civil War History* 59 (Summer 2013): 279–319.

Smith, William Henry, ed. *The St. Clair Papers.* Cincinnati: Robert Clarke, 1882.

St. Jean, Wendy. *Remaining Chickasaw in Indian Territory, 1830s–1907.* Tuscaloosa: University of Alabama Press, 2011.

Stonefish, Darryl K. *Moraviantown Delaware History.* Thamesville, Ont.: Moravian Research Office, 1995.

Strack, George, George Ironstrack, Daryl Baldwin, Kristina Fox, Julie Olds, Robbyn Abbitt, and Melissa Rinehart. *myaamiaki aancihsaaciki: A Cultural Exploration of the Myaamia Removal Route.* Miami, Okla.: Miami Tribe of Oklahoma, 2011.

Sturtevant, William. "Oklahoma Seneca-Cayuga." In *Handbook of North American Indians,* edited by Bruce Trigger, 15:537–38. Washington, D.C.: Smithsonian Institution, 1978.

Sugden, John. "Early Pan-Indianism; Tecumseh's Tour of the Indian Country." *American Indian Quarterly* 10 (Fall 1986): 273–304.

———. "Tecumseh's Travels Revisited." *Indiana Magazine of History* 96 (June 2000): 151–68.

Swieranga, Robert P., and William Van Appledorn, eds. *Old Wing Mission: Cultural Interchange as Chronicled by George and Arvilla Smith in Their Work with Chief Wakazoo's Ottawa Band on the West Michigan Frontier.* Grand Rapids, Mich.: Eerdmans Publishing, 2008.

Tanner, Helen Hornbeck. *Atlas of Great Lakes Indian History.* Norman: University of Oklahoma Press, 1987.

———. "The Glaize in 1792: A Composite Indian Community." *Ethnohistory* 25 (Winter 1978): 15–39.

Taylor, Alan. *The Divided Ground: Indians, Settlers, and the Northern Borderland of the American Revolution.* New York: Alfred A. Knopf, 2006.

Thompson, Charles N. *Sons of the Wilderness: John and William Conner.* Indianapolis: Indiana Historical Society, 1937.

Thompson, Joseph J. "The First Catholics in and about Chicago." *Illinois Catholic Historical Review* 3 (January 1921): 231–40.

Thornbrough, Gayle, ed. *Letterbook of the Indian Agency at Fort Wayne.* Indianapolis: Indiana Historical Society, 1961.

———, ed. *Outpost on the Wabash.* Indianapolis: Indiana State Historical Society, 1957.

Thwaites, Reuben Gold, ed. "American Fur Company Employees—1818–1819." *Collections of the State Historical Society of Wisconsin* 12 (1892): 154–69.

———, ed. "American Fur Company Invoices—1821–1822." *Collections of the State Historical Society of Wisconsin* 11 (1888): 370–79.

———, ed. "Narrative of Peter J. Vieau." *Collections of the State Historical Society of Wisconsin* 15 (1900): 458–69.

Tiro, Karim M. "The View from Piqua Agency: The War of 1812, the White River Delawares, and the Origins of Indian Removal." *Journal of the Early Republic* 35 (Spring 2015): 25–54.

Trask, Kerry A. *Black Hawk and the Battle for the Heart of America.* New York: Henry Holt, 2006.

Trennert, Robert A., Jr. "The Business of Indian Removal: Deporting the Potawatomi from Wisconsin, 1851." *Wisconsin Magazine of History* 63 (Autumn 1979): 36–50.

———. *Indian Traders on the Middle Border: The House of Ewing, 1827–54.* Lincoln: University of Nebraska Press, 1981.

Unrau, William E. *The Rise and Fall of Indian Country, 1825–1855.* Lawrence: University Press of Kansas, 2007.

Usner, Daniel, Jr. *Indians, Settlers, and Slaves in a Frontier Exchange Economy: The Lower Mississippi Valley before 1783.* Chapel Hill: University of North Carolina Press, 1992.

Viola, Herman J. *Thomas L. McKenney, Architect of America's Early Indian Policy: 1816–1830.* Chicago: Swallow Press, 1974.

Wallace, Anthony F. C. *Jefferson and the Indians: The Tragic Fate of the First Americans.* Cambridge, Mass.: Harvard University Press, 1999.

Walsh, Martin W. "The 'Heathen Party': Methodist Observation of the Ohio Wyandot." *American Indian Quarterly* (Spring 1992): 189–211.

Warren, Stephen. *The Shawnees and Their Neighbors, 1795–1870.* Urbana: University of Illinois Press, 2005.

———. *The Worlds the Shawnees Made: Migration and Violence in Early America.* Chapel Hill: University of North Carolina Press, 2013.

Way, Royal B. "The United States Factory System for Trading with the Indians, 1796–1822." *Mississippi Valley Historical Review* 6 (September 1919): 220–35.

Weslager, C. A. *The Delaware Indians: A History.* New Brunswick, N.J.: Rutgers University Press, 1972.

West, Elliott. *The Last Indian War: The Nez Perce Story.* New York: Oxford University Press, 2009.

White, Richard. "Creative Misunderstandings and New Understandings." *William and Mary Quarterly* 63 (January 2006): 9–14.

———. *The Middle Ground: Indians, Empires, and Republics in the Great Lakes Region, 1650–1815.* New York: Cambridge University Press, 1991.

Whitney, Ellen M., comp. and ed. *The Black Hawk War 1831–1832.* 3 vols. Springfield: Illinois State Historical Library, 1973.

Willig, Timothy D. *Restoring the Chain of Friendship: British Policy and the Indians of the Great Lakes, 1783–1815.* Lincoln: University of Nebraska Press, 2008.

Wilson, George R., and Gayle Thornbrough. *The Buffalo Trace.* Indianapolis: Indiana Historical Society, 1946.

Winfrey, Dorman H., ed. *The Indian Papers of Texas and the Southwest, 1825–1916.* 5 vols. College Station: Texas State Historical Association, 1995.

Wishart, David J. *An Unspeakable Sadness: The Dispossession of the Nebraska Indians.* Lincoln: University of Nebraska Press, 1994.

Witgen, Michael. *An Infinity of Nations: How the Native New World Shaped Early America.* Philadelphia: University of Pennsylvania Press, 2013.

Wolfe, Patrick. "Settler Colonialism and the Elimination of the Native." *Journal of Genocide Research* 8 (December 2006): 387–409.

Wunder, John. "Native American History, Ethnohistory, and Context." *Ethnohistory* 54 (Fall 2007): 591–604.

Young, Mary. "The Exercise of Sovereignty in Cherokee Georgia." *Journal of the Early Republic* 10 (Spring 1990): 43–63.

———. *Redskins, Ruffleshirts, and Rednecks: Indian Allotments in Alabama and Mississippi, 1830–1860.* Norman: University of Oklahoma Press, 1961.

INDEX

Abbot, James, 223
Adams, Robert, 64
Adams-Onis Treaty of 1819, 109
adaptive resistance, 13, 66, 72, 178,
    240n32
allotment, 17, 211–12, 220–23,
    225–26, 228–29. *See also* Dawes
    Act (General Allotment Act of
    1887)
American Anti-Slavery Society, 212
American Board of Commissioners of
    Foreign Missions (ABCFM), 60
American Fur Company, 41, 173, 175
Amherstburg, Ontario, 31, 33, 36, 37,
    42; Indian visits to, 39–40, 100; site
    of Wyandot reservation, 115, 133
Anderson, John, 143–45
Anderson, William, 78, 91, 95, 97,
    103–104, 107, 110–11, 125
Anishinaabe (Anishinabek, pl.), 182,
    184, 185, 200, 204, 205, 207, 210;
    avoiding removal, 185, 186, 187,
    191, 202; explanation of term,
    267n1; at Treaty of Washington
    (1836), 194. *See also* Ojibwes
Armstrong, Arthur, 228–29
Armstrong, Henry, 228–29
Armstrong, John, 144

Articles of Confederation, 23, 50, 52,
    63, 152
Ashkum, 164
Assagon, 208
Atkinson, Henry, 47–48
Auglaize River, 25, 31, 86, 99;
    center of Northwestern Indian
    Confederacy, 25, 86
Austin, Stephen F., 109–10

Balestier, Joseph, 177
Baptists, 60, 61, 69, 168, 175, 177, 192,
    194, 202. *See also* McCoy, Isaac,
    Rev.; Slater, Leonard, Rev.
Barclay, Robert, Capt., 37
Barnett, John, 142
Barron, Joseph, 171
Battle of Fallen Timbers, 25, 29–31,
    35, 92
Battle of Lake Erie, 37, 118
Battle of San Jacinto, 214
Battle of Stillman's Run, 46
Battle of the Bad Axe River, 19, 48,
    154
Battle of the Thames, 37, 42, 102
Battle of Tippecanoe, 33–34, 54, 96,
    98
Baylor, John, 220